Exploring Economics

Ray Notgrass

Exploring Economics
Ray Notgrass

ISBN 978-1-60999-094-7

Copyright © 2016 Notgrass Company. All rights reserved.
No part of this material may be reproduced without permission from the publisher.

Front Cover: Container ship photo by Alex Kolokythas Photography / Shutterstock.com
Back Cover: Background by Sinngern / Shutterstock.com
Author photo by Mev McCurdy

All product names, brands, and other trademarks mentioned or pictured
in this book are used for educational purposes only.
No association with or endorsement by the owners of the trademarks is intended.
Each trademark remains the property of its respective owner.

Unless otherwise noted, Scripture quotations taken from the New American Standard Bible,
Copyright 1960, 1962, 1963, 1971, 1972, 1973, 1975, 1977, 1995
by the Lockman Foundation. Used by permission.

Cover design by Mary Evelyn McCurdy
Interior design by John Notgrass
Weekly projects and literature selection by Bethany Poore
Charts and graphs by Nate McCurdy and John Notgrass
Project managers Charlene Notgrass and John Notgrass

Printed in the United States of America

Notgrass Company
1-800-211-8793
www.notgrass.com

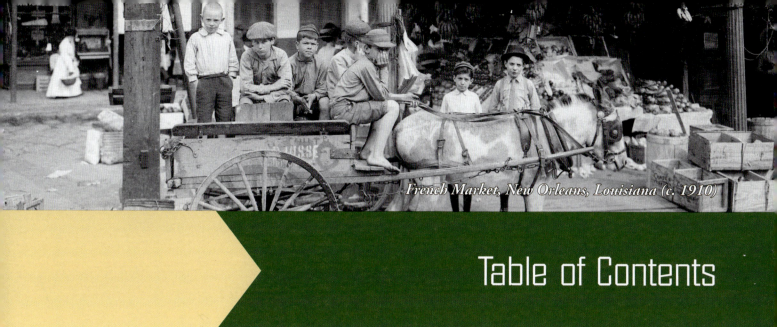
French Market, New Orleans, Louisiana (c. 1910)

Table of Contents

Introduction vi

How to Use This Curriculum ix

1 Getting a Grasp of Economics 1

1 - What Would You Do with Five Hundred Dollars? 3
2 - Big Topics in Economics 9
3 - More Big Topics 17
4 - Superstars of Economics 23
5 - More Big Names 31

2 God's Economics, Part 1 37

6 - The Lord Provides 39
7 - Rich and Poor in Ancient Israel 45
8 - The Righteous Will Flourish 49
9 - God Owns It All 53
10 - The Radical Economics of Jesus 57

3 God's Economics, Part 2 63

11 - To Each as Any Had Need 65
12 - Economics in Church History, Part 1 69
13 - Economics in Church History, Part 2 73
14 - Economics for Today's Christian 77
15 - The Love of Money 82

4 A Brief Economic History of the United States 87

16 - From Exploration to Confederation 89
17 - Money and the New United States 95
18 - Wars and Panics 101
19 - Prosperity and More Panics 106
20 - The Economy As We Know It 112

5 Choices 117

21 - Chocolate or Vanilla? 119
22 - Economic Choices 123
23 - Producers Choose 129
24 - We Choose 135
25 - Uncle Sam Chooses 141

6 Markets 147

26 - How Markets Work 149
27 - Supply and Demand 156
28 - How Much Does It Cost? 164
29 - When Markets Change 171
30 - When Markets Fail 179

7 Money 187

31 - What Is Money Worth? 189
32 - How Banks Work 196
33 - Wise Investing 203
34 - Inflation (Not Our Friend) 209
35 - What Is the Fed? 216

8 Trade 223

36 - Trade Is Good 225
37 - Restrictions on Trade 231
38 - The Case for Free Trade 237
39 - Have We Been Exported? 243
40 - Money Changes Clothes 251

9 Business 257

41 - Building Blocks of Business 259
42 - Small Business, Big Dream 265
43 - So You Want to Start a Business? 269
44 - It Comes Down to Profit and Loss 275
45 - The Economy-Go-Round 282

10 Labor 287

46 - Now Hiring 289
47 - Workers and Their Jobs 293
48 - Unions 299
49 - Income 305
50 - Out of Work 313

11 Government 317

51 - Government Departments and Agencies 319
52 - Government Policies 325
53 - Regulations, Regulations 331
54 - Taxes, Taxes 337
55 - Making and Breaking the Budget 344

12 Measuring the Economy 349

56 - What's Gross About the Domestic Product? 351
57 - A Few Important Numbers 356
58 - What Goes Up Must Come Down 361
59 - What's a Recession? 367
60 - Rich and Poor 371

Table of Contents   v

13 Economic Issues, Part 1   379

61 - The Business of Health Care   381
62 - Social Security and Medicare   388
63 - Energy   393
64 - On the Road Again   400
65 - O Give Me a Home   405

14 Economic Issues, Part 2   411

66 - Old MacDonald Had a Farm   413
67 - The Environment   418
68 - Productivity and Growth   425
69 - What Happened in
       the Great Depression?   430
70 - What Happened in the
       Great Recession?   435

15 ME-conomics: The Ultimate Microeconomy   441

71 - What Difference Can
       One Person Make?   443
72 - What Should I Do?   447
73 - Me and My Money   451
74 - When I Grow Up   455
75 - "Seek Ye First . . ."   459

Hunter Plant in Castle Dale, Utah, is a coal-fired power generation station.

Gray's General Store, Little Compton, Rhode Island (2008)

Introduction

A factory closes in your town. Three hundred people lose their jobs because the company has decided to move its production to Mexico. What will all of those former employees do for work?

You are thinking about applying for a summer job at a new clothing store because they carry attractive but modest apparel. However, it is the seventh clothing store in the same shopping area. If it doesn't stay in business, you may be out of work for the rest of the summer. What should you do?

A family that lives down the street is moving to a less expensive house. The mother in that family had to have surgery for a brain tumor, and they are having a hard time paying all of the medical expenses. What economic issues are they facing?

In the early 1960s, gasoline cost twenty-five or thirty cents a gallon. Today, gasoline prices change constantly and can go from two dollars a gallon to four dollars a gallon and back again in a year. What causes these changes?

The promises that a presidential candidate makes regarding economic policy sound good—but the promises of another candidate sound good also, even though they embody the opposite policy priorities. Which candidate should you support? Are either candidate's proposals realistic?

You hear people at church talking about an increase in taxes that the government is considering. They say that it will be a one percent increase. That doesn't sound like very much. What's the problem?

Every day the news reports some statistic: the unemployment rate, new housing starts, a change in the Consumer Price Index, the Dow Jones average. What do all of these numbers mean?

You want to be a good steward of the resources, including the money, that God provides for you. You want to live, work, and think about the world around you in a way that will honor God. What do you need to understand in order to accomplish these goals? All of these are reasons you need to study economics.

Goals and Purpose

Exploring Economics provides a thorough survey of the basic terms and concepts of economics. However, our goal has been not just to assemble the required definitions, statistics, and charts, but to provide an understanding of what economics is, what it means to you now, and what it will mean to you in your adult life.

Some of you who study this course will go on to take an economics course in college. Probably very few of you who study this curriculum will become economists. But everyone who studies this course will face economic issues and decisions. Having a grasp of the basic issues in the field will be helpful.

Introduction

If you shop for clothes or groceries or gasoline, if you buy imported goods, if you start a business, if you read the headlines, if you support and vote for political candidates, economics will affect you. If you are ignorant of the subject, people who have all sorts of agendas can mislead you. The danger of ignorance is real in many areas of life, but it is especially dangerous when it comes to your money.

Content and Structure

This curriculum begins with an overview of economic terms and concepts and some of the more important economic theories. Two units (ten lessons) are devoted to what we call God's Economics: what the Bible says about economics, business, and wealth; a survey of economic ideas in church history; and economic issues that Christians face today. One unit (five lessons) provides a brief survey of the economic history of the United States to put our present situation in context. Eight units (forty lessons) present economic ideas, terms, and realities in greater detail. Two units then discuss vital economic issues that confront America today and show how the ideas presented earlier in the curriculum relate to these issues.

We hope to make the field of economics more clear by this three-fold presentation: brief overview, detailed discussion, and application to contemporary issues. The final unit in the curriculum puts all of what we discussed on a personal level by presenting economic priorities and decisions that affect individuals and families.

Our Perspective

We approach the subject of economics from a perspective of faith in God and a reliance on the Bible as God's infallible Word. Since issues involving money are so important and can have such a huge impact on a person's walk with the Lord, the teachings of the Bible are essential to a proper understanding of economics.

We believe in the strengths of the capitalist free-market system. We believe that the free market system has done more than any other economic system to help people live well in material terms; to provide outlets for them to use their God-given talents and resources; and to enable them to know personal, political, and economic freedom. By contrast, command economies that central government bureaucrats run have proven to be an inefficient and sometimes destructive way to guide the economic life of a country.

At the same time, we recognize the imperfections of capitalism. Capitalists are humans, and humans are sinners. Capitalists can be greedy, unjust, and exploitative. Sometimes people take advantage of a free system to do wrong for personal gain, just as those who are committed to or involved with a socialist or government-planned economy can do wrong and be selfish. Sometimes, for any number of reasons, the free market does not work completely smoothly. As a result, economic difficulties occur.

The human factor is why some government regulations are necessary even in free-market economies. However, unreasonable or ineffective government regulations that go too far are hurtful and counterproductive. The dynamic of imperfect people seeking to live by (and sometimes work around) economic principles makes economics fascinating and leads to lively debates.

Economics is not the study of business administration, although business activity is a vital part of the economy. You will not learn about the best way to organize a business, how to hire and motivate employees, good bookkeeping and accounting practices, or other matters related to running a business.

Economics is also not a study of personal finance. You will not learn how to balance a checkbook or how to shop wisely. These are important topics, but you can learn about these and other such issues in a course on consumer math. This course considers personal financial matters in the context of broader economic activity.

The World of Economics Today

We live in a time when economic events and government policies have challenged the classic definitions of economics. For instance, the communist nation of China, which has a history of central economic planning, is promoting capitalist enterprises within its borders (the Chinese call it socialism with a Chinese flavor). At the same time, the traditionally capitalist United States has seen a great increase in government involvement in economic planning and oversight in recent decades. Understanding the classic definitions is important, but we must also understand the changing economic realities of today.

Economic developments are constantly in the news. The times in which we live should encourage your generation to realize that a study of economics is relevant and vital. We hope that this curriculum will help you understand current economic realities while you gain an insight into topics that have long been associated with the study of economics.

In addition, please note that the websites and specific Internet sources cited in the text were current when this curriculum was written. Websites change and sources can be taken down at any time. We do not control the content accessed through these links, and a link to any site does not imply our endorsement. Please use care and discretion while browsing the Internet, and let us know if any of the links are outdated or inappropriate.

Acknowledgments

The materials we publish are always family projects. We have all had a hand in helping this curriculum come to fruition. John and Charlene Notgrass provided essential input on lesson content. John also did the graphic design of the book layout and helped with the editing of the volume of original sources. Nate McCurdy produced the charts and graphs. Mary Evelyn McCurdy designed the covers. Charlene reworked the review and test questions from the first edition. Bethany Poore developed the literature component and the lesson assignments and activities.

We have also benefited from the work of others. Ellen Petree, who is state certified in economics, reviewed the first edition and offered valuable insights. Larry Raper, who understands economic issues well because of his career with a major insurance company, also read the lessons and made many helpful suggestions. I am grateful for the help that these and other people have provided, but any errors and shortcomings are mine.

May we all be wiser stewards (the Greek word is *oikonomoi*, from which we get the English word economics) of the great gifts God gives us, and may He be honored through this curriculum.

Ray Notgrass
Gainesboro, Tennessee
December 2016
ray@notgrass.com

Clothing factory in Bangladesh (2012)

How to Use the Curriculum

Exploring Economics is a one-semester high school course that helps students understand economic terms and issues that have an impact on the United States and its citizens. This course introduces both microeconomics and macroeconomics. In states where a year-long course is considered one high school credit, the economics and English components count as one-half credit each. In states where a year-long course is considered two high school credits, each course is counted as one credit.

To earn credit for both economics and English, the student should:

- Read the lessons in the text.
- Read the assigned documents in *Making Choices*.
- Complete a project for each unit (see explanation below).
- Read the four assigned books.
- Read the literary analysis for each book in the *Student Review*.
- Complete the assignments found at the end of the literary analysis for each book.
- **Optional:** Complete daily review questions, quizzes, and exams in the Student Review Pack.

If you do not wish to use *Exploring Economics* for English credit, you can omit half of the projects and the four assigned books, but we encourage you to include them because they greatly enhance your student's understanding of economics.

Unit Projects. Our design for students earning one-semester credits in both economics and English is for the student to complete one project per week as suggested in the unit introductions. The student can choose to do *either* a writing assignment or a hands-on project. For students completing the one-semester English credit, we recommend that the student choose the writing assignment at least six times during the semester.

Time Required. A student should complete each day's assignments, listed at the end of each lesson, on that day. The actual time a student spends on a given day might vary, but you should allow your student about one hour each day for economics and one hour for English. If you are using the *Student Review* material, the work for the last day of each unit includes the unit quiz, which will require a few more minutes that day. Three days in the semester will include taking an exam over the previous five units, so you should allow some more time for this activity.

We Believe in You. We believe that you are in charge of your child's education and that you know how best to use this material to educate your child. We provide you with tools and instructions, but we encourage you to tailor them to fit your child's interests and abilities and your family's situation and philosophy. Being able to do this is one of the benefits of homeschooling!

Course Descriptions

You can use the following course descriptions as you develop your school records, produce a high school transcript, or report grades.

Economics. The student will receive an introduction to Biblical teaching related to economics, economics in church history, and the economic history of the United States. The student will then explore the basics of macroeconomics and microeconomics, learning about markets, money, trade, business organization, and labor. The student will also learn how government is involved in the economy and look at modern economic challenges. The student will read a significant number of original source documents and essays about economics while studying the lessons.

English (Economics in Fiction and Non-Fiction). The student will read two novels, one book about the global economy, and one autobiography (see list below). The student will read literary analysis of the books and discuss them in writing. The student will also complete a project each week, either an essay or another creative project related to the study of economics.

Student Review Pack

The *Student Review Pack* has material that you might find helpful for increasing your student's understanding of the course and for giving you a way to know and grade your student's grasp of the content. It is an optional supplement that contains the following three components.

The *Student Review* includes review questions on each lesson, literary analysis of the books assigned in the curriculum, and essay questions on the books. The literary analysis is also available at notgrass.com/ee.

The *Quiz and Exam Book* has a quiz to be taken at the end of each unit that is based on the lesson review questions. In addition, after every five units, it has an exam that is based on the quizzes from those five units. This makes a total of fifteen quizzes and three exams over the course of the semester. The lesson review questions can serve as a study guide for the quizzes, and the quizzes can serve as a study guide for the exams.

The questions at the end of the literary analysis for the four books provide the material needed for grading English.

The *Answer Key* contains answers for the lesson review questions, literary analysis questions, and the quizzes and exams.

Assigned Literature		
Units 1-3	*Silas Marner*	George Eliot
Units 4-7	*The Rise of Silas Lapham*	William Dean Howells
Units 8-11	*The Travels of a T-Shirt in the Global Economy*	Pietra Rivoli
Units 12-15	*Mover of Men and Mountains*	R. G. LeTourneau

Wall Street and Broadway, New York City (1911)

1 Getting a Grasp of Economics

Economics is about life. It is about how people make choices, produce and use goods and services, work, spend money, and interact with each other in a local setting and around the world. An economy involves many participants, including business owners, workers, and the government. Each one plays a role in how that economy works. Economists have identified principles that describe how an economy works. Adam Smith and Karl Marx are two of the most influential economists in history, but many other economists and schools of economic thought have influenced our understanding of economics. This unit provides a survey of basic economic ideas and introduces some of the most influential economists and their ideas.

Lesson 1 - What Would You Do with Five Hundred Dollars?
Lesson 2 - Big Topics in Economics
Lesson 3 - More Big Topics
Lesson 4 - Superstars of Economics
Lesson 5 - More Big Names

Books Used

The Bible
Making Choices
Silas Marner

Project (choose one)

1) Write 300 to 500 words on one of the following topics:

- What would you do with five hundred dollars? Explain your reasons (see Lesson 1).

- Explain the ways that your household is involved in economics (jobs held; stores and other businesses patronized; property owned; charities supported, etc.).

2) Create a poster-sized work of art that represents the concept of supply and demand. Use the medium of your choice (paint, pastels, pencil, colored pencil, marker, ink, chalk, collage, etc.).

3) Conduct an interview with a parent or (with your parents' permission) another adult in your parents' or grandparents' generation. Ask your interviewee how he or she views economics; what his or her financial priorities are; major economic events in his or her own life and that they have experienced historically. Prepare at least seven questions ahead of time and try to keep the conversation within one hour to respect your interviewee's time. Use video or audio to record the interview.

Literature

Mary Ann Evans was born in Warwickshire, England, in 1819. She chose the male pen name George Eliot to help give her novels credibility at a time when female authors were associated with lightweight romantic literature. The 1864 portrait below is by Sir Frederick Burton.

Eliot's first novel, *Adam Bede*, published in 1859, was a success. Other acclaimed novels followed: *The Mill on the Floss* in 1860, *Silas Marner* in 1861, *Romola* in 1863, *Middlemarch* in 1872 and *Daniel Deronda* in 1876. Her realism and insights into the human mind set her work apart.

Silas Marner, set in an out-of-the-way English village, has a gentle pace and a somber mood. The main characters guard secrets which isolate them from healthy relationships. The unexpected arrival of a small child teaches the title character and his community the power of giving and receiving love.

George Eliot was one of the leading novelists of the 19th century, a rich period in English literature. She died in 1880.

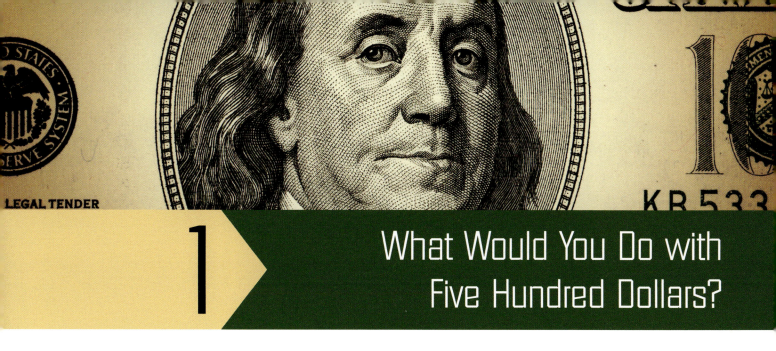

1 What Would You Do with Five Hundred Dollars?

Economics is a study of mankind in the ordinary business of life.
— Alfred Marshall, Principles of Economics *(1890)*

Suppose you had five hundred dollars. What would you do with it? This is one way to look at some of the basic issues of economics.

The five hundred dollars are a resource that you obtained from somewhere. Perhaps you worked for someone who put a value of five hundred dollars on your labor. Perhaps your parents gave it to you over time as an allowance. You might have inherited the money from a relative. However you came to have it, someone earned it. Economics concerns how people acquire wealth.

Maybe you don't have five hundred dollars in cash; maybe you have a resource worth five hundred dollars in another form. It might be a tree on your property that you could cut down and sell for the lumber. Your resource might be a skill that you could offer to perform for others, such as doing plumbing work or mowing lawns. Economics deals with the value that people place on goods and services.

Your five hundred dollars is a resource, but it is limited. This means that you must decide what you are going to do with it from among several alternatives. Even if you had a million dollars, or a trillion dollars, your resource would still be limited. Economics is about making choices about what to do with limited—or scarce—resources.

You might put the money in the bank, which would mean that you could earn interest on it. This would also allow the bank to loan some of your five hundred dollars to someone else. You would make money on the interest you receive, the bank would make money on the interest it charges for the loan, and the recipient of the loan could make money by investing the money in a business. How the banking system works is part of economics.

You might decide to invest the five hundred dollars in a business of your own. If you buy some tools, you could increase your productivity and do work for others who would pay you for your labor. You could print flyers to advertise your services as a babysitter and get more babysitting jobs. You might buy ingredients to make lemonade, set up a stand, and sell the lemonade at a profit. A key topic in economics is productivity.

You might decide to buy something for yourself with the five hundred dollars. If you do, the owner of the store will make a profit, and the store owner will pay the person who made the item so that he or she also makes a profit. The store owner and the

3

Lemonade stand at the Zapata County Fair, Zapata, Texas (2014)

maker of the item will then use their profits to buy things they want or need, so the impact of your five hundred dollars is multiplied many times over. Economics studies this circulation of money. If you do buy something, you will want to make the wisest purchase you can and one that will benefit you the most. This is being a good steward of your resources.

You might decide to give some of the five hundred dollars to your church, or to a charity, or to an individual you know who is in need. The way you spend your money—whether as a purchase, a gift, or an investment—reflects what you think about God.

But you can't save it all, invest it all, spend it all, and give it all. You have to make choices about how you are going to use your resource.

So far, we have just talked about you, your five hundred dollars, and what you and other participants in the economy might do with it. But other players are involved with your five hundred dollars. We have to consider the government's interest in your money. The government plays a major role in economics. If you earned the money as income, you might have to pay income tax on it. You probably won't have to pay taxes on it if you only make five hundred dollars in a year; but if it is the last five hundred dollars of a much larger total amount of earnings, you probably will have to pay taxes on it. This involves the reality of marginal tax rates, which we will discuss later.

If you buy something with the money, you will probably have to pay sales tax. Government policies will determine if you have to pay more income or sales tax than you paid last year. If the people in charge of government decide to start a new program, they will want more tax revenue to pay for it. Unfortunately, governments rarely want decreasing amounts of tax revenue. In general, taxes discourage economic activity and growth; but governments must obtain revenue from somewhere.

So far we have assumed that you have a choice about what you do with your five hundred dollars. The kind of government and economy in which you live will affect what choices you have. If you live in a country where the government runs the economy (often called a command economy), government bureaucrats would decide what gets produced and what gets put on the store shelves for you to buy. This kind of economy limits a person's choices, and it limits the economic activity that takes place in that country. If you wanted to start a business, you would have to get government approval for the kind of business you wanted to start. But because of the nature of a command economy, you would be less likely to have five hundred dollars with which to make economic choices anyway.

If you buy something with your five hundred dollars that has been made in another country, you enter into the realm of international trade. Our government allowed a business to import that item from another country through a trade treaty or trade agreement with that country. The person who made the item in that other country may have received a lower wage than a worker making the same item in the United States would have received. An American company might have built the factory in the other country because it can pay workers there less than it would have to pay workers in the United States. All of these elements are issues in economic policy.

Here's an even more basic question: What is the five hundred dollars? What you have are small pieces of paper printed with green ink that have "United States of America," "Federal Reserve Note," "In God We Trust," and other phrases, numbers, and pictures on them. You might be able to create a piece of paper that is more attractive, but it would be worth nothing economically unless another person also considered it valuable. Who says that these pieces of paper have a value of five hundred dollars?

Money is an agreed-upon medium of exchange, whether it is metal coins, pieces of paper printed by the government, or electronic records in a bank. Money allows you to buy things more easily than if we had a barter economy, in which people exchange goods and services directly instead of buying and selling them with money.

When making plans about using your money, you must keep in mind inflation. Inflation is a decline in the value of money, which is evident in a rise in prices for goods and services. A year from now your pieces of green paper that add up to $500.00 might be worth only $490.00 in relative purchasing power because of the impact of inflation.

Economics can be a complicated subject, but this simple situation illustrates many of the issues involved in economics:

You have five hundred dollars. What are you going to do with it?

Origin of the Word Economics

The terms economics, economist, and economy come from the Greek word *oikonomos* (oy-ko-NO-mos), which means steward. This compound Greek word is formed from two shorter words, *oikos*, meaning house, and *nemein*, meaning to manage (the word *nomos*, law, is related to *nemein*). An *oikonomos* was the manager or steward of a household, a position of responsibility that a slave often held. His work was an *oikonomia* (oy-ko-no-ME-ah), or stewardship. The New Testament uses the Greek words in this sense in Luke 12:42-48, Luke 16:1-8, and Galatians 4:2.

The terms came to have a broader application that involved the stewardship or carrying out of any responsibilities related to an office, even the leadership of a country. Romans 16:23 mentions Erastus, the city treasurer or *oikonomos* of Corinth.

Paul used the word to describe the stewardship or the carrying out of responsibilities that God entrusted to him as an apostle (1 Corinthians 4:1-2, 9:17). Paul also used it in describing the role of an overseer, bishop, or elder as a steward carrying out a responsibility in the church (Titus 1:7). Peter used it for the stewardship or proper handling of the grace of God that God expects of all Christians (1 Peter 4:10-11). Another occurrence with a slightly different meaning was the way Paul used the term in Ephesians 1:10, where *oikonomia* means God's working out of His plan for "the summing up of all things in Christ."

In generations previous to ours, the English word *economy* referred primarily to the management of a household. People later applied it to the carrying out of any responsibility, and then to the fiscal life of a country.

Words related to the term economics, such as the adjective *economical* or the verb *economize*, refer to being wise or frugal—that is, being a good manager—in financial matters. In spite of the original meaning of the word, an economist does not necessarily manage the financial affairs of a country. Economists for the most part study the field of economics. They might teach in universities, work for investment companies, write books, or give speeches. Some economists are in positions of responsibility within government. These positions enable them to influence or manage economic activity.

The Meaning of Economics Today

People have defined economics in various ways. Economist Jacob Viner (1892-1970) said, "Economics is what economists do." This is true, but it does not help much. The definition by Alfred Marshall (1842-1924) at the start of this lesson, "Economics is a study of mankind in the ordinary business of life," is also true and broadly descriptive, although we would still like more specifics.

Shoe factory in Borovo, Croatia (2015)

Lesson 1 - What Would You Do with Five Hundred Dollars?

Many economists emphasize the fact of scarce or limited resources and the choices people make concerning them. British economist Lionel Robbins (1898-1984) said, "Economics is a science which studies human behavior as a relationship between ends and scarce means which have alternative uses." Merriam-Webster's Collegiate Dictionary, Eleventh Edition, defines economics as "a social science concerned chiefly with description and analysis of the production, distribution, and consumption of goods and services." Let's think about that last definition some more.

Production issues involve the supply of goods and services available in a society. Production deals with such matters as what to make, who makes or who should make it, what they give up in order to make it (a decision that economists call the opportunity cost), the resources needed to make it (such as labor, raw materials, and technology), the production of capital goods (the machinery required to make other goods), and the desire to keep the cost of production as low as possible. Production also involves the organization of business, issues related to the employment of workers, and the desire that companies and workers have for ever-greater productivity. Many of these questions involve the production of goods, but the production of services—such as health care, education, and transportation—is also a vital part of this topic.

Distribution deals with getting goods and services to the public. This gets into the demand side of the supply-and-demand equation. How will producers distribute goods and services: through sale in the market or by the government providing them? Who will get them? At what price can people obtain them? Will the producer or provider set the price to generate a profit? Distribution issues involve transactions within a country and trade among the nations of the world.

Consumption takes place by individuals, households, businesses, and governments as they purchase and use goods and services. What price will a consumer be willing to pay? What goods and services provide a consumer with utility, which in economics means satisfaction?

Economics obviously has to do with money. Production, distribution, and consumption generate income for individuals and for businesses; and this income enables more production, distribution, and consumption. Banks and other financial institutions provide people with a place to keep their money safely. Banks use that money to invest in mortgages and in loans to businesses so that banks can earn more money.

Behind these issues are policy questions that the government addresses. What trade policies and regulations of business should the government pursue to enable the most effective production, distribution, and consumption of goods and services? What policies regarding money should the government pursue to encourage a stable and growing economy? How should the government generate funding for its programs through taxes on the production, distribution, and consumption of goods and services?

As you can see, economics deals with the ways that many aspects of life work together.

Economics as Science and Art

Economics is a science, but not in the same way that chemistry is a science. As a social science, economics identifies principles, which are sometimes even called laws, based on what has generally happened in financial or business activity. But economics studies human behavior, and humans have the ability to choose their behavior whereas chemical compounds do not. The economic behavior being studied might be that of an individual, a group, a locality, a business, an industry, a nation, or even the entire world. Moreover, economics assumes that people make rational decisions; but of course they do not always do so. Economists can attempt to predict the outcomes of certain behaviors and patterns of activity, but (1) they might be wrong and (2) the outcomes might take years to occur.

As you study economics, you need to remember that the world economy is constantly changing. New economic realities, such as major technological changes, come into existence. Traditionally accepted definitions run up against new situations. For instance, the classic simple distinction between a capitalist economy and a command economy does not have a clear category for what happened during the economic recession of 2007-2009, when the capitalist American government oversaw the merger of investment companies and took over private enterprises. Economic assumptions often have to change to meet these new realities.

Economists have their own opinions about why certain things have happened and what they think should happen. Two economists can come to quite different conclusions about what caused a particular economic trend or event, and they can offer different ideas about what they think should happen in the future. In other words, economists are interested in the way things are; but they are also interested in the way they think things ought to be. In this curriculum we will try to offer a basic understanding of how the economy works, and we will try to present fairly opposing ideas on economic issues; but we too have opinions about certain matters, and those opinions will be obvious from time to time.

So get ready for a study of a field that is constantly changing, a field that examines financial activities which affect the entire globe, but a field that also has something to say about your personal resources. After all, God cares about the decisions you make regarding what He places in your care.

And the Lord said, "Who then is the faithful and sensible steward, whom his master will put in charge of his servants, to give them their rations at the proper time? Blessed is that slave whom his master finds so doing when he comes. Truly I say to you that he will put him in charge of all his possessions."
Luke 12:42-44

Assignments for Lesson 1

Literature — Read "Who, What, How, Why, and Why Not: A Primer for Literary Analysis of Fiction," available on page 3 of the *Student Review* or on our website.

Begin reading *Silas Marner*. Plan to finish it by the end of Unit 3.

Project — Choose your project for this unit and start working on it.

Student Review — Answer the questions for Lesson 1.

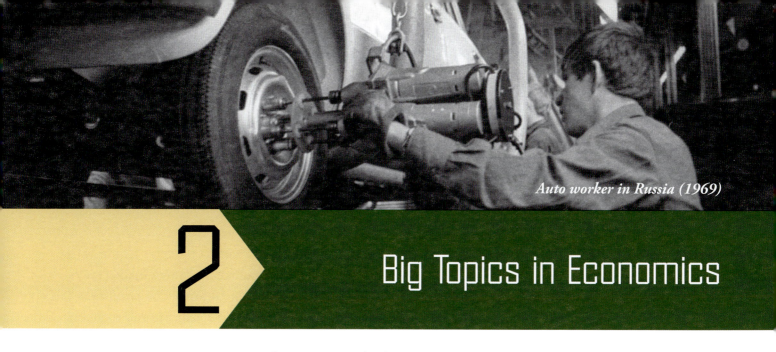

Auto worker in Russia (1969)

2 Big Topics in Economics

There's no such thing as a free lunch.

— *Anonymous*

Webster defines an economy as "the structure or conditions of economic life in a country, area, or period." Economists recognize two basic kinds of economic systems. One is called the *market*, *free market*, or *capitalist* economy. In this system, private individuals own the means of production, meaning the capital by which people produce goods and services. Suppliers are free to offer whatever goods and services they wish, and buyers are free to obtain whatever goods and services they can afford. The only limitation that suppliers have is their production capability, and the only limitation buyers have is what producers offer in the market and what buyers can afford. The United States has traditionally had a market economy.

The other major type of economic system is the *command* economy, in which some authority (usually the government) dictates what and how much producers will produce. Another term that people often use to describe this kind of economy is *socialist*. Under socialism, the state or the government, in the name of the people as a whole, owns the means of production. Everyone works for the government in a command economy, since the government has final say over what people do. The decisions that people in government make regarding what workers produce do not necessarily reflect what buyers actually want. Instead, those decisions reflect the priorities or wishes of government leaders, which might have little to do with the actual economic wants and needs of the people.

A command economy limits what buyers will be able to obtain because the government, not suppliers or the marketplace, determines what producers will produce. In addition, because a command economy does not consistently reward productivity and does not provide the motivation for profits, goods are not as readily available and the system hampers innovation. Buyers in a command economy on average have less money to buy goods and services than do people in market economies because the government sets wages, which often do not accurately reflect workers' effort or ability. This is another limitation on what people can obtain. Also, governments can ration goods and services to the people, even if the people pay for them. The government can declare, for instance, that an individual can purchase no more than ten gallons of gasoline per week. This is yet another way in which a command economy limits choices for buyers.

However, modern economies are usually not purely market or purely command. An economy that has elements of both market and command economies is called a *mixed* economy. This describes most national economies today, although most economies lean toward either being more free market or more command. In countries that most people consider to be capitalist, for instance, the government owns or oversees parts of the economy to varying degrees. Examples are socialized health care and government-owned transportation systems. This is common in the countries of Western Europe. In the United States, the federal government has created businesses such as Amtrak for passenger rail service and the Tennessee Valley Authority, which generates electricity for much of the southeastern part of the country.

A free market economy also has government regulations that affect supply and demand. For instance, ever since the New Deal policies President Franklin Roosevelt instituted during the Great Depression of the 1930s, farmers have deliberately grown lower quantities of certain crops than was possible. The federal government pays subsidies to farmers for not growing more as a way to boost farmers' income. This policy limits supply and causes prices for consumers to be higher.

On the other hand, though China has traditionally had a command economy, market forces are growing within that country. The government has allowed a limited number of private, capitalist enterprises to operate alongside the government-controlled businesses.

Countries that once had command economies but are now developing market economies are sometimes called *transition* economies. Former Communist countries in Eastern Europe are in this category. They are moving toward free markets, but

Amtrak train in Bakersfield, California, celebrating the 40th anniversary of the rail service in 2011.

the change from a command economy is neither quick nor painless. People who have been subject to government dictates for decades have to learn how to operate in freedom.

A Focus on the American Economy

In this curriculum, our main emphasis is on the economy of the United States. We examine such topics as the production and distribution of goods and services; the supply of and demand for these goods and services in the marketplace; the prices that these goods and services bear; competition in the marketplace among those who supply the same or similar goods and services; the income that people receive; how the operation of businesses in the marketplace affects business owners, workers, and the public; how money works in an economy; the role of banking, saving, and investment; government policies regarding taxation, regulations that deal with business activity, and government spending for its operation and for programs that the government decides to fund; matters such as inflation, economic expansions, economic recessions, and the business cycle; agricultural production and sales; international trade, which includes government policies that encourage or discourage trade and the exchange rate for the various national currencies; and much more.

But what comes first in a study of economics? How does an economy develop and grow? How did we get where we are in our economy, and how should we go on from here? In this lesson and the next, we outline a basic approach to understanding economics. To do this, we will use some simple, idealized models. A common practice in economics is the creation of a simple model that illustrates principles. Real life doesn't usually happen exactly the way that the model describes, but the model isolates important principles so that we can understand how those principles work in the complex web of economic life.

Specialization, Interdependence, and Choices

Imagine a society in which each person works to support himself. Each person sees his well-being as completely a matter of personal responsibility. He grows his own food, makes his own clothes, and builds his own house. If an individual wants a horse, he captures it and tames it himself. If a family wants meat, someone in the family goes hunting to kill an animal or captures animals to domesticate them. Individuals might claim property as their own; or the community might hold property as a tribe and challenge the claims that other tribes make for that property.

Economic interdependence comes when people begin specializing in certain kinds of work that they perform for others and for which they receive payment of some kind. For instance, people might recognize one person for his good work in building houses, so they ask him to build houses for them. Community members recognize someone else as a skilled hunter, yet another for making clothes or pottery. The people of this society realize that they will be better off if they trade the goods or services that they each do well (meaning what they do more efficiently or with better quality). This is called *specialization of labor*. When people begin concentrating on their specialized skills, they become interdependent on each other for their well-being and sometimes even for their existence.

This interdependence requires some adjustments and some new decisions. Making a decision to do something involves, by default, deciding not to do other things. In other words, whenever anyone makes a decision to do A, they are also deciding not to do B, C, or D. This introduces the principle of *opportunity cost*: the real cost of doing or making one thing includes the cost of not doing or making something else.

Economics involves choices. If you choose to buy a soft drink, you give up the ability to use that same money to buy a candy bar or to save it in a bank. When people realize that they are better off concentrating on certain skills and depending on others for other goods and services, they begin to experience the principle of *comparative advantage*. Producer A has a comparative advantage over Producer B when Producer A has a smaller opportunity cost (that is, when he gives up less) than Producer B. We'll talk more about these terms and their meaning later in the curriculum.

As we mentioned earlier, an economy never stands still. The issues never stay the same. Someone develops a better way to build houses, someone discovers iron and others discover ways to use it, someone invents the automobile, someone else develops the personal computer, and on it goes. When someone develops a better, faster, or cheaper way to accomplish a goal, once-thriving industries—such as the production, distribution, and use of typewriters or film cameras—can shrink dramatically.

These examples demonstrate the role of innovation and productivity in an economy. Increased demand for goods and services means that more people can find jobs in those industries; decreased demand (or greater efficiency or moving a factory overseas) means that fewer people work in a given industry, at least in a certain country. We will discuss other ways that an economy grows or shrinks in a later lesson.

In the past, a society might have operated for some time with little concern that any resource they need might be in short supply. It might appear that there is no shortage of animals, trees, grain, or any other resource. At some point, however, the society will likely realize that the resources it wants and needs are not limitless. Perhaps the population grows to the point that the people need more grain or wood or land than the country has. Perhaps those who have been hunters can no longer provide meat for the growing population. These shortages mean that the people in this society have to make choices about what they do with their limited resources.

The Circular-Flow Diagram

One way to illustrate how an economy operates is with a circular-flow diagram, as seen below. The simplest form has two entities—households (which includes individuals) and businesses. The arrows indicate the direction in which the elements flow.

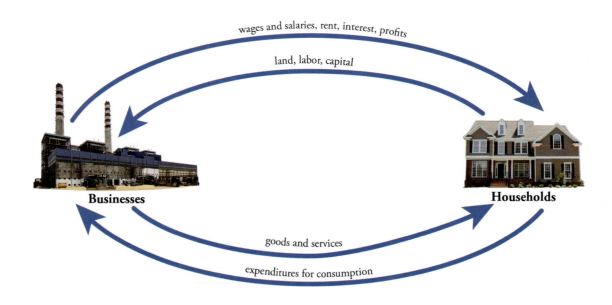

Lesson 2 - Big Topics in Economics

People provide the land, labor, and capital (which includes machinery and other means of production) that create businesses. Businesses produce goods and services which they offer to the people. The people expend their resources to consume the goods and services that businesses provide. Businesses use the income they receive from these sales to pay for the land and facilities and to pay workers with salaries or wages. Businesses pay back any loans they have taken out that enable them to operate, plus interest on those loans. After paying for these expenses and the cost of the materials of the goods and services they have produced, anything left over is profit. A business might share its profit among its owners, but the owners will likely reinvest some of the profit back into the business so that it can produce more goods and services or produce them more efficiently.

The flows that the arrows in the diagram on page 12 indicate are continuous and enable the other flows to occur. Households must provide businesses with people and resources in order for businesses to be able to produce goods and services. Businesses must provide goods and services for people to have something to buy and consume. People must buy goods and services for businesses to be able to pay salaries and expenses. Businesses must pay salaries and wages for households to be able to buy goods and services. And on and on it goes.

The circular-flow diagram on this page is more complex but more realistic because we have added three more elements. First, all of the arrows flow through markets, which are places where goods and services are bought and sold. Businesses offer goods and services in a market, where households buy them. Households offer land, labor, and capital in real estate, labor, and financial markets. Individuals consider where they can earn the most money and businesses try to find the best labor at the lowest price. Businesses try to minimize their costs and maximize their profits.

Second, some of these activities go through the sphere of international trade. People invest in companies that operate in other countries, companies ship their products to consumers in other countries, some of what people buy comes from other countries, and some companies pay workers in other countries. Some of that overseas activity comes back to the country from which it originated. For instance, companies sometimes invest profits in countries other than where they make those profits. Many people outside of the United States, for instance, invest in American companies.

Furniture store

Third, another sphere through which the arrows flow is the government. From the buying and selling that takes place in the markets, government takes money in the form of taxes. Government then spends that money by paying government workers (who then become consumers) and by providing certain services to certain people. Sometimes businesses provide goods and services to the government, such as military equipment. In these transactions, the government is a consumer.

As a general rule, government does not create wealth. Instead, the wealth that people create in the market provides funding for government operations. Government might enable people to create wealth, by funding certain experimental projects, for instance; but the work and ingenuity of people create the wealth.

The Market, Supply and Demand, and Prices

People who specialize their efforts in certain ways and who offer their goods and services to others for a price create a market. A market operates on the principle of supply and demand. A market involves the relationship between the supply of goods and services that people want to sell, and the demand for those goods and services by people who want to buy. The market enables the transaction to take place. In the market, suppliers learn what people want and are willing to pay for, and consumers reward with their purchases those suppliers who provide what they want and need. Of course, the same people can be both suppliers and

Lesson 2 - Big Topics in Economics

consumers. For instance, the person who supplies horses will also want food and clothes.

The law of supply and demand works because of the power of prices. Prices in the marketplace determine whether an individual or a company can survive in the marketplace by supplying goods or services at a certain price and then obtaining other goods and services from other suppliers at certain prices. Prices also determine whether customers will be able to afford the goods and services offered.

A supplier charges a price for his goods or service such that, when he receives payment, it makes it worth his effort. If, for example, someone who does lawn care charges less than his expenses for gasoline and equipment, he will soon go out of business. At the same time, the price he charges must be reasonable given the level of competition in the marketplace. If he charges significantly more than what others who supply lawn care charge for comparable service, he will likewise soon go out of business. His charges must be low enough given the competition in the marketplace and high enough for him to make a profit from his work.

Money as a Medium of Exchange

Barter involves the exchange of goods or services in which people determine equivalent values. For instance, if I make a table for you in exchange for your providing me with a horse, that is a barter exchange. This process works well in some situations.

Paper currency from various countries

However, if I need a horse but you do not need a table, what do I do? The resolution of this dilemma is the use of a common medium of exchange that has value to all parties involved. This medium of exchange is called money.

Money has no value in and of itself. If someone had a million U.S. dollars on a desert island or in a society that did not accept American money, those dollars would be worthless. Money only has value in terms of what it enables a person to obtain. In our society, money is a medium of exchange that enables a person to obtain goods and services that he or she wants or needs. Money makes economic activity easier because people only have to determine the value of something in terms of money and not in terms of pigs, chickens, ears of corn, car washes, piano lessons, or anything else they might exchange for the item.

As we study economics, we should remember that all we have is a gift and a trust from God.

Furthermore, as for every man to whom God has given riches and wealth, He has also empowered him to eat from them and to receive his reward and rejoice in his labor; this is the gift of God.
Ecclesiastes 5:19

Assignments for Lesson 2

Making Choices — Read "I, Pencil" (pages 1-6).

Literature — Continue reading *Silas Marner*.

Project — Continue working on your project for this unit.

Student Review — Answer the questions for Lesson 2.

Port of Singapore

3 More Big Topics

Labor can do nothing without capital, capital nothing without labor, and neither labor nor capital can do anything without the guiding genius of management; and management, however wise its genius may be, can do nothing without the privileges which the community affords.
— W. L. Mackenzie King, Canadian politician (1919)

International Trade

The American economy involves more than the goods and services produced within our own country. Our economy is engaged in the world market of international trade. For instance, some of the oil we use comes from outside of our country; and the demand for oil by other countries affects the supply of oil that is available to us. In addition, many of the products that American stores offer for sale come from foreign countries. At the same time, people in other countries buy much of what producers make in this country. The United States exports more merchandise than any other country except China.

Some American companies have found that it is more profitable for them to manufacture their products overseas where labor is cheaper, while workers in the United States do the research and development and marketing of those products.

The story of international trade is complex. It involves what happens in many nations, not just ours. Some of those countries do not share our commitment to freedom and do not play by the same rules we prefer regarding free trade. In addition, political instability is a reality in many places around the globe; and war and revolutions can affect trade. Besides the heartwrenching personal impact, such instability affects the economy. Workers may have to leave their work to fight in the army. They might even be wounded or killed as a result of war. Conflict destroys factories and farmland and disrupts business within the country and trade with other countries.

Business and Labor

In the American economy, individuals offer goods and services to others, submitting themselves to the law of supply and demand, and depending on the principle of prices to help them make a profit. But the situation is much more complex than that.

Individuals do offer goods and services, but our economy also involves thousands of companies that employ millions of workers. The dynamics of business and labor in the United States create most of the energy that runs the engine of our economy.

Owners of companies make goods and services available to American consumers. This process has many steps. Beyond the cost of making the goods themselves, businesses have to deal with additional costs of production such as the expense of building and maintaining a factory. They have to cope with competition from other companies, which might make newer or more innovative versions of the products. Companies grow because of investments—money that allows them to build more production capacity and hire more workers. Investments happen when people part with money that they could spend on something else in order to take a risk on a business venture.

Workers produce goods and services. These laborers want to be paid at a level that is commensurate with their efforts. Workers want a decent wage and usually some fringe benefits, which companies have to pay for out of the income they receive by selling the goods and services that they offer. These workers have to receive training to do the work that a constantly-changing economy needs. Many workers organize themselves into labor unions, which negotiate with business owners as large groups of workers who want higher wages and benefits. However, in the United States, most workers choose not to be members of unions. We will examine the pros and cons of labor unions later.

Government

Government has an impact on the economy in several ways. One way is through taxation. For instance, when government places high taxes on income, this discourages efforts by individuals to generate more income, since much of what they earn has to go to the government. High taxes on corporate profits mean that corporations have less money to invest in their own growth.

Taxes placed on imported goods are called tariffs. These cause imported goods to cost more. The higher price means that fewer of these imported goods will likely be sold in the importing country. High tariffs also discourage exports, since people in other countries will have less money to buy goods that we might export if Americans buy few of the goods they produce. Tariffs sometimes cause trade wars, in which a country retaliates against another country for a high tariff placed on its exports by imposing tariffs on what the other country wants to export. Tariffs tend to cause higher prices for goods made within a country, since domestic manufacturers have protection from competition with cheaper imports. Domestic companies therefore have less incentive to reduce their production costs. Higher prices usually mean that consumers will buy fewer goods.

Another way that government affects the economy is through the policies it enacts. For instance, a government might ban completely the importation of certain goods. That country will then find it hard to sell its goods to countries which produce the banned goods. Also, most economists believe that a government policy of setting a minimum wage discourages the hiring of young, low-skilled workers. This contributes to higher unemployment, even though raising the minimum wage is often a politically popular action. If the government has a practice of spending more than the revenue it receives, it has to borrow money to fund some of its programs. This obligates some of the money that could be invested in business growth.

A third way that the government influences the economy is through regulations that it places on businesses. If the government requires a factory to install a sprinkler system and place fire extinguishers every seventy-five feet, the company has to pay for those items. The company passes on the costs to consumers in the form of higher prices, which can discourage buying. If the government requires

Officials use x-rays to scan a cargo truck crossing the border from Germany into Switzerland.

pollution control systems on cars, carmakers will pass on the cost for these systems to the consumer. If the government requires companies to complete many documents regarding hiring practices, safety measures, or other matters, companies might have to hire additional workers to comply with those requirements, which again increases the cost of production.

Sometimes these regulations are worthwhile in the overall picture. For instance, the government might require that factory owners install pollution control systems. These will add to the cost of producing goods. However, without regulation companies may poison streams and air, which increases health problems among the population. These health problems have an economic cost as well as a personal cost. Environmental impacts are *externalities*. This term refers to economic effects external to the direct production of goods but which are a reality nonetheless. As you can see, even a government policy of doing nothing still reflects an economic policy decision and has an impact.

A fourth way that government influences the economy is by its monetary policy. Most countries have a central bank, which oversees the money supply. Governments also have treasury departments that develop and apply monetary policies. We will see that monetary policy has a significant impact on the economy.

Surf shop in Kona, Hawaii

Economic Institutions

In a free economy, producing goods and services to meet the demands of consumers, creating markets for the sale or exchange of goods and services, and setting prices for those goods and services, all take place without coordination by any individuals or groups. However, when people perceive a need, they take action to organize institutions to meet those needs, including institutions that help the economy operate. Among these institutions are corporations, labor unions, banks and other financial establishments.

In addition, people develop rules for the just and orderly operation of the market. The legal system codifies rules which participants in the economic system must follow for the good of everyone involved. These laws deal with such matters as truthfulness in advertising, the forbidding of actions that would hinder free and fair trade, the sanctity of contracts, the safety of goods sold in the market, and other issues that relate to the operation of the economy.

The institution of the rights of property owners is a vital element of a successful market economy. Property owners have rights because of their status as owners, and they have legal protection against individuals or the government encroaching upon their property or unreasonably seizing their property. If property were subject to whatever the government or another individual might want to do, property ownership would have little value and property owners would have little motivation to use their property to contribute to the economy.

Lesson 3 - More Big Topics

Measuring and Defining the Economy

Anecdotes about a factory closing or a business doing well are not sufficient to give us an accurate picture of the overall economy. Economists, government officials, and the public want to know in specific, objective terms how the economy is functioning. Economists have devised several ways to measure economic activity. The single statistic that provides the broadest picture is the gross domestic product or GDP, which is a measure of the value of all of the finished goods and services produced within a country.

Economists have devised many other means of evaluating the state of the economy, including the rate of inflation, the unemployment rate (the percentage of potential workers who do not have jobs), household income, the poverty rate (the percentage of the population that lives below what the government determines to be the minimum income to provide needed goods and services), home sales, and home construction activity.

Moreover, economists have developed many terms that they use to analyze economic activity. For instance, economists talk about macroeconomics and microeconomics. Macroeconomics looks at the big picture of the economy as a whole. It emphasizes such elements as a country's GDP, the rate of inflation, the unemployment rate, and the level of productivity. Macroeconomics considers how the various parts of an economy work together, whether that economy is local, national, or global. Microeconomics, by contrast, considers the small picture. It examines how individual households and companies make decisions, how buyers and sellers interact in the market, and other individual elements of an economy. We will discuss other specialized terms that economists use in later lessons.

Economics and You

One goal of a study of economics is to help you think the way an economist thinks. That might not sound very exciting, but thinking the way an economist thinks helps you to be engaged with the world in which you live. Life should be more than just reacting to situations around you. You will live more successfully if you don't just complain about high gasoline prices or shake your head when the government announces a new tax policy or a new regulation.

Street vendor and general store in Corozal, Belize

When you understand more about economics, you will realize that what seems like a good idea or a good development might not be so good after all, and that what might appear to be a step backwards could actually be helpful in the long run. With a better grasp of economics, you won't be in the dark, just working for a living, watching your money come in and go out, and voting for whoever makes the promises that you want to hear.

However, we also want to encourage you to think about economics as a Christian. That is, we hope that a commitment to God's principles in the Bible will guide your study of economics and all of your financial dealings throughout your life. These principles teach us how God wants us to view people, money, decisions, natural resources, and all other aspects of economic life. We hope that you will commit yourself to the way of honesty, righteousness, and trust in God instead of trusting in riches. "The earth is the Lord's, and all it contains; the world, and those who dwell in it" (Psalm 24:1). Since this is true, economics belongs to Him.

We should respect and seek to understand the value that God places on human beings and on all other aspects of His creation.

Are not two sparrows sold for a cent?
And yet not one of them will fall to the ground apart from your Father.
But the very hairs of your head are all numbered.
So do not fear; you are more valuable than many sparrows.
Matthew 10:29-31

Assignments for Lesson 3

Literature — Continue reading *Silas Marner*.

Project — Continue working on your project for this unit.

Student Review — Answer the questions for Lesson 3.

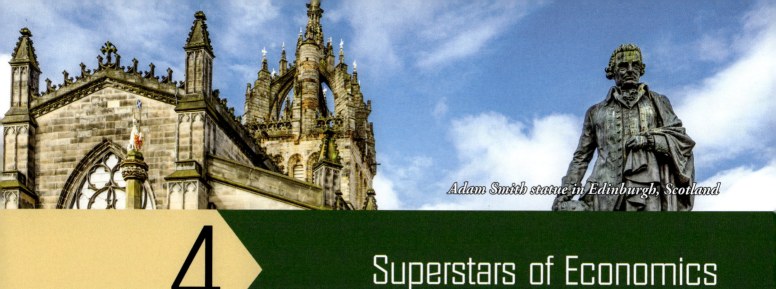
Adam Smith statue in Edinburgh, Scotland

4 Superstars of Economics

Little else is requisite to carry a state to the highest degree of opulence from the lowest barbarism but peace, easy taxes, and a tolerable administration of justice: all the rest being brought about by the natural course of things.
— Adam Smith, 1755 lecture

Many people have studied economics. Some have had a significant and lasting impact on the field. Two men, one who lived in the eighteenth century and one who lived in the nineteenth century, represent two major schools of economic thought. One man's work was the basis for capitalism, while the other provided the foundation for command economies or socialism. Each man has had devoted followers who believe that his ideas best describe how a healthy economic system should work.

This lesson introduces these men and their ideas. While economics includes a great deal about theories and numbers, we should not forget—as these men did not forget—that in economics we are talking about human beings and how they think and act.

Life of Adam Smith (1723-1790)

Adam Smith, a Scottish philosopher, is often called the father of modern economics. In 1776 he published *An Inquiry into the Nature and Causes of the Wealth of Nations* (commonly shortened to *The Wealth of Nations*). Many people see this as the beginning of the study of economics as an independent discipline.

Adam Smith was born in Kirkcaldy, Scotland, in 1723. His father died about six months before he was born. Adam enrolled at the University of Glasgow at the age of fourteen. In 1740, he undertook studies in Oxford, England; but Smith was not happy there and left in 1746.

With help from a patron, Smith began giving lectures in Edinburgh on various subjects. In 1751, he began teaching at Glasgow University. Smith published *The Theory of Moral Sentiments* in 1759. In this book, he claimed that the human ability to develop moral thinking and demonstrate concern for others came from a person's interaction with other people. He claimed that this ability to interact with others overcame a person's basic self-interest.

Smith also developed his thinking about economics. In 1763, he accepted an offer to be the private tutor to Henry Scott, the Duke of Buccleuch, at a salary much greater than what he received at Glasgow University. In this new role, Smith traveled with Scott to Europe, where he met many intellectuals, such as French philosopher Voltaire and American statesman Benjamin Franklin.

Smith's work as a tutor ended in 1766, when he returned to his hometown and began work on a treatise on economics. He published *The Wealth of Nations* ten years later, and it met with immediate success. The book went through five editions during his lifetime.

In 1778, Smith received an appointment as a commissioner of customs. He moved to Edinburgh and lived with his mother. Adam Smith never married. He died in 1790.

The Wealth of Nations

Like many influential books and leaders, Smith's work both reflected the tide of the times and also furthered important concepts. The prevailing economic philosophy in the 1700s was mercantilism, in which the king and his small group of advisors guided and encouraged economic development by granting favors to certain individuals and groups. Mercantilism envisioned an economy that operated from the top down. The primary determinant of the wealth that a nation possessed was the amount of gold and silver that a king or government controlled. A country could increase its holdings of gold and silver by exploring and by trading with other countries.

Smith challenged this belief by proposing that the real "wealth of nations" lay in the labor that its citizens supplied in producing the "necessaries and conveniences" which the nation either consumed or traded with other nations. Rather than taking a top-down view of economic activity, Smith said that the economy actually developed from the bottom up, as the labor of the people of a nation powered the economic machine that generated wealth. Smith claimed that, rather than economic success coming from the decisions of the king, the most significant economic growth occurred when the government stayed out of the way and let the operations of an unhampered market produce profits for its participants (and also for the king).

In Smith's view, a natural order exists in the world which, when people respect it and allow it to function, produces what is good. A part of this natural order is the right of people to pursue the work they want to do or feel a need to do. What people produce by their labor is the result of each person's self-interest. The butcher, for instance, sells meat not primarily because he wants to provide food for other people but because he wants to have enough income to feed his own family. The baker sells bread for the same reason.

This pursuit of mutual self-interest by all of those in a free market leads not to chaos or merciless competition but to the availability of goods and services that all people can purchase with the profits of their own labor. The goods and services

Engraving of Adam Smith by John Kay (1790)

The Author of the Wealth of Nations

The Baker's Cart, *Jean Michelin (French, 1656)*

that producers offer, the amount of each that they produce, and the prices they charge for those goods and services are best established not by government decree but by what Smith called the "invisible hand" of the market. Just as these principles apply to economic activity within a nation, they also apply to trade among the nations. Thus, Smith advocated free trade, regulated only by the forces of supply and demand in the international market.

After laying down these principles, Smith examined such topics as money, prices, wages, capital, and the role of government. Government, he said, influenced economics by its policies, by treaties between nations, by maintaining subservient colonies, by the nature and amount of revenue it collected, and by the debt that it accumulated.

Throughout his book, Smith advocated respect for man's freedom and warned against government action that hindered national (and thus individual) well-being. However, Smith also warned that the self-interest of businessmen can hurt people when that self-interest limits competition and access to goods and services. Government's best remedy for such injuries is not intervening in the market any further than simply preventing a monopoly. Competition, he said, is part of the natural order and will rectify any inequities.

Smith's ideas had wide influence. They were a key foundation of what became known as *laissez faire* economics. The term is French for "allow to do," and those who advocated this policy wanted government to refrain from any regulation of economic activity.

As a result of Smith's insights, government control of the economy through mercantilism gave way in much of the western world to capitalism and greater freedom of economic activity for individuals and companies, although tariffs continued to be a common way for governments to try to generate revenue and to control international trade.

Critics of Smith's ideas have questioned whether the "invisible hand" really exists. They have noted that Smith assumed that producers and consumers always make rational decisions, which they do not. Critics have also pointed to decisions by business owners in unregulated economies that have exploited workers and consumers who lacked basic protections that government can offer.

Life of Karl Marx (1818-1883)

The best-known economic theorist of the nineteenth century, Karl Marx, was born in Trier, Prussia, in 1818. His father was ethnically Jewish but converted to Lutheranism in order to be able to practice law. Marx was educated at home until he was thirteen and then at the Trier Gymnasium school. He later studied at the University of Bonn and Humboldt University in Berlin. Marx received a doctorate in 1841.

During his university studies, Marx became a radical revolutionary thinker. The philosophy of George W. F. Hegel (1770-1831) was a major influence on Marx. According to Hegel's theory of the historical dialectic, an idea, which Hegel called the thesis, becomes dominant in some field of thought. Then people arise who oppose this idea; their thinking is called the antithesis. The result of the debate between proponents of the two ideas is a new idea, or the synthesis. The synthesis then becomes the new thesis, and the process begins anew. Marx believed that this is how philosophies develop. He also believed that he was part of the movement proposing the antithesis to traditional political and economic thinking.

In 1843, Marx moved to Paris, where he lived among political radicals and worked for a radical

Statue of Karl Marx (left) and Friedrich Engels in Bishkek, Kyrgyzstan

newspaper. While there, he developed a close working relationship with Friedrich Engels, with whom he collaborated for the rest of his life. Marx was expelled from Paris in 1848 after he wrote an article that praised an assassination attempt on the king of Prussia.

Marx relocated to Brussels, Belgium, where he and Engels co-wrote a relatively short book called *The Communist Manifesto*. They wrote this statement of revolutionary principles on behalf of a labor organization. Marx was thereupon expelled from Brussels. He settled in London, where he lived from 1849 until his death in 1883.

Marx had a relatively secure financial situation until he moved to London. There he and his family lived in largely impoverished conditions, being supported in great measure by Engels while Marx did research on his ultimate work on economics, *Das Kapital* (*Capital*). Marx had married in 1843; he and his wife had seven children, three of whom lived to adulthood. Marx suffered from poor health during his declining years.

The first volume of *Das Kapital* was published in 1867. Two further volumes were published during his lifetime, and Engels helped to edit a fourth volume after Marx died.

The Economic Theories of Marx

Two important assumptions lay behind Marx's theories. First, he denied the spiritual realm. In 1843 he wrote, "Religion is the sigh of the oppressed creature, the heart of a heartless world, and the soul of soulless conditions. It is the opium of the people." As a result, Marx's dialectical theory of history has been called dialectical materialism. Second, as he said in *The Communist Manifesto*, "The history of all hitherto existing society is the history of class struggles," namely the ongoing struggle between the working class (the proletariat [pro-leh-TARE-e-aht]) and the ownership class (the bourgeoisie [bur-zwah-ZEE]).

In his day, as Marx saw it, owners controlled all of the means of production, including the machinery and the raw materials. The bourgeoisie needed the labor of the workers to enable the owners to make their profits, but the workers had no ownership in the fruits of their labor other than the wages for which they worked. As a result, the working class was exploited as well as alienated from their labor, the product of their labor, and other human beings.

Marx spoke of the labor theory of value. The value of a product—what society says it is worth—is derived from the labor needed to produce it. (This idea is somewhat similar to Smith's regarding the wealth of nations as coming from the labor of the people.) Profit, Marx said, is the surplus value charged by capitalist owners; but the workers do not receive any part of this. This arrangement handicapped the working class by putting them in a limited economic condition. According to Marx, this conflict between laborers who do not share in profits and capitalists who exploit the workers creates conditions of class struggle.

The working class, according to Marx, needed to develop a class consciousness. This awakening of workers to their true condition was a primary motivation for Marx's work. He wrote, "The workers of the world have nothing to lose but their chains. They have a world to win. Workers of the world, unite!" (*The Communist Manifesto*). Marx urged the overthrow of the bourgeoisie-controlled society, economy, and government, by force if necessary.

In his theory, the working class would then establish Communism, a socialist state run by the proletariat—actually, run on behalf of the people by central planners, an intellectual elite of whom Marx considered himself to be a member. In this Communist state, the workers themselves would own the means of production. As workers shared in the profits of the economy, states or governments around the world would wither away and society would be transformed into a utopian commune in which the workers would no longer be alienated from their labor or from other people.

Failings of Marxist Theory

Karl Marx began with faulty assumptions. He ignored the reality of the spiritual realm and its profound effect on the actions of mankind. His emphasis on class struggles is too simplistic an explanation for all of history. Society is more complicated than just two classes. The middle class was already emerging as Marx wrote, and the role of the middle or management class in the economy is significant. Also, people move from class to class depending on their circumstances. Some workers earn and save and become managers and even owners. Meanwhile, some owners lose what they have and become workers.

Labor is an important component of the value of what is produced. Owners have sometimes exploited workers. But that is not the whole story. For instance, thousands of farm and factory workers in Europe during the 1800s and early 1900s took matters into their own hands. They moved to the United States and greatly improved their circumstances. Moreover, profit does not just go into the pockets of owners. Instead, owners reinvest much of it into other business activities, which produce still more jobs. Profit margins for most businesses are fairly small, often about five percent or less of gross sales. In addition, profit is the reward for someone who takes the risk to create or invest in a business opportunity. Many such risks fail, and the result in those situations is not profit but loss.

Workers share in the value of goods above their wages. This sharing came about through years of conflict between labor and management; but many workers now have numerous benefits, such as health care, disability insurance, and retirement funds. Marx failed to anticipate the strength of the labor union movement, which gave workers more power within the capitalist system. In Western democracies, workers have been for the most part suspicious of Marxist ideas. Laborers have generally understood that democracy, not authoritarianism, gives them the best opportunity to enjoy better economic conditions.

Shoppers wait outside a store in Santa Clara, Cuba (2016)

The experience in many countries that have established command economies since the Russian Revolution of 1917 has been that such economies do not work as well as capitalist economies in bettering the economic conditions of the people. The absence of market conditions generally ruins an economy, while freedom and competition generally stimulate economic growth. Central planners who sit in offices in the national capital cannot possibly have enough information to guide a vast and complex farm economy or industrial economy throughout a large country. The information that an economy needs to operate successfully is held in small bits and pieces by millions of owners, managers, workers, and consumers who participate in and help maintain and grow a free economy.

Finally, no socialist state has ever withered away into utopian Communism. Communism became an authoritarian, non-democratic political system. In Communist countries, huge new socialist bureaucracies developed, including planners, propagandists, a security (spy) apparatus, and military personnel, all of whom prop up the tiny ruling clique that develops its own elite lifestyle and self-perpetuating control of power in the name of the people.

No Communist country has evolved into a worker's paradise. The excuse that Communist leaders give for the continuation of the command state is the supposed threat of greedy capitalists and imperialists who stand in the way of the well-being of the innocent millions in the people's republics. But the movement toward capitalism that has been taking place even in Communist countries is further evidence that Marx's theories are of dubious relevance to today's economic realities.

Contrasting Perspectives

Economic policies in the United States have generally reflected capitalist ideas. According to polls, a majority of Americans continue to support capitalism over socialism, though younger Americans are more likely to have a negative view of capitalism and a positive view of socialism. However, a very high percentage of Americans, including young Americans, say that they are in favor of free markets.

Many people do not understand from historical experience the difference between capitalism and socialism and the long-term effects of each. They may not understand that capitalism and a free-market economy are essentially the same thing. How some people were taught in school might have made socialism more attractive and capitalism more suspect. Some people might think of the widespread and increasing involvement of the government in the economy as a positive development and thus be favorable toward socialism. The economic difficulties during the recession of 2007-2009 might have led more people to be critical of capitalism.

Capitalism and socialism divide over a basic question: Who should make economic decisions? Adam Smith believed that these decisions should be spread as widely as possible throughout the economy. Producers and consumers are capable of making those decisions. They have the information they need to make those decisions, and they are directly affected by those decisions. Capitalism is based on a belief in human dignity and human freedom, a belief that individuals have the character and knowledge necessary to bring about the best results for the most people.

Karl Marx, on the other hand, believed that economic decisions are best made by a select few within the government for the benefit of all the people. These leaders would supposedly know best what needed to happen throughout the economy as a whole and would have a loyalty to the system. The basis of socialism is the belief that people need to be managed and regulated—managed and regulated, of course, by other people who are subject to the same selfish drives that all people have.

Adam Smith and Karl Marx also gave opposing perspectives on the role of government. Smith advocated that the role of government in economic activity should be as limited as possible. Marx, on the other hand, advocated complete government control of the economy. According to Marxist theory, this would only be needed until the state withered away into utopian Communism. Since this has never happened, the reality is that the government controls the economy of Communist or socialist systems.

We do not have to choose either unregulated capitalism or a completely government-planned command economy. Capitalism has accomplished much good and has provided the most economic gain for the most people. At the same time, capitalists have not always treated workers, consumers, or the environment with respect. Experience has shown that the best approach is to have a basic policy of economic freedom that is guided by reasonable government regulation and oversight. This simple statement sounds good enough in theory, but how such an economy works in reality and the extent to which freedom and regulation should exist in an economy are questions that fuel the ongoing economic debate.

The Bible sometimes conveys spiritual truths in economic terms.

Ho! Every one who thirsts, come to the waters;
And you who have no money come, buy and eat.
Come, buy wine and milk without money and without cost.
Why do you spend money for what is not bread,
And your wages for what does not satisfy?
Listen carefully to Me, and eat what is good,
And delight yourself in abundance.
Isaiah 55:1-2

Assignments for Lesson 4

Making Choices Read the excerpts from *The Wealth of Nations* (pages 7-15).

Literature Continue reading *Silas Marner*.

Project Continue working on your project for this unit.

Student Review Answer the questions for Lesson 4.

Statues at the University of Vienna

5 More Big Names

Give me a one-handed economist. All my economists say, "On one hand... on the other..."

— *Attributed to Harry Truman*

Economists have lively and continuing discussions and debates, especially on the causes of economic growth and decline as well as what policies governments should implement to help the economy. These discussions and debates are often variations on the two poles of economic thought, the free market on one hand and government control on the other.

The Austrian School of Economics

A group of economists living and teaching in Vienna, Austria, in the late nineteenth and early twentieth century came to be called the Austrian School of Economics. Most economists see the 1871 publication of *Principles of Economics* by Carl Menger as the beginning point of this group's influence. The Austrian School, which continues in existence today, generally follows the principles of Adam Smith. They advocate the power of prices as the organizing principle of economics in the marketplace.

Adherents of the Austrian School advocate as little government involvement in and regulation of the economy as possible and tend toward libertarian ideas. Ron Paul, former Republican congressman from Texas and sometime candidate for the Republican presidential nomination, has been a strong advocate of the economic ideas of the Austrian School.

One of the best-known proponents of this position in the twentieth century was Ludwig von Mises (1881-1973). Mises was born to Jewish parents in Austria-Hungary (now the Ukraine). His family moved to Vienna when he was a child. Mises received a doctorate from the University of Vienna in 1906. He then taught at the university and was an economic advisor to the Austrian government. In 1934 Mises left Austria in the face of Nazi aggression and moved to Switzerland. In 1940 he took up residence in the United States. From 1945 to 1969 he taught at New York University. He did not hold a salaried position with the school, but was supported by individual businessmen.

Among the ideas for which Mises was known was his belief that command economies would eventually fail because government planners cannot organize a strong, complex economy. He believed that the absence of free-market competition

Ludwig von Mises

would make a command system unworkable. The downfall of the Soviet Union and Eastern European Communist countries near the end of the twentieth century vindicated Mises' beliefs.

One young man who studied under Mises in Vienna was Friedrich Hayek (1899-1992), a native of the city. Hayek began teaching at the London School of Economics in 1931 and eventually became a British citizen. In 1950, he began teaching at the University of Chicago. Like Mises, he was supported by individuals and was not a member of the economics faculty.

Hayek's most famous work is *The Road to Serfdom* (1944), in which he argued that a government-planned and government-controlled economy led to tyranny over the population because of the increasing amount of power that such a policy demanded. Economic control, Hayek claimed, would lead to the loss of political and personal freedoms as well. Hayek saw the Soviet Union and Nazi Germany as examples of countries that followed this path. The book had a profound impact on the thinking of U.S. President Ronald Reagan and British Prime Minister Margaret Thatcher.

Hayek was corecipient of the 1974 Nobel Prize in Economics. In 1991 President George H. W. Bush awarded Hayek the Presidential Medal of Freedom.

John Maynard Keynes (1883-1946)

The most influential economist of the twentieth century was John Maynard Keynes of England. Keynes (pronounced CANES) proposed government intervention to help overcome times of economic recession. Many consider him the father of the modern study of macroeconomics.

Keynes was the son of a Cambridge economics lecturer. The younger Keynes studied at Cambridge and became a lecturer in economics there as well. He was an economic advisor to the British government during the First World War and at the Versailles Peace Conference of 1919. Following the conclusion of the treaty, Keynes issued warnings about the harsh reparations that the victorious nations demanded of Germany. He feared that the payments would ruin the German economy and lead to renewed conflict in Europe. Unfortunately, his predictions came true.

In 1936, Keynes published his landmark book, *The General Theory of Employment, Interest, and Money*. A major emphasis in Keynes' work was the idea of aggregate or overall demand in an economy. Published during a world-wide depression, the book advocated government action, including deficit spending and the funding of public works, to stimulate aggregate demand when unemployment was high (aggregate demand is the total desire for all goods and services at one time by all groups within a nation).

Lesson 5 - More Big Names

Keynes only favored deficit spending in times of emergency and not as a general policy. These ideas influenced Franklin Roosevelt's New Deal policies, although the ideas had been circulating for some time. During World War II, Keynes advocated higher taxes instead of deficit spending to finance the war effort. He rejected Marxism as an obsolete theory "which I know not only to be scientifically erroneous but without interest or application to the modern world" (*Essays in Persuasion*, 1931).

Keynes was involved in the 1944 conference at Bretton Woods, New Hampshire, that created a global postwar economic system. The conference led to the creation of the World Bank, the International Monetary Fund, and the General Agreement on Tariffs and Trade. The Bretton Woods conference did not adopt Keynes' own specific proposals, but he endorsed the results of the conference. What happened at Bretton Woods took government involvement in the economy beyond the national level to the world level. Keynes died in 1946.

The idea of government involvement in and oversight of the economy has gained widespread acceptance since the New Deal of the 1930s. In 1965, during the growth of the Great Society programs of President Lyndon Johnson, *Time* magazine ran a cover story that highlighted Keynesian (pronounced CANES-ee-un) economics. In 1971, Republican President Richard Nixon said, "We are all Keynesians now," by which he meant that almost everyone supported the idea of government involvement in the economy to some degree.

For many people the debate has become not whether government should be involved in the economy, but to what extent it should be. Government has found that deficit spending as an ongoing policy, not just in emergencies, enables programs that lead to people becoming dependent on the government. Many will want to vote for candidates who propose continuation and expansion of government programs. The question of how to address the resulting government debt usually remains unaddressed. Liberals want to tax the rich, while conservatives want to cut spending. They seldom reach more than a short-term compromise, while the debt and the dependence on government both increase.

The pendulum swung back toward less government oversight of the economy during the 1980s. In his 1981 inaugural address, President Ronald Reagan said, "In this present crisis, government is not the solution to our problem; government is the problem." In his 1996 State of the Union speech, President Bill Clinton said, "The era of big government is over," although Clinton went on to say that citizens should not be left to fend for themselves. The economic meltdown of 2008, however, renewed calls for greater government involvement in the economy, a central Keynesian idea.

Harry Dexter White (left), Assistant Secretary of the U.S. Treasury, and John Maynard Keynes were attendees at the March 1946 inaugural meeting of the International Monetary Fund in Savannah, Georgia. Keynes died of a heart attack a few weeks later.

Milton Friedman (1912-2006)

A conservative economist who exerted significant influence in the last half of the twentieth century was Milton Friedman. He was born in Brooklyn, New York, of Jewish immigrants from Hungary (now the Ukraine). He attended Rutgers, the University of Chicago, and Columbia University, where he received a doctorate in 1946.

Friedman was originally a Keynesian and supported Franklin Roosevelt's New Deal programs, in which he was a participant. However, he came

Milton Friedman, pictured at right, influenced Gary Becker (1930-2014), his student and later colleague at the University of Chicago. Saieh Hall, pictured below, is home to the Becker Friedman Institute for Research in Economics at the University of Chicago.

to believe that those programs did not really help the economy or the long-term recovery from the Depression. Friedman taught at the University of Chicago for thirty years, beginning in 1946, and was a leader in what became known as the Chicago School of Economics. He later worked with the Hoover Institution at Stanford University in California.

One of the key ideas that Friedman developed was that of monetarism, which highlights the role of money in the economy. Friedman believed that the Great Depression was primarily caused by a failure of the Federal Reserve System to maintain an adequate supply of money to help the economy grow. This contraction of the money supply prolonged and deepened the effect of the business downturn that began in 1929. We will study the Federal Reserve System in Lesson 35, and we will discuss the Great Depression in Lesson 69.

Paul Krugman in Stockholm, Sweden, to receive his Nobel Prize in economics.

Friedman advocated a steady expansion of the money supply as a policy to promote strong but manageable economic growth. He opposed almost all government regulation of any kind.

Friedman received the Nobel Prize in economics in 1976. In 1980, Friedman and his wife Rose (also an economist) published *Free to Choose* and produced a ten-part PBS series by the same name, both of which promoted his free market views. The book was the best-selling non-fiction title of the year. Ronald Reagan awarded Friedman the Presidential Medal of Freedom in 1988.

The Debate Continues

The field of economics has many advocates who promote a wide variety of ideas and policies.

Gregory Mankiw (MAN-kew) is a professor of economics at Harvard University. He was chairman of the Council of Economic Advisors from 2003 to 2005 under President George W. Bush. Mankiw has been described as a New Keynesian economist. He sees some value in limited government intervention in the economy; but he supports free trade and limited government regulation. Mankiw's college economics textbooks have sold over one million copies.

Thomas Sowell is a fellow at the Hoover Institution at Stanford University. He has written numerous books and columns that reflect his conservative views on economics and politics. The Foundation for Economic Liberty and the Library of Economics and Liberty are two organizations that provide resources which support free market economic ideas.

One of the more prominent voices of liberal economics is Paul Krugman, a columnist for the *New York Times* and recipient of the 2008 Nobel Prize in economics.

You can hear many different and conflicting ideas from economists. Your challenge is to discern the truth amid all the varying opinions.

Without consultation, plans are frustrated,
But with many counselors they succeed.
Proverbs 15:22

Assignments for Lesson 5

Literature   Continue reading *Silas Marner*.

Project   Finish your project for this unit.

Student Review   Answer the questions for Lesson 5 and take the quiz for Unit 1.

Jacob travelling to Egypt, *Wenceslaus Hollar (Czech, c. 1650)*

2 — God's Economics, Part 1

This unit is the first of two that survey the teachings of Scripture regarding money and how the church has dealt with economic issues. How people think about and handle money is a major theme in Scripture. God promised His people that He would provide for them, and He taught His people to trust Him above material wealth. The Law of Moses included several provisions about economic issues that Israel would face. The Old Testament Scriptures and the Old Testament prophets spoke with convicting words about Israel's failure to handle money with godliness, and they taught many lessons about how God's people were to handle economic and financial issues. Money matters were a major topic in Jesus' teachings.

Lesson 6 - The Lord Provides
Lesson 7 - Rich and Poor in Ancient Israel
Lesson 8 - The Righteous Will Flourish
Lesson 9 - God Owns It All
Lesson 10 - The Radical Economics of Jesus

Books Used

The Bible
Making Choices
Silas Marner

Project (choose one)

1) Write 300 to 500 words on one of the following topics:

- How would the economy change if people understood that they are stewards of the property, possessions, and money that belong to God instead of owners of them?

- Respond to the teaching of Jesus, "You cannot serve both God and wealth."

2) Discuss with your parents a specific project your family can do to help the poor. Consider programs organized by your church or other local churches (such as a food pantry, clothing distribution, or home repair) or with a local organization. With your parents involvement, plan and carry out this project.

3) Memorize Matthew 6:19-24.

6   The Lord Provides

For the Lord your God is bringing you into a good land ... a land where you will eat food without scarcity, in which you will not lack anything.
— Deuteronomy 8:7-9

A basic principle of economics is that people have to make choices among alternative uses for scarce or limited resources. We do not have a limitless supply of everything we want, so we have to choose how to use the things we do have.

For instance, a person can use a particular piece of wood either to heat his home or to make a piece of furniture; but he cannot use the same piece of wood to do both. That person has to make a choice. The same is true with a quantity of oil. A person can use it to power a car or to make plastic, but he has to make a decision regarding which use he wants to make of it. Economics analyzes how and why people choose to use scarce or limited resources and what the consequences of those choices are.

The goal of this curriculum is to help you understand economics from a Biblical point of view. While it is true that you cannot make a fire and a table from the same piece of wood, God presents Himself in Scripture as the God not of scarcity but of abundance, as the verse above indicates. Thinking based on the assumption of scarcity can lead to an attitude of fear. On the other hand, thinking based on the assumption that God will provide leads to an attitude of trust.

Scripture tells us that, from the beginning, God provided abundantly for mankind in general and for His people in particular. When God created man, He placed him in a well-watered garden which produced everything of a material nature that Adam needed (Genesis 2:8-17). Even after Adam and Eve sinned, God provided them with clothes and with the opportunity to produce food from the ground (Genesis 3:21-23). After the flood, God gave animals and plants into the hands of Noah and his sons for their use (Genesis 9:2-3).

God continues to create resources. An acorn from an oak tree produces another oak tree. A kernel from a corn plant produces another corn plant. The winter snows in the mountains melt into the waters that irrigate the fields for another growing season. The compost that a gardener collects becomes the soil for next year's garden.

39

God's People Will Have Enough

God's will for His people is that, by His provision and as they live faithfully before Him, His people will have enough:

> I have been young and now I am old,
> Yet I have not seen the righteous forsaken
> Or his descendants begging bread.
> Psalm 37:25

> And my God will supply all your needs according to His riches in glory in Christ Jesus. Philippians 4:19

Material resources are indeed limited. Even with God's promise that His people will have enough, God's people still have to be good stewards and make wise choices regarding how they use the resources God gives them. His people might not always have everything they want, but they can count on having what they need.

> Make sure that your character is free from the love of money, being content with what you have; for He Himself has said, "I will never desert you, nor will I ever forsake you," so that we confidently say, "The Lord is my helper, I will not be afraid. What will man do to me?" Hebrews 13:5-6

These assurances do not mean that Christians will never face scarcity. Sometimes they have. In the book of Acts, a famine impoverished Christians in Jerusalem (Acts 11:27-28); but God provided what they needed. Believers in Antioch took up a collection to help them (Acts 11:29-30). Several years later, when Paul was on his third missionary journey, he collected money from churches to help "the poor among the saints in Jerusalem" (Romans 15:26; see also 2 Corinthians 8-9). The Christians in Jerusalem apparently dealt with scarcity for some time, but other Christians provided their needs by choosing to use their limited resources to help others.

At other times, when God's people have suffered from scarcity, it has been because of their unfaithfulness:

> "But I gave you also cleanness of teeth
> in all your cities
> And lack of bread in all your places,
> Yet you have not returned to Me,"
> declares the Lord. Amos 4:6

God's people can have a good life even without an abundance. The psalmist wrote that having a little with righteousness is better than having an abundance with wickedness:

> Better is the little of the righteous
> Than the abundance of many wicked.
> For the arms of the wicked will be broken,
> But the Lord sustains the righteous.
> Psalm 37:16-17

God's Economics in Genesis

In the book of Genesis, Canaan experienced a severe famine; but Abram was able to survive it by going to Egypt for a time (Genesis 12:10). Upon Abram's return, he and his nephew Lot were so wealthy that the same land could not support them both (Genesis 13:2-12). This was a case of abundant resources but scarce land.

By God's leading, Abraham's great-grandson Joseph was able to oversee the production of abundant food in Egypt to prepare for the years of famine that God had foretold (Genesis 41:46-49). Joseph's father Jacob and Joseph's brothers and their families in Canaan had enough wealth to buy grain in Egypt more than once during the famine (Genesis 42:1-5, 43:1-15). Canaan as a whole experienced scarcity, but Abraham's descendants had enough.

Lesson 6 - The Lord Provides

The economic conditions in Egypt during this famine illustrate the economic principle of supply and demand. The country experienced a scarcity of food. The supply of food was limited and the demand was great. As a result, the price of grain was high. The people of Egypt paid all of their money, then their livestock, and finally themselves to purchase grain. Then Joseph bought the land on behalf of Pharaoh, except for that which the priests owned. The people of Egypt became sharecroppers on the land that Pharaoh now owned. The people kept four-fifths of the crops for themselves and gave one-fifth to Pharaoh. While kings have often seen themselves as owning all of the land in their realms, in Egypt it became literally true (Genesis 47:13-26).

God's Provision for Israel

After the passage of time, another pharoah enslaved Abraham's descendants (the Israelites) because he feared their numbers (Exodus 1:8-14). Pharaoh thus exercised complete economic and physical control over the Israelites. However, God continued to care for them. When the plagues that God sent laid waste to Egypt, He spared the Israelites (see, for instance, Exodus 9:4). As the Israelites prepared to flee from Egypt in the exodus, God enabled them to gain significant wealth by allowing them to plunder the Egyptians simply by asking the Egyptians for silver, gold, and clothing (Exodus 3:21-22, 12:35-36).

God promised that He would provide for Israel by bringing them into a land "flowing with milk and honey" (Exodus 3:17). Before they got there, however, God led them through the wilderness for forty years. This was a time of scarcity that they had to endure because of their faithlessness (Numbers 14:33-34). Even there, God took care of the Israelites by giving them manna each morning, and He even kept their clothes from wearing out (Deuteronomy 8:3-4).

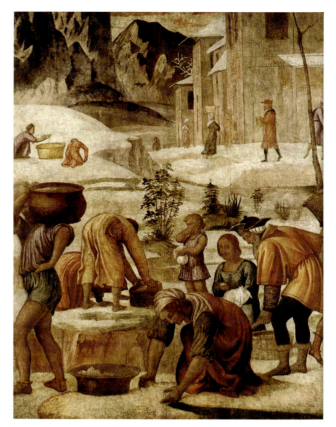

The Gathering of the Manna
Bernardino Luini (Italian, c. 1521)

The Lord promised that, in the land He was giving them, they would have an abundance of grain, wine, oil, and herds (Deuteronomy 7:13). Canaan would be for them a land that produced abundantly, "a land where you will eat food without scarcity, in which you will not lack anything," including even iron and copper (Deuteronomy 8:7-9).

Economic Aspects of the Law

While the Israelites camped at Mount Sinai, the Lord gave them the Law by which they were to live. Certain principles in the Law guided the economy that God established in Israel. First, Israel needed to remember God, "for it is He who is giving you the power to make wealth" (Deuteronomy 8:18). Second, the Israelites were to understand that God actually owned the land and that they were simply stewards of it, using it as aliens and strangers to produce crops (Leviticus 25:23).

Field in Israel

Third, they were to trust God enough to let the land lie fallow regularly to let it rest, during which time God would continue to provide for them (Leviticus 25:1-7). Fourth, Israel was to demonstrate holiness in their economic activity by being fair and honest, by not taking advantage of their fellow Israelites, and by being considerate of the poor (see especially Leviticus 19:9-18).

The Israelites were to plant and harvest for six years, but every seventh year was to be a sabbath rest for the land. In addition, every fiftieth year was to be a jubilee year. They were not to plant crops that year either, and land that had been sold was to be returned to the family to whom the Lord had given it originally (Leviticus 25:8-12). The 49th and 50th years would thus constitute a two-year sabbath, but the Lord assured Israel that they would still have enough to eat during this period. Some Bible scholars question whether Israel ever observed the jubilee year because Scripture makes no mention of its being observed. On the other hand, we know that Israel did observe other festivals and sabbaths that the Lord commanded.

Whenever an Israelite sold a parcel of land, the parties in the transaction were to take into account the nearness of the jubilee year in determining the purchase price (Leviticus 25:15). God explained that the buyer was not really buying the land but merely buying the right to raise a certain number of crops on it (Leviticus 25:16). The number of crops that the buyer could expect to harvest before its return in the jubilee year would determine the purchase price. If an Israelite became poor and had to sell some of his land, a kinsman was to buy back or redeem the land so that it would stay in the tribe. At the jubilee it would revert to the family of the original owner (Leviticus 25:25-28).

Lesson 6 - The Lord Provides

The Israelites were to treat each other with kindness and consideration. They were to care for and not take advantage of an Israelite who became poor (Leviticus 25:35). Israelites were not to charge interest on loans they made to their fellow countrymen. Instead, they were to "revere your God, that your countryman may live with you" (Leviticus 25:36). If an impoverished Israelite had to sell himself into the service of another, the purchasing Israelite was to treat the impoverished one as a hired man and not as a slave; and the owner would set the man free in the year of jubilee (Leviticus 25:39-43). However, Israelites could own slaves from the nations around them (Leviticus 25:44).

If an Israelite sold himself to a foreigner, a kinsman could redeem him, with the price to be determined by the nearness of the jubilee year. In the jubilee, he was to go free (Leviticus 25:47-54). These provisions prevented a permanent Israelite slave class from developing in Israel, a class that would see itself as being subservient to and dependent on others. God wanted Israel to remember that, "the sons of Israel are My servants; they are My servants whom I brought out from the land of Egypt. I am the Lord your God" (Leviticus 25:55).

When a Hebrew man or woman served a fellow Israelite for six years, he or she was to be set free in the seventh year and provided for liberally by his former owner (Deuteronomy 15:12-15). The guideline for how the owner was to provide for the former servant was the way that the Lord had provided for him. "You shall give to him as the Lord your God has blessed you" (verse 14). Alternatively, the servant had the choice of voluntarily renouncing his freedom and remaining a servant permanently (Deuteronomy 15:16-17).

Thus we see that the Israelites could build wealth, but not in land or in Israelite slaves. God did not want the Israelites to think that their power or status came from owning the land or people, when in fact God owned the land and the people.

The sabbath year also brought about a cancellation of debts that Israelites owed to each other, though not of debts that foreigners owed (Deuteronomy 15:1-3). This provision was intended to prevent a permanent debtor class in Israel. It was God's will that, "there will be no poor among you, since the Lord will surely bless you in the land which the Lord your God is giving you as an inheritance to possess, if only you listen obediently to the voice of the Lord your God, to observe carefully all this commandment which I am commanding you today" (Deuteronomy 15:4-5). If a man did suffer poverty, his fellow Israelites were to open their hearts toward him and give him what he needed, "for the poor will never cease to be in the land" (Deuteronomy 15:7-11).

Verse four ("There will be no poor among you") and verse seven ("The poor will never cease to be in the land") seem contradictory on the surface, but they describe God's will for taking care of those in need. There will always be people who need economic assistance. God's people are to take care of those in need so that they do not remain impoverished. If the Israelites followed God's commands to be compassionate and generous, there would not be poor people who fell through the cracks (verses 4-6).

God wanted the Israelites to conduct themselves in every aspect of their lives, including business and economics, with an attitude of holiness. The commandments in Leviticus 19 demonstrate this. The Israelites were not to be greedy for every last stalk of grain, but instead were to leave the gleanings in the fields for the needy and the foreigner (Leviticus 19:9-10). They were to deal honestly with each other in their business dealings. They were to use standard and accurate weights and measures (Leviticus 19:11, 35-36). An employer was to pay his hired men at the end of the day and not hold their pay until the next day (Leviticus 19:13). This avoided many potential problems. The employer might say in the morning, "Didn't I pay you last night? I thought I did." The worker might say, "I worked ten hours yesterday, not eight." The owner might lose the money, or either person might die before payment was completed.

God promised the Israelites that they would enjoy prosperity if they kept His commandments (Deuteronomy 28:1-14), but He warned that they would suffer in many ways, including economically, if they were unfaithful (Deuteronomy 28:16-68).

*All these blessings will come upon you and overtake you
if you obey the Lord your God.
Deuteronomy 28:2*

Assignments for Lesson 6

Literature — Continue reading *Silas Marner*. Plan to finish it by the end of Unit 3.

Project — Choose your project for this unit and start working on it.

Student Review — Answer the questions for Lesson 6.

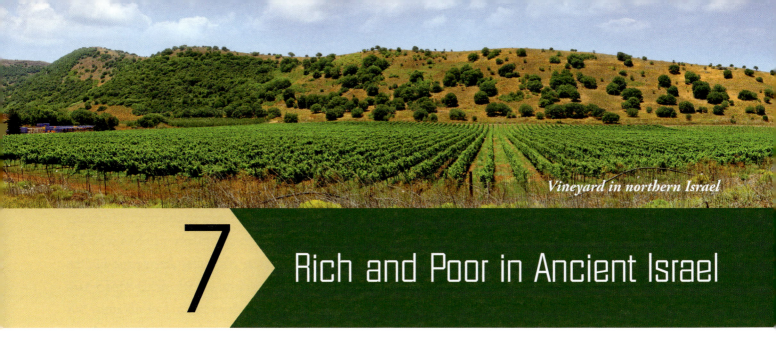
Vineyard in northern Israel

7 Rich and Poor in Ancient Israel

Hear this, you who trample the needy, to do away with the humble of the land, saying, "When will the new moon be over, so that we may sell grain, and the sabbath, that we may open the wheat market, to make the bushel smaller and the shekel bigger, and to cheat with dishonest scales, so as to buy the helpless for money and the needy for a pair of sandals, and that we may sell the refuse of the wheat?"

— *Amos 8:4-6*

God was Israel's king and provider, but the time came when that did not satisfy the people of Israel. When Samuel was old, the elders of Israel came to him and asked him to appoint a king to rule over them. God assured Samuel that they were rejecting Him, not Samuel. The Lord told Samuel to give them what they asked for but also to warn them of the consequences of having a king (1 Samuel 8:1-9). Those consequences included economic ramifications:

So Samuel spoke all the words of the Lord to the people who had asked of him a king. He said, "This will be the procedure of the king who will reign over you: he will take your sons and place them for himself in his chariots and among his horsemen and they will run before his chariots. He will appoint for himself commanders of thousands and of fifties, and some to do his plowing and to reap his harvest and to make his weapons of war and equipment for his chariots. He will also take your daughters for perfumers and cooks and bakers. He will take the best of your fields and your vineyards and your olive groves and give them to his servants. He will take a tenth of your seed and of your vineyards and give to his officers and to his servants. He will also take your male servants and your female servants and your best young men and your donkeys and use them for his work. He will take a tenth of your flocks, and you yourselves will become his servants. Then you will cry out in that day because of your king whom you have chosen for yourselves, but the Lord will not answer you in that day." (1 Samuel 8:10-18)

The people did not listen to Samuel's warning, so Samuel anointed first Saul and then David to be their king. David's son Solomon followed him on the throne.

The reign of Solomon was a time of great wealth in Israel. Solomon asked the Lord for wisdom to rule Israel well, and the Lord responded by giving him not only wisdom but also "both riches and honor" (1 Kings 3:13). "Judah and Israel were as numerous as the sand that is on the seashore in abundance; they were eating and drinking and rejoicing" (1 Kings 4:20). This was especially true for the royal household. "Solomon had 40,000 stalls of horses for his chariots, and 12,000 horsemen" (1 Kings 4:26). Solomon built a magnificent palace and temple (1 Kings 7). He engaged in foreign trade that increased his wealth (1 Kings 10:11-12, 14-15).

King Solomon and the Queen of Sheba
(Persian, 16th century)

When the queen of Sheba visited Solomon because of the report she had heard about him, she was amazed at what she saw. "[T]he half was not told me. You exceed in wisdom and prosperity the report which I heard" (1 Kings 10:7).

Much of Solomon's wealth was the result of what the people of Israel produced. The king's daily provisions were abundant (1 Kings 4:22-28). Forced laborers from Israel provided the labor for Solomon's projects (1 Kings 5:13-16). Most people in Israel apparently had enough, but Solomon used his position to make sure that he had more than enough.

When Solomon's son Rehoboam became king, he foolishly decided to make the government's oppressive hold on the economic life of the nation even tighter so that the people would know who was boss. This turn of events was from the Lord to fulfill a prophecy made earlier (1 Kings 12:13-15). Because of Rehoboam's harshness, the ten northern tribes rebelled against him and set up their own kingdom (1 Kings 12:16-19).

After Israel divided into the Northern Kingdom (also called Israel and the Southern Kingdom (also called Judah), the Northern Kingdom of Israel experienced great prosperity, especially in the early part of the eighth century (800-750 BC). Archaeological discoveries show evidence of the great wealth present in the area at the time. However, this wealth came at a heavy price socially and spiritually. First, the ruling class enjoyed their prosperity at the expense of the poor; and second, the Northern Kingdom abandoned the worship of the one true God for the worship of idols. The Lord's prophets, especially Hosea and Amos, condemned these practices. The Lord spoke through Hosea, saying:

> For [Israel] does not know that it was I who
> gave her the grain, the new wine and the oil,
> And lavished on her silver and gold, which
> they used for Baal.   Hosea 2:8

Lesson 7 - Rich and Poor in Ancient Israel

Amos used especially pointed phrases to condemn the exploitation of the poor by the rich in Israel:

> Thus says the Lord, "For three transgressions of Israel and for four I will not revoke its punishment, because they sell the righteous for money and the needy for a pair of sandals." Amos 2:6

> Hear this word, you cows of Bashan who are on the mountain of Samaria, who oppress the poor, who crush the needy, who say to your husbands, "Bring now, that we may drink!" The Lord God has sworn by His holiness, "Behold, the days are coming upon you when they will take you away with meat hooks, and the last of you with fish hooks." Amos 4:1-2

Amos warned of a coming exile in both Israel and Judah:

> Woe to those who are at ease in Zion and to those who feel secure in the mountain of Samaria, the distinguished men of the foremost of nations, to whom the house of Israel comes. . . . Those who recline on beds of ivory and sprawl on their couches, and eat lambs from the flock and calves from the midst of the stall . . . who drink wine from sacrificial bowls while they anoint themselves with the finest of oils, yet they have not grieved over the ruin of Joseph. Therefore, they will now go into exile at the head of the exiles, and the sprawlers' banqueting will pass away. Amos 6:1-7

Hosea also warned of a punishment coming upon Israel (Hosea 10).

During the time of Elisha in the Northern Kingdom, the Arameans laid siege to Samaria and a famine occurred. 2 Kings 6:25 describes extremely

This carving of the prophet Amos by Jörg Syrlin the Younger (c. 1493) is located at Blaubeuren Abbey in Germany.

high prices for even the most disgusting items. However, Elisha prophesied that prices would return to normal (2 Kings 7:1). After the Lord scattered the Arameans and the siege ended, food prices did return to normal (2 Kings 7:18). This account serves as another Biblical example of the principle of supply and demand.

True to God's word, Assyria conquered Israel and carried many of its people into captivity in 721 BC. Babylon conquered the southern kingdom and carried captives away beginning in 606 BC.

Every Man Under His Vine and Fig Tree

A phrase that the Old Testament uses several times exemplifies the ideal of security, prosperity, freedom, and property rights. During Solomon's reign, "Judah and Israel lived in safety, every man under his vine and his fig tree, from Dan even to Beersheba, all the days of Solomon" (1 Kings 4:25). Micah used the same idea to describe the Messianic ideal in this way:

> Each of them will sit under his vine and under his fig tree, with no one to make them afraid, for the mouth of the Lord of hosts has spoken. Micah 4:4

Zechariah used a similar phrase:

"In that day," declares the LORD of hosts, "every one of you will invite his neighbor to sit under his vine and under his fig tree."
Zechariah 3:10

The Lord through Jeremiah used an inverse form of the phrase to describe the punishment that was coming upon Israel:

"I will surely snatch them away," declares the Lord; "There will be no grapes on the vine and no figs on the fig tree, and the leaf will wither; and what I have given them will pass away."
Jeremiah 8:13

Economic issues are not just a factor in modern times. They were present during the time of the Bible in the land of Israel, just as they have been present in all of the nations of the world throughout human history. The issues of God's promise of prosperity to His faithful, His call to practice economic justice, and the economic consequences of unrighteousness are timeless.

"If you consent and obey,
You will eat the best of the land;
But if you refuse and rebel,
You will be devoured by the sword."
Truly, the mouth of the LORD has spoken.
Isaiah 1:19-20

Assignments for Lesson 7

Making Choices — Read "Socialism, Capitalism, and the Bible" (pages 16-22).

Literature — Continue reading *Silas Marner*.

Project — Continue working on your project for this unit.

Student Review — Answer the questions for Lesson 7.

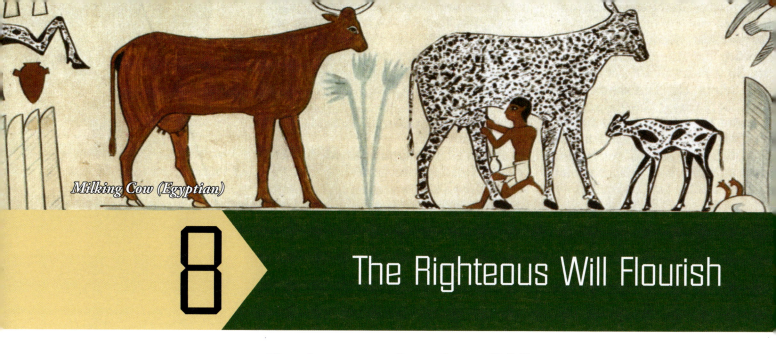
Milking Cow (Egyptian)

8 > The Righteous Will Flourish

*He who trusts in his riches will fall,
But the righteous will flourish like the green leaf.*
— Proverbs 11:28

Many passages in the Old Testament, especially in Proverbs, address the issues of wealth, business, and economics.

The Importance of Humility

The Lord taught Israel that the most important attitude to have concerning financial matters is humility.

> The rich and the poor have a common bond,
> The Lord is the maker of them all.
> Proverbs 22:2

> It is the blessing of the Lord that makes rich,
> And He adds no sorrow to it.
> Proverbs 10:22

The Blessings of Faithfulness

Several Old Testament Scriptures teach that faithfulness tends to lead to economic well-being.

Honor the Lord from your wealth and from the first of all your produce; so your barns will be filled with plenty and your vats will overflow with new wine. Proverbs 3:9-10

The reward of humility and the fear of the Lord are riches, honor and life.
Proverbs 22:4

The Value of Hard Work

The Bible teaches many specific principles that apply to economics. For instance, hard work (an economist might say productivity) pays off.

He who tills his land will have plenty of bread, but he who pursues worthless things lacks sense. Proverbs 12:11

In all labor there is profit, but mere talk leads only to poverty. Proverbs 14:23

First Things First

A person needs to keep his priorities straight. He needs to look to his productive resources first.

> Prepare your work outside and make it ready for yourself in the field; afterwards, then, build your house. Proverbs 24:27

Another practical lesson in Scripture is that the wise person stays in touch with the condition of his economic resources.

> Know well the condition of your flocks, and pay attention to your herds; for riches are not forever, nor does a crown endure to all generations. Proverbs 27:23-24

Warnings Against Sin and Laziness

On the other hand, the Bible is also clear that laziness and sin (a lack of productivity) lead to poverty.

> "A little sleep, a little slumber,
>   A little folding of the hands to rest"—
> Your poverty will come in like a vagabond
>   And your need like an armed man. Proverbs 6:10-11

> Poverty and shame will come to him who neglects discipline, but he who regards reproof will be honored. Proverbs 13:18

> Ill-gotten gains do not profit, but righteousness delivers from death. Proverbs 10:2

> Great wealth is in the house of the righteous, but trouble is in the income of the wicked. Proverbs 15:6

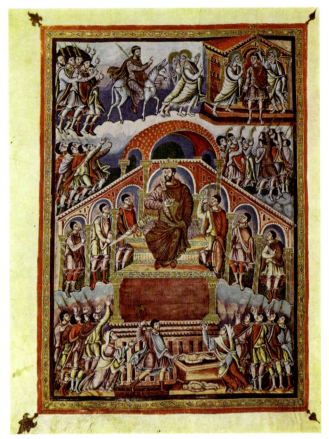

Illustration of King Solomon's court
Ingobertus (French, c. 880)

Give and You Shall Receive

The Scriptures teach that generosity leads to wealth.

> There is one who scatters, and yet increases all the more, and there is one who withholds what is justly due, and yet it results only in want. Proverbs 11:24

God's people are not to give in order to receive. That is mercenary and selfish. Instead, God's people are to give because God has given generously to them. They are to give when they see a need, not worrying about their own needs. In this way they will reflect the heart of God. They are to trust that, as God has given to them, so they can give to others, God will continue to provide for them as they are generous and ready to share.

Lesson 8 - The Righteous Will Flourish

The Deceptiveness of Wealth

Wealth is attractive, but it is deceptive and will one day pass away. The writer of Ecclesiastes sought wealth and pleasure in his pursuit of the meaning of life, but this is what he found:

> All that my eyes desired I did not refuse them. I did not withhold my heart from any pleasure, for my heart was pleased because of all my labor and this was my reward for all my labor. Thus I considered all my activities which my hands had done and the labor which I had exerted, and behold all was vanity and striving after wind and there was no profit under the sun.
> Ecclesiastes 2:10-11

The psalmist said that the righteous would laugh at:

> [T]he man who would not make God his refuge, but trusted in the abundance of his riches and was strong in his evil desire.
> Psalm 52:7

Wealth is attractive not only to the person who pursues it but also to those around him. It brings the wealthy person many so-called friends who want to take advantage of that person's money.

> Wealth adds many friends, but a poor man is separated from his friend.   Proverbs 19:4

But the pursuit of wealth is simply not worth it.

> Do not weary yourself to gain wealth, cease from your consideration of it. When you set your eyes on it, it is gone. For wealth certainly makes itself wings like an eagle that flies toward the heavens.   Proverbs 23:4-5

> Riches do not profit in the day of wrath, but righteousness delivers from death.
> (Proverbs 11:4)

> The one who gains wealth by unrighteous means will leave it to be enjoyed by others.

> He who increases his wealth by interest and usury gathers it for him who is gracious to the poor. (Proverbs 28:8)

God Will Make Things Right in the End

The wicked sometimes are able to become wealthy (perhaps by using devious means), but God warned them that they would one day get their just recompense. The psalmist agonized:

> For I was envious of the arrogant as I saw the prosperity of the wicked.

But then he "came into the sanctuary of God" and "perceived their end":

> Surely You set them in slippery places; You cast them down to destruction. How they are destroyed in a moment! They are utterly swept away by sudden terrors!
> Psalm 73:3, 17, 18-19

Economic principles are consistently true in the conduct of business, but God's principles are even more sure. We should conduct our business dealings in a way that is consistent with our claim of being God's people.

Ecclesiastes tells us that labor is good and that it enables us to enjoy life while we realize that our ability to work and the fruit of our labors come from God.

There is nothing better for a man than to eat and drink and tell himself that his labor is good. This also I have seen that it is from the hand of God. For who can eat and who can have enjoyment without Him?
Ecclesiastes 2:24-25

Assignments for Lesson 8

Making Choices — Read the excerpts from the Precepts of Ptah-Hotep (pages 23-24).

Literature — Continue reading *Silas Marner*.

Project — Continue working on your project for this unit.

Student Review — Answer the questions for Lesson 8.

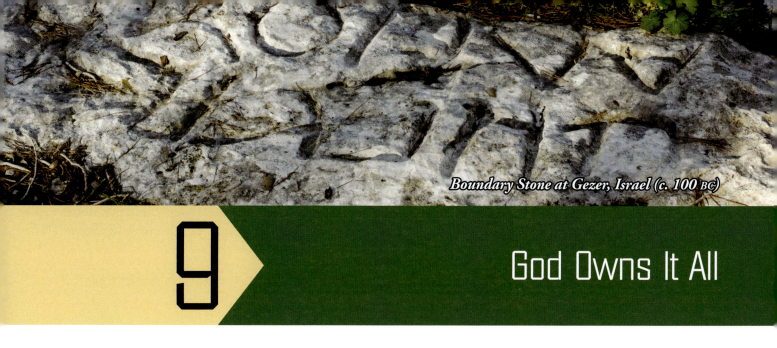

Boundary Stone at Gezer, Israel (c. 100 BC)

9 God Owns It All

Better is a little with righteousness than great income with injustice.
— Proverbs 16:8

God wants to rule over the economic part of our lives as much as He wants to rule over every other aspect of our lives. Indeed, how we handle money and business transactions says a great deal about whether our hearts are truly devoted to God or whether we give lip service to God's instructions and then do whatever we want in everyday life. The Lord taught important financial principles throughout the Scriptures.

Honesty Is Essential

Honesty is essential to the proper conduct of business. In economic terms, dishonesty, bribery, and manipulation of goods interrupt the proper operation of supply and demand.

> A false balance is an abomination to the Lord, but a just weight is His delight.
> Proverbs 11:1; see also 16:11 and 20:23

> A wicked man receives a bribe from the bosom to pervert the ways of justice.
> Proverbs 17:23

> Do not move the ancient boundary which your fathers have set. Proverbs 22:28

> He who withholds grain, the people will curse him, but blessing will be on the head of him who sells it. Proverbs 11:26

People tend to complain about a deal while they are making it but then they go away and boast about the great deal they had made. Another proverb describes this tendency in this way:

> "Bad, bad," says the buyer, but when he goes his way, then he boasts. Proverbs 20:14

Debt Is Dangerous

Debt is enslaving and should be avoided.

> The rich rules over the poor, and the borrower becomes the lender's slave.
> Proverbs 22:7

53

Becoming surety for the debt of another (today we call it co-signing for a loan) means that the co-signer is responsible for paying off the debt if the person to whom the loan is made does not pay the creditor. A person should avoid making such a commitment. If someone needs to have a co-signer to obtain a loan, that is a strong indication that the lender does not think that the person receiving the loan is a good risk. It is difficult to get out of being a co-signer on a loan, so the better approach is to avoid making such a commitment at all.

> My son, if you have become surety for your neighbor, have given a pledge for a stranger, if you have been snared with the words of your mouth, have been caught with the words of your mouth, do this then, my son, and deliver yourself; since you have come into the hand of your neighbor, go, humble yourself, and importune your neighbor. Give no sleep to your eyes, nor slumber to your eyelids; deliver yourself like a gazelle from the hunter's hand and like a bird from the hand of the fowler.   Proverbs 6:1-5

Beggars in Jerusalem (late 1800s)

Be Concerned About the Poor

God's people should not simply seek as much financial gain as possible without regard for how our actions affect others. Instead, in our financial activities we should be concerned about the rights of the poor; and we should not take advantage of them.

> The righteous is concerned for the rights of the poor, the wicked does not understand such concern.   Proverbs 29:7

> Do not rob the poor because he is poor, or crush the afflicted at the gate; for the LORD will plead their case and take the life of those who rob them.   Proverbs 22:22-23

> One who is gracious to a poor man lends to the Lord, and He will repay him for his good deed.   Proverbs 19:17

More Important Than Money

The Lord considers other things to be more important than wealth.

> Better is a little with the fear of the Lord than great treasure and turmoil with it.
>   Proverbs 15:16

> A good name is to be more desired than great wealth, favor is better than silver and gold.   Proverbs 22:1

> Better is the poor who walks in his integrity than he who is crooked though he be rich.
>   Proverbs 28:6

Ruth in Boaz's Field, *Julius Schnorr von Carolsfeld (German, 1828)*

The Essentials Are All We Need

What each of us really needs is simply what he needs today. Anything more or less can become a problem.

> Two things I asked of You, do not refuse me before I die: Keep deception and lies far from me, give me neither poverty nor riches; feed me with the food that is my portion, that I not be full and deny You and say, "Who is the Lord?" Or that I not be in want and steal, and profane the name of my God.
> Proverbs 30:7-9

Everything Belongs to God

All that anyone ever has comes from the Lord. He is the Maker of everything, it all belongs to Him, and ultimately it will return to Him.

"I will shake all the nations; and they will come with the wealth of all nations, and I will fill this house with glory," says the Lord of hosts. "The silver is Mine and the gold is Mine," declares the Lord of hosts.

Haggai 2:7-8

Everything belongs to God the Creator. He gives people various amounts of His possessions to manage (as a steward or *oikonomos*) for a relatively few years. This realization should humble us. The psalmist recognized that the way a person conducts financial matters reflects his heart before God.

O Lord, who may abide in Your tent?
Who may dwell on Your holy hill?
He who walks with integrity, and works righteousness,
and speaks truth in his heart. . . .
He does not put out his money at interest,
nor does he take a bribe against the innocent.
He who does these things will never be shaken.
Psalm 15:1-2, 5

Assignments for Lesson 9

Literature — Continue reading *Silas Marner*.

Project — Continue working on your project for this unit.

Student Review — Answer the questions for Lesson 9.

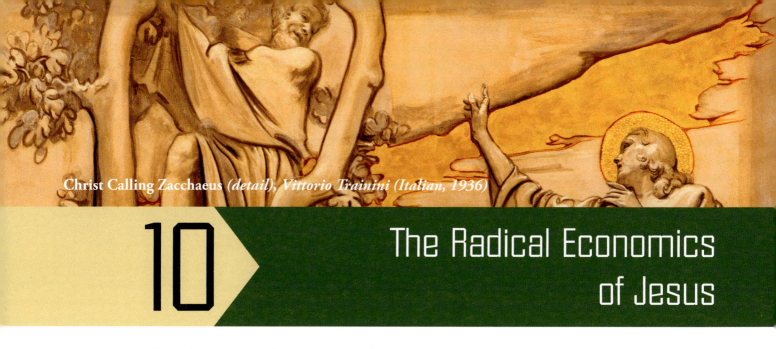

Christ Calling Zacchaeus *(detail), Vittorio Trainini (Italian, 1936)*

10   The Radical Economics of Jesus

Blessed are you who are poor, for yours is the kingdom of God . . . .
But woe to you who are rich, for you are receiving your comfort in full.
— *Luke 6:20, 24*

Jesus came into a world and a society that grappled with economic issues. Some Jewish religious leaders of His day were hungry for wealth. Luke 16:14 describes the Pharisees as "lovers of money." The Pharisees and scribes reinterpreted the Law to encourage people to make contributions to the temple instead of using their money to take care of their parents (Mark 7:9-13). Scribes would "devour widows' houses" (Mark 12:40), probably a reference to the practice of pressuring widows or their survivors into donating the widow's house to the temple.

The rich young man who came to Jesus with an important question was probably a synagogue ruler (Luke 18:18). Perhaps part of the reason he had been given a position of prominence and leadership was his financial success. Zaccheus was a chief tax collector whom Luke describes as being rich (Luke 19:2). This taxman's desires were not all that different from those of most people; he had just learned how to play the game more successfully that most.

Rome controlled the area of Israel to enhance its political and economic security. The Roman government siphoned off wealth from Israel (and from other areas that it controlled) in the form of taxes, which the Romans used in part to finance their occupation army.

A New View

Jesus came to teach a new way of living, which required a new way of thinking. As a part of His teaching, the Lord urged a radical reorientation in the way people thought about wealth. During His ministry on earth, Jesus talked about money more than any other single subject except the kingdom of God.

In the Sermon on the Mount, He told people not to store up treasures on earth, but rather to store up a different kind of treasure in heaven because, "Where your treasure is, there your heart will be also" (Matthew 6:21). Jesus wanted total commitment from His followers, and that included an undivided loyalty to Him instead of to money. Jesus was not satisfied with partial loyalty because He knew that such divided allegiance would not work in reality.

Ancient Roman and Greek Coins

"No one can serve two masters; for either he will hate the one and love the other, or he will be devoted to one and despise the other. You cannot serve God and wealth" (Matthew 6:24). In the parable of the sower, Jesus warned that the person who is preoccupied with "the worry of the world and the deceitfulness of wealth" will find the word choked in his life; and as a result that person will be unfruitful (Matthew 13:22).

The Lord taught His followers not to be worried about food and clothing. He said that God will take care of those who follow Him, in the same way that God feeds the birds and clothes the lilies of the field. Fretting about possessions is the faithless (that is, pagan) way of thinking. Instead, Jesus said, "Seek first His kingdom and His righteousness, and all these things will be added to you" (Matthew 6:33). In other words, Jesus told us that God meets the needs of His faithful people.

Jesus counseled the paying of taxes because it was the fulfillment of a proper obligation (Matthew 17:24-27 and 22:15-22). However, Jesus taught that people had an even more important obligation to fulfill. "Render to Caesar the things that are Caesar's; and to God the things that are God's" (Matthew 22:21).

The test of faithfulness in Jesus' teachings is what we do with our possessions, not how much we have or acquire. In the parable of the talents, a master gave his servants talents (a talent was worth about fifteen years' wages for a worker) "each according to his own ability." The master praised the two who invested the talents wisely, but he condemned the one who hid his talent out of fear (Matthew 25:14-30).

Two of Jesus' parables used economic situations in a surprising way to make their point. In the parable of the workers in the vineyard (Matthew 20:1-16), a landowner hires men at various times through the day; but when the landowner pays them, they all receive the amount for which those hired earliest had agreed to work. The men who had worked all day grumble at what they perceived to be unfair treatment. "These last men have worked only one hour, and you have made them equal to us who have borne the burden and the scorching heat of the day" (verse 12).

The landowner tells the men that he had done nothing wrong. The land and the money were his, and he could do with them as he wished. "Is your eye envious because I am generous?" the landowner asks (verse 15). The lesson of the parable is that God can bless people and dispense grace according to His wisdom without answering to anyone else. Everything belongs to Him, and He can use it as He wills. This means that in some cases, those whom we would think of as first will be last and the last will be first (verse 16).

In the parable of the unrighteous steward (Luke 16:1-12), a rich man's household steward was found to have squandered his master's possessions. After the steward had been given his dismissal notice, he apparently played fast and loose with his master's accounts and discounted the debtors' obligations to the master in order to win favor from those debtors after he left his stewardship position. The master praises the steward for his shrewdness in his last official acts as steward.

Jesus' point is not to justify manipulation of accounts. Instead, He used the steward's actions as a point of comparison in what is called a "light and heavy" parable: if something is true in a less important situation, certainly it is true in a more important situation. Here Jesus is saying that if an unjust steward can be considered shrewd for monkeying with his master's accounts, certainly God's people, "the sons of light" (verse 8), need to be wise in preparing for heaven by how they handle the resources that God gives them in this life:

> And I say to you, make friends for yourselves by means of the wealth of unrighteousness, so that when it fails, they will receive you into the eternal dwellings. He who is faithful in a very little thing is faithful also in much; and he who is unrighteous in a very little thing is unrighteous also in much. Therefore if you have not been faithful in the use of unrighteous wealth, who will entrust the true riches to you? And if you have not been faithful in the use of that which is another's, who will give you that which is your own?
> Luke 16:9-12

Parable of the Workers in the Vineyard (German, c. 1040)

The Parable of the Rich Fool, *Rembrandt (Dutch, 1627)*

Rich and Poor

Jesus did not praise the wealthy; instead, He warned them. The Lord told a parable about a rich fool who stored up treasure for himself but who was not rich toward God. The man died suddenly and left to others all that he had worked so hard to acquire (Luke 12:16-21). In other words, as important as productivity is, it is not the most important trait for a person to have. In another incident, Jesus praised Zaccheus only after the tax collector promised to give half of his possessions to the poor and to make things right with anyone he had defrauded (Luke 19:8-10).

The Lord told the rich young ruler to sell all that he had and give to the poor (Matthew 19:16-21). When the young man went away sorrowful because he had great wealth, Jesus told his disciples, "Truly I say to you, it is hard for a rich man to enter the kingdom of heaven. Again I say to you, it is easier for a camel to go through the eye of a needle, than for a rich man to enter the kingdom of God" (Matthew 19:22-24). This amazed the disciples. In their eyes, the rich young ruler was the model of success and godliness. If he did not qualify for salvation, they wondered, "Then who can be saved?" Jesus reminded them that God does the saving, not man (Matthew 19:25-26).

Lesson 10 - The Radical Economics of Jesus

Many people have wondered whether Jesus' command to the rich young ruler to sell his possessions applies to all Christians. Apparently it does not. Jesus accepted financial assistance from people, apparently without requiring them to give away all that they owned (Luke 9:3). When Zaccheus promised to give half of his possessions to the poor and to make fourfold restitution to anyone he had defrauded, Jesus said salvation had come to that house (Luke 19:1-10). He did not insist that Zaccheus divest himself of all of his possessions.

People in the early church sold property and gave the money to be distributed to the poor (Acts 4:34-37); however, we have no indication that the centurion Cornelius or the businesswoman Lydia did that (Acts 10:1-48, 16:14-15). Paul instructed Timothy to teach those who were "rich in this present world . . . to be generous and ready to share" (1 Timothy 6:17, 19), but the apostle did not insist that those Christians sell everything they owned.

The heroes in many of Jesus' parables and in many of the encounters with Him that the gospels relate are not the wealthy but the poor. Jesus said that He came "to preach the gospel to the poor" (Luke 4:18). The men in Jesus' teachings who exemplified the kingdom of heaven were the man who sold all he had to buy a field that contained a treasure and the man who sold all he had to buy the pearl of great price (Matthew 13:44-46). In one story, the man who rested in Abraham's bosom after his death had been a poor man in this life, while the man in torment had been rich in this life (Luke 16:19-31). Jesus took note of and complimented the poor widow who gave to the temple treasury two copper coins, all she had in her poverty, not the people who gave larger amounts out of their abundance (Luke 21:1-4)

In Luke 6, Jesus said that the poor and the hungry were blessed; but He uttered woes upon the rich and well-fed (Luke 6:20-25). He taught His followers that their goal should not be to acquire and to possess but to "lend, expecting nothing in return" (that is, not expecting to receive a favor in return; Luke 6:35). Jesus promised His listeners, "Give, and it will be given to you. They will pour into your lap a good measure—pressed down, shaken together, and running over. For by your standard of measure it will be measured to you in return" (Luke 6:38). Jesus told His followers, "Sell your possessions and give to charity" (Luke 12:33).

When a woman anointed Jesus with costly perfume, the disciples were outraged at what they saw as a waste. The perfume could have been sold and the money given to the poor, which they thought would have been a wiser use of the resource. But Jesus gently reminded them, "You always have the poor with you." In other words, you always have the opportunity to serve others. The poor are not just to use in scoring points in a discussion. Jesus knew that the woman who anointed Him had better insight into what was truly valuable, and she made the best use of her scarce resources (Matthew 26:6-13).

This altarpiece at the Church of St. Vincent in Heiligenblut, Austria, depicts Mary Magdalene washing the feet of Jesus.

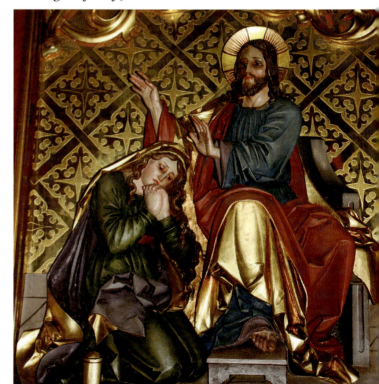

What It Means to Follow Jesus

In His best-known call to discipleship, Jesus described the meaning of following Him in economic terms:

> Then Jesus said to His disciples, "If anyone wishes to come after Me, he must deny himself, and take up his cross and follow Me. For whoever wishes to save his life will lose it; but whoever loses his life for My sake will find it. For what will it profit a man if he gains the whole world and forfeits his soul? Or what will a man give in exchange for his soul?" (Matthew 16:24-26)

In presenting this challenging summons, Jesus did not ask anyone to do what He had not already done. The Lord could have come to earth to be a powerful political ruler or a wealthy businessman; instead, He lived as one who did not even have a place to lay His head (Luke 9:58). It is to this radical system of economics that Jesus calls us. Whoever has been given much—and Americans have been given much—has a greater responsibility to be a good *oikonomos* or steward of what he has been given.

From everyone who has been given much, much will be required; and to whom they entrusted much, of him they will ask all the more.
Luke 12:48

Assignments for Lesson 10

Literature Continue reading *Silas Marner*.

Project Finish your project for this unit.

Student Review Answer the questions for Lesson 10 and take the quiz for Unit 2.

Volunteers from the U.S. Navy work with Habitat for Humanity in San Antonio, Texas (2011)

03 God's Economics, Part 2

Wealth and poverty were significant spiritual issues in the early church. Early Christian teachers had much to say regarding how believers were to handle money. The monastic movement was a reaction to the influence of the world. Later movements, such as the Protestant Reformation and Puritanism, also dealt with how believers conducted economic activities. Nineteenth and twentieth century theologians introduced new ideas on how Christians should view economic and financial matters. Following Jesus includes how a disciple thinks about and uses money. Greed is one of many issues regarding wealth that a Christian must confront in his own heart.

Lesson 11 - To Each as Any Had Need
Lesson 12 - Economics in Church History, Part 1
Lesson 13 - Economics in Church History, Part 2
Lesson 14 - Economics for Today's Christian
Lesson 15 - The Love of Money

Books Used

The Bible
Making Choices
Silas Marner

Project (choose one)

1) Write 300 to 500 words on the first topic or write a poem:

   - Write about the relationship the church as a body should have with material wealth. Should a church own possessions? Should a church have debt? Are large buildings and large budgets evidence of faithfulness? How can a church best steward finances? If possible, use Scripture to support your answers.

   - Write a poem of at least twelve lines about the fellowship described in Acts 4:32-35.

2) Research and make a list of at least ten national Christian-owned companies. Include a brief description of the business and the location of the headquarters.

3) Write and perform a skit that creatively explores the topic of greed. Recruit siblings or friends to perform with you.

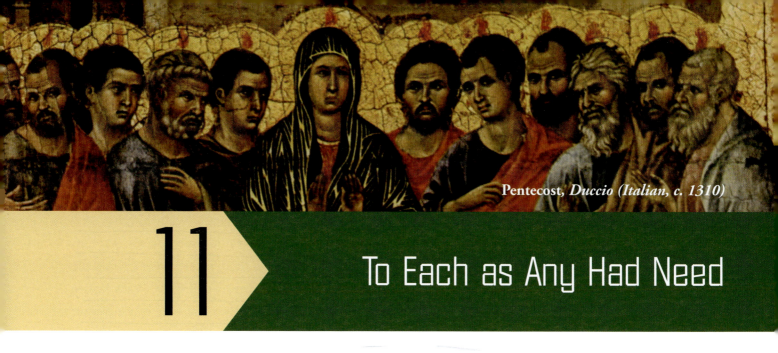

Pentecost, Duccio (Italian, c. 1310)

11 — To Each as Any Had Need

> *For there was not a needy person among them . . .*
> — Acts 4:34

The revolution in living that Jesus offered to people affected their economic lives. When a person is transformed by the renewing of his or her mind (Romans 12:2), that person's thinking about finances is changed along with everything else.

Economics in Acts

The Holy Spirit led the first believers in Jerusalem to see their possessions in a new way because of the fellowship of disciples that had just been formed.

> And the congregation of those who believed were of one heart and soul; and not one of them claimed that anything belonging to him was his own, but all things were common property to them. And with great power the apostles were giving testimony to the resurrection of the Lord Jesus, and abundant grace was upon them all. For there was not a needy person among them, for all who were owners of land or houses would sell them and bring the proceeds of the sales and lay them at the apostles' feet, and they would be distributed to each as any had need.   Acts 4:32-35

Those Christians did not look at their fellow believers who were poor and think that those people just needed to pull themselves up by their own sandal straps. Instead, the disciples sold some of what they had to generate money that they gave to help the needy in the fellowship.

Some have said that the early church practiced Communism, but this is not true. Communism involves state ownership of the means of production and the forced distribution of scarce resources that government workers direct. This was not how the early church operated. First, the government did not carry out the distribution; second, the early church did not take over the operation of farms and shops that Christians owned; and third, the sharing of resources was not compulsory. The sharing that took place was the result of personal conviction based on the new view of life and material possessions that Jesus created in His followers.

Helping the poor was a major issue in the early church. The fellowship in Jerusalem oversaw a daily distribution of food to widows (Acts 6:1).

In that day, widows received no government assistance, so if they needed help other individuals had to provide it. Christians in Antioch—again voluntarily—collected assistance that Barnabas and Saul took to the elders in Jerusalem to distribute to Christians there who needed relief during a famine (Acts 11:27-30). Paul collected money on his third missionary journey to help the poor in Jerusalem (see Romans 15:25-27).

This emphasis on the needs of the poor in the early church reminds us that the gospel had a major appeal among people in the first century world who were poor (see 1 Corinthians 1:26), although certainly some who became Christians had a degree of wealth. Two examples of those with considerable means are the centurion Cornelius (Acts 10:1-2) and the businesswoman Lydia (Acts 16:14-15).

Economics in the New Testament Letters

The inspired letters written to churches in the first century discussed economic and financial issues. In Philippians, Paul said that he had "suffered the loss of all things" for the sake of Christ, but that for him knowing Christ Jesus as his Lord held "surpassing value" (Philippians 3:8). Paul sincerely thanked the Christians in Philippi for their assistance to him, but he noted:

> Not that I speak from want, for I have learned to be content in whatever circumstances I am. I know how to get along with humble means, and I also know how to live in prosperity; in any and every circumstance I have learned the secret of being filled and going hungry, both of having abundance and suffering need. I can do all things through Him who strengthens me.
>
> Philippians 4:11-13

Paul also assured the Philippians that, in response to their generosity toward him, "My God will supply all your needs according to His riches in glory in Christ Jesus" (Philippians 4:19). Those needs might not have been financial, but Paul understood the power of the God of abundance.

Paul addressed the social and economic arrangement of slavery in several letters. He encouraged slaves and masters to have a new perspective on their relationship. Slaves were to serve their masters as though they were serving the Lord. Masters were to treat their slaves with justice and kindness, remembering that they had a Master in heaven (Ephesians 6:5-9, Colossians 3:22-4:1).

In 1 Corinthians 7, Paul addressed several life situations. The general theme in the chapter is encouragement for people to remain in the status they were when they became Christians (1 Corinthians 7:20). Regarding slavery, Paul said a Christian should be satisfied to remain in the condition he was in, although if a believer had the opportunity to become free he should take it (verses 21-23). Paul did not initiate a campaign to abolish slavery, but through him the Lord introduced a new way of viewing others. Centuries later this new way of thinking led some to become convinced that slavery was incompatible with the Christian life and people with this conviction organized abolitionist efforts.

This fresco depicting early Christians sharing a meal is from a catacomb in Rome.

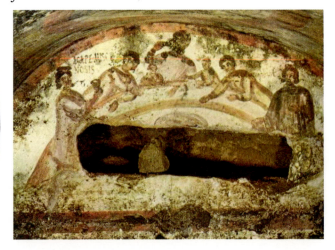

Mosaic of merchant ship in Tunisia (c. 3rd century AD)

In 2 Thessalonians, Paul addressed the problem of Christians not working and thus not providing for their own needs as they should. Paul had words of warning for those who led an unruly or undisciplined life. Many have interpreted this to mean that some in the church in Thessalonica had quit work and were waiting for what they thought would be the Lord's imminent return. When that did not happen, and when those who had quit work continued to need food and covering, they began to depend on other Christians for their needs. Paul gave them these admonitions:

> Now we command you, brethren, in the name of our Lord Jesus Christ, that you keep away from every brother who leads an unruly life and not according to the tradition which you received from us. For you yourselves know how you ought to follow our example, because we did not act in an undisciplined manner among you, nor did we eat anyone's bread without paying for it, but with labor and hardship we kept working night and day so that we would not be a burden to any of you; not because we do not have the right to this, but in order to offer ourselves as a model for you, so that you would follow our example. For even when we were with you, we used to give you this order: if anyone is not willing to work, then he is not to eat, either. For we hear that some among you are leading an undisciplined life, doing no work at all, but acting like busybodies. Now such persons we command and exhort in the Lord Jesus Christ to work in quiet fashion and eat their own bread.
> 2 Thessalonians 3:6-12

James gave special emphasis to the matter of how the gospel affected the rich and the poor and how the fellowship of believers was to respond to those in different economic situations. "The brother of humble circumstances," James said, was to rejoice in the spiritual riches he had in Christ, while the rich man was to rejoice in the fact that one day all of his wealth would be gone (James 1:9-11).

James also condemned treating people with partiality on the basis of their economic status. If the members of a church paid special attention to a rich man who came into its assembly but brushed aside a poor man, James said that they had become "judges with evil motives." James reminded his readers that God had chosen the poor "to be rich in faith and heirs of the kingdom," while it was rich people who had persecuted and oppressed them (James 2:1-7). Later, James condemned the unjust rich who took pride in their wealth and mistreated laborers who worked for them (James 5:1-6).

James admonished believers to engage in business activity with humility, subjecting themselves to the will of God and realizing the brevity and uncertainty of life:

> Come now, you who say, "Today or tomorrow we will go to such and such a city, and spend a year there and engage in business and make a profit." Yet you do not know what your life will be like tomorrow. You are just a vapor that appears for a little while and then vanishes away. Instead, you ought to say, "If the Lord wills, we will live and also do this or that." But as it is, you boast in your arrogance; all such boasting is evil. Therefore, to one who knows the right thing to do and does not do it, to him it is sin.
> James 4:13-17

The Economic Downfall of Rome

Under the inspiration of the Holy Spirit, the apostle John wrote the book of Revelation to give encouragement to first-century Christians who were suffering under persecution by Roman authorities. Information in Chapter 17 and elsewhere identifies the evil force that is described as Babylon the great, the great harlot, and the beast (among other things) as being Rome. Revelation 17:9 says that the seven heads of the beast are the seven mountains on which the woman sits (Rome was built on seven hills). Revelation 17:18 says that, "The woman whom you saw is the great city, which reigns over the kings of the earth," a description that only fits Rome.

Chapter 18 predicts the downfall of Babylon the great, which the Bible describes as the woman of immorality (Revelation 18:2-3). This chapter contains several references to the end of the city's wealth and to grieving merchants who had been engaged in trade with it (including verses 3 and 11-15). The economic power and influence of Rome were indeed destroyed when it fell, in keeping with the prophecy of this passage in Revelation.

Paul described the grace of Christ and what it gives to believers in economic terms.

> *For you know the grace of our Lord Jesus Christ,*
> *that though He was rich, yet for your sake He became poor,*
> *so that you through His poverty might become rich.*
> *2 Corinthians 8:9*

Assignments for Lesson 11

Literature — Continue reading *Silas Marner*. Plan to finish it by the end of this unit.

Project — Choose your project for this unit and start working on it.

Student Review — Answer the questions for Lesson 11.

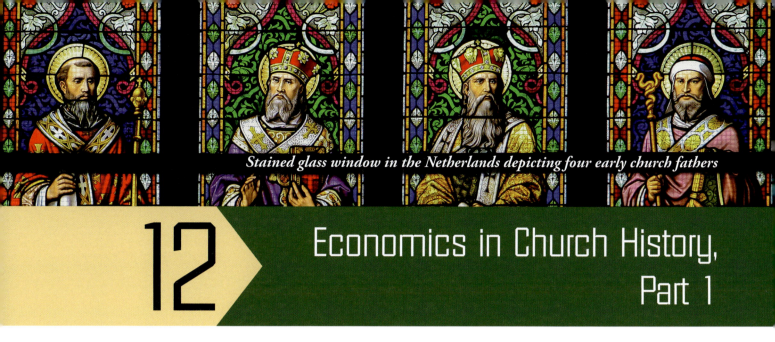
Stained glass window in the Netherlands depicting four early church fathers

12 Economics in Church History, Part 1

Nothing that is God's is obtainable by money.
— *Tertullian (c. 160 - 220 AD)*

The church of our Lord has included many different teachings and movements over the centuries. Christians have gone from one extreme to the other in their views of wealth, from advocating absolute poverty to the glorification of possessions. Many of these diverse doctrines have reflected one particular aspect of Christian teaching but not all of God's truth. This is why these teachings have had an appeal to various people but do not completely reflect the whole counsel of God.

The Church Fathers

After the age of the apostles, Christians continued to share material goods with their needy brethren. Leaders who are today known as the church fathers warned against greed and the accumulation of wealth and decried the practice of usury (charging interest on loans) as being hurtful to the poor. They also described generosity to others as a way for Christians to demonstrate their faith in God.

Falsehood is not found among them; and they love one another, and from widows they do not turn away their esteem; and they deliver the orphan from him who treats him harshly. And he who has gives to him who has not, without boasting. And when they see a stranger, they take him in to their homes and rejoice over him as a very brother; for they do not call them brethren after the flesh, but brethren after the spirit and in God. And whenever one of their poor passes from the world, each one of them according to his ability gives heed to him and carefully sees to his burial. And if they hear that one of their number is imprisoned or afflicted on account of the name of their Messiah, all of them anxiously minister to his necessity, and if it is possible to redeem him they set him free. And if there is among them any that is poor and needy, and if they have no spare food, they fast two or three days in order to supply to the needy their lack of food.
— Aristides (c. 125 AD)

But those, moreover, whom you consider rich, who add forests to forests, and who, excluding the poor from their neighborhood, stretch out their fields far and wide into space

69

without any limits, who possess immense heaps of silver and gold and mighty sums of money, either in built-up heaps or in buried stores. Even in the midst of their riches those are torn to pieces by the anxiety of vague thought, lest the robber should spoil, lest the murderer should attack, lest the envy of some wealthier neighbour should become hostile, and harass them with malicious lawsuits. Such a one enjoys no security either in his food or in his sleep. . . . And oh, the odious blindness of perception, and the deep darkness of senseless greed! Although he might disburden himself and get rid of the load, he rather continues to brood over his vexing wealth. He goes on obstinately clinging to his tormenting hoards. From him there is no liberality to dependents, no communication to the poor.

— Cyprian (c. 250 AD)

[Possessions] are good if you open up the granaries of your righteousness, so that you may be the bread of the poor, the life of the needy, the eye of the blind, the father of orphaned infants. . . . Whoever, then, does not use his property as a possession and knows not how to give and dispense to the poor is the slave and not the master of his goods, for he watches over what belongs to others like a servant and does not use what is his like a master. When it comes to a disposition of this kind, then, we say that the man belongs to the wealth and not the wealth to the man.

— Ambrose (c. 375 AD)

The Monastic Movement

At some point, perhaps in the second century after Christ but certainly by the third, some believers wanted to escape the influence and defilement of the world to such an extent that they began living as hermits. They sold or gave away almost all of their possessions and lived completely or almost completely cut off from contact with the world. This approach to the Christian life became known as monasticism, and those who engaged in it were called monks, from the Greek word *monos*, which means one or alone. In the fourth century, these monastics, as people who had decided to live apart from the world, began gathering into communities called monasteries. These monks committed themselves to a life of voluntary poverty and devoted themselves to prayer and fasting.

The monastic movement began as a way for individuals to live with repentance and humility before God. Monks who were not completely cut off from the world often served the communities in which they were located. Some of them tried to teach and influence society in an evangelistic way.

The Roman Empire eventually tolerated Christians and then established Christianity as the official religion. When Christians were no longer an outcast group, many in the church came to regard the monastics as possessing a higher level of spirituality compared to others. As Christians acquired wealth and the church began to gain social standing, some saw the monastics as evidence that the church had

Church Fathers (Russian, c. 1076)

This image of monks working in a field is by Jörg Breu the Elder (German, c. 1500)

not lost its soul while it acquired an ever greater portion of worldly goods.

What began as a movement of penance became a way for a person to try to do enough good to merit God's salvation. As believers began giving money and bequeathing property to the church (again, often in an attempt to earn God's favor), what began as a movement of poverty came to be part of a system that controlled significant wealth. During the Middle Ages, the Roman Catholic Church was the richest institution in Europe and had significant influence in the political realm. Kings sometimes appealed to the pope for financial support for their military undertakings.

The Protestant Reformation

Martin Luther and other leaders in the Reformation Movement rejected many traditional Roman Catholic teachings and practices, including the view that poverty was especially meritorious in the eyes of God. Luther, himself a former monk, rediscovered the idea of a personal calling available to everyone. The person who was, for example, a carpenter, baker, or wife and mother and who lived to the glory of God was fulfilling his or her calling from God at least as much as someone who lived in poverty and cut himself off from the world. Luther understood that a person could live in the mainstream of life and business and still serve the Lord. Such Christians had to guard against greed, dishonesty, and other sins; but they were not to be seen (nor were they to see themselves) as second-class Christians, as compared to those living a monastic lifestyle.

As the Protestant movement diversified in the ensuing years, teachings and practices went in many directions regarding money. John Calvin, for instance, was not opposed to Christians accumulating wealth or even loaning money as a way to build wealth, as long as they did not oppress the poor in doing so. Anabaptists criticized other Reformers for not doing enough to help the poor. Many Quakers were successful businessmen. People made attempts from time to time to establish utopian communities with communal economic arrangements.

The Puritans

The Puritans of sixteenth and seventeenth century England, some of whom settled in the Massachusetts Bay colony and elsewhere, had a significant influence in America because of their successful New England colonies. Their views of religious truth and economic realities helped to shape the thinking of American Christians about faith and money.

On the whole, Puritans saw money as a good thing because it is part of God's creation. Money was a gift from God, they said; and people are to be good stewards of what God gives them. Thus the Puritans believed that using one's God-given talents to earn money was faithful stewardship. Besides, the more money one had, the more good he could accomplish. However, financial success was not a matter of one's own merit. Instead, they saw success as a gift of God.

In the Puritan mindset, poverty was also from God. Enduring poverty could be a trial to bring about needed spiritual growth. Puritans knew from their own experience that "all who desire to live godly in Christ Jesus will be persecuted" (2 Timothy 3:12), and this persecution could involve the loss of material possessions. In addition, the reality of people in poverty provided an opportunity for believers who had wealth to get out of themselves and help others.

Still, most Puritans did not sell themselves out to the acquisition of wealth. They understood that money can be dangerous because it can replace God as the object of chief devotion in a person's heart. Money can cause a person to rely on himself instead of God. The Puritans sought a balance between honoring God as their first love and honoring God in their working lives, even as they realized that this balance is often difficult to maintain. Their priorities of hard work, simple lifestyle, and moderation led to economic success.

This lesson has touched on just a few of the ideas and movements that emerged from the second through the seventeenth century. Many Christians through the centuries have given serious thought to money and economics out of a desire to serve God faithfully in all aspects of life. Surely Christians today should do no less.

We should plan our economic activities while remembering that success is in the Lord's hands.

The mind of man plans his way,
But the Lord directs his steps.
Proverbs 16:9

Assignments for Lesson 12

Making Choices — Read the excerpts from "A Model of Christian Charity" (page 25).

Literature — Continue reading *Silas Marner*.

Project — Continue working on your project for this unit.

Student Review — Answer the questions for Lesson 12.

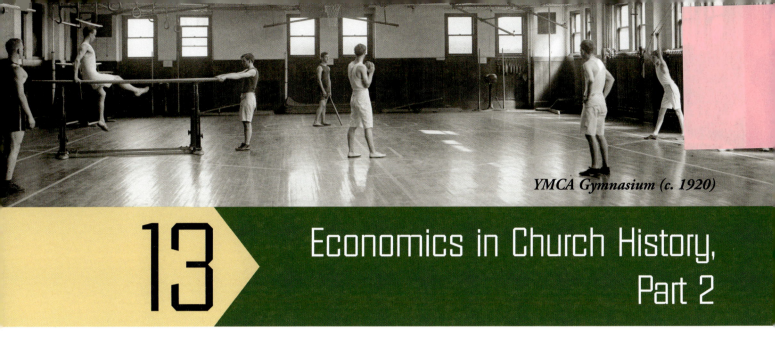
YMCA Gymnasium (c. 1920)

13 Economics in Church History, Part 2

My Lord is not limited; He can again supply; He knows that this present case has been sent to me; and thus, this way of living so far from leading to anxiety, is rather the means of keeping from it.

— George Müller

Nineteenth Century America

The great cause for many Christians in the middle of nineteenth century America was the abolition of slavery. The slavery issue involved moral, political, spiritual, and economic questions. Slaveowners feared that an end to slavery would bring about their financial ruin, while opponents of slavery were ashamed that any part of the country's wealth was built on the institution. Before the Civil War, American churches were divided over whether to support slavery, champion abolition, or remain silent on the issue.

Following the Civil War and the ending of slavery, the last quarter of the nineteenth century and the first quarter of the twentieth century was a period that saw a number of rapidly developing movements. American industrial growth was immense. At the same time, workers often felt exploited and began to demand better wages and working conditions. Evangelists such as Dwight L. Moody and Billy Sunday drew huge crowds. Through their ministry, thousands of people made decisions to follow Christ. Meanwhile, many Christians took up causes for social reform that had economic impact, such as prohibition, better working conditions, and a graduated income tax. The focus on social and economic causes in the name of Christ came to be called the social gospel.

Many wealthy businessmen gave financial support to Christian causes such as the YMCA, Moody Bible Institute and other training centers, as well as foreign missions. Undoubtedly the financial success of American business enabled greater funding for these efforts.

The Protestant Ethic and Capitalism

In 1904-05, German economist and sociologist Max Weber published *The Protestant Ethic and the Spirit of Capitalism*. The book was translated into English in 1930. Weber noted that capitalism developed and grew during the same period that Protestant (particularly Calvinistic) theology was gaining acceptance. In fact, two countries that

73

were leaders in the development of both capitalist business and international trade were the Protestant Netherlands and Protestant Britain.

Weber defined capitalism as economic activity that expects a profit through peaceful, voluntary, and mutually beneficial exchanges. He saw the spirit of capitalism as the rational (that is, the reasoned or well thought-out) pursuit of economic gain. Weber's thesis was that Protestant thought was a strong influence (though not the only influence) on capitalism and capitalistic thinking. According to Weber, some of the aspects of Protestant thought that influenced the development of capitalism were:

- The idea of seeing one's vocation in life, not just service within the church, as a calling (an idea we mentioned in the previous lesson).

- The belief that discipline and hard work (sometimes called the Protestant work ethic), which led to making money, were legitimate ways to honor God and to fulfill one's calling.

- The rejection of personal luxury, which led to businessmen investing their profits in further growth of their businesses.

- The worth of the individual, which led to greater economic activity (and which also led to a commitment to political freedom, which in turn enabled greater economic activity).

Since the publication of Weber's book, many scholars have challenged and critiqued his theory. It is true that most of the industrial leaders in Europe and America at the time that Weber wrote were Protestants. Protestant thought probably did influence capitalistic activity. However, one might also argue that capitalism grew because it is an effective way to conduct business and to make a profit, and that Protestant thought justified what business owners wanted to do anyway.

Max Weber

Other Philosophies

The twentieth century saw various groups and individuals put forth several other approaches to money and economics in the name of Christ. We will look briefly at two of these as examples of how Christian people have tried to combine Biblical teaching with economics.

Liberation Theology. Liberation theology developed in the mid-twentieth century among some Roman Catholics, particularly in Latin America. Its advocates have largely adopted Marxist thought and taken a politically liberal stance. Liberation theology uses ideas from Scripture to support what it calls the liberation of the poor from their poverty by opposing those whom liberationists call the oppressors of the poor. To liberationists, the oppressors are capitalists, the government, and sometimes the Catholic hierarchy. Scriptures they use to justify this philosophy include Isaiah 61:1

(often translated, "The Lord has anointed Me to bring good news to the poor"—and what could be better news than liberation from poverty?) and Matthew 10:34 ("I did not come to bring peace, but a sword," which they interpret as supporting political revolution).

It appears that liberation theologians had their goal of political revolution to begin with, and then they found passages in Scripture that they used to give religious justification for it. This theology has several problems. First, Jesus did not come to bring about a political revolution. He disappointed all of those in His own day who expected this. Second, capitalism has not oppressed people. To the contrary, capitalism has been the way that many people have gotten out of poverty. It is true that Latin American governments have sometimes oppressed people, and some of those governments have worked with capitalists; but capitalism as an economic system is not the problem. Third, Marxism is not the way that people have found political liberation and release from poverty. Instead, Marxism brings greater power and wealth to the few who have political or military power. It has failed to bring greater wealth to the people for whom Marxists claim to speak. Fourth, liberation theology focuses on political and economic conditions in this world and has little or nothing to say about spiritual realities.

Church in Malata, Peru

Theonomy or Reconstructionism. Theonomy or Christian reconstructionism is the school of thought promoted by R. J. Rushdoony (1916-2001) and others. Christian reconstructionists maintain that the church should rule society. Their goal is the reconstruction of governmental, legal, and economic systems on the basis of their interpretation of Biblical teaching from both the Old and New Testament Scriptures.

Reconstructionism is a controversial philosophy, and many Christians have expressed reservations about it. First, the Bible nowhere teaches that the goal of the church is to rule society. Instead, the Bible indicates that the church would face persecution by the forces of worldly power (see, for instance, John 16:33 and 1 Peter 4:12-19). At the same time, the New Testament teaches that Christians should respect government (Romans 13:1-7 and 1 Peter 2:13-17). Second, reconstructionists fail to see the difference between (1) the Old Testament Law that God intended for the nation of Israel in preparation for the coming of the Messiah and (2) the new covenant in Christ that is the basis for the church which exists in many nations (Ephesians 2:14-22, Hebrews 9:11-28). Third, it is unclear who would lead such a reconstructed society, unless it would be those committed to Rushdoony's ideas. If this were the case, all others who might have different ideas would be relegated to the role of enemies or infidels. This latter group would eventually include those who began as insiders and at some point took exception to the ideas and interpretations of the leader. We would all like to think that our ideas are the best and only true ideas, but many people have suffered at the hands of leaders who have insisted that their perception of truth is the only acceptable way to think.

As we consider how Christians should live in the world without being part of the world, we should remember these words of Jesus:

Jesus answered, "My kingdom is not of this world. If My kingdom were of this world, then My servants would be fighting so that I would not be handed over to the Jews; but as it is, My kingdom is not of this realm."
John 18:36

Assignments for Lesson 13

Literature — Continue reading *Silas Marner*.

Project — Continue working on your project for this unit.

Student Review — Answer the questions for Lesson 13.

Beggar outside a church in St. Petersburg, Russia

14 Economics for Today's Christian

The world asks, "What does a man own?"
Christ asks, "How does he use it?"
—Andrew Murray

The study of economics is not just a theoretical endeavor, nor is it merely an academic exercise that uses big words and complicated ideas. Economics involves how we live and how we make decisions every day. It affects individuals as well as nations. The personal consequences of national and global financial issues remind us that economic practices and decisions have immediate impact on millions of people.

Because economics affects everyone, because it involves decisions that reflect our priorities, and because the economy is constantly changing, Christians face many decisions. In making these decisions, we look to Scripture as our guide; but we have to apply the teachings of Scripture in situations today that the Bible does not directly address (the Bible doesn't talk about multinational corporations, stock markets, or hedge funds, for instance). These decisions are not always easy, and the answers are not always clear. Well-meaning Christians can arrive at different conclusions in all good conscience. But not wrestling with these issues is not an option for those who want to follow Jesus in every aspect of their lives. This lesson presents some of the economic issues that Christians face.

For the sake of clarity, we can divide these issues into ones that primarily involve individual actions and ones that involve system-wide or economy-wide policies. However, the distinction is not always clear-cut. Actions by an individual can affect the economy as a whole, and economy-wide policies and actions have an impact on individuals. We need a Christian perspective at both levels. Certainly one person can make the greatest difference in matters that he or she can control individually. You can decide to avoid debt, for example, whether or not your government decides to avoid debt.

It will be helpful to keep these and other personal, practical issues in mind as you study the rest of the lessons in this curriculum. Economics makes a difference for your life every day.

Issues Involving the Individual

What standard of living should be a Christian's goal? Should a Christian aim for a subsistence-level existence or a more "comfortable" lifestyle?

Chick-fil-A restaurants are closed on Sundays to give operators and employees time to rest, spend time with family and friends, and worship if they choose. Founder Truett Cathy (1921-2014) was a Christian who sought to build the business in keeping with his faith.

Should a Christian strive for the greatest income he or she can acquire, with the goal of using profits or income above a certain level to help others in some way? What price or sacrifice should Christians be willing to pay to achieve the standard of living they want to have? Is job satisfaction more important than level of income?

How should a Christian be engaged with the world in terms of economics? Should we withdraw from the world as much as possible and try to develop an individual or small group economy? Should we store up supplies and cash to tide us over a period of time in case of an emergency? What is the best way that an individual Christian or a church can help the poor? Should we campaign for candidates whose economic proposals we support? Should Christians boycott or picket businesses that use or exploit undocumented foreign workers or that sell materials that Christians believe are indecent?

Assuming that a Christian business person will be committed to honesty and integrity, what other principles should he or she follow in business? Should she limit her work hours (for instance, not working on Sunday or in the evenings)? Should he avoid using or selling products made in countries that do not respect human rights? Should she always try to grow her business, or should she be satisfied at a certain level of income? Can a person be a Christian and a (fill in the blank: capitalist? socialist? clerk at a convenience store or movie theater?). Should a Christian business person's main goal be making a profit or serving the community (whether it be the church community or the community at large)? Does a Christian have to choose one or the other?

Lesson 14 - Economics for Today's Christian

How should a Christian business person use his profit? Should he make a capital investment to expand his business? Should she pay a bonus to her workers? Should he take his family on a vacation? Should she give it to the poor or to missions?

Is a Christian guaranteed financial success? We have discussed several verses in the Old and New Testaments that say the Lord will provide for His faithful. However, Christians do from time to time get laid off from their jobs or suffer other economic hardship. Christians have to endure scarcity like everybody else. Job is an example of someone who was faithful to God but who suffered severe economic reversal.

Here are some thoughts on these questions. First, we have to make sure that we understand God's definition of success. Spiritual success in His eyes is most important. Having everything we want is not within God's definition of success.

Second, God does promise to take care of His people (see, for example, Psalm 37:25, Matthew 6:33, Luke 6:38, and Philippians 4:19).

Third, God will sometimes provide for His people through the generosity of other Christians when a brother or sister has a need.

Fourth, God provides, but we still have to work. He does not promise abundance as a reward for laziness. He expects people to invest their time, labor, and other assets wisely.

Fifth, God indicated early on that His will for abundance can be thwarted by disobedience (Deuteronomy 28:15-68). Sin that causes problems in an economic system can adversely affect individuals within that system.

Sixth, Job did suffer economic reversal; but it was for a divinely-guided purpose.

Silk factory in Dalat, Vietnam (2012)

Jesus said that giving would result in blessings to the giver (Luke 6:38), but Jesus did not say that giving to Him was the way to obtain the blessings. The lesson from Scripture is that if you are generous you will have plenty (Proverbs 11:24, 19:17). Moreover, a faithful Christian who goes through an economic reversal might inaccurately blame the problem on a lack of faith. The fact is that we have struggles in this world. God has His good purposes in this world and for each individual life. He sends rain on the righteous and the unrighteous (Matthew 5:45), and He disciplines those whom he loves (Hebrews 12:6). God is not a cosmic gumball machine that dispenses prizes to the one who puts his money in just the right non-profit slot.

Issues Involving the Broader Economy

What standards characterize a just economy? For instance: Should every person in that economy be able to feed and clothe his or her family? What is the responsible use of natural resources? Should every citizen have a voice in choosing leaders and thus in directing economic policy?

How should a Christian, or the church, or the economy address certain issues? These issues include poverty, the environment, equal pay for workers doing the same job, discrimination against certain categories of people in the workplace, energy usage and development, and relationships with developing nations (should we utilize their workers; should we provide aid and, if so, in what form?).

Do you want to see a smaller, more efficient, and less intrusive government, or a larger, more activist government? Issues involved in this question include the protection of personal liberties; government regulations on business; inefficiencies in government; appropriate levels of taxation; and the government's role in helping the poor, protecting property rights, providing economic stimulus, and encouraging business initiative.

Should wealth be redistributed? If not, what are the prospects for the poor? If so, to what extent should it be done and who should do it: individuals, the church, charities (all through direct donations or the creation of programs), or the government (through collecting taxes and then providing payments and programs)?

What is your view of corporate executives who have large pay and benefits packages? Should the government impose any limits on their income and benefits, especially in companies that are government contractors or that are filing for bankruptcy?

These questions remind us that we cannot leave our faith outside of the bank, investment office, workplace, or voting booth. Living completely for Christ means seeking God's will and wisdom in these and other economic questions. The prophet Micah taught God's people the basics that God requires:

> *He has told you, O man, what is good;*
> *And what does the Lord require of you*
> *But to do justice, to love kindness,*
> *And to walk humbly with your God?*
> *Micah 6:8*

John Searcy started selling car batteries in the Dallas/Fort Worth area in the 1950s. He named his business the Interstate Battery System. Norm Miller, an Interstate employee, took over leadership in 1978 when Searcy retired. Miller is an outspoken Christian who has sought to run the business in accordance with his faith. Their company purpose is "to glorify God and enrich lives as we deliver the most trustworthy source of power to the world."

Assignments for Lesson 14

Making Choices   Read "The Use of Money" by John Wesley (pages 26-33).

Literature   Continue reading *Silas Marner*.

Project   Continue working on your project for this unit.

Student Review   Answer the questions for Lesson 14.

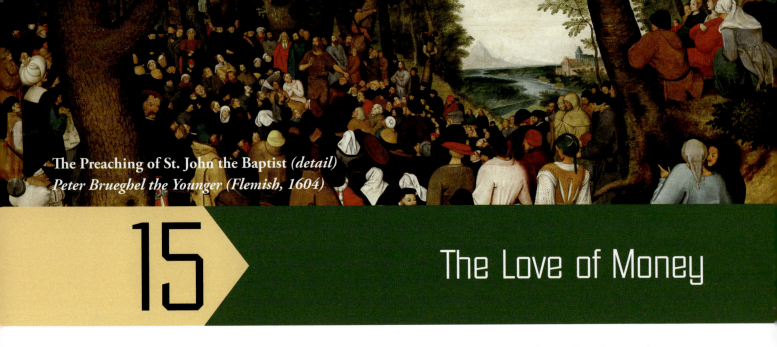

The Preaching of St. John the Baptist (detail)
Peter Brueghel the Younger (Flemish, 1604)

15 ▸ The Love of Money

> *Long Island, New York: A Walmart employee is trampled to death on the morning after Thanksgiving as crowds of shoppers anxious to get into the store on "Black Friday" break down the front door.*
>
> — *News item, November 2008*

One of the main causes of problems and unhappiness with regard to money is greed. According to the Merriam-Webster dictionary, greed is "a selfish and excessive desire for more of something (as money) than is needed." Greed is the desire to have more of something for a selfish reason, such as to have more than someone else has or to have more in order to enjoy more power and status.

Biblical Teachings About Greed

The Bible has much to say about greed. When Abram and Lot separated in Canaan, Lot selfishly chose the better land. He chose to live in wicked Sodom, a decision based on a selfish desire that caused him great sorrow and loss (Genesis 13:1-13, 19:1-38).

The Ten Commandments prohibit coveting anything that belongs to one's neighbor (Exodus 20:17). God knew that greediness toward what a neighbor had would cause strife and unhappiness.

Amos condemned those of Israel who trampled the needy, who were eager for a religious festival to be over so that they could trade dishonestly again, and who were willing to treat the poor as things in order to have more themselves (Amos 8:4-6).

John the Baptist told the tax collectors who came to him to collect only what they were supposed to. He instructed soldiers who came to him not to extort money from people and to be content with their wages (Luke 3:12-14).

Jesus warned a man who was being greedy about an inheritance to be on his guard "against every form of greed; for not even when one has an abundance does his life consist of his possessions." The Lord then told the parable of the rich fool who wanted bigger barns but who died suddenly and left all that he possessed to others. "So is the man who stores up treasure for himself, and is not rich toward God," concluded Jesus (Luke 12:13-21).

Lesson 15 - The Love of Money

Ananias and Sapphira conspired to lie to the church and to the Holy Spirit about the sale price of some property they sold, so that it would appear they were giving all of the proceeds of the sale to the church when in fact they were keeping back part of what they had received. They paid for their greed with their lives (Acts 5:1-10).

Paul said that greed "amounts to idolatry" (Colossians 3:5). James explained the tangled web that results from the wrong kind of desires:

> What is the source of quarrels and conflicts among you? Is not the source your pleasures that wage war in your members? You lust and do not have; so you commit murder. You are envious and cannot obtain; so you fight and quarrel. You do not have because you do not ask. You ask and do not receive, because you ask with wrong motives, so that you may spend it on your pleasures.
>
> James 4:1-3

John said that the "lust of the eyes" is not of the Father but is of the world and is passing away (1 John 2:16-17).

Examples of Greed from the American Economy

The men who oversaw the companies that built the transcontinental railroad in the 1860s received huge fortunes from the project, even though the workers on the line were paid relatively little and sometimes got paid late. In the late nineteenth and early twentieth centuries, many American manufacturers used cheap child labor and did not want to pay adult workers what many considered to be a decent wage.

To say that the poor are poor because the rich are rich is too simplistic. However, greed for more money has characterized the decisions and actions of many businessmen.

This young man lost his legs in a West Virginia coal mining accident when he was fourteen (1910)

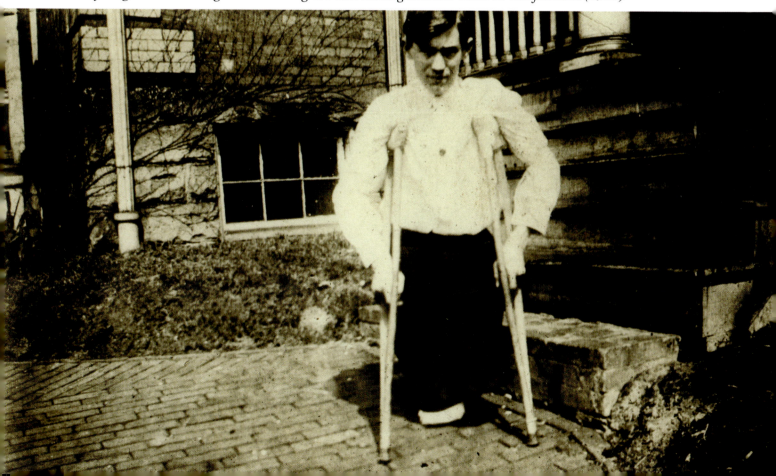

Crowd outside the New York Stock Exchange after the crash of 1929

Throughout American history, the free market has allowed greedy and sometimes unscrupulous people to try to get rich; but their attempts have often resulted in catastrophic losses for many people. Greed was a factor in the stock market crash of 1929 and the Great Depression that followed. Consumers wanted more and more stuff, investors wanted more and more profit, and the economic system let people gamble on the possibility of ever-higher stock prices. When prices fell, many people were hurt.

Many American businesses have moved their production facilities to other countries where labor is cheaper. The result has been the loss of thousands of American jobs while some executives keep their jobs and continue to receive large salaries. The decision regarding where to locate production facilities is one factor in a complicated process. Moving production overseas can help a company remain competitive. But another motive for such a move could be greed.

On the other hand, American consumers have not consistently been willing to pay higher prices for American-made goods, at least in part because they have wanted to hold on to a little more of their money.

Many stories have come to light telling of executives receiving enormous pay and benefits packages even as their companies were failing. Some cases involve outright fraud and deceit, while in other situations executives were able to make the best of a bad situation for themselves because of their position of power.

Some businesses use strong-arm tactics with their suppliers so that those businesses can pay less for what the suppliers produce and thus have greater profit. People can get over their heads in debt because they are greedy. They want to own more stuff than they can realistically afford with their income.

Lesson 15 - The Love of Money

Greed was a major factor in the recession of 2007-2009. People wanted to own homes that were beyond what they could afford to buy, banks wanted to make a profit by making loans to those people, and politicians encouraged looser mortgage practices so that they could get credit for enabling more people to own their own homes. When people could not afford to make the payments on their mortgages, they lost their homes and banks got stuck with homes worth less than what the banks could sell them for (we will study this financial crisis in more detail in a later lesson).

Principles at Work

Money (we might also call it riches or wealth) is not evil in itself. Like so many things in our world, people can use money for good or for ill. Wealth is a gift from God, but it is not to be a god (Matthew 6:24). Although many people seem to worship money or what it can provide, money is a poor god because it does not really satisfy our desires. Not only can it easily be lost, it can also leave us spiritually impoverished even in the midst of material abundance.

Maurice Sterne, born in Latvia in 1878, emigrated to the United States in 1889. Sterne's painting entitled Greed *(1939) is displayed in the main library of the Department of Justice building in Washington, D.C.*

The problem is with the attitude of greed. A person's attitude toward money reveals a heart condition—what that person truly desires. Someone could be greedy and not have much money, or that person could have a great deal of money and not be greedy. Paul gives us the solution when he instructs us to be content, thankful for what we have and confident that God will continue to provide:

> But godliness actually is a means of great gain when accompanied by contentment. For we have brought nothing into the world, so we cannot take anything out of it either. If we have food and covering, with these we shall be content. But those who want to get rich fall into temptation and a snare and many foolish and harmful desires which plunge men into ruin and destruction. For the love of money is a root of all sorts of evil, and some by longing for it have wandered away from the faith and pierced themselves with many griefs. (1 Timothy 6:6-10)

Greed is an issue in our economy because it is so commonly present in the hearts of people. Many factors play a part in a nation's economic life; but at the core, people like you and me far too often make decisions on the basis of greed instead of contentment and trust. The Bible frequently reminds us that greed has negative consequences.

*The righteousness of the upright will deliver them,
But the treacherous will be caught by their own greed.
Proverbs 11:6*

Assignments for Lesson 15

Literature — Finish reading *Silas Marner*. Read the literary analysis of the book beginning on page 19 in the *Student Review* and answer the questions over the book.

Project — Finish your project for this unit.

Student Review — Answer the questions for Lesson 15 and take the quiz for Unit 3.

Erie Canal in New York State (1829)

04 A Brief Economic History of the United States

Economic issues were involved in the founding of colonies in North America and in colonists' decision to separate from Great Britain. The new nation grappled with economic problems, and the Constitution laid out specific fiscal powers that Congress could exercise. The United States has experienced significant economic growth, spurred by new industries and inventions and helped by a framework of laws that protects property rights and intellectual property. Wars and economic downturns have brought periods of hardship and economic adjustment. The past one hundred years brought unprecedented growth and also brought the unprecedented downturns of the Great Depression of the 1930s and the Great Recession of 2007-2009.

Lesson 16 - From Exploration to Confederation
Lesson 17 - Money and the New United States
Lesson 18 - Wars and Panics
Lesson 19 - Prosperity and More Panics
Lesson 20 - The Economy As We Know It

Books Used

The Bible
Making Choices
The Rise of Silas Lapham

Project (choose one)

1) Write 300 to 500 words on one of the following topics:

- What are good strategies to prepare for economic recessions and depressions?

- What do you think are the most important changes in the American economy in the last 100 years? Why are they important?

2) Make a commercial about one minute long encouraging people in Europe to settle in the American colonies (as if video commercials were possible at the time). Focus on the economic benefits of relocating.

3) Design a poster recruiting workers for American textile mills of the late 1700s and early 1800s.

Literature

William Dean Howells was born in 1837, the son of a printer and publisher in Ohio. When he was older, Howells himself went into printing and publishing and became a writer. President Lincoln named Howells U.S. consul to Venice as a reward for supporting him in the 1860 election.

Upon his return, Howells returned to publishing. From 1871 to 1881, he was the editor of the influential *Atlantic Monthly* magazine. He wrote several novels, the best-known of which was *The Rise of Silas Lapham* (1885). The book was one of the first to explore the topic of the American businessman. Set in Boston during the Victorian era, the story follows the financial and romantic upheavals of the Lapham family, with a focus on the personal development of the title character as his rise unfolds.

Howells became known as the dean of American letters. The photo at right shows him in 1906. He died in 1920.

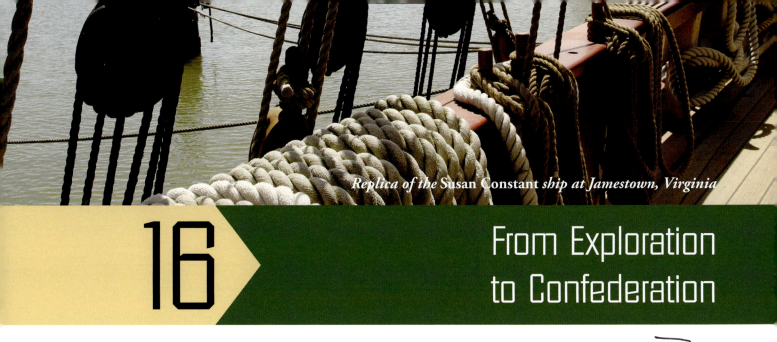

Replica of the Susan Constant *ship at Jamestown, Virginia*

16 From Exploration to Confederation

To prohibit a great people [i.e., the American colonies], however, from making all that they can of every part of their own produce, or from employing their stock and industry in the way that they judge most advantageous to themselves, is a manifest violation of the most sacred rights of mankind.
— Adam Smith, The Wealth of Nations *(1776)*

] Amen!

Before we take up our discussion of economic terms and principles, we want to give you an overview of American economic history. We do this to show you why it is important to understand economics. Economic issues have always been a major part of American life, just as they are today. Knowing history prepares us for making better economic choices.

The Colonial Period

By the late 1400s, a growing European market wanted spices and other imports from Asia. The demand was greater than the supply, and European traders found that using overland routes to Asia was slow, expensive, and dangerous. Interest in Europe turned to possible sea routes to Asia, at first around Africa. Spain and Portugal led these efforts. Thus, economic benefit was a strong motivation for naval exploration.

Christopher Columbus sailed west on behalf of Spain in 1492 in the hope of finding a water route to Asia. What he found instead was another continental mass. For many years the main goal of European explorers was to find a way around or through America to reach Asia. Spain began establishing settlements in the New World during the first half of the 1500s. The purpose of the settlements was to control the areas being settled and to extract as much wealth as possible to send to Spain.

Europeans eventually realized that North and South America were more than just a roadblock to Asia. England and France sought to establish settlements in North America in the hope that they might bring profits back to businessmen and the crown. The common thinking among political leaders was that foreign empires were a way to increase the wealth of the homeland. As a result, the government encouraged and assisted businessmen in establishing colonial outposts. This government policy is called mercantilism.

Unit 4: A Brief Economic History of the United States

The First Slave Auction at New Amsterdam in 1655, *Howard Pyle (American)*

During the 1500s and early 1600s, many Europeans longed for religious freedom. In addition, as Christians learned about the native peoples living in America, they wanted to carry the gospel to those tribes. Thus we should recognize both the economic and the spiritual motives behind the founding of European colonies in North America. Moreover, leaders at the time did not see the two motives as mutually exclusive. Many saw economic success as evidence of God's blessing and a way to honor God with one's life.

The Virginia colony of 1607 was primarily an economic venture. The Separatist settlement at Plymouth in 1620 and the Puritan settlement at Massachusetts Bay in 1630 were begun primarily for spiritual reasons, but in both of those cases some settlers wanted to turn a profit by developing the resources that settlers could find there. The founders of other colonies, such as Pennsylvania, Maryland, and Georgia, had strong religious motives as well as a desire to make the colonies profitable.

The economic foundation of the American colonies was agriculture. An estimated eighty percent of colonists were small farmers. Traders profited by taking agricultural products—tobacco, rice, and indigo—back to Europe for sale along with furs trapped on America's frontiers and lumber cut from abundant forests. The colonies also provided a market for goods that England and Europe produced.

Besides exporting goods to Europe, the colonies developed economies of their own. New England colonies emphasized trade, shipbuilding, fishing, and small businesses such as sawmills. Colonies in the South developed plantations that produced agricultural crops. The Middle colonies were a mixture of farming and trade.

The primary standard of wealth in America was ownership of land, and abundant land was available to those who could buy it and develop it. Land served several purposes. A landowner could support his family with what the land produced, he could grow crops or harvest timber to sell to others, or he could use his land as a medium of exchange to buy other land or goods.

Most colonists, even small farmers, saw in America a greater opportunity for economic advancement than they would ever have had in Britain. Many settlers began their time in America as indentured servants, who sold their services to larger landowners for a period of years. When indentured servants completed that obligation, they received their freedom and a parcel of land to start out on their own. In addition to small farmers and large landowners, a middle class of traders and small businessmen grew in the colonies.

However, another group in the colonies did not enjoy these rising expectations. These were African slaves, who were important participants in the American economy. Slaves were present in all thirteen of the original British colonies that became the United States, but slavery was a major part of the southern plantation economy.

The American economy grew slowly but steadily during the colonial period. By the mid-1770s, seacoast towns were busy with international trade, the continent was home to numerous successful farms and plantations, and the first efforts at industry were taking shape. It was an economy that the British government thought worth trying to keep.

American Independence

The American colonies were a part of Britain's expanding empire. The French and Indian War (1754-1763) eliminated France as a competitor in North America, but it was a costly effort for the British government. As its empire grew, Britain wanted to exercise greater control over its colonies. In 1763, King George III forbade further settlement west of the Appalachians to avoid provoking conflict with the Indians. This restriction frustrated the Americans, who had helped fight the war so that they could have the freedom and security to settle the western lands. In addition, Britain imposed new taxes on the colonies to pay for the war and for the British security forces in the colonies. Parliament also enacted political restrictions on the freedoms of the American colonists. These policies of the London government angered American colonists.

The colonies' economic life was intertwined with their political life. The desire for independence in America grew both from the economic conflict with the mother country but also out of a desire for political and personal liberty. Britain's control of the colonies' economic activities (such as the London government deciding with which countries the colonies could trade) was a vivid demonstration to many colonists of the practical adverse effects of British domination over the colonies.

The 1773 Boston Tea Party incident occurred because of frustration over London's control of the tea trade in the colonies. A growing number of colonists agreed with the sentiment of Thomas Paine, published in early 1776, that the colonies' connection with Britain was a detriment—politically and economically—and "'Tis time to part."

The colonies formed a Continental Congress, which met to discuss American complaints. The Congress voted on July 2, 1776, to separate from Britain and adopted Thomas Jefferson's Declaration of Independence two days later.

View of Salem *(Massachusetts), Balthasar Friedrich Leizelt (German, c. 1774)*

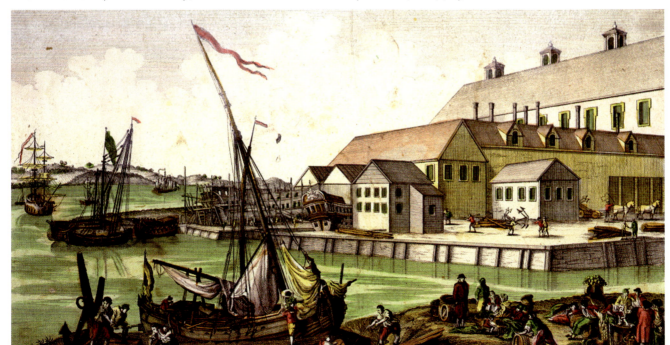

In order to secure "life, liberty, and the pursuit of happiness," the new nation fought a war with Great Britain. The war, which lasted over six years from Lexington to Yorktown (1775-1781) was a costly one for the United States in many ways, especially in the lives that were lost. In addition, thousands of men had to leave their farms and shops for extended periods to fight in the army. The war disrupted American society and the American economy, and the needs of the army caused a scarcity of goods and inflated prices for the rest of Americans.

The colonists were not united on making war with Britain, and many of those who opposed independence were members of the upper economic class. An estimated 100,000 colonists who were loyal to Britain left the United States to live in Canada, Britain, or the West Indies, taking with them a great deal of money and talent.

Troubles in the Confederation

The United States accomplished the goal of independence. The necessities of war had led to the growth of domestic American industries, especially those related to military purposes. The new nation developed new international trading partners since the war had interrupted trade with Great Britain.

However, the United States faced significant economic difficulties. First, the national government from 1776 to 1789 was in the form of a confederation or loose association of the states. The Articles of Confederation that America's leaders wrote to govern the confederation gave no power of taxation to the national government. It could only request payments from the states, and the states were free to ignore such requests.

Re-enactment of the Battle of Monmouth in New Jersey (2010)

Lesson 16 - From Exploration to Confederation

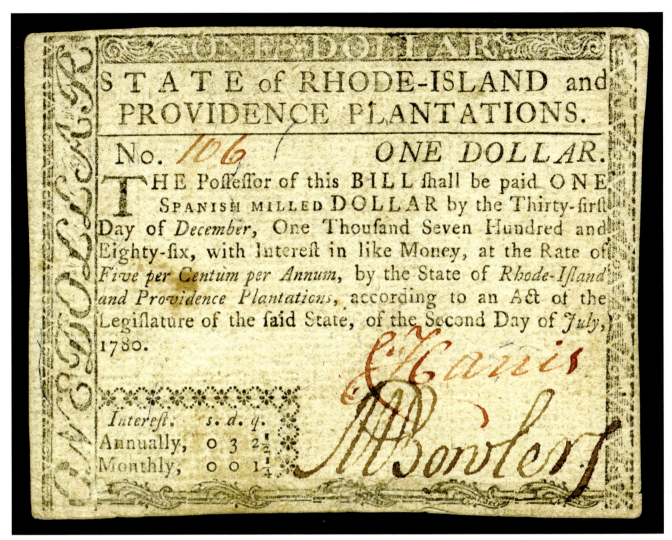

This bill of credit issued by the State of Rhode Island in 1780 promises to pay the bearer "one Spanish milled dollar," plus interest, by December 31, 1786.

Second, the country was deeply in debt. Congress had financed the war effort by issuing bonds (by which wealthy individuals loaned money to the United States with the expectation of getting their money back plus interest), obtaining loans from foreign governments, requesting assistance from the states, and printing paper money. Only the first two ways worked, but these caused the growth of debt. The states, not having much money themselves, did not provide the central government with significant financial assistance. Since the country had minimal gold and silver reserves, the Continental dollars that Congress had printed were not a reliable currency and thus were not worth much.

Third, the states had their own fiscal crises. Hard money (made of gold or silver) was in short supply, and inflation raised prices for scarce commodities. In 1786, Daniel Shays led a rebellion of Massachusetts farmers against what they felt was unfair treatment by creditors to whom they owed money. The farmers marched on the state capital and demanded relief from the legislature. The state militia dispersed the rebellion, but fears arose that more violent revolts might develop in other colonies.

A fourth difficulty was instability in the West, the area between the Appalachian Mountains and the Mississippi River. Frontiersmen worried about Native American attacks. They were also frustrated that the federal government could not guarantee them access to the port of New Orleans to sell their goods. Some Americans in the West wanted to go to war with Spain, which controlled the port city, while others wanted to pursue more friendly relations with Spain to gain access to the port, even to the point of trying to make secret alliances with that country.

A meeting of representatives from five states took place in Annapolis, Maryland, in 1786, ostensibly for the purpose of discussing sea trade and interstate commerce. With Shays' Rebellion fresh in their minds along with their knowledge of the other problems the young nation faced, the delegates went on record favoring a convention to revise the Articles of Confederation. Later that year, Congress also called for a special convention. The Constitutional Convention that met in Philadelphia in 1787 was the result.

The new nation was struggling. The answer to every struggle is to rely on the Lord.

Now I know that the Lord saves His anointed;
He will answer him from His holy heaven
With the saving strength of His right hand.
Some boast in chariots and some in horses,
But we will boast in the name of the Lord, our God.
Psalm 20:6-7

Assignments for Lesson 16

Making Choices — Read Letter 4 of the Letters from a Farmer in Pennsylvania (pages 34-36).

Literature — Begin reading *The Rise of Silas Lapham*. Plan to finish it by the end of Unit 7.

Project — Choose your project for this unit and start working on it.

Student Review — Answer the questions for Lesson 16.

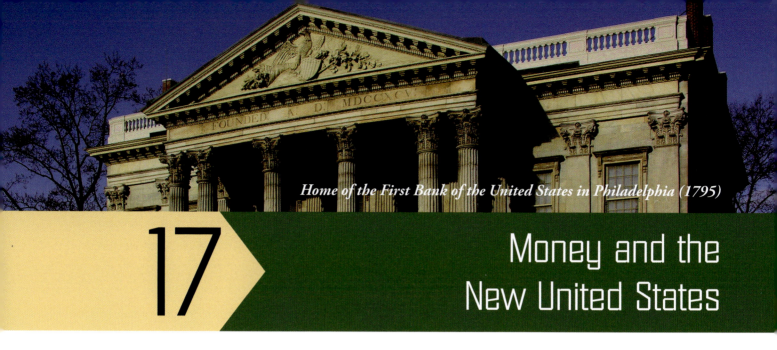
Home of the First Bank of the United States in Philadelphia (1795)

17 Money and the New United States

To cherish and stimulate the activity of the human mind, by multiplying the objects of enterprise, is not among the least considerable of the expedients, by which the wealth of a nation may be promoted.
— Alexander Hamilton, Report on Manufactures (1791)

Economic Provisions of the Constitution

The delegates who gathered for the Constitutional Convention in Philadelphia in the summer of 1787 knew the serious situation that the young nation faced. Once they decided to abandon the Articles of Confederation in favor of a new governing document, the delegates spent weeks debating the exact form that the new national government would take and the powers it would have. The men in the convention sought to achieve a delicate balance. They wanted to give the new central government more power than had been available under the Articles, but not so much power that it would be a threat to individual liberty and the authority of the states.

The fiscal powers of the proposed national government were significant, but they were limited. This authority included powers listed in Article I, Section 8:

- To lay and collect Taxes, Duties, Imposts and Excises, to pay the Debts and provide for the common Defence and general Welfare of the United States; but all Duties, Imposts and Excises shall be uniform throughout the United States;

- To borrow Money on the credit of the United States;

- To regulate Commerce with foreign Nations, and among the several States, and with the Indian Tribes;

- To establish . . . uniform Laws on the subject of Bankruptcies throughout the United States;

- To coin Money, regulate the Value thereof, and of foreign Coin, and fix the Standard of Weights and Measures;

- To provide for the Punishment of counterfeiting the Securities and current Coin of the United States.

Section 9 forbade Congress from imposing a capitation or direct tax except in proportion to the census enumeration. The convention assumed that the federal government could lay a direct tax on the states in proportion to their population, and the states could come up with the revenue as they saw fit. The next section forbade states from coining money and from imposing any duties on items brought into them through interstate commerce. This ban on internal tariffs between states created a common market and helped unify the nation's economy.

Even at this early date, slavery was a subject of bitter debate. Northern states had abolished slavery, while southern states maintained the practice and staunchly defended it as crucial to their economic well-being. This conflict resulted in a series of compromises in the Constitution that gave slavery de facto recognition, even though the Constitution as the delegates wrote it did not use the word slavery. (The Thirteenth Amendment, ratified in 1865, was the first use of the word in the Constitution.) The delegates to the convention left slavery as an issue for the states to regulate. This debate exposed the conflict between the nation's stated devotion to freedom and the denial of that freedom to slaves.

Hamilton's Plan

In his tenure as first Secretary of the Treasury, Alexander Hamilton helped to establish a national economy with the central government playing a key role. Hamilton proposed that the new national government assume the debts that the states and the Continental Congress had incurred under the Articles of Confederation. He proposed that the federal government issue bonds for the face value of older certificates of debt. The sale of additional bonds provided revenue for government expenditures.

A stock is a small share of a company. When someone purchases a stock, he becomes a part-owner in that company. Twenty-four stock brokers and merchants made an agreement in 1792 to promote their common interests. The signed agreement is shown at right and a diorama depicting the event is shown below. Four of the original brokers worked with others to create the New York Stock and Exchange Board in 1817.

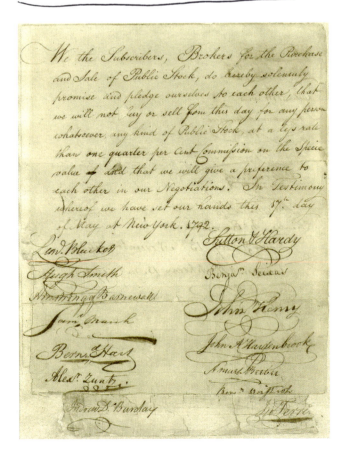

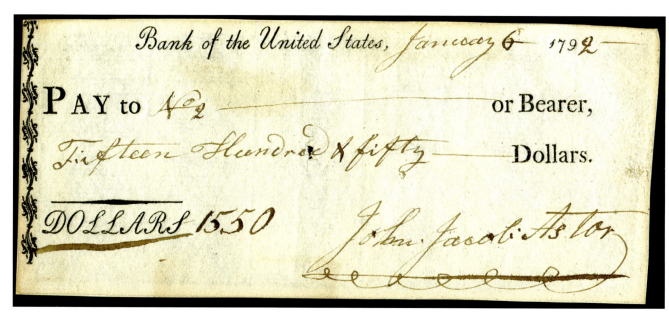

John Jacob Astor (1763-1848), a German immigrant, started a fur-goods business in New York City after the American Revolution. This 1792 check for $1,550 was drawn on the Bank of the United States. Astor grew wealthy through the fur trade and real estate and was the wealthiest person in the United States at the time of his death.

The purpose of Hamilton's proposals was to demonstrate that the new government would stand by its obligations. It also gave the buyers of bonds a strong reason to support the new government. The plan also made bond redemption more reliable, since some state governments were financially unstable. Congress passed Hamilton's proposal, and the bonds sold well in the United States and in Europe.

A second part of Hamilton's plan involved government assistance in the creation of a manufacturing economy. Whereas the American economy was centered on agriculture, Hamilton saw that domestic economic growth and competition in the world market depended on the development of American industry. Hamilton proposed import tariffs on foreign goods and an outright ban on the importation of some items in order to protect American manufacturers. He also proposed that raw materials not be exported out of the country, and he offered other ideas to encourage industry and inventions.

Congress rejected much of this part of Hamilton's plan, although it did enact several individual tariffs. Tariffs became the main source of federal revenue for many years. Most modern economists believe that tariffs hurt economic development, but in Hamilton's day tariffs were a common part of the trade policies of many governments.

Finally, Hamilton proposed the creation of a national bank, similar to central banks in Europe, to handle the government's fiscal affairs and to provide loans to commercial customers and to the national government. Eighty percent of the bank's initial assets were to come from private investors. On the basis of its assets, the bank could issue notes that would serve as a national currency. Hamilton's purpose was to provide economic stability for the new nation.

During the colonial period, merchants were the most common source of credit for their individual customers. In 1789 only three commercial banks existed in the entire country. Some Americans saw value in greater accessibility to money and credit for expanding economic activity. Thomas Jefferson was one prominent opponent to Hamilton's proposal for a national bank. Not only did Jefferson and his followers think the bank was unconstitutional, they saw it as a dangerous concentration of economic power in the hands of a few people. However, the economic instability of the country led Congress in 1791 to charter the Bank of the United States for twenty years.

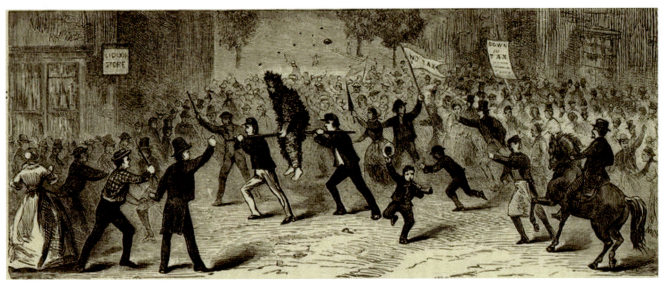

This 1880 illustration depicts tax protesters during the Whiskey Rebellion forcing a federal tax collector to ride a rail after they had tarred and feathered him.

Economic Growth in the New Nation

The ideas that Hamilton proposed and Congress enacted succeeded in helping the American economy grow. After a sluggish period during the 1780s, Federal revenues increased from $3.6 million in 1792 to over $10 million in 1800. The states chartered over one hundred banks during the life of the first Bank of the United States, which indicates the amount of economic activity taking place. The country finally had a reliable national currency.

A tax that Congress imposed on whiskey sparked the Whiskey Rebellion of 1794. Farmers in western Pennsylvania rebelled because they feared that the increased cost would hurt their sales. President Washington ordered a large military force to move against the rebels, who dispersed and went home. The incident reinforced the authority of the national government to maintain order and enforce its economic policies.

However, we should not think that the nation's economic growth was solely the result of government actions. The entrepreneurial spirit was alive and active, and the freedom that the country provided encouraged the economic growth that has become the hallmark of our nation.

During the latter half of the 1700s, Britain experienced significant growth in manufacturing, especially in making cloth or textiles. Several inventions in Britain improved production during this period. British manufacturers brought machinery, workers, and a power source (at first, water from streams) together in factories, a move that dramatically increased production and quality while lowering costs.

To protect the textile industry, the British government made it illegal to take the machines or their plans out of the country or for skilled workers to leave the country. Meanwhile, Americans offered bounties to anyone who could introduce the new technology here.

In 1789 Samuel Slater memorized the plans for a water-powered spinning frame and secretly left England. A businessman eventually brought Slater to Rhode Island, where the Englishman built the water frame according to the plans he had memorized. Slater's Mill opened in 1790. Slater went on to build other factories, and those whom he trained created even more. The mass production of textiles became a major industry in the United States.

Lesson 17 - Money and the New United States

The textile mills greatly increased the demand for cotton. In 1793 Yale graduate Eli Whitney was visiting a plantation in Georgia. There he heard about the difficulties of separating seeds from cotton fibers. Whitney developed a gin (short for engine) that combed out seeds, separating them from the fibers.

The cotton gin dramatically increased the productivity of workers and made cotton a much more attractive investment for plantation owners. In 1793 the United States exported about a half-million pounds of cotton to overseas textile makers. By 1801 cotton exports totaled over twenty million pounds.

The South found another market for cotton in the New England textile industry. Unfortunately, the dramatic growth of cotton production caused southern plantation owners to increase their reliance on slave labor. Had they chosen to hire free workers instead, whether white or black, the social and economic history of the country would have been profoundly different.

In transportation, Robert Fulton's steamboat revolutionized water travel and trade in 1807. The movement of people and goods was no longer at the mercy of wind and water currents. The Erie Canal, constructed by the state of New York, in 1825 opened the region west of the Appalachians to eastern markets. The canal connected the Great Lakes to the Hudson River, which flows south to New York City. This enabled New York City to become the chief financial center of the country.

Slater Mill in Pawtucket, Rhode Island

Invention and innovation. Buying and selling. Profit and loss. These have been part of the history of the world since almost the very beginning. Those who seek to build new businesses should remember our reliance on the One who gives us natural resources and creative abilities to use them.

*But you shall remember the Lord your God,
for it is He who is giving you power to make wealth . . .
Deuteronomy 8:18*

Assignments for Lesson 17

Literature — Continue reading *The Rise of Silas Lapham*.

Project — Continue working on your project for this unit.

Student Review — Answer the questions for Lesson 17.

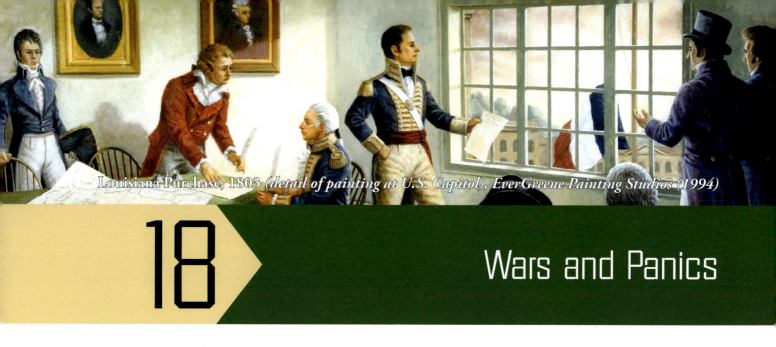

Louisiana Purchase, 1803 *(detail of painting at U.S. Capitol)*, EverGreene Painting Studios (1994)

18 Wars and Panics

No sooner do you set foot upon the American soil than you are stunned by a kind of tumult; a confused clamor is heard on every side; and a thousand simultaneous voices demand the immediate satisfaction of their social wants. Everything is in motion around you . . . .
— Alexis de Tocqueville, Democracy in America *(1835)*

Trade Wars and the War of 1812

The American economy went through several alternating periods of growth and recession in the 1800s. The purchase of the Louisiana Territory for $15 million in 1803 added significantly to the country's land wealth. This opened the door to major economic opportunities, while also contributing to continued oppression of Native American tribes.

For a period of about sixteen years (1807-1823), the United States economy faced many trials. America depended greatly on foreign trade, and Great Britain and France were two of the country's best trading partners. Unfortunately, Britain and France were at war with each other; and one tactic in that war was to interfere with vessels headed to the enemy's ports. The United States was officially neutral regarding the conflict between England and France, but the French and British navies (especially the latter) routinely intercepted American vessels.

At the same time, the British apparently stirred up trouble among Native Americans in the frontier region between the Appalachians and the Mississippi River. The resulting insecurity on the frontier, and the lack of foreign markets for agricultural products grown in that region (a situation which frontiersmen blamed on British attacks on American shipping), led to many people calling for war against Great Britain.

The first step that the United States took against Britain was an economic one. Upon President Thomas Jefferson's urging, Congress passed the Embargo Act in 1807, which forbade American ships from traveling to foreign countries. Jefferson hoped that the loss of trade with America would convince Britain to leave American shipping alone. The embargo caused a serious loss of trade in America. American ships languished in port, overseas markets for American goods dwindled, and domestic production declined.

101

The Embargo Act was widely unpopular; and Congress repealed it in 1809, just before Jefferson left office. The issues with Great Britain did not go away, and in 1812 Congress declared war.

The War of 1812, which ended with the Battle of New Orleans in January of 1815, primarily accomplished a confirmation of the status quo between the two countries. It did give Americans a sense of national pride and strength; but as we shall see, it cost the United States in economic terms.

John Reubens Smith (1775-1849) was born in London. As a young man, he moved to the United States and built his career as an artist. Smith created this image of Peace *to commemorate the end of the War of 1812.*

Panic of 1819

The economic downturn that began in 1819 had many elements that have occurred repeatedly in American history. It was the first incidence in the United States of what has become known as the boom and bust cycle (also called the business cycle) in capitalism. One factor was significant federal debt. Other contributing factors included greed for quick wealth and unwise extensions of credit.

The Bank of the United States (BUS) had ceased operation in 1811. Republican opposition to it prevented Congress from renewing the Bank charter that year when its initial life of twenty years had ended. Because no central bank existed, the federal government borrowed hodgepodge from state banks to finance the War of 1812. Following the war, the federal government sold off a large portion of the frontier lands to help pay off the debt.

Most of the buyers who purchased these lands were speculators who bought largely on credit. Most of these speculators sold smaller tracts to individuals, also on credit. The state banks that financed these sales (banks that were sometimes owned by the same land speculators) took unnecessary risks in the hope that everyone would become more wealthy. The banks had holdings of gold and silver money, but in order to encourage economic expansion they often printed paper money far in excess of their specie (gold and silver, or hard money) deposits.

Sensing the need for a more secure national economy, President James Madison and the Republican-led Congress renewed the charter for the Bank of the United States in 1816 for another period of twenty years. At first, however, the Bank had irresponsible management and engaged in the same risky behavior as state banks. A notable case of fraud in one branch of the Bank also hurt the institution's credibility.

Then in 1819, a new director of the Bank attempted to clean up its operations. The Bank issued fewer loans and demanded redemption in hard money of the state bank notes it received. This put pressure on the state banks, which in turn put pressure on individual debtors who owed them money. When those debtors were land speculators, the speculators put pressure on individuals to pay for the land they had purchased.

In boom times, these individuals would have had the income to pay their debts. However, the general economy turned sour. Demand in Europe for American agricultural products declined as the continent recovered from the Napoleonic Wars that ended in 1815. Britain found cheaper sources for cotton in the East Indies and Asia, so the demand for southern cotton also declined. These declines impacted sales of American manufactured goods, which caused a cutback in industrial output.

The nation experienced a panic in 1819. Debtors defaulted on their loans, state banks defaulted on their obligations to the Bank of the United States, and the BUS was not of a mind to bail people out. An easing of credit terms might have alleviated the economic trend, but the BUS stood firm. Property was foreclosed, banks failed, and many Americans were unemployed.

President Madison suspended the requirement that debtors make their payments in specie, but he did little else. Later under President James Monroe, Congress passed laws that eased the pressure on debtors. The Bank of the United States remained solvent, but many people (especially in the West) blamed the BUS for the hard times. Better conditions returned by 1823.

Nicholas Biddle (1786-1844)

In 1824, the United States Supreme Court in *Gibbons v. Ogden* gave a broad interpretation of the right of Congress to regulate interstate commerce. The decision struck down a steamboat monopoly granted by the state of New York that affected travel to New Jersey. The decision effectively created a national U.S. economy based on free trade and guided only by Congress instead of being hindered by a patchwork of conflicting state regulations.

The Bank War and the Panic of 1837

Andrew Jackson was elected president in 1828 as the champion of the common man and the enemy of power and privilege. He opposed the Bank of the United States and favored a hard money economy (meaning gold and silver only, no paper currency). Jackson failed to appreciate the stabilizing effects of the Bank on the economy, but he was correct in his criticism of the Bank for using its power to wield political influence.

The Bank's charter did not have to be renewed until 1836. In 1832 Republicans in Congress, led by their presidential candidate Henry Clay, decided to bring the charter up for renewal to make it an issue in the campaign. The renewal passed Congress; but Jackson vetoed it and Congress was not able to override his veto. Jackson easily defeated Clay in the election.

During his second term, Jackson weakened the bank by ordering the removal of federal funds from the Bank. Federal officials deposited those funds in over twenty different state banks (derisively called pet banks). The director of the BUS, Nicholas Biddle, tried to fight back by limiting loans and demanding payment in specie for state-issued notes. His goal was to show how vital the Bank was by causing an economic recession.

However, the new influx of federal funds let state banks print money and make loans at an even more unrestrained rate. This activity made whatever strength the Bank still had largely irrelevant. The Bank's charter finally expired in 1836.

This illustration by Edward Williams Clay was printed in 1837 by Henry R. Robinson in New York. It depicts the economic hardship faced by many Americans and alludes to the political debates of the times.

Meanwhile, the federal government operated at a surplus because of revenue from tariff collections and the sale of western lands. In 1836, Congress passed a law that distributed these surplus funds directly to state governments. A month later, the Jackson Administration changed federal policy and ordered that buyers make payments for land sales only in hard money. These actions weakened state banks in two ways:

- The federal government withdrew funds from state banks, and thus state banks could not use those funds as assets, and

- specie reserves in state banks diminished because of the federal requirement for hard money land payments.

When Martin Van Buren became president in 1837, the country was headed for another panic. An economic downturn in Britain resulted in lower prices there for American cotton and less British investment in American business. Once again, creditors in America pressed debtors for payments on the risky loans they had obtained.

State governments cut spending and sometimes defaulted on their debts, and many state banks closed (causing, among other things, the loss to the United States government of several million dollars it had deposited in them). It is estimated that by the fall of 1837, one-third of American workers were without jobs, a rate not even seen in the Great Depression of the 1930s. No federal programs provided relief to individuals in financial straits.

The economy recovered by 1843. America's abundant natural resources and labor supply, the movement to settle and utilize the country's vast western lands, and developing technology such as railroads and the McCormick reaper, helped to bring about the upsurge. In succeeding years, events such as the invention of the telegraph (1844) and the discovery of gold in California (1848) further fueled the American boom.

The federal government would not resume such a direct role in the nation's banking system for many years. Democrats retreated from the policy of placing federal funds in unreliable state banks. Under Van Buren in 1840, Congress created the Independent Treasury, a system of depositories (sometimes called the Subtreasury System) that simply accepted payments to the government in specie only and also paid the government's bills. The new Whig majority repealed the arrangement in 1841, but a Democratic majority renewed it in 1846. The subtreasury system remained largely unchanged until the creation of the Federal Reserve System in 1913.

The nation suffered another, shorter panic in 1857 and 1858. Factors included a weaker world market for American agricultural goods, the overproduction of manufactured goods in the United States relative to their potential market, the collapse of land investment schemes that speculators devised based on guesses at possible railroad routes, and a major case of embezzlement that brought down the New York office of a life insurance company. Some 5,000 businesses and several banks failed within a year. The South fared better during this downturn because of the relative strength of the world cotton market.

Average people have had to deal with economic ups and downs since ancient times. Some of these were caused by greedy businessmen and some by natural disasters.

Behold, seven years of great abundance are coming in all the land of Egypt; and after them seven years of famine will come, and all the abundance will be forgotten in the land of Egypt, and the famine will ravage the land. So the abundance will be unknown in the land because of that subsequent famine; for it will be very severe.
Genesis 41:29-31

Assignments for Lesson 18

Literature — Continue reading *The Rise of Silas Lapham*.

Project — Continue working on your project for this unit.

Student Review — Answer the questions for Lesson 18.

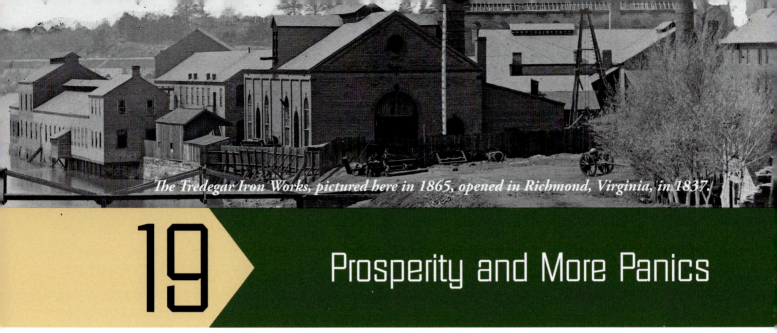

The Tredegar Iron Works, pictured here in 1865, opened in Richmond, Virginia, in 1837.

19 Prosperity and More Panics

The lessons of paternalism ought to be unlearned and the better lesson taught that while the people should patriotically and cheerfully support their government, its functions do not include the support of the people.
— *Grover Cleveland, 1893*

The cycle of boom and bust continued for the country. The devastating Civil War caused a social revolution in the South and economic hardship both for former slaves and for those who had been free. Following the war, a great period of industrialization led to significant growth in the United States economy. The country suffered through a series of panics, saw the creation of the Federal Reserve System, struggled through the Great War (World War I), and rebounded in the 1920s, only to endure the devastating stock market crash of 1929 and the Great Depression of the 1930s.

Economic Impact of the Civil War

The Civil War affected the American nation in many ways, not the least of which was in terms of economics. The war and its aftermath were really a tale of two economies. When the war began, the North had a greater population than the South, more farm production than the South, twice as much railroad mileage as the South, and 92% of the nation's industry. The war enabled northern industrial and agricultural output to grow while the South suffered tremendous losses in both categories.

During the war, existing railroads in the South were mostly destroyed, and agricultural output declined sharply. The South produced two billion pounds of cotton in 1860, over half of the world's supply. It did not reach that level again until 1879. Tobacco production did not regain its pre-war level until 1880. Although the South began to build more industry in the late 1800s, the region's economy was primarily agricultural until World War II.

The North financed its war effort through increased taxes and tariffs, by printing greenbacks as currency (more about that later), and by issuing bonds. The South raised only a small amount in taxes and bonds. For the most part the Confederate government resorted to the printing press to produce currency that was nearly worthless. This led to serious inflation.

Lesson 19 - Prosperity and More Panics

While the South struggled, the North began an economic transformation. Congress authorized the transcontinental railroad during the war, and workers completed the line in 1869. The Morrill Land Grant Act enabled the establishment of state agricultural and mechanical universities through the sale of public lands. The Homestead Act encouraged settlement of the Great Plains. The National Bank Act asserted some federal control over banking without establishing a national bank. The Civil War increased the size of the federal government and broadened the types of activities it became involved in. The war also greatly increased the national debt.

Postwar Prosperity

The transformation of the American economy in the decades following the Civil War was truly astounding. By the 1890s—a mere three decades after the devastation of the Civil War—the United States surpassed Great Britain as the largest economy in the world. Several factors came together to produce an economic machine the likes of which the world had never known.

America's natural resources played a big part. Abundant land made many things possible, such as greater farm production. The size of the country encouraged the creation of a network of railroads. The nation's deposits of iron, coal, and oil fed the growth. The American working population, increased by an ever-growing number of immigrants, provided the labor to make and the market to buy the goods that industry produced.

American businessmen dreamed big, and they created companies that dwarfed the size of businesses that existed before the Civil War. The first big business was railroads. Government on all levels assisted railroad construction with special favors and deals. The railroads themselves were major operations, and the attendant industries (such as iron and steel production for rails and engines, construction of rail cars, and telegraph lines that paralleled the tracks) also employed thousands of workers. Andrew Carnegie's steel company grew in the last quarter of the 1800s to the point that it produced one third of all American steel by 1900.

Advances in technology fueled American economic growth. It was the period when electricity became a practical source of energy, and electric lights became common. Refrigerated railroad cars gave producers of even perishable goods a national market. Henry Ford's innovations such as the assembly line transformed American car manufacturing, and automobiles for the masses transformed American life and the American landscape.

Bankers such as J. P. Morgan built large enterprises that were not in the business of making things directly. Rather, they invested huge sums of money in companies that did. This type of business is called investment capitalism.

Annual picnic of the Carnegie Steel Company in Pittsburgh, Pennsylvania (c. 1908)

Not everything that happened during the period was good. Some business leaders (some railroad tycoons are notable examples) as well as some powerful politicians acted in corrupt and unethical ways. With all of that money circulating, some of it found its way into certain pockets illegally. In some ways the business world told government at all levels what to do. Labor organizations, on the other hand, were not very powerful and were widely unpopular.

The government's first major attempts at regulation, such as the Interstate Commerce Commission (1887) and the Sherman Antitrust Act (1890), were tentative steps at guiding the actions and power of business along ethical lines. Reforms under Theodore Roosevelt, such as the Pure Food and Drug Act (1906), and court decisions such as the 1911 Supreme Court verdict against Standard Oil of New Jersey were more effective in limiting corporate power. Regulating business to protect American consumers without dampening the free enterprise that helps American consumers is a delicate balancing act.

Monetary Policy

The country's amazing economic growth took place despite the fact that the government's monetary policy often shifted and was the subject of considerable and contentious debate. When the Civil War started, the United States government had a hard money policy. During the Civil War, Congress approved the printing and circulation of millions of dollars in paper money.

This 1911 cartoon from Puck *magazine depicts J. P. Morgan as having a dominating influence on the economy of the United States, represented by Uncle Sam.*

Lesson 19 - Prosperity and More Panics

Because the Treasury printed the money with green ink, the bills were called greenbacks. The use of paper money tends to cause some degree of inflation, but it also enables more flexible economic growth. When money is easier to come by, it makes the payment of debt easier; but those debts are paid with dollars that are usually worth relatively less than when the debtor took out the loan.

Following the Civil War, the government began withdrawing greenbacks from circulation. Farmers and debtors opposed this move toward a renewed hard money policy since it took money out of circulation. The Treasury Department stopped withdrawing greenbacks in 1868. A few years later, the Grant Administration again began withdrawing greenbacks.

In addition, the government ceased coining silver money in 1873 in order to go to a gold-only standard. The minting of silver coins began again in 1878, and in the early 1890s the federal government minted even more silver. Silver dollars soon became commonplace. The increased supply of silver lowered its value relative to gold. The government ceased minting silver in 1893, but then government-held gold reserves fell as people increasingly redeemed paper money for gold. In 1895 a group of bankers led by J. P. Morgan agreed to help the government protect and increase its gold reserves.

Panics

A series of panics punctuated the general trend of prosperity and growth. These panics slowed the economy and brought serious financial setbacks.

The Panic of 1873. Following the Civil War, the country embarked on an expansionist boom fueled by businesses borrowing money in amounts beyond their ability to pay and based on unrealistic hopes for sales. This was especially true in the railroad industry. The decision to stop minting silver led to a reduction in the money supply.

This print shows the Janeway & Carpender Wall Paper Manufactory in New Brunswick, New Jersey (c. 1895). The company was founded in 1844.

In 1873 a major investment company led by Jay Cooke was unable to sell bonds to finance a second transcontinental railroad. The company declared bankruptcy, which led to huge losses and widespread uncertainty. The New York Stock Exchange closed for ten days. About one fourth of the nation's railroad companies went bankrupt and some 18,000 businesses failed over the next two years. By 1876 unemployment reached 14%. Economic expansion resumed in the 1880s.

The Panic of 1893. Unfortunately, risky speculation again fueled this economic expansion. Too many rail companies, some of which were shaky, competed for not enough business. The Philadelphia and Reading Railroad declared bankruptcy in February of 1893. Many people rushed to withdraw their money from banks. This is called a bank run.

With that money withdrawn, banks were unable to extend as much credit to businesses, which slowed the economy even more. The continuing uncertain monetary policy (changes from gold-only to the minting of both gold and silver) also caused fears. Several banks and rail companies failed, thousands of other businesses also went under, unemployment rose again, and homeowners abandoned the houses for which they could not make payments. Despite these setbacks, the economy recovered by 1896.

Copper mining in Butte, Montana (c. 1905)

The Panic of 1907. Frederick Augustus Heinze, son of a German immigrant, had become the Copper King through his copper mining business in Montana. He came to New York that year and began a scheme to corner the market on copper in order to drive up the price. (To corner the market means to control the available supply.) Heinze's scheme backfired.

This event weakened banks that had lent money to the scheme and runs took place on several banks. In response, some banks became reluctant to loan money, which meant that some investors were not able to borrow money to buy stocks. This caused stock prices to go down, and a general panic began to unfold. New York's third largest trust company went bankrupt. (A trust company holds and manages money or property for others, usually for a set period of time.)

J. P. Morgan organized a group of bankers who invested money in the stock market. This move eased the crisis. Many in the financial industry as well as government were concerned about the lack of a central bank to oversee monetary policy. Congress created the Federal Reserve System in 1913 to serve as the central bank of the United States. One major goal was to avoid crises such as the Panic of 1907.

The Great Depression. American involvement in the Great War (later called World War I) was costly to the country, and a difficult economic recovery followed. However, the national economy rebounded in the 1920s. President Calvin Coolidge (1923-1929) cut federal spending, proposed several tax cuts that Congress passed, and lowered the federal deficit by a third. Once again, though, overspeculation in the stock market ended in a dramatic drop in stock prices, and the country faced another crisis in 1929 that mushroomed into the Great Depression.

The major difference with this economic downturn was that the federal government under Franklin Roosevelt played an active role in trying to recover from the collapse. He instituted reforms intended to help prevent a recurrence. We will look at the Great Depression and Roosevelt's response in the New Deal in more detail in a later lesson.

The American Friends Service Committee (AFSC), a Quaker organization, supplied food for children in Germany and Austria after World War I. During the Great Depression, the AFSC sought to help mining communities in Appalachia, and Eleanor Roosevelt took an interest in their work. A federal program overseen by Clarence Pickett, an AFSC leader, established a planned community in what is now Arthurdale, West Virginia, in 1934. This is one of the 165 homes built for displaced mining families to get a new start.

Stronger economic activity finally returned when the United States got involved in World War II. Industries adapted to supply what was needed in the war effort. Unfortunately, as in all wars, much of what was built was quickly destroyed.

At times the United States has had an abundance, and at times it has endured scarcity. During both general conditions, individual Americans have had abundance and others have had scarcity. The Lord expects faithfulness to Him in every circumstance.

He who is faithful in a very little thing is faithful also in much;
and he who is unrighteous in a very little thing is unrighteous also in much.
Therefore if you have not been faithful in the use of unrighteous wealth,
who will entrust the true riches to you?
Luke 16:10-11

Assignments for Lesson 19

Making Choices — Read the Letters to John P. Nicholson (pages 37-38).

Literature — Continue reading *The Rise of Silas Lapham*.

Project — Continue working on your project for this unit.

Student Review — Answer the questions for Lesson 19.

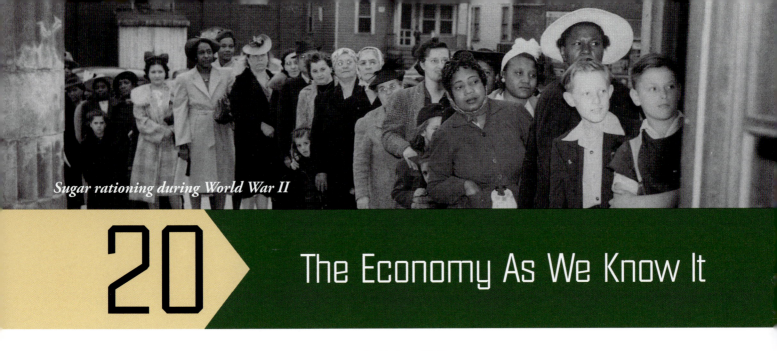

Sugar rationing during World War II

20 › The Economy As We Know It

A rising tide lifts all boats.
— President John F. Kennedy, explaining why his proposed tax cuts would help the overall economy

In the fifty years following World War II, the gross domestic product of the United States grew at a healthy average annual rate of 3%. Though the United States had several periods of recession, our country's free market economy, subject to limited government regulation, has produced the strongest economy in the world.

Postwar Prosperity

Most of the country's production capacity during World War II was focused on military needs. The government managed the wartime economy in several ways. Production controls and rationing limited what consumers on the home front had available. The government put price controls in place to prevent profiteering on scarce goods.

Following the war, the economy roared into high gear. Production turned quickly to domestic goods (goods citizens need as opposed to goods the government, especially the military, needed). However, America's Cold War with the Soviet Union kept military spending at a high level, too.

Men and women who had served in uniform were eager to get back to their civilian jobs and everyday lives, and consumers were eager to buy goods that had been unavailable during the war. Workers wanted higher wages than they had been able to receive during the war. Businesses wanted to charge higher prices than they had been permitted during the war but balked at paying workers more. The major problem after the war was inflation, which was the result of demand outpacing supply. Wage and price controls ended for the most part in late 1946.

Prosperity extended into the 1950s as the consumer economy grew by leaps and bounds. The growth of credit cards and a large increase in homeownership, funded by home mortgages, encouraged consumers to spend more. The administration of Republican Dwight Eisenhower basically maintained the increased level of federal spending that Franklin Roosevelt had begun.

Democratic President John Kennedy proposed a large tax cut to further stimulate economic growth. The measure passed in early 1964 and did spur expansion. President Lyndon Johnson's social

Lesson 20 - The Economy As We Know It

programs, such as Medicare and Medicaid, as well as the country's involvement in Vietnam, dramatically increased federal spending during the 1960s. This occurred without a tax increase, which meant that federal deficits grew significantly.

Inflation Woes

A major economic problem that developed in the early 1970s was inflation. As mentioned in Lesson 1, inflation is a decline in the value of money, reflected in higher prices for goods and services. In 1967 the country's inflation rate was 3%, which means that, at the end of the year, prices for the same goods and services were an average of 3% higher than they had been at the start of the year. In 1973, however, the inflation rate tripled to 9%. Inflation rose to 12% for 1974 and remained a serious issue for the rest of the decade.

Along with inflation, unemployment rose and production declined in the 1970s, in part because of competition from foreign goods. To try to ease the economic woes, in 1971 President Nixon imposed a 90-day wage and price freeze. However, because the government allowed previously agreed-upon contracts to go into effect, wages and prices actually rose during the three-month period.

Then in 1973, because of the United States' support of Israel in a war against its Arab opponents, the Organization of Petroleum Exporting Countries (OPEC) refused to sell oil to the United States. This meant that the supply of oil in the United States could not keep pace with demand. Prices rose quickly and gasoline shortages were common for a time. Nixon's successor, Gerald Ford, spearheaded a "WIN" campaign: Whip Inflation Now. It didn't work. Inflation continued to be a major problem during the Ford and Carter Administrations.

After the Iranian revolution in 1979, another oil crisis developed. This again led to long lines at gas stations.

Reaganomics

In 1980 inflation was running at an annual rate of about 13.5%. The benchmark prime interest rate that banks charge for loans to their best customers hit 20% that year. Unemployment was also high. All of these factors made for a slow economy. The nation seemed unable to regain the prosperity that it had enjoyed in the 1950s and 1960s.

Ronald Reagan campaigned for the presidency in 1980 talking about the prospect of better days that he believed would come by putting the economy back on track and getting government off of the people's backs. He proposed a broad and deep tax cut that he believed would stimulate the economy and would provide even more tax revenue because of greater business activity.

The basis for Reagan's tax proposals were the ideas of economist Arthur Laffer. Laffer believed that a tax cut would actually raise government revenue. According to this idea, lower taxes would give people the incentive to work harder and to save and invest more, which would stimulate economic growth. This increased economic activity would then generate more tax revenue, even with lower tax rates. This idea is called supply-side economics. George H. W. Bush, a rival for the Republican nomination that year, called the idea "voodoo economics." Nevertheless, Bush eventually became Reagan's running mate.

Reagan and Bush won in a landslide, and Congress passed the tax cuts. After a recession in the early 1980s, the rate of inflation fell to just over 3% by 1983. Unemployment, which stood at 10.8% of the workforce in late 1982, declined to 5.4% by the end of Reagan's second term. Revenue increased after the tax cuts, but it did not keep pace with increased federal spending.

The Republican Reagan and the Democratic Congress did not agree on the spending cuts that Reagan had advocated, so the federal government spent well beyond its means. As a result, some of the renewed prosperity was paid for with borrowed money. The national debt, which stood at $930 billion in 1981, almost tripled to $2.6 trillion by 1988. The country also registered large continuing trade deficits as we bought more from overseas than we sold to other countries.

The personal computer became a major part of the worldwide economy during the 1980s. The Commodore 64, first released in 1982, was the bestselling individual model with some 15 million units sold worldwide.

Lesson 20 - The Economy As We Know It

The 1990s

The country experienced difficulties during the tenure of George H. W. Bush as President (1989-1993). One was the failure of the savings and loan industry. For several years, through the Carter and Reagan presidencies, the federal government had been deregulating certain industries, such as trucking, airlines, communication, and savings and loan institutions.

Because of looser regulations, S&Ls began granting loans for riskier real estate purchases and engaging in other uncertain investments. Many of those loans and investments failed, which meant that the S&Ls which had made the loans lost money. Hundreds of these thrift institutions closed, and the federal government devised a plan to cover the losses of the failed institutions or sell off their assets. The cost to the federal government of the S&L collapse was well over $100 billion.

When he ran for the presidency in 1988, George H. W. Bush promised that if Congress proposed tax hikes, he would not agree. "Read my lips," he said, "no new taxes." By 1990, however, the mounting deficits were creating a serious economic problem. Bush and Democratic congressional leaders agreed on a package of tax increases and budget cuts that they hoped would reduce the deficit over several years. Nevertheless, the country was mired in a recession for the last half of 1990 and the first quarter of 1991.

America experienced significant prosperity in the 1990s. The dot-com boom in Internet businesses created millionaires quickly and transformed the way Americans shop, connect with each other, and get information. The North American Free Trade Agreement led to freer trade among the United States, Mexico, and Canada. It also allowed many American companies to move production to Mexico where labor costs are cheaper. Still, the growing domestic economy enabled unemployment to remain below 5%. President Bill Clinton oversaw

The NASDAQ Stock Market opened 1971 using all-electronic trading. It handles the stocks of many technology companies such as Microsoft, Apple, and Amazon.com. The composite value of NASDAQ stocks reached an all-time high in March 2000, during the dot-com boom. The value of the stocks dropped more than 75% by October 2002. The NASDAQ composite did not reach similar levels again until 2015.

the enactment of tax increases to help lower federal deficits. By the end of the decade, the federal government ran annual budget surpluses; and the government made payments that decreased the national debt.

The Twenty-First Century

In 2000, George W. Bush campaigned on a promise to cut taxes if he became president. After he was elected, Congress did pass significant tax cuts. However, the September 11, 2001 terrorist attacks led to both a slowdown of economic growth and an increase in military spending as the country began a protracted war on terrorism. Economic growth was slow during the first years of the new century, and real family income declined during the Bush presidency. As we have seen several times in American history, much of the growth that occurred during the decade was the result of a speculative bubble that finally burst in 2008. We will discuss the financial meltdown of that year in a later lesson.

Summary

For over two centuries, the United States economy has seen many good times and many difficult times; but the overall trend has been one of growth. This has happened because of the freedom that the United States has offered people to pursue dreams, run their own businesses, work where they wanted to, and change jobs when they so desired. The actions of the federal government have helped at times and have caused problems at times. The free market has worked, although some people have taken advantage of the system and hurt others by their greed. The implementation of regulations has been an attempt to make participants in the economy operate on the basis of justice and honesty; but regardless of the number of regulations, some will try to cut corners and beat the system.

The economic principles that we will be discussing in the next several units are not just theory. They reflect the real-life, everyday issues with which Americans have wrestled for years, issues that have brought great financial success and also great heartache. This reality is what makes economics a vital topic that is worth your effort to understand.

As we try to understand how our economy works, however, we should remember the reassuring words of Jesus.

So do not worry about tomorrow; for tomorrow will care for itself. Each day has enough trouble of its own.
Matthew 6:34

Assignments for Lesson 20

Literature — Continue reading *The Rise of Silas Lapham*.

Project — Finish your project for this unit.

Student Review — Answer the questions for Lesson 20 and take the quiz for Unit 4.

05 Choices

Economics involves the need and the opportunity to make choices regarding alternative uses of limited resources. Choices have consequences, sometimes unintended ones. The need to make choices means that we must perform cost-benefit analysis of the alternatives before us. Most economic choices involve marginal decisions, which means deciding to a little more or a little less of something. Producers make choices about what and how much they produce. Factors such as incentives, substitute goods, and utility or satisfaction influence consumers' choices. People in government make choices based on their goals or ideals.

Lesson 21 - Chocolate or Vanilla?
Lesson 22 - Economic Choices
Lesson 23 - Producers Choose
Lesson 24 - We Choose
Lesson 25 - Uncle Sam Chooses

Books Used

The Bible
Making Choices
The Rise of Silas Lapham

Project (choose one)

1) Write 300 to 500 words on one of the following topics:

   - Write a short story about a choice that had significant impact.

   - Write about your ideas for what you will do after you finish high school. You can discuss one plan or multiple possibilities. Write about the costs and benefits. Write about the motivations behind your goals and dreams.

2) Make a photo essay of at least twenty photos illustrating economic choices that are an everyday part of your family's life, both the ones you make and the ones that are made for you. Write captions for the photos.

3) Create a children's book with the title "Choices." Illustrate it yourself in the medium of your choice (photography, painting, drawing, etc.). The book can have words to accompany the pictures, or only pictures. Create a cover and at least 20 pages.

21 Chocolate or Vanilla?

Did You Ever Have to Make Up Your Mind?
— song by The Lovin' Spoonful (1966)

God has endowed us as human beings with the ability to consider alternatives, to make choices, and to realize that we are making choices. Sometimes having to make a choice is agonizing, but the ability to make choices is a blessing.

We Get to Make Choices

Think about some of the choices you can make. Every morning you have a choice about what you will wear. When you go to a restaurant, you have many choices of what you can eat. You have a choice about the type of work you will go into as an adult. When you are old enough to vote, you will have a choice about which candidate you will support in an election.

Beyond these matters, you have choices about significant issues in your life. You can decide to believe in God. You can decide what your attitude will be, even in hard circumstances. You can decide how you are going to treat other people.

You should always remember this fact: You do not have to live as a victim. Regardless of how much you feel hemmed in or limited by your circumstances, you do not have to live your life as a victim. When you think of yourself as a victim, you are putting a limit on what you can accomplish and how successfully you can live. When you live as a victim, you are making a choice. You are choosing to let circumstances control your life.

Not all possible choices are open to everyone. Previous choices can limit future choices. If you choose not to be trained in medicine, you cannot legally write prescriptions and sign your name with the letters M.D. after it. Despite some limitations on the choices you can make, you can choose to make the most of your situation despite these limitations.

We Have to Make Choices

Not only do we have the ability and opportunity to make choices, but we also have the responsibility to make choices about many things. No one has the time or money to do absolutely everything he or she would like to do, so he or she has to make choices. The richest person in the world can only be in one place at 9:00 on Monday morning.

The person with no work responsibilities only has the same 24-hour day that the busy person has. A person has the responsibility to choose some way to provide food for himself or herself; otherwise he or she is choosing to starve or to depend on someone else. The most important choice that a person has to make is whether or not to confess and obey Jesus Christ as Savior and Lord.

When you decide to live as a Christian and be faithful to that calling, you cannot also choose to live any way you want. Jesus said that following Him involves serious choices every day. You must choose whether or not you will love your enemy (Matthew 5:44). You must choose how you pray (Matthew 6:5-15). You must choose whether to store up treasure on earth or treasure in heaven (Matthew 6:19-20). You must choose not to judge others (Matthew 7:1-5). You must choose whether you will go through the narrow gate of life or the wide and popular gate of destruction (Matthew 7:13-14). You must decide whether you are merely going to listen to Jesus or whether you will act upon His words (Matthew 7:24-27). The point of the parable of the sower (Matthew 13:1-9, 18-23) is to challenge the listener to choose what kind of soil he or she is going to be.

How to Make Good Choices

The choices you make are not a coin toss or a blind shot in the dark. Some decisions will be difficult, and the best alternative might not be absolutely clear to you. Still, you can take steps that will help you make the best decisions possible.

You can seek to determine if at all possible what God's will is in a particular situation. You will need to study Scripture to see what God has said that will inform your decision. If He has directly spoken on a topic in Scripture, the choice that a Christian should make is clear. If God has not directly spoken on a certain topic in Scripture, you have to apply Biblical principles and use the best-informed and most God-oriented discernment you can.

You need to decide what will bless others the most. Decisions that a person makes out of a selfish heart are not good decisions.

You need to decide what will best accomplish the goals that God has for you. To recognize and accept goals but then to make decisions that are contrary to attaining those goals is unwise.

You need to decide what will be best in the long run. Decisions that a person makes with only the immediate or short-term consequences in mind are usually not wise.

You need to get wise counsel. Other people have probably faced the same or similar decisions, and their experience can help you see a little further into the fog.

You need to pray about decisions. James told us to pray for wisdom and to pray in faith that God will answer (James 1:5-6). Jesus said that if we ask, seek, and knock, we will receive (Matthew 7:7-8).

Realities About Choices

Actions have consequences. Ideas have consequences. Choices have consequences. The reason that choices are so important is that they make a difference. They really matter. Here are some ways in which this is true.

Bad choices make good choices harder to make and result in fewer good options before you. When you decide to go down the wrong road, turning around and going back to where you can make a better choice is difficult. You have to admit that you were wrong, which can be hard. Sometimes you have to deal with the consequences of the bad choice even after you decide to start doing what is right.

Having made bad choices might mean that you have to start over by taking the time to get more training before you can get a job, or pay off some debt that you have accumulated by making bad choices,

Ice cream shop in Hatyai, Thailand

or take a lower-paying job for a while, or appear in court to answer for mistakes you have made, or do other things to rectify the mess you have made. Paul said that we reap what we sow (Galatians 6:7). You have a choice about what you sow, but you do not have choices about what you reap as a result of what you have sown.

Choices have more at stake the longer you go through life. A child's choice between chocolate and vanilla ice cream is not an earth-shaking matter (unless he is allergic to chocolate!). By contrast, whom a person decides to marry will have consequences that last a lifetime and even longer. Deciding whether to start a career or go to college is a big decision; deciding whether to go to work or go to graduate school can be an even bigger decision. The longer you live, the more you become responsible for. Bigger responsibilities mean that your choices tend to affect more people. You should get into the pattern of making good choices early in your life.

Choices often have unintended consequences. You should think through the consequences of your decisions as clearly and as carefully as possible, but even then you will likely be surprised. When you decide to eat more than you should, you don't mean to give yourself a stomach ache or to gain weight; but that is what can happen. The framers of the Treaty of Versailles following the Great War in the early twentieth century did not intend for the harsh treatment of Germany to lead to another world war, but most historians believe that World War II was at least partly the result of the terms of that treaty. The people at lending institutions who approved loans that were larger than what customers could afford to pay back did not mean to contribute to a worldwide economic meltdown, but their actions did play a part in the Great Recession.

Making choices is a big part of life. Many of the choices that you, the people around you, people in business, and people in government make have to do with economics. Joshua encouraged Israel to make a good choice in the most important decision they had before them.

> *. . . choose for yourselves today whom you will serve . . . .*
> *Joshua 24:15*

Assignments for Lesson 21

Making Choices — Read "Free to Choose: A Conversation with Milton Friedman" (pages 39-47).

Literature — Continue reading *The Rise of Silas Lapham*. Plan to finish it by the end of Unit 7.

Project — Choose your project for this unit and start working on it.

Student Review — Answer the questions for Lesson 21.

22 Economic Choices

You can't have your cake and eat it too.

— *American Saying*

Choices about Scarce Resources

We said in Lesson 1 that economics involves a study of the choices that people make regarding the production, distribution, and consumption of products and services made from scarce resources for which alternative uses exist. People in a society—including producers, consumers, and people in government—make choices about three basic economic issues:

1. What goods and services, and in what quantities, will an economy produce? In other words, what goods and services do potential consumers value and desire? Producing goods and services is pointless if no one wants them or is willing to pay for them. Once producers decide what to make, the quantity part of the question involves determining how much of that product the market will bear. It is poor economic planning to produce more than what people want or to produce less than what people want if the producers are capable of producing more.

Product

2. How will people produce goods and services? This question involves determining the nature and quality of the raw materials that will go into goods. It also involves the standard of training for those who provide services: do we expect nurses, accountants, and electricians, for instance, to receive training and certification? Another production issue involves determining whether domestic businesses will produce the goods and services or if foreign sources will provide them.

Service

3. How will people distribute the goods and services across the population? Will a producer find it worthwhile to pay for national marketing and distribution, or does the producer want only a local or regional market? Will the goods or services only be available to people who are able to pay for them, or will the government make them available by paying for them through tax revenues (as happens with public education and, for many people, with health care)? Or will the government subsidize production—that is, pay for part of the cost—so that the goods and services will be available at a lower cost to consumers? This is what happens with mass transit and the production of ethanol.

Distribution

Ethanol plant in West Burlington, Iowa

You might think that at least some of these choices are simply business decisions, a discussion of which might be more appropriate in a course on business. However, remember that in Lesson 4 we said that the knowledge about how the economy works is held in small bits by billions of people who participate in the market. The choices we have described are business decisions, but they reflect economic realities that we discuss in this curriculum, such as:

- The demand and supply for goods and services that people might produce,

- The availability of resources to produce the goods and services, and

- The role of labor and government in the economy.

Scarcity or Abundance: How Do We Act?

We face economic choices because we have limited resources. We do not have an unlimited supply of gasoline, food, clothes, or any other product or service. Nor do we have an unlimited supply of time and money that would allow us to do and to have everything we might want. Producers cannot produce and consumers cannot consume anything and everything. This is why we have to make choices. The way we make those choices has an impact on our economic life.

We admit the reality of scarce resources in general; but in practical terms, people often do not think or act with an assumption of scarcity. In one sense this is good, and in another sense this is not good.

First, the good part. We believe that sufficient resources exist in the world for everyone to have a decent standard of living. We believe that as the population grows, creative people come up with new ideas to help more people meet their basic needs. People have the potential to make good choices, and the economy can expand to provide what people need. The land of the United States once fed, clothed, and housed only a few million people; it now feeds, clothes, and houses over 300 million people. More importantly, as we discussed in Lesson 6, God has promised to supply all the needs of His people.

People generally believe that the market for goods and services is large enough for people to start a new business or expand an existing business. People have found ways to make the economic pie larger. A healthy way to make economic decisions regarding limited resources involves believing that there is enough of the pie for me if I work hard and live responsibly. Thinking that there is only a limited economic pie that people can divide into only so many pieces is thinking on the basis of fear.

Second, the bad part. Some people do make irresponsible decisions about limited resources. Those who do not want to make hard choices about how to use the limited resource of their money buy more than they should and go into debt. They are trying to buy a bigger piece of the pie with borrowed money, hoping that they will earn enough later to pay off the debt. This approach often gets them into financial trouble.

Many families have saddled themselves with thousands of dollars in credit card debt. Many college students, some of whom do not even graduate from college, accumulate tens of thousands of dollars in student loan debts. In 2008 after many people bought houses that were more expensive than they could afford, this mindset contributed to the entire economy going into recession when millions of people could not make their mortgage payments.

Believing that the Lord of abundance will provide does not mean going deeply into debt for material things and then trusting that the Lord will provide the money for the payments. Economic responsibility means making wise choices about your scarce resources.

Cost-Benefit Analysis

One step in making wise economic decisions is doing a *cost-benefit analysis* of the choices you face. This involves making a list of the costs and the benefits of taking a particular step before you take it. You want to determine if the benefits outweigh the costs, making the choice worthwhile.

Many times a day we conduct a cost-benefit analysis unconsciously. Is the benefit of more sleep worth the cost of being late for work? Is the benefit of saving a few moments by turning into the line of traffic now worth the risk of an accident, or would it be better to wait until there is more room in the lane? Is the benefit of talking to my friend now worth the cost of having to do my chores later in the evening?

Sign advertising foreclosure home sale (2009)

Candy shop in Tokyo, Japan

Here are three examples of cost-benefit analysis related to consumer purchases. Remember that a cost can be something other than money.

Buying a candy bar carries a cost. The benefit is being able to enjoy eating the candy bar. However, if you do this too often, you might gain weight or have other health problems that result from eating too much sugar. Does the benefit of enjoying this candy bar outweigh the financial and potential health costs for you?

Buying a coat involves a cost. The benefit is that you can have protection from cold weather, so that you can go places in the cold and so that you will not run the risk of becoming ill. Do those benefits outweigh the financial cost of the coat?

Both saving and spending have a cost and a benefit. If you have a certain amount of money, you need to decide what are the relative benefits of spending it on something now compared to saving it so that you can buy something of greater value later.

Businesses have to do cost-benefit analysis of their plans. Will the benefit of increased sales outweigh the cost of creating a new product (costs such as paying for planning and engineering, creating production facilities in which to make the product, and so forth)? Will the cost of an advertising campaign result in the benefit of more sales? Might the company find that the advertising that it plans to do will not influence most potential customers?

People in government should engage in cost-benefit analysis of programs and proposals. Do they have sufficient evidence that, if a city or a county buys property for an industrial park, owners of industries will want to build there and generate enough tax revenue to recoup the cost of the land? Sometimes the benefit of a decision by people in government is not a financial benefit, but the benefit is real nonetheless. If government leaders are thinking about expanding the public library, they might want to survey library patrons and the general public to see if the community will see a benefit from having more educational resources available.

Failing to do a cost-benefit analysis can result in significant losses. If a person does not do cost-benefit analysis before purchasing items, that person can wind up with a lot of stuff that he or she does not really need and not enough money to achieve more important goals. If people in a business fail to do cost-benefit analysis, they might wind up with a big warehouse with nothing to fill it or with significant losses from buying too much equipment. Elected officials sometimes do not want to conduct a cost-benefit analysis of a proposed or existing program if the program is politically popular. However, when government funds a program without a cost-benefit analysis, the government might spend money for something that is not worth the expense.

Margins

In economics, a *margin* is a small step that makes a big difference in an action being taken. Few decisions that we make are all-or-nothing decisions. Most of the time we make choices about doing a little more or a little less of something. For instance, once you have decided to exercise, you have to decide whether you have the time and energy to jog one more lap around the block. That is a marginal decision. Economists spend a great deal of time studying margins because that is where important economic decisions are made. One way to think of margin is the next one: the next worker hired, the next dollar earned, the next unit of a product consumed. What are the consequences or effects of the next one?

The owners of a widget-making business know that they can make and sell 5,000 widgets with the workers and machinery they have. To make the 5,001st widget, they would have to hire an additional worker or buy more machinery. Would that additional expense be worth it? With another worker, they could make an additional 1,000 widgets, but could they sell enough of the widgets to make hiring the additional worker worth the expense of producing them? Determining the point where a change in behavior occurs (such as hiring an additional worker to make more widgets) is a marginal cost-benefit decision. *Marginal benefit* is the change in total benefit that results from an action. *Marginal cost* is the change in total cost that results from an action. All else being equal, it is better to take the action if the total benefit is greater than the total cost.

Economists refer to the *marginal propensity to consume*, which is the fraction or decimal part of extra income that an individual or household is likely to spend instead of save. For instance, if the marginal propensity to consume is .6, this means that the public, on average, will spend 60 cents of every dollar of extra income and save 40 cents. This statistic is helpful in estimating the effect of additional income, such as that which might come from higher wages or working overtime, on the economy as a whole.

Clothing manufacturer in Oromia, Ethiopia

We are going to look at economic choices that producers, consumers, and people in government make involving scarce resources, cost-benefit analysis, marginal thinking, and other economic realities that influence our choices.

Jesus reminds us that we have an important choice to make regarding Who or what will be our master. This is not a marginal decision involving just the next step, but it is a basic decision about the direction of a person's entire life.

> *No one can serve two masters;*
> *for either he will hate the one and love the other,*
> *or he will be devoted to one and despise the other.*
> *You cannot serve God and wealth.*
> *Matthew 6:24*

Assignments for Lesson 22

Literature — Continue reading *The Rise of Silas Lapham*.

Project — Continue working on your project for this unit.

Student Review — Answer the questions for Lesson 22.

Quebec, Canada, produces about three-fourths of the world's maple syrup.

23 Producers Choose

Would you like fries with that?
— *a question of economics*

We divide what producers offer in an economy into goods and services. *Goods* are tangible items that companies or individuals produce for consumption, such as cars, computers, clothes, and food. *Services* are intangible duties that people perform for pay, such as house cleaning, child care, legal counsel, and medical care.

People who operate businesses decide what goods and services they want to offer. Decisions about production can take many forms, and they have significant impact. For instance, a farmer has to decide what crops he wants to plant and determine the cost for machinery and seed, as well as what price he can expect to get for his crop. Automakers have to decide what models they think people will want to buy: will the automaker emphasize large, comfortable cars or small, economical cars? Someone who wants to start a home health business has to determine if the community needs such a business, what will be involved in finding and hiring qualified personnel, and how difficult it will be to collect payment for services from individual customers, insurance companies, or government agencies.

People who engage in retail sales have other choices to make regarding the distribution of goods. A retailer has to decide if he wants to offer his product line in a physical store, from a mobile stand, on the Internet, or through a combination of methods. A store owner has to decide if she is going to concentrate on one kind of product, such as clothes or office supplies, or whether she will open a store that carries many product lines.

Production Resources

Production resources are the elements that producers use to create goods and services. Also called factors of production, these include material resources, human resources, and capital.

Material resources are those things found in nature or processed from things found in nature that people use to manufacture goods. Material resources include petroleum and other mineral deposits, trees, rock, maple syrup, and many other things. People who operate a business have to determine the cost of the material resources that are available for the production of goods. They might obtain the resources themselves, or they might pay someone else for preparing and delivering them.

129

Human resources include labor, creativity, and technology. People provide the labor to produce goods and provide services, and human creativity has generated the technology that makes new products and more efficient production possible.

When we hear the word capital with reference to financial matters, it usually refers to money (as in, "He now has the capital to start his business."). In economics, however, *capital* refers to the materials used to produce goods, such as machinery and factories. Someone might use the word to refer strictly to money, but remember that money only has worth as it can provide other things. Money does not produce goods and services. Money can buy equipment, land, offices, and factories that people can use to produce goods and services.

People who produce goods and services make many choices about production resources. They decide what materials they want to use, how much they are willing to pay, and how to obtain the materials. Producers decide how many workers they want to hire, what skills they want the workers to have, and how much they are going to pay the workers. They decide about the technology in which they want to invest to have the most efficient production process they can.

Business owners are also consumers. They choose the property where they want to build a factory or open an office, what machinery they want to purchase, and what other materials they need to start and run their business.

Production Possibilities

One aspect of production that economists examine is the *production possibilities curve (or frontier)*. This is the maximum production that an economy can have, given its production resources.

Imagine an economy that can produce only two goods: cell phones and MP3 players. The economy can produce 750 cell phones if it produces no MP3 players, and it can produce 750 MP3 players if it produces no cell phones. If it produces both cell phones and MP3 players, it can produce lesser amounts of both. This is illustrated on Production Possibilities Curve #1.

A production possibilities curve illustrates several key economic concepts. One is efficiency.

Production Possibilities Curve #1

Production Possibilities Curve #2

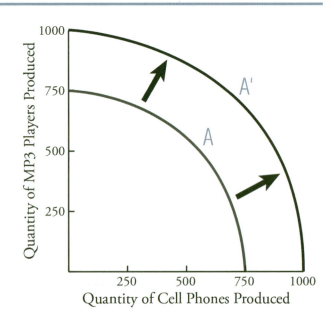

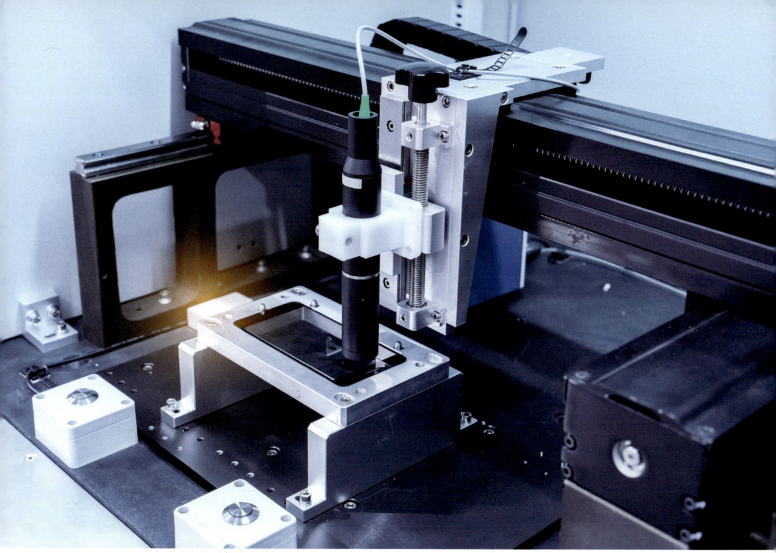

Robotic manufacture of a cell phone

If new technology enables the economy to produce more MP3 players with the same or less labor, the economy becomes more efficient with regard to MP3 players. Another economic concept that the graph shows is that, if the actual production of goods falls somewhere below the curve, the economy is not producing at maximum efficiency.

If new technology enables more of one or both of the products to be produced, the production possibilities curve moves outward or to the right. This is shown by the curve A' on Production Possibilities Curve #2.

Another principle involved in production decisions is opportunity cost. When a person decides to do one thing, he or she is deciding not to do everything else he or she could do. *Opportunity cost* is defined as the greatest benefit that a producer gives up when he makes a choice. When you decide to visit Aunt Stella from 2:00 to 4:00 on Monday afternoon, you are deciding not to do many other things, such as reading a book or mowing a neighbor's yard during those two hours. When you decide to take an online college class, you are deciding not to do other things during the time it takes to complete the class.

Opportunity cost is the greatest benefit a producer gives up in taking an action. If you decide to sell lemonade and make $50.00, you are giving up the opportunity to mow a lawn and make $35.00, bake cookies for a farmer's market and make $25.00, or babysit and make $20.00. Your opportunity cost would be $35.00, the greatest alternative you are giving up. Your opportunity cost would not be $80.00, the total of the three alternatives, because you could not do all three of the alternatives at the same time.

To take the opportunity to do or make or sell one thing could be the best decision you can make, but in making that decision you are paying the price of not doing or making or selling something else. Wise decision-makers want to make their opportunity cost as small as possible compared to what they gain from the decision.

Still another economic concept illustrated by the production possibilities curve is that of tradeoffs. A *tradeoff* is what you have to accept when you make a decision. If the people in the economy described above decide to focus exclusively on MP3 player production, they face the tradeoff of having to import cell phones or do without them. If producers decide to import oil instead of exploring for domestic sources, they are facing the tradeoff of being dependent on the oil production policies of other countries.

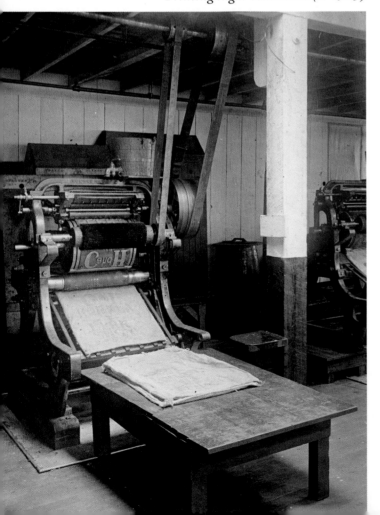

Printing sugar containers (c. 1915)

If people in a society decide to minimize environmental restrictions on producers, they are deciding to have less expensive goods but with the tradeoff of possible environmental damage. If the people of that society's government did not consider potential environmental impact when they decided to place as few regulations as possible on producers, the environmental damage could be seen as an *unintended consequence* of the decision.

Economies of Scale and Scope

Economy of scale occurs when the average total cost per item decreases as the number of units produced increases. A print shop usually operates on the basis of economies of scale. If a customer wants 200 copies of a brochure, the printer might charge 30 cents per copy. The cost for the print job would be $60. However, the printer could produce 1,000 brochures for 20 cents each. The cost for the larger print job (five times as many) would not be five times as much ($300) but only $200.

A single small retail clothing store, Mr. Little's Fine Clothing Emporium, might have to pay 38 cents per pound to have a truck deliver garments to his one store. However, if a trucking company delivers goods to many locations in the Big Box Store chain, the chain might only have to pay 20 cents per pound because of the economy of scale in delivering to Big Box. Therefore a shirt will likely cost more at Mr. Little's.

Some tradeoffs would be that Mr. Little would always be there to give personal service and you would be more likely to find a good selection at his store, while Big Box's employees may be hard to find and the merchandise may be largely picked over.

In another illustration, production is cheaper per item if the goods are made in a single factory than if they are made in several factories, since the cost of building and maintaining several factories is much greater than the cost for one factory.

Amazon.com has used economies of scale to grow its business with a large network of fulfillment centers.

When a business owner has to decide whether to build another factory or expand production at the current facility, he is dealing with issues of economy of scale.

A related but separate issue is *economy of scope*. This is when a company's average total cost of production decreases as it produces more related products. For example, it is cheaper for one factory to produce shampoo and conditioner than it would be for two companies to build and maintain facilities to produce them separately. If a company becomes known for paper goods or computer peripherals, it can probably obtain material resources and utilize advertising more cheaply to develop full lines of products than the total cost incurred by several companies making and advertising individual though related products.

Another way that a company might utilize economy of scope is by expanding the scope of activities related to what it produces. For instance, some companies have found that it is more efficient to own sources for raw materials and trucks for distribution instead of just producing the product and paying other companies to provide the other steps in the supply chain.

These are just some of the choices that producers make. We will consider other decisions they make in Unit 9.

Jesus placed a choice before the rich young ruler. Unfortunately, the young man decided that the tradeoff was too great for him to choose the way Jesus wanted him to choose.

---

*Looking at him, Jesus felt a love for him and said to him,
"One thing you lack: go and sell all you possess and give to the poor,
and you will have treasure in heaven; and come, follow Me."
But at these words he was saddened, and he went away grieving,
for he was one who owned much property.
Mark 10:21-22*

Assignments for Lesson 23

Making Choices — Read the letter to Eli Whitney Sr. (pages 48-50).
Read the letter to Eli Whitney Jr. (page 51).

Literature — Continue reading *The Rise of Silas Lapham*.

Project — Continue working on your project for this unit.

Student Review — Answer the questions for Lesson 23.

Shoppers wait for a sale in Zurich, Switzerland (2015)

24 We Choose

Paper or plastic?
— another question of economics

You might think that the choices consumers make play only a small role in the economy. The tendency might be to believe that corporate and investment activity make up the lion's share of what goes on in the economy. However, economists estimate that personal consumption makes up seventy percent of economic activity in the United States. So much of what companies produce is geared toward the consumer, and so many consumers live in the country, that understanding the choices that consumers make is a major part of understanding economics.

The fundamental choice that consumers make is what to buy. That simple decision, however, has many factors. One factor is the choice between spending or saving. The consumer might not want to buy. He or she might want to save instead, either while waiting for a better deal on a particular product or while waiting to buy something else entirely.

Incentives

Incentives influence the choices that consumers make. Economists believe that people act out of self-interest, though sometimes a person's self-interest involves serving or sacrificing for others. An *incentive* is a benefit that motivates action. People behave differently because of incentives that producers provide which appeal to a person's self-interest.

The most common example of an incentive is a reduction in price. People generally buy more when prices are lower because people are interested in saving money. Another incentive is a subsidy in one form or another, which means that someone else is paying part of the cost. A common subsidy for consumers is the rebate. With a rebate, the seller does not lower the purchase price, but the company offers to refund part of the purchase price if the customer completes and submits a rebate form. The practice of offering rebates generally increases sales. In addition, companies have found that some of those who buy at full price do not send in the rebate form, and this increases the company's profit.

Some consumers respond to the incentive of conspicuous consumption, which means buying goods in order to display one's wealth or prestige. Producers encourage this by adding a distinctive logo or charging a higher price so that consumers will view their products differently.

Workers making blue jeans in Istanbul, Turkey (2014)

People also respond to disincentives, which discourage purchases. One common disincentive is an additional tax on an item. The federal government, state governments, and some local governments place excise taxes on cigarettes, partly to discourage people from smoking. The health warnings in cigarette advertisements are another disincentive. Since producers want people to buy their goods and services, disincentives usually come from the government to accomplish some goal other than the sale of goods, such as a decrease in smoking.

Incentives can have unintended consequences. For instance, if a computer company cuts its prices to encourage more sales, the demand might exceed the company's ability to supply the goods. This can frustrate consumers, who might not want to wait for weeks until they can get a computer at the lower price, so they buy another brand. Disincentives can also have unintended consequences. For example, if government raises taxes on gasoline to encourage lower consumption, the resulting drop in sales can cause lower gasoline tax collections, which means that the government loses revenue.

Substitute Goods

Another factor in consumer choices is the presence of substitute goods. A *substitute good* is an alternative to the item that the consumer would otherwise buy. A consumer might buy apples instead of bananas (or vice versa), or one brand of soft drink instead of another. A common example of substitute goods are store brands or generic items that compete with name brand goods. Instead of buying a pair of jeans made by a company that has spent big money on an advertising campaign that gives the impression that fashionable people only buy this brand, a consumer might decide to buy a cheaper pair of jeans made by a company that does not have a big marketing budget and that only sells to a particular retailer.

Lesson 24 - We Choose

Choosing substitute goods is not just a shopping or a personal budget issue. Producers know that a sizable market exists for non-name brand items. Some producers decide to try to make a profit not by offering the best known or most expensive goods, but by offering items that appeal to consumers who are more interested in saving money.

Substitute goods raise the issue of tradeoffs. Sometimes the cheaper store brand of an item is of lesser quality than the more expensive name brand. The consumer has to decide whether to pay more for higher quality or pay less for what she believes will be good enough quality. Then, of course, there is the tradeoff that other people may not think of you as cool if you do not have a pair of designer jeans!

Substitute goods also have to do with the issue of marginal decisions. The *marginal rate of substitution* involves how much of one product a consumer is willing to give up in exchange for another product to maintain the same level of satisfaction. For me personally, buying four books would bring me a certain level of satisfaction. Buying three books and two CDs would bring me an equivalent level of satisfaction. Thus, my marginal rate of substitution would be two CDs for one book.

Consumer Choice Theory

One specialized area of economic study is *consumer choice theory*, which examines how consumers decide what to buy. In economics, *utility* does not mean usefulness but satisfaction. Economists assume that customers want satisfaction and that they seek the greatest utility or satisfaction in their purchasing. Economists study what brings about the maximum utility for consumers.

One factor in consumer choice is what the consumer wants. The second factor is what the consumer can afford, given his or her budget restraints. The third factor is what the consumer actually chooses. Since economists focus on margin, consumer choice economists study a fourth factor, which is how changes in price and changes in consumer income affect the choices that consumers make. The people who operate businesses have an interest in knowing all of these factors.

A principle that economists have developed is the law of *diminishing marginal utility*. One application of this law says that, as someone consumes more of an item, each unit has less value to the consumer, to the point at which one more unit provides no utility. An example is potato chips. The first few potato chips that a person eats at one sitting are tasty and satisfying. Additional chips are less and less satisfying, until the person reaches the point that another chip would not provide any additional satisfaction beyond what he already feels.

Calbee is a snack food manufacturer based in Japan that operates in many other countries. Popular items include Pizza Potato chips in the Philippines, ketchup-flavored Jaxx potato sticks in Thailand, and Snapea rice sticks in the United Kingdom and Spain. A worldwide favorite is Kappa Ebisen, made with shrimp. This display in Hong Kong features bags of Kappa Ebisen snacks.

This might seem like a trivial issue unless your business is producing and distributing potato chips. Then you will want to know how many chips to put into an individual serving bag to achieve maximum average consumer utility, since putting in more than that amount would increase your cost without increasing positive customer response. The point of diminishing marginal utility for a particular product or service changes from time to time, which we can see in the fact that portion sizes of chips, soft drinks, and other food items have increased in recent years.

Economists refer to *utility-maximizing conditions* as those conditions (usually influenced by government policies) that bring about the most utility (satisfaction) for the greatest number of people. This might include the creation of more public parks or taxing the wealthy at higher rates to provide income or service benefits to the poor. The theory behind this idea is that a dollar of benefits to the poor will increase their utility (satisfaction) more than a dollar more in taxes will decrease the utility of the wealthy.

Looking at the College Choice from an Economic Standpoint

High school students face the choice of whether or not they will attend college. Colleges offer a service—education—that many people want. About fifty to sixty percent of high school graduates go on to attend college for some length of time. The choice that a young person makes will have a major impact on his or her life, so it is wise to consider the decision carefully.

Lewis Hines photographed these students at the West Virginia Collegiate Institute in 1921. Now known as West Virginia State University, the school was established in 1891 as a segregated school for African Americans.

Lesson 24 - We Choose

Cost-benefit analysis. The financial costs for attending college include tuition, books, room and board, transportation, and discretionary spending. College students pay an opportunity cost, since they sacrifice the income they could have made at a full-time job in order to attend college. The primary financial benefit of attending college is that, on average, college graduates earn more over their lifetime than high school graduates who do not attend college. During the recession of 2007-2009, the unemployment rate for college graduates was reportedly about half that of the general public. College graduates generally had more stable jobs and had more options open to them when looking for jobs.

Attending college also has intangible costs and benefits. The potential costs include a student compromising his or her spiritual principles under pressure from friends, media, and the campus culture to adopt an ungodly lifestyle. Potential intangible benefits from attending college, besides the college education itself, include gaining a broader view of the world. In addition, many people meet their spouse while at school. And some come to Christ during their college careers.

A primary cost-benefit factor that potential college students will want to consider is whether attending college will help them achieve their life goals. If someone wants to obtain a professional degree or to be trained in a particular area of study and work, a college degree will help him or her with that goal. If a person wants to operate the family business or to be a full-time wife and mother, a college education might or might not be worth the cost.

Payment options. If a person decides to attend college, he has many choices for paying for it. Colleges offer incentives such as scholarships, grants, and work-study arrangements. Many college students take out loans to pay for college expenses, under the expectation that they will earn enough after graduating to repay the loans.

R. L. "Rube" Goldberg published this cartoon in Puck *magazine in 1914. The title asks the question "Can a college man be successful in spite of his 'education'?" It points out that achievement and popularity in college do not always lead to greater success in later life.*

A student might decide to support himself by working and paying cash for college expenses. Several options for substitute services are available, such as trade schools, online degree programs, and attending a less expensive community college for the first two years.

Unintended consequences. A student who borrows money to go to college may face the unintended consequence of not having enough income to make the necessary payments on a large debt (often tens of thousands of dollars). On the other hand, the person who does not go to college might find himself at a disadvantage if he applies for jobs for which a college degree is preferred.

Tradeoffs. By going to college, a person accepts less income now for the prospect of greater income later. The person who does not attend college soon after high school faces the reality that going back to school later is often more difficult than continuing his or her education directly after high school. However, other people have found that, after being out of school for a period of time, they are more highly motivated and have a clearer life purpose when they do attend college later. The person who goes to work instead of college can use the money he would have spent on college to start his own business, buy a home, or invest for the future.

Jesus described the ultimate choice that every person must make, including its costs and benefits.

And He summoned the crowd with His disciples, and said to them,
"If anyone wishes to come after Me, he must deny himself,
and take up his cross and follow Me.
For whoever wishes to save his life will lose it,
but whoever loses his life for My sake and the gospel's will save it.
For what does it profit a man to gain the whole world, and forfeit his soul?
For what will a man give in exchange for his soul?"
Mark 8:34-37

Assignments for Lesson 24

Making Choices — Read the Letters to Theodore and Martha Roosevelt (pages 52-54).

Literature — Continue reading *The Rise of Silas Lapham*.

Project — Continue working on your project for this unit.

Student Review — Answer the questions for Lesson 24.

Utah State Senate (2011)

25 Uncle Sam Chooses

> Ginger: "We'll either die free chickens or die trying!"
> Babs: "Are those the only choices?"
>
> — dialog from the movie *Chicken Run*

Many people talk about "the government deciding" to do this or that, or they say that "society disapproves" of this or that, but these expressions can cause us to forget an important truth. "Government" and "society" as institutions do not do anything; people make choices. People in government, people in business, and people in society make decisions. In this curriculum, when you read something about what government, business, or another group does, remember that this is a shorthand way to express the fact that people make decisions.

Who Decides?

In an earlier lesson, we said that the two models of economies are capitalist and command. Another way to express this is to say that the two poles or ideals of economic systems are market economies and command economies. The difference between them primarily involves the question of who makes economic decisions. In a market economy, the people who participate in the market of buying and selling goods and services make the decisions about who gets what and for what price. In a command economy, government officials make the decisions about who gets what and for what price.

Economists have identified and defined six broad economic goals that people in government pursue. Both command economies and market economies pursue these goals, but they do so in different ways.

Choices of Efficiency and Equity

Efficiency. Economic efficiency is the goal of encouraging the people in an economy to be as productive as possible in making goods and services available for consumers. Leaders of command economies believe that they can best decide how to make an economy efficient.

In a market economy, producers and consumers work in the freedom of the marketplace to make the most goods and services available. In this atmosphere of competition, some will be successful and some will not. Those who are not can regroup and try again. Some people are not productive, so they will not have as much as those who are. Historically, market economies are far superior to command economies in achieving efficiency.

141

Equity. Economic equity is the goal of having people in a society share goods and services as equally as possible. Those who lead a command economy believe it is better for all to have somewhat less but be more equal in what they have than to have some who are very rich and some who are very poor. (In practice, this applies to everyone except the elite leaders of the command economy and those whom the leaders favor!)

In a market economy, people have a wide range of income and wealth depending on how they participate in the market. People in a market economy are free to work for great wealth. It is also possible that some will be poor, for a number of reasons. Experience has shown that market economies give people the greatest opportunity for acquiring wealth, and even middle and lower class people in market economies have more than the vast majority of people in command economies. The average standard of living in a market economy is much higher than the average standard of living in a command economy.

These first two principles can be in conflict to some degree because an efficient economy (getting the most produced) is not necessarily an equitable economy (making sure that most people have about the same amount of wealth and income).

The government of North Korea is one of the strictest in the world. It censors the news media, regulates movement within the country, and enforces a dress code. It spends large amounts of money to build its military while many North Koreans struggle to get enough food.

Lesson 25 - Uncle Sam Chooses

Choices of Freedom and Security

Freedom. The goal or principle of economic freedom involves allowing people to do what they want to do in an economy. A market economy highly values this principle, which influences such questions as whether individuals can decide where they live, what work they do, and whether they may start their own businesses.

A command economy, by contrast, does not highly value this principle. In a command economy, what people produce and who works where are decisions that the central planning office makes. In a market economy, supply and demand and personal choice provide the answers to these questions.

Security. A command economy places higher value on economic security than freedom. The government has a stated goal of meeting the basic needs of all citizens. However, because of limited economic resources, the average income for most people will be relatively low.

In a market economy, it is possible that some people might slip through the economic cracks. However, even in market economies people in government have provided significant human and social services to the population.

Market economies give people the chance to achieve higher economic success, but people also have the risk of failing. In command economies, people generally cannot fly as high, so they do not have as far to fall. Again, though, the vast majority of people in market economies have more than the vast majority of people in command economies. The goals of freedom and security can be in conflict. Being free economically means that you give up a degree of economic security, while the promise of economic security means that you give up a degree of economic freedom.

Choices of Growth and Stability

Growth. Economic growth, the expansion of production and consumption, takes place in command economies in the segments of the economy that central planners target for growth, often in such areas as heavy industry and military armaments. Often this growth takes place at the expense of growth in consumer goods and other parts of the economy.

By contrast, growth in a market economy takes place primarily as a function of market demand and productivity. In countries with market economies, people in government can encourage or discourage productivity; but generally real growth takes place in the market, not through government action. These governments can spur growth more directly by providing subsidies to certain industries, such as "green" technology, or by spending government money in a certain industry, such as the manufacture of military equipment.

Stability. Market economies experience "boom and bust" business cycles, which involve periods of significant growth that alternate with periods of recession and shrinkage. Command economies have fewer such dramatic swings, again because the economy has less productivity to begin with. Market economies enable growth by risking stability. Command economies try to ensure stability while sacrificing the possibility of significant growth.

Decisions That People in Government Make

People in government create policies that affect the economy. Here are some of the kinds of decisions that people in government make.

Priorities. As with a family budget, the areas of expenditure in a government's budget and the amounts allotted for each reflect the priorities of the people in government.

President Lyndon Johnson signed the bill creating the Medicare program in 1965. Seated at the table with him is former president Harry Truman, who had pushed for a federal health care plan in the 1940s.

For many years after World War II, during the Cold War between the United States and the Soviet Union, military spending accounted for about half of the federal budget. Spending on social programs became a greater budget priority in the 1960s. When politicians talked about choosing whether to spend money on defense or social programs, they called it a choice between "guns and butter." A top priority of the federal government had always been guns (that is, national defense). The idea of the federal government being responsible for providing butter (that is, social welfare) reflected a new budget priority.

Incentives. People in government can provide incentives that can influence the actions of producers and consumers. For instance, a state or local government can try to attract new industry by offering to forgo collecting property or business taxes from the industry for a period of years or by offering to build new roads to the factory. The federal government offers a significant incentive for owning a home by allowing homeowners to deduct from their taxable income the interest they pay on a home mortgage loan.

Limitations. People in government can put limitations on business activity in order to achieve some social or economic goal. Environmental regulations limit what a business can do, but it also limits pollution in order to help the environment. Governments put tariffs and embargoes on imported goods to help domestic producers. These policies serve to limit the choices that producers and consumers have in order to meet other goals that the people in government value.

Allocation. People in government can determine who gets what goods and services. Will they be available only to those who can afford them, or will they be available to all, regardless of their ability to pay, by means of government funding for them? This policy involves the government redistributing money from one part of the population to another to pay for some goods and services.

Lesson 25 - Uncle Sam Chooses

In the 1930s, for instance, people in the federal government decided to allocate more of the nation's wealth to the elderly through the Social Security program by taxing workers to pay for retirement pensions. In the 1960s, the federal government expanded this policy of redistribution to include medical services for the elderly through Medicare, paid for through Medicare premiums and payments that participants paid, taxation to pay what premiums and payments did not cover, and borrowing money to pay what payments and taxes did not pay. This borrowed money added to the federal debt.

Public Choice Theory

Public choice theory is a field of study that applies principles of economics to political science. Just as people act on the basis of their self-interest in economic matters, public choice theory holds that voters act politically on the basis of their self-interest and that—lo and behold!—elected and appointed government officials act on the basis of their self-interest as well. Government officials do not always act benevolently on the basis of some so-called "higher public good." This helps to explain why many elected officials promote spending and other policies that further their own interests (namely, re-election) and why government bureaucracies become entrenched and seem almost impossible to reduce in size.

When the party out of power convinces enough voters to "throw the rascals out," the "new rascals" that come into power tend to do the same things for which they criticized the previous majority when they exhibit the same basic motivation of self-interest. This premise of basic self-interest also helps explain why special interest groups pressure elected officials to support their programs: their basic self-interest motivates them as they seek to influence government policy.

2016 presidential campaign memorabilia

The economic impact on the public of policies determined by self-interest is significant because the government collects tax revenue from the public at large but funds many programs that are of particular interest to relatively few, namely those who are in positions of power and those who support these elected representatives. Public choice scholars also study other factors, such as possible ways of changing the constitutional rules by which government representatives make decisions. One proposal involves placing constitutional limits on annual spending increases. The spending increases would be tied to growth in the economy.

In this unit we have discussed the process of making choices, particularly the economic choices that consumers, producers, and people in government make. We hope you can see why making choices is a central aspect of economics.

The Bible says that even God makes choices and that one of His choices reflected the different economic conditions that people have.

Listen, my beloved brethren: did not God choose the poor of this world to be rich in faith and heirs of the kingdom which He promised to those who love Him?
James 2:5

Assignments for Lesson 25

Literature — Continue reading *The Rise of Silas Lapham*.

Project — Finish your project for this unit.

Student Review — Answer the questions for Lesson 25, take the quiz for Unit 5, and take the first exam.

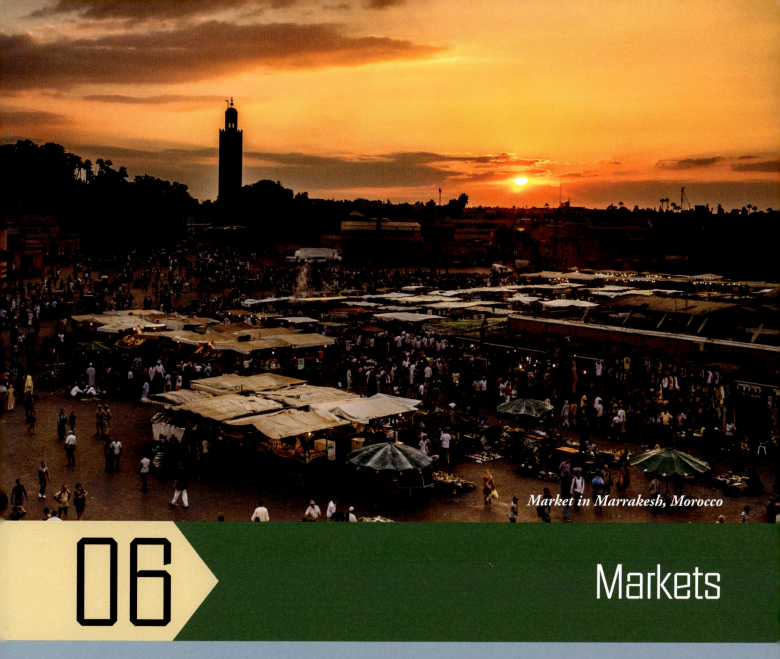
Market in Marrakesh, Morocco

06 Markets

A market is any context in which sellers offer products and services and buyers purchase them. Markets define the extent of freedom in an economy. Markets enable sellers and buyers to compete. The laws of supply and demand in markets determine the allocation of resources and establish prices for goods and services. Buyers and sellers can affect competition through such actions as sellers forming a cartel or buyers organizing a boycott. Prices are a powerful factor in a market. Markets are always changing because the goods and services that sellers offer change and because consumer choices change. Markets experience failure when they do not allocate resources efficiently.

Lesson 26 - How Markets Work
Lesson 27 - Supply and Demand
Lesson 28 - How Much Does It Cost?
Lesson 29 - When Markets Change
Lesson 30 - When Markets Fail

Books Used

The Bible
Making Choices
The Rise of Silas Lapham

Project (choose one)

1) Write 300 to 500 words on one of the following topics:

   - Why is the price system the best way to distribute goods and services and satisfy the most people?

   - Reflect on this quotation of Henry David Thoreau, "The price of anything is the amount of life you exchange for it."

2) If you know someone who owns a business supplying goods or services, ask to interview him or her (with your parents' permission). Ask about how they make decisions regarding supply and demand; how they set prices; their peak times and off-peak times; how they use advertising to influence supply and demand; and any other ideas you have. Prepare at least seven questions ahead of time and try to keep the conversation within one hour to respect your interviewee's time. Use video or audio to record the interview.

3) Make a chart with the following items along the left column: gallon of milk, dozen eggs, bath towel, adult sneakers, and coffee mug. Locate those items at 5 different stores in your area. You do not have to locate products of the same type or brand. For each product that you locate, list the store, price, place of manufacture, and your perspective of the quality on a scale of 1 to 5. After you have completed the research, write a paragraph about each product and give your theories and opinions on the reasons for prices, quality, and the marketing behind each of these products and the stores that sell them.

Sardine auction in Kochi, India (2007)

26 — How Markets Work

> *We who live in free market societies believe that growth, prosperity and ultimately human fulfillment, are created from the bottom up, not the government down. Only when the human spirit is allowed to invent and create, only when individuals are given a personal stake in deciding economic policies and benefiting from their success—only then can societies remain economically alive, dynamic, progressive, and free. Trust the people. This is the one irrefutable lesson of the entire postwar period contradicting the notion that rigid government controls are essential to economic development.*
> — Ronald Reagan

How should a society distribute bread among the people? How about health care? If someone cannot afford bread or health care at the going price, should that person simply not be able to get them?

Since economics is the study of the production, distribution, and consumption of goods and services about which people must make choices; and since everyone cannot have everything he or she wants, societies create formal or informal methods of distributing goods and services. Several different means of distribution are possible. Societies have tried to use the following methods at various times and places.

Majority rule. The majority decides who gets what, perhaps on the basis of characteristics such as family connections or skin color.

Force. A small group with guns tells everybody else who gets what.

First come, first served. Under this system, those with physical or mental limitations would be more likely to go without.

Lottery. A random drawing determines distribution. Sometimes people receive tickets to a special event or a child's placement in an exclusive school in this way.

Government mandate. The government might decide that it will distribute goods and services equally to all. Whether it is actually able to do this is another matter.

Price system. Producers set prices for the goods and services they want to offer, and buyers who have the ability to pay purchase them.

Offshore oil platform in the Norwegian sector of the North Sea

No method of distributing goods and services satisfies all the wants of all the people, but the best method of distribution that helps the most people is the price system. The dynamic that makes a free market work is supply and demand. The chief factor in creating supply and demand is the prices at which producers offer goods and services. If you understand markets, supply and demand, and the effect of prices, you will understand a great deal about economics.

Definition of Market

A *market* is anywhere sellers offer goods and services and buyers purchase them. It might be a real, physical location such as Wall Street or a Saturday morning farmers' market; it might be in the virtual space of the Internet; or it might range across the country or the world and take various forms, as is the case with the labor market. Some markets involve face-to-face transactions, while in other markets buyers and sellers never see each other.

People sometimes talk about the market in general, referring to all buyers and sellers; but individual markets exist for many specific goods and services. Economists might refer to the lumber market, the cell phone market, the home health services market, and many others. You might hear people talk about money markets or the housing market. The agricultural market is a broad term, while the corn market is more specific.

Every market has a structure, which is the way that market operates. Market structures vary depending on what people are buying and selling in it and how specialized that market is. The stock market, for example, operates differently from the market for antiques, even though both deal with supply and demand and prices. The number of producers in a market can vary depending on the goods or services they provide. The number of buyers in a market will vary also.

Markets are interrelated, in that what happens in one market can affect what happens in other markets. Increased demand in the oil market, for instance, can raise prices in the corn market. This is because companies can make ethanol, which is a substitute for gasoline, from corn. Ethanol is more attractive when oil prices go up. In another example, a decrease in the price for a video streaming service might lead to a decrease in the price for movies on disc. If more people pay for a streaming service, the demand for movies on disc may fall, which would lead to a price reduction.

People offer goods and services in markets. Services involve the performance of work or professional activity. An attorney offers legal services. A lawn care company offers lawn service to individual customers and to businesses. In neither case does the buyer purchase a material item (except perhaps a legal document, such as a will). Instead, the buyer pays for work that the provider does for him or on his behalf.

We can define goods in several ways. *Capital goods* are things like machinery for which people make a major investment and then use to produce other items. *Producer goods* include tools and raw materials that people use to make other products. *Consumer goods* are what end users purchase to meet their wants and needs and what they consume, such as candy bars and light bulbs. We can further divide consumer goods into *durable goods* such as cars and refrigerators, which are intended to last a long

Lesson 26 - How Markets Work

time, and *non-durable goods* (sometimes called *soft goods*) such as cleaning supplies and clothing. People consume these items in the short term and thus these non-durable goods do not last long. Generally, durable goods are more expensive.

Markets involve producers and consumers. Individuals and companies are both producers and consumers. A toy company, for instance, consumes energy and produces toys. A worker at the toy company provides the labor that produces toys and consumes food and clothing.

What Markets Do

Markets accomplish several key functions in the economy. First, markets define the nature and extent of economic freedom in an economy. The kinds and amounts of the goods and services that are available in the market, the ability of consumers to obtain those goods and services in the market, and the ability of producers to bring new and improved goods and services to the market are all indicators of the economic freedom that is present in an economy.

Second, markets accomplish the allocation of resources and the distribution of goods and services that most fairly reflect what buyers and sellers value. In other words, a free market provides what sellers want to offer and what buyers want to obtain. People sometimes call a market economy a consumer economy or a consumer-driven economy because the driving force is what consumers want and are willing and able to buy.

Third, markets determine the amount of goods and services that producers offer and the prices that they charge for those goods and services. In the United States, no bureaucrat sits in Washington or in a state capital and decides how many toy stores, for instance, can open in a city and what each store can charge for each item. Bureaucrats do make those kinds of decisions in a command economy such as North Korea.

In a market economy, what determines those amounts is what the toy market will bear; in other words, whether there are enough consumers in the toy market in a city to support the number of toy stores that are open and the prices that toy buyers are willing to pay. No bureaucrat decides what businesses can charge for a computer or for a dress. The market also determines this. If computers cost more than what most people are willing and able to spend, fewer people will buy them. If the price that consumers are willing to pay is too low, producers will not be able to continue making them profitably.

Toys "R" Us store in Newport News, Virginia (2014)

Competition

Markets enable both sellers and buyers to compete. *Competition* takes place when there are many sellers and many buyers for the same or similar goods and services. Economists use the term *perfect competition* for the situation in which there are many sellers and buyers and where each individual seller and buyer has a negligible effect on the price that sellers charge and buyers pay. *Imperfect competition* is when there is a limited number of suppliers or buyers and one of either can have a significant effect on price. We will discuss examples of imperfect competition such as monopolies in Lesson 30.

Sellers compete in several ways. They compete in terms of price, quality, product design, product variety, customer service, and advertising effectiveness. If the Alpha Company produces widgets for 49 cents each, the Beta Company will look for ways to make comparable widgets for 44 cents (perhaps by using less expensive materials or more efficient machines) or ways to make widgets for 49 cents that have more features or come in a wider variety of colors than those that Alpha produces. If the Gamma Company ships orders for widgets in five days, the Delta Company will offer to ship orders in two days. The Epsilon Company, which produces a comparable widget, might develop an advertising campaign that appeals to buyers more effectively than the advertising campaigns of other companies. These are all ways in which sellers compete with each other.

Several factors affect the level of competition in a market. These factors include the number of buyers and sellers in the market, the ease with which new products can enter the market, the information consumers can obtain regarding the goods and services that sellers offer, and the quality and quantity of substitute goods and services.

Competition benefits buyers or consumers in several ways. Competition motivates suppliers to

Farmer's Market in Portland, Oregon

improve product quality and availability and to offer better customer service. It encourages greater productivity, which leads to lower costs of production, which leads to lower prices. Competition motivates people and companies to invest in more advanced technology that will improve the operation of the business, such as in production or record-keeping.

Competition also fosters economic growth. If widgets become popular, more people will want to get into the widget business and build new factories which will employ more workers. This leads to a better quality of life as people benefit from owning widgets and as more people have jobs producing them. As we discussed in an earlier lesson, the self-interest of suppliers in producing items that people want leads to more choices being available, which increases the national level of well-being. Markets enable this dynamic to happen.

A command economy is not built on the principle of competition, but even a command economy will usually have some limited form of competition. When goods are scarce because of command policies, a black market or illegal market will often develop for goods for which there is high demand. Black market sellers might import goods illegally or sell goods that are stolen from government factories and sold to black marketeers. These goods will provide competition for items available in state-run stores.

Ways of Influencing the Market

In a market economy, sellers are supposed to compete on the basis of the value they offer buyers. Sometimes, however, sellers get together behind the scenes to influence the market in a practice called *collusion*. Collusion is defined as secret cooperation for a dishonest purpose. Providers in a market (say the passenger airline industry) might decide that they will all raise their prices ten percent, or the companies in collusion with each other (say the retail home improvement industry) might decide to allow each company to take over the market in a particular region of the country (Company A in the South, Company B in the Midwest, and so forth). Collusion that uses artificial constraints other than the competitive market to fix prices or reduce competition in order to raise prices is a restraint of trade. Such action reduces competition and is against the public interest. Collusion is often difficult to detect. In the United States, collusion is illegal.

Collusion is relatively more difficult in a market with many sellers because it is unlikely that many providers will agree to such an arrangement. One or more sellers would likely not participate and would try to take business away from those who made the collusion agreement.

A group of providers that engage in collusion to increase profits is called a *cartel*. One of the best known world cartels is the Organization of Petroleum Exporting Countries (OPEC). No international law forbids such collusion. The number of countries that export petroleum is relatively small, and OPEC representatives meet regularly to set production goals in order to limit supply, increase demand, and thus maximize profits.

The actions of OPEC have contributed to an overall increase in oil prices, but the cartel has historically not been effective in maintaining discipline among its members. A primary principle by which countries operate is that of national self-interest. One or more OPEC members will routinely decide that their self-interest is better served by ignoring the cartel agreement and increasing production in an attempt to increase their profits.

A *boycott* is an organized action by buyers to bring attention to what they see as a wrong policy in an attempt to change that policy. Boycotts are legal as long as they are voluntary and nonviolent. The right to buy includes the right not to buy. However, coercion to enforce a boycott, such as a union intimidating or expelling members who do business with a particular company that the union leadership opposes, is an action that is in restraint of trade and is illegal in the United States.

Rosa Parks receives the Congressional Gold Medal (1999)

In 1955, the Montgomery, Alabama, bus system practiced racially-segregated seating. Rosa Parks, a black woman, refused to give up her seat to a white man. This was a violation of city law, and Parks was arrested. In response, black residents boycotted the Montgomery city bus system. This boycott caused a significant loss of revenue for the city and highlighted its unjust policy of segregation and discrimination. The boycott lasted over a year, at which time the Montgomery city government agreed to end segregation and discrimination on city buses.

For many years some nations and companies participated in a boycott against the Republic of South Africa because of that country's policy of apartheid or racial segregation. Various groups have organized boycotts to promote particular causes. For instance, some groups encourage people not to buy the products of companies that sponsor what the group sees as immoral television programs or programs with hosts that are advocates of positions with which the group disagrees.

Do Markets Exploit the Poor?

A common charge made against market economies by those who favor a command or socialist economy is that markets exploit poor people. These advocates say that the capitalist desire to offer goods and services at the lowest possible price drives down wages for workers who produce goods that the workers themselves cannot afford at their income level.

A typical scenario that these advocates describe is that of an American company paying workers in a foreign country a few dollars per day to produce goods that it will sell in America for many times what the company pays the worker. In addition, critics charge that markets exploit poor buyers who do not have the education or discernment to reject crass or misleading advertising appeals.

However, competitive markets are the best way for the poor to become better off. Market economies

Lesson 26 - How Markets Work

tend to make life better for more people than do command economies. The freedom of a market economy allows and encourages technological progress, makes more and cheaper goods available to more people, and gives entrepreneurs the opportunity to develop new products that can create wealth for owners and workers.

Poverty is present in market economies for several reasons, which we will explore later, but the evidence is overwhelming that widespread and chronic poverty is more common in command economies because they lack the competition that motivates providers to offer better goods and services at lower prices. In a command economy, a larger percentage of people are poor because only the relatively few leaders and planners have the opportunity to get the best of things.

Companies generally pay workers in other countries less than what they pay workers in the United States, but when a factory is built in a third-world country people flock to it hoping to get a job. The wages they hope to earn are better than what many other people earn in those countries.

Wages and working conditions have improved in the United States since the late 1800s. This did not happen because of a command economy but because of a free economy with agreed-upon regulations. The same kind of progress is taking place in many developing countries today. Markets, not bureaucratic management of the economy, offer the best opportunity for the poor.

Jesus had a different purpose for going to a market. When Jesus went to a physical market place, others heard about it and brought their sick to Him there. All those who touched the fringe of His cloak were healed.

Wherever He entered villages, or cities, or countryside,
they were laying the sick in the market places, and imploring Him
that they might just touch the fringe of His cloak;
and as many as touched it were being cured.
Mark 6:56

Assignments for Lesson 26

Making Choices   Read "The Markets and Human Values" (pages 55-61).

Literature   Continue reading *The Rise of Silas Lapham*. Plan to finish it by the end of Unit 7.

Project   Choose your project for this unit and start working on it.

Student Review   Answer the questions for Lesson 26.

Greeting card display, Toronto, Canada (2013)

27 Supply and Demand

> *Advice is the only commodity on the market where the supply always exceeds the demand.*
> — Anonymous

Markets work on the principle of supply and demand. Suppliers or producers offer goods and services in the market, and consumers purchase the goods and services they want and need. The circular flow diagrams on pages 12 and 13 illustrate this dynamic.

Supply

Supply is the total amount of a product or service that is available for purchase. The factors that a producer considers when deciding what product or service to supply in the market and in what amount to supply it are called *determinants of supply*. These factors include:

Price of the product. Can a supplier receive a price for his product or service that will make it worthwhile for him to offer it?

Price of substitute goods. Will he be able to make a profit despite competition from other similar goods or services?

Disposable income. Do potential buyers have the money to purchase it?

Price of resources. Can the producer afford the materials needed to make the product at a price consumers can afford?

Changes in technology. Can new technology, such as the invention of better manufacturing equipment, make production less expensive?

Expectation of future price increases. Can the producer reasonably expect to continue making a profit, especially if that locality experiences a rising cost of living?

Number of suppliers. Is the market for this good or service already crowded?

Consumer tastes. Do people want this good or service?

Taxes and subsidies. Does the government offer any incentives or disincentives for producing this good or service?

The law of supply states that, all else being constant, as the price for a product or service increases, production will increase. Producers have an incentive to supply more when they believe that they will make more profit by doing so. On the other hand, as the price for a product or service decreases, production will decrease. In addition,

Lesson 27 - Supply and Demand

when the cost for what a supplier has to pay for resources or ingredients or any factor of production increases, production falls, meaning that producers produce fewer products to sell. Conversely, when the cost of production falls, supply increases. In other words, supply is directly related to price and inversely related to the cost of production, which means that as cost of production increases, supply decreases.

Suppose the average retail price of a greeting card at a discount store is $2.00. At this price, the Howdy-Do Greeting Card Company prints 100,000 cards per year. But then a rage for sending greeting cards sweeps the country, and the increased demand causes cards to begin selling for $2.50 each, with no immediate increase in the cost of production. Howdy-Do begins to produce another 50,000 cards per year. The supply increased as the price increased.

However, eventually Howdy-Do has to hire an additional worker, which increases its production cost. Then, because of the increased demand for cards, the demand for cardstock on which the company prints the cards also increases and the price of cardstock goes up. This causes the production cost of Howdy-Do cards to increase further.

The owners of Howdy-Do decide that they will lay off the additional worker and only print 100,000 cards. The supply decreased because the cost of production increased. However, since the demand for cards is still high, the company now can actually make more money printing fewer cards and having fewer employees than when it was at maximum production.

Graphing Supply

Two graphics commonly portray supply. The first is a *supply schedule*, which is a chart showing how much of a product or service a company will supply at a given price. Look at the supply schedule at the top of the next column.

Supply Schedule for the Howdy-Do Greeting Card Company

Retail Price Per Card	Quantity Supplied
1.00	0
1.50	50,000
2.00	100,000
2.50	150,000
3.00	200,000

If the retail price per card was $1.00, the company could not afford to produce any cards; but as the retail price per card increases, the company is willing to produce an increasing supply of cards.

The graph below that illustrates supply is called a *supply curve*. This is a graph with x and y axes showing the relationship between price and quantity supplied. Again, as the price increases, production increases. In economics, the price is always the y or vertical axis and the quantity supplied is always the x or horizontal axis. The graph is called a curve even though it is a straight line.

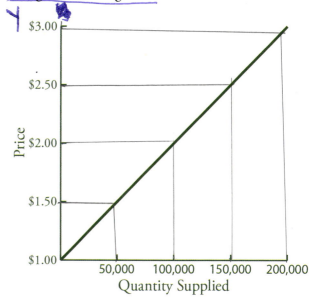

Note that the supply curve slopes upward from the lower left to the upper right and is typically drawn as a straight line for illustrative purposes. This graph illustrates the law of supply (as price increases, production also increases).

Demand

The other side of the principle of supply and demand is *demand*, which is the total amount of a product or service that consumers are willing to purchase at a given price. The factors involved in causing consumers to purchase goods and services are called *determinants of demand*. The main determinants of demand are:

- **Price.** How much does a product or service cost?
- **Price of substitute goods.** What is the cost of another product or service that could satisfy my needs and desires?
- **Price of complementary goods.** What additional goods or services will I have to buy if I buy this one? (See additional explanation below.)
- **Population.** What is a reasonable estimate of the number of people who will want to buy this product or service?
- **Level of income.** Can those people afford it?
- **Personal tastes.** Will they want it?
- **Government policies.** Will buying this good or service force me to complete government paperwork? Can I get a tax deduction if I buy it? Will I have to pay an additional tax if I buy it? Are there any government health or safety warnings that discourage me from buying it?

The law of demand states that, all else being equal, when the price of a good or service rises, demand falls. Likewise, when prices fall, demand increases. Demand is inversely related to price. Returning to the greeting card example, increased demand led to the retail price rising to $2.50 each. Then some companies began producing fancier cards for $3.00 each. As a result, the average price for all cards began rising toward $3.00. Card companies were happy to produce more cards at this price; but as a result of this development, consumers started changing their habits. They began using plain paper, making phone calls, and sending emails. The demand for greeting cards fell as the price increased.

Economists have classified four kinds of goods. *Normal goods* are those for which demand rises when income rises. People generally want more of these goods when they are more able to purchase them. *Inferior goods* are goods for which demand rises as income falls. If people have less income, they settle for products that are inferior to what they had bought previously, such as cheaply-made clothes rather than ones of higher quality. *Substitute goods* are comparable but slightly different from (and often of a somewhat lesser quality than) another product. Substitute goods are those for which demand rises when the price for another product rises. Because of an increase in the price for one product, consumers buy something else instead. *Complementary goods* are products that people commonly purchase together, so much so that a change in price for one product leads to a change in demand for the other. For instance, a decrease in the price of spaghetti will lead to an increase in demand for tomato sauce.

Derived demand is the demand by a producer for a factor of production related to consumer demand. For example, producers who make shirts have a derived demand for more sewing machines to produce more shirts.

Lesson 27 - Supply and Demand

Graphing Demand

Like supply, we can illustrate demand in two ways. The *demand schedule* is a chart that shows the relationship between price and demand. As seen below, this schedule shows that cards offered at $1.00 each would generate a large demand. At the other end of the price range, shoppers at discount stores would not want to pay $3.00 per card.

Demand Schedule for the Howdy-Do Greeting Card Company

Retail Price Per Card	Quantity Demanded
1.00	200,000
1.50	150,000
2.00	100,000
2.50	50,000
3.00	0

A *demand curve* on a graph also shows this information.

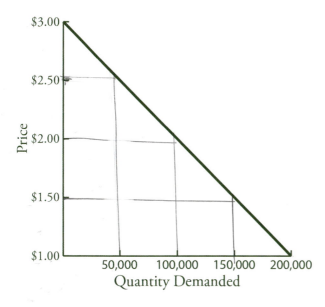

The demand curve (line) slopes downward from upper left to lower right. It is the opposite of the supply curve. Thus we see that, as the price rises, demand decreases. The dramatic changes in gasoline prices during 2008 demonstrated this reality. As the price for gasoline rose to about $4.00 per gallon, consumers decreased their demand for it. They took fewer pleasure trips, consolidated shopping trips, and used alternative means to get to work instead of driving their cars. Eventually gasoline prices fell, in part because of this lower demand that resulted in a greater supply of gasoline on the market. The greater supply caused prices to decrease.

How Supply and Demand Work Together

In a free market, *sellers determine supply and buyers determine demand*. As we noted earlier, as price increases, suppliers are motivated to increase supply; as price decreases, buyers are motivated to increase demand. When the price is too high, suppliers have a *surplus* or excess supply on the market because consumers do not want to pay that much. When the price for a product or service is too low, buyers face a *shortage* because the excess demand is greater than suppliers' willingness or ability to produce goods and services at lower prices.

The conflicting principles regarding supply and demand are:

1. Suppliers tend to offer more when prices are high; but

2. Consumers tend to buy more when prices are low.

The law of supply and demand states that the price of a product or service adjusts to bring supply and demand into balance. We can demonstrate this by putting the supply curve and the demand curve on the same graph.

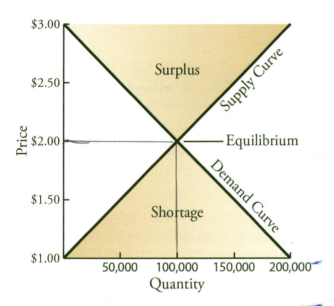

The point at which the supply curve and the demand curve cross is called the *equilibrium price* or *market clearing price*. This is the price for which suppliers are willing and able to offer their goods and services and the price that consumers are willing to pay. Theoretically, this is the price that will bring about the sale of all of a particular product or service in the market. Thus we see that supply and demand affect the quantity of goods and services offered in the market and the price charged for those goods and services.

In our example, consumers would be happy to buy a large quantity of cards at $1.00 each, but Howdy-Do could not supply them at that price and make a profit. On the other hand, Howdy-Do would be happy to supply a large amount of cards at $3.00 each, but the company would not sell any. On the graph, we see that the equilibrium price for greeting cards is $2.00. The conflicting principles mentioned above intersect at the equilibrium price. We also see the illustration of surplus and shortage. Surplus exists when supply exceeds demand, and shortage exists when demand exceeds supply.

The example used here and the laws of supply and demand are a simple theoretical construct designed to help us see how the complex economic market works. Things usually do not work out this neatly. It is rare that exactly 100,000 greeting cards are sold for exactly $2.00 each and then the shelves are bare. Some cards will not be sold even at the equilibrium price, perhaps because the supply of cards in one location exceeds the demand there.

These leftover cards might be sold at a deep discount to a bargain store, where they are offered at a much lower price; or they might be collected by the distributor and sold to a recycling company that will turn them back into plain paper to be used for some other product. On the other hand, the supply could theoretically be exhausted and some consumers would have to use plain paper or email to send their greetings.

Which Comes First: Supply or Demand?

Does a producer develop a product or service and then develop a market for it among buyers, or does a demand for a product or service arise among consumers and then producers respond by making goods that meet that demand? The answer is yes; it can happen both ways. Few producers will pursue an idea for a product just on the hope that sufficient demand will develop. History is littered with inventors' big ideas that went nowhere with the public. Instead, producers usually try to meet the wants and needs that they perceive already exist among potential customers.

Sometimes products come to market because of accidental discoveries. This was the case with Post-It Notes. In 1970 a 3M Company researcher was trying to develop a strong adhesive, but instead he came up with a weak adhesive that didn't stick very well and thus didn't seem to have a market. Then four years later, another 3M scientist was singing in his church choir. The markers he used to help him find the songs kept slipping out of his book. He remembered his co-worker's weak adhesive, applied some of it to small pieces of paper, and the Post-It Note was born. Through 3M's effective marketing

Lesson 27 - Supply and Demand

and promotion, the company was able to identify and help develop a demand for note paper that stuck, but not too tightly.

More often, producers respond to a demand—or at least a perceived demand—from consumers. The increase in the number of women working outside of the home contributed to a greater demand for house cleaning services, which today is a multi-million dollar industry.

Scientists developed the first computer in response to a need by the United States Army during World War II to calculate artillery trajectories quickly. Advances in computer speed and capacity moved relatively slowly until people saw the possibilities for computers performing many kinds of functions using digital technology. Besides performing calculations, computers could handle word processing, information storage and retrieval, graphic design, and eventually communication among many computers. Technological improvements in memory capacity and processor speed made computers faster, smaller, and more powerful. The supply of more advanced computers has increased to keep pace with the growing demand for faster, smaller, and more powerful computers.

Say's Law

French economist Jean-Baptiste Say (1767-1832) proposed a principle that relates to supply and demand, which has since become known as Say's Law, which asserts that the production, or supply, of products creates a demand for products. People often rephrase this, somewhat inaccurately, as "supply creates its own demand."

According to Say, the pay that workers receive for producing goods provides those workers with the means whereby they can purchase what they produce as well as what others produce; and thus demand grows as supply grows. As many industries across the economy follow this principle, the economy grows. Supply sometimes exceeds demand in some segments of the economy, which results in a surplus and therefore temporary unemployment for some workers; but Say believed that the market generally corrects itself such that supply and demand remain in fairly close balance.

In this view, the economy grows by increasing supply or production, not by increasing consumption. This view holds that production creates consumption. Pay people to work and produce, and that will generate demand.

The Electronic Numerical Integrator And Computer (ENIAC), built during World War II, filled an entire room and required extensive training to use. Six women performed most of the early programming of the machine, including Ruth Teitelbaum and Marlyn Meltzer (pictured below). Today approximately two billion people around the world, such as these men in India, carry a smartphone that has much more computing power and many more capabilities than the ENIAC.

Price controls and other government policies in Venezuela have led to product shortages for many years. Though this supermarket had an excess of some products, it was completely out of others.

By contrast, classic Keynesian theory (mentioned on page 33) emphasizes aggregate demand. For Keynesians, demand determines the amount supplied. Keynes advocated government programs to stimulate demand during periods of recession by providing relief payments to individuals so that consumers would be able to purchase goods. This demand, Keynesians say, will enable producers to hire people and put them to work. Proponents of Say's Law would say that such programs take potential investment money that could stimulate production and instead direct it to the government's use. Such programs slow down or even prevent the recovery that would result from the stimulation of production.

Stimulating demand or stimulating production might sound like two sides of the same coin, but the difference it makes relates to the kind of economic policies the government should pursue. Should government encourage an increase in production, which then will produce demand among consumers? Or should government try to stimulate demand by focusing on assistance to individuals who can then increase consumption? In determining what to do, politics gets involved because some elected officials believe that, if government assistance is spread throughout a larger segment of the voting public, the people will re-elect those representatives who supported government assistance programs to them. We will discuss this topic more in the lesson on the Great Depression.

Lesson 27 - Supply and Demand

Aggregate Demand and Aggregate Supply

While economists talk about supply and demand in terms of a particular product or service, such as computers or health care; the terms they use for the overall economy are *aggregate supply* and *aggregate demand*. The *aggregate supply* is the total quantity of goods and services that all sellers are willing and able to provide at any price. *Aggregate demand* is the total of all goods and services that all households, companies, and the government are willing and able to buy at any given price in a given period of time. The four components of aggregate demand are consumption, investment, government spending, and net exports.

Aggregate supply and aggregate demand are macroeconomic (big picture) terms. They are especially important when discussing government policies that affect the overall economy. People involved in making economic policy for the government consider changes that would increase production or increase disposable income. They also evaluate how changes in tax laws might affect aggregate supply or aggregate demand.

Sometimes we human beings have to do things to stimulate supply in order to meet our demands. By contrast, we can count on the greatest Supplier to meet all our needs out of His great abundance.

> *And my God will supply all your needs according to His riches in glory in Christ Jesus.*
> Philippians 4:19

Assignments for Lesson 27

Making Choices — Read the excerpt from the interview with the Soviet refugee (pages 62-65).

Literature — Continue reading *The Rise of Silas Lapham*.

Project — Continue working on your project for this unit.

Student Review — Answer the questions for Lesson 27.

Gas prices in Indiana (2011)

28 How Much Does It Cost?

The price of anything is the amount of life you exchange for it.
— *Henry David Thoreau*

Price is what consumers pay when they buy a product or service and what suppliers receive when they sell a product or service. Price is a powerful factor in economics. Consider some of the roles that prices play.

The Power of Price in a Market Economy

Price influences supply and demand. The quantity supplied varies directly with price (that is, the higher the price, the more that is produced). The quantity demanded varies inversely with price (the higher the price, the less that is demanded).

Price determines who does what work, or even what work is done at all. Goods that do not command a price that generates a profit for the supplier do not get produced. Costlier goods are generally produced by more skilled workers, who usually get paid more.

Price determines who is able to have the goods and services that are produced, according to consumers' ability to pay. Those who are not able to pay as much do not have as much.

Price affects consumers' buying habits. Consumers will buy less or will buy substitute goods when prices are high.

Price is an efficient way to allocate scarce resources. Prices reflect the value that people place on resources. Higher prices mean a higher perceived value, sometimes because a resource is scarce or because it is expensive to produce. As we noted earlier, price is a more efficient way to allocate scarce resources than having central planners make guesses.

Price is the determining factor in creating market equilibrium, the point at which supply matches demand.

While these are ways in which price is a cause for certain things to happen in economics, price can also be an effect. Various factors can have an

Lesson 28 - How Much Does It Cost?

effect on prices. Competition has an impact on prices. Competition among buyers for the same amount of goods supplied leads to higher prices because prices rise when demand exceeds supply at the existing price. Competition among suppliers for the same number of buyers leads to lower prices because prices fall when supply exceeds demand at the existing price.

Facts About Prices

Everything has a price. Price reflects what consumers value and the choices they are willing to make. People commonly think of prices in terms of the prices they pay for goods and services, such as the price of bananas or the price a plumber charges for a service call; but everything has a price. The price for money is called interest. The price for labor is expressed in terms of wages and salaries.

In everyday conversation, price and cost are practically synonyms ("How much did that jacket cost?" "The price was thirty dollars.") However, in economics, price is what a consumer pays for a product or service; while cost refers to the supplier's cost of production.

Markets determine prices. In the market, generally speaking, buyers want the lowest price possible and sellers want the highest price possible. A producer of gourmet candy bars does not simply decide that it will charge $5.00 for its candy bar. The producer has to determine the minimum price it can charge to make production worthwhile, as well as what price the market will bear by considering the price of competing candy bars, the price of substitute goods such as other candy, and how many bars the company is likely to sell at given prices.

A *price maker* is a producer who has enough influence in the market to have an impact on what price is charged for its product or service. A *price taker* is a producer who has little influence on the market by itself and is forced to charge the prevailing price for its product or service. Rolls-Royce is a price maker. The company can essentially set its own price for its luxury cars—within reason—because it has little or no direct competition and because of the perceived luxury and exclusivity of its cars. People who want and can afford a Rolls-Royce aren't usually worried about the price. Milk producers, on the other hand, are price takers because they have to sell their milk at the prevailing price in the market, where consumers are concerned about price.

2014 Rolls-Royce Wraith in Hong Kong

A *relative price* is the price of one product or service expressed as the price for another product or service. An economist might say that the relative price of one apple is two potatoes. Relative prices demonstrate the value that one product or service has compared to another.

Relative prices are also helpful in measuring the relative scarcity of goods and services. For instance, the fees that medical specialists charge are usually higher than those that general practitioners charge. Specialists must have additional training that adds to the cost of their education, and they have a relatively smaller field of potential patients that they will see. Suppose the price for a consultation with a specialist is $300 and the price for an office visit with a family doctor is $100. The relative price of a trip to a specialist is expressed as three office visits to the family doctor.

Price and Prosperity

A common assumption is that business owners build wealth by being able to charge higher prices for a particular product or service. However, America's great wealth and economic strength have actually come about largely because American businesses have lowered prices for goods and services, which has brought more buyers into the market.

Sam Walton opened Walton's 5-10 (five and dime) in 1951 in Bentonville, Arkansas. He opened his first Walmart store in 1962. The original Walton's store is now home to the Walmart Museum.

Before Henry Ford developed assembly line production of automobiles, cars were primarily playthings for the rich. The assembly line made lower-price autos available to more people, and this development is what built Ford's great wealth. There are only so many rich people a company can sell to, but being able to sell to the mass market enables business owners to build greater wealth. *TRUE*

In the same way, Sam Walton did not become a multi-billionaire by raising prices at Walmart stores. Instead, he became wealthy by lowering prices and making the goods at Walmart stores accessible to a greater number of people.

These and many other examples show that price is indeed a powerful tool in the marketplace. They also show that, many times, the smaller tool is more effective in getting a job done.

Price Discrimination

You might think that setting a price for a product or service would be simple: determine the cost of production, decide how much profit you want to make, set the price, and put the product or service on the market. But setting prices in order to make the most profit is not that simple. A variable factor is the willingness of different consumers to pay a given price. Producers respond to this different level of willingness by the practice of *price discrimination*, which is selling the same product to different consumers at different prices. This might seem unfair; but companies do it all the time, and we consumers accept it. Let's see how the process works.

First, imagine a monopolist who can charge any price for his product. He sets a price for the product, and some people buy it while others do not. Some who buy it would have been willing to pay more for it, and some who didn't buy it would have been willing to pay a lower price for it, so the producer's profit is less than it could be. But now let's also assume that the monopolist knows how much each consumer is willing to pay for the product. The

Passengers board a Ryanair plane at Lech Walesa Airport in Gdansk, Poland, in 2015. Ryanair is a budget airline that started in Ireland in 1985 and now carries passengers across Europe.

monopolist will charge those various prices, and the result will be a greater profit.

We can be thankful that true monopolists are rare in our economy. However, companies still practice price discrimination to increase their profit on the basis of consumers' willingness and ability to pay different prices. For instance, most museums, amusement parks, and other businesses that charge an admission fee charge less for children. Parents might not be willing to pay the adult rate for a child and would choose to stay home, but the lower children's rate is an incentive for parents to bring their children. The result is greater profit for the amusement park or other business.

One of the great mysteries of life is the wide variation in airline ticket prices. It is possible that no two people on a plane paid exactly the same price for their tickets, even though they all got on the same plane and went to the same destination. Airlines know that some people are willing to pay any price for a ticket, that some business travelers don't care what the ticket costs because the company is paying for it, and that some travelers are cost-conscious and want the best deal possible. Some people use a travel agent (who gets a fee from the airline for providing their services to the customer), others just want to do business with their favorite airline, and still others scour the Internet themselves for cheap tickets. Airlines set prices at different levels for a certain number of seats on each flight. As the time for departure nears, the price for unsold seats might change. The whole process is price discrimination. It works because the flying public accepts it.

Some companies sell goods to high-price stores, the same companies sell some goods (sometimes the same goods) to mid-price stores, and still other goods to discount stores. If they put all of their goods in one kind of store, they might not be able to make a profit because they wouldn't have enough customers in one kind of store. However, by distributing their goods to a wide range of consumers and using price discrimination as they determine the market for their goods in each kind of store, the company can make a profit.

Artificial Price Controls

Many economists believe that the best way to bring about economic growth and improved economic well-being for the greatest number of people is to allow markets to operate by supply and demand so that prices will approach equilibrium without government intervention or other artificial attempts to control prices. People who impose artificial price controls say they want to help consumers, but in most cases they actually hurt the people they are claiming to help. They distort what would be normal price incentives for the transactions between producers and consumers.

As we indicated in the previous lesson, the market-clearing price is the price at which supply and demand intersect. A *price ceiling* is a maximum-allowable price set by the government that is below the market-clearing price. When the government sets a price ceiling, the price that a business charges consumers cannot go above the ceiling.

A common example of a price ceiling is rent control, which sets into law a maximum allowable amount of rent. This is a policy in many large cities. The stated intention of the law is to ensure the availability of affordable housing for the poor. What actually happens is that, over the long term, landlords have no incentive to maintain or improve housing units they own (usually apartments) because they cannot recover their expenses the way they could if they could raise rent to the level that the market would allow. If a landlord cannot earn a profit by charging only the legally allowable rent, he or she will close the building instead of operate it at a loss. The result is that, instead of creating a supply of affordable housing, there is a shortage of decent, affordable housing because of the market distortion caused by rent control. Price ceilings lead to consistent shortages of goods and services because many providers do not find it worthwhile to offer the goods and services at the allowed price.

On the other hand, a *price floor* is a minimum-allowable price set by law that is above the market-clearing price. When a price floor is decreed, prices cannot go below the floor. The United States government sets a price floor for many agricultural products. The government guarantees farmers a minimum price; and over the years the government has limited production or bought up the surplus at the artificial minimum price floor to keep the price at or above the floor. A price floor creates a surplus because farmers grow more to take advantage of the guaranteed minimum prices and because some people cannot afford to pay the resulting higher prices for food.

Agricultural price supports were supposed to help small farmers, but today large agricultural corporations actually receive the bulk of government assistance. Although agricultural price floors are poor economic policy, they enable elected officials to brag about helping two voting groups: farmers, who receive government payments, and the poor, who receive government assistance for buying food.

The Diamond-Water Paradox

A common brain teaser for students of economics is the paradox of value, also known as the diamond-water paradox. The paradox is that, although water has greater practical value than diamonds—in other words, it is more necessary to life—water is much less expensive than diamonds. Why is this vital commodity so cheap?

Many philosophers and writers have mentioned this paradox. Adam Smith discusses it this way in *The Wealth of Nations*:

> The word VALUE, it is to be observed, has two different meanings, and sometimes expresses the utility [usefulness, or ability to provide satisfaction] of some particular object, and sometimes the power of purchasing other goods which the possession of that object conveys. The one may be called "value in

This worker in Sri Lanka is grinding a diamond. A Chinese billionaire paid the highest price ever for a diamond at an auction in 2015: $48.4 million.

use;" the other, "value in exchange." The things which have the greatest value in use have frequently little or no value in exchange; and on the contrary, those which have the greatest value in exchange have frequently little or no value in use. Nothing is more useful than water: but it will purchase scarce anything; scarce anything can be had in exchange for it. A diamond, on the contrary, has scarce any value in use; but a very great quantity of other goods may frequently be had in exchange for it.

Several factors help to resolve the apparent paradox. Generally speaking, people have to expend less labor to acquire water than the labor needed to obtain diamonds. This explains the apparent paradox from the perspective of the labor theory of value, but other and more sufficient explanations exist.

The supply of water is much greater than the supply of diamonds, so we would expect water to have a lower price. Water is necessary for life, and the Lord provided it in sufficient amounts for living things to have. For most people in the world today, the supply of water exceeds the demand. The very thirsty person in a desert would give many diamonds to have even a little water, but that is an exceptional case that proves the general truth.

The theory of marginal utility helps to explain the apparent paradox. Marginal utility is the satisfaction that the next unit of something provides. Generally speaking, society values a unit of water less than a unit of diamond. The marginal utility or usefulness of one unit of diamond is greater than the marginal utility of one unit of water. People value another diamond more than they value another cup or gallon of water. In addition, the next unit of water is more easily available and thus worth less than the next unit of diamond. Supply and demand explain a great deal in economics, but other principles, such as the theory of marginal utility, are important as well.

The apparent diamond-water paradox actually proves the truth of supply and demand. Although the demand for water is great, the supply is greater. This keeps the price of water comparatively low. The supply of diamonds is limited and the demand is great. This drives up the price of diamonds.

Another reminder from this discussion is that, however much we try to define economics in terms of objective principles, we cannot escape the subjective human element of the topic. People want water and they want diamonds, but they want these goods in different ways and thus they value them differently.

The Influence of Price

Price is a powerful motivation for economic activity. It influences what goods and services producers make available, how they produce the goods, and who obtains them. Prices reflect how people value goods and services. Because of the power of price for consumers, businesses and individuals can be tremendously successful on the basis of what they charge for goods and services. Interference with the operation of price can have a detrimental effect on the process of supply and demand. Never underestimate the power of price.

Jesus told two parables that described the joy of people who learned the true price of the kingdom of heaven. Even though the price was very great, these people willingly paid the price because they understood the value of the kingdom. The price is significant in these parables because the price reflects the immense value of what carried the price.

The kingdom of heaven is like a treasure hidden in the field, which a man found and hid again; and from joy over it he goes and sells all that he has and buys that field. Again, the kingdom of heaven is like a merchant seeking fine pearls, and upon finding one pearl of great value, he went and sold all that he had and bought it.
Matthew 13:44-46

Assignments for Lesson 28

Literature Continue reading *The Rise of Silas Lapham*.

Project Continue working on your project for this unit.

Student Review Answer the questions for Lesson 28.

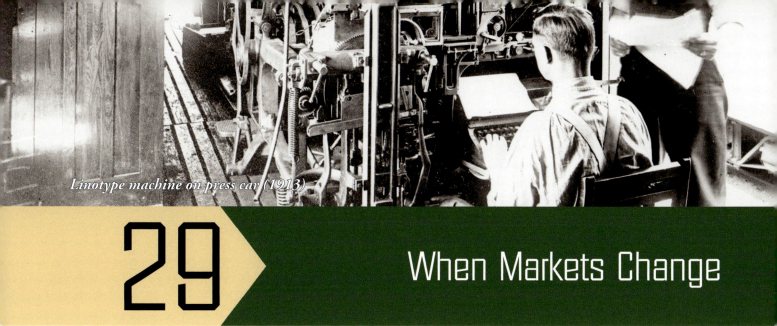
Linotype machine on press car (1913)

29 When Markets Change

I lost my job ten months ago. I am a printer by trade. The new linotype machines are beautiful specimens of invention, but . . . . Of course, I don't blame the newspapers for getting the machines. Meanwhile, what can a man do? I've never learned but the one trade, and that's all I can do. I've tramped all over the country trying to find something. There are a good many others like me. . . .

— Unemployed typesetter in the novel In His Steps

In the novel *In His Steps*, the desperate man who came first to Henry Maxwell and then to Maxwell's church looking for help revealed by these words that he had been a victim of economic change. Printing technology had changed from handset type to linotype machines, and men whose work was once essential to the publishing industry were now unnecessary. In previous centuries, the economy did not change much over long periods of time. Today the rate of change is rapid.

Changes in Markets

Markets are constantly changing because the goods and services that producers supply and the goods and services that consumers want are constantly changing. Existing companies as well as start-up entrepreneurs are continually bringing new products to the market. Much of what consumers have to choose from today was not available twenty or thirty years ago. In addition, producers constantly improve production methods; and developers create new technologies to produce and sell goods. These changes are a form of competition, as new goods and services compete with and sometimes replace existing ones.

At one time, the mark of an up-to-date office was whether it had a new model typewriter. Today, typewriters are hard to find; almost all offices rely on computers. The mainstay of American transportation used to be the horse-drawn carriage. Now it is the automobile. The production of iron was once a major part of the American economy; but after steel came onto the scene, steel production soon dwarfed America's iron output. The markets for typewriters, horse-drawn carriages, and iron are quite different today from what they were many years ago.

171

Three college students in Finland made a mobile game in 2003 and started a company together. When they released Angry Birds in 2009, it was their 52nd project. As of 2016, people around the world have downloaded Angry Birds games three billion times. The headquarters of Rovio Entertainment is pictured in this office complex in Espoo, Finland, in 2012.

The methods of producing and delivering goods and services have changed dramatically also. Production of certain goods for the American market has shifted to other countries such as Mexico and China because labor costs are significantly lower there than they are in the United States. On the other hand, companies in the United States and around the world are creating completely new goods such as mobile apps. The small general store used to provide customers in most small towns with goods that they needed. Catalog sales introduced a new way of shopping that eliminated the need for even going to stores for many items. In turn, the Internet changed the importance of catalogs.

Farming used to be all-natural, and distribution only involved a farmer's local area. Railroads, especially refrigerated cars, vastly expanded the market for agricultural goods. Chemicals increased yield, but they have also brought problematic health side-effects. Today a growing segment of farming involves, of all things, a return to the past: all-natural methods and a focus on local markets.

Even the companies that offer goods and services change. New businesses come into being, and existing businesses fold every day. The number and identity of auto companies that offer products to American car buyers have changed significantly over the years. Pontiac and Oldsmobile have joined Studebaker and Hupmobile as automobile makers that once were but now are no more. New companies such as Hyundai and Kia have earned a place in the American market.

Fortune magazine began publishing a list of America's top 500 public corporations in 1955, focusing on manufacturing, mining, and energy companies. The list started including service companies in 1994. Of the original 500 companies, only 61 (12%) remained on the list in 2015.

These changes do not come without an impact on the economy and on individuals and families. Change is difficult. The typesetter in *In His Steps* illustrates this impact. The alternative to changing, however, is failing to improve and grow. Jobs will be lost as production methods and markets for goods and services change; but new jobs requiring new skills will appear as the economy grows and changes.

Adjusting to the changes take time and effort. In the short run people do suffer economically. State and federal governments provide job retraining programs to help workers make this transition. Meanwhile, some of the people affected by these changes will decide to go into business for themselves.

By the way, my father operated a linotype machine for a newspaper for a number of years. When I first read *In His Steps*, I was unsettled by the thought that a machine that Dad had used to support his family had, when it was first introduced, caused some men to lose their ability to support their families. Dad worked for the newspaper long enough to see another technological change, when computer-driven typesetting machines replaced linotype machines.

Changes in Supply and Demand

Several factors affect the supply of goods and services in the market. These factors have a primary influence on suppliers. One leading factor is price. A change in the price of an item, or a change in the price of the factors of production, can change supply. As we noted in an earlier lesson, as the price of a product or service increases, supply increases because producers expect more profit. However, as the price for resources to make the product increases, supply of the product decreases because the producer expects less profit (unless the price for the product increases also to match the higher cost). Changes in technology that lessen the cost of production tend to increase supply.

The number of sellers in the market can affect supply, since more sellers will tend to offer a greater aggregate supply. The opportunity for profit by the seller, which any number of factors can influence, can change supply as well. Factors affecting profit include increased government regulations that add additional expense and new or increased taxes that discourage purchases.

Factors that affect demand center on consumers. In addition to changes in price, demand can change because of a change in consumers' income, changes in consumer preferences, the number of consumers in the market, and the price of related goods and services. Related goods and services are those things that consumers will probably need to buy in order to use another product or service. For instance, if the price for streaming music decreases significantly, the demand for earbuds will likely increase even if the price of the earbuds themselves does not change.

Effects of Changes in Price

An increase in the price of a good or service causes consumers to look for substitutes, and demand for the original item decreases. Often an increase in the price of goods or services is an attempt by suppliers to cover increased costs of production, usually materials and labor.

A price increase for one product or service can lead to price increases for other products and services. An increase in electricity rates will likely cause an increase in the price of labor, because workers in many industries will likely demand higher wages in order to pay their electricity bills. The cost of these higher wages will likely be passed on to consumers who purchase the goods and services that those workers produce in the form of higher prices.

Price stability exists when prices in an economy do not change significantly over a long period of time. Such a situation implies that neither inflation nor deflation is a problem. Unfortunately, price stability is rare. The long-term trend in the United States has been for prices to increase; however, products and services offered in the market are constantly changing, and prices for some products (such as computers) can decrease at times.

Changes in the Supply and Demand Curves

Recall the supply and demand graph from Lesson 27:

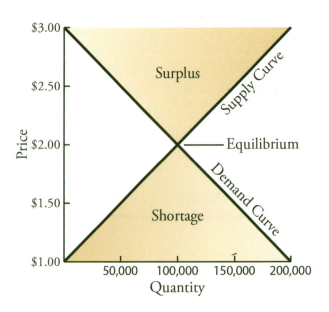

We can change the graph to show changes in supply, demand, and price. First, we'll consider the demand curve. When price changes, demand simply moves up or down along the demand curve. This is what the graph is intended to show.

However, when a factor other than price changes, the demand curve shifts left (inward) or right (outward). For instance, if consumer income increases, people will be more willing to buy greeting cards whether at a higher price or at a lower price. Thus, the curve shifts outward.

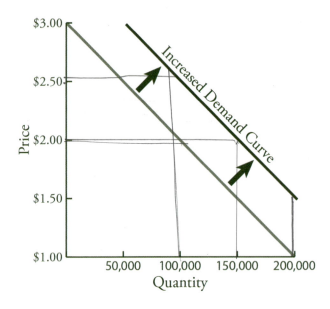

The same principle is true for the supply curve. When price changes, supply moves up or down the supply curve. When another factor affects supply, the supply curve itself shifts left or right. Suppose a new printing technology enables printers to print more cards at the same cost. The supply curve shifts outward. With this change in production cost, suppliers would be willing to produce more cards at both lower prices and higher prices.

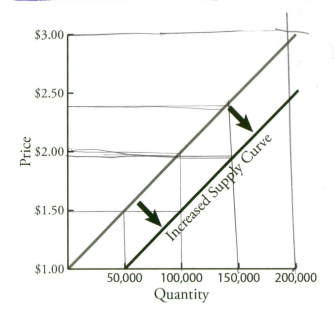

When either the supply curve or the demand curve shifts, or when they both shift, the result changes the equilibrium or market-clearing price.

Lesson 29 - When Markets Change

Elasticity

So, markets change; and buyers and sellers respond to changes in the market. But how much do factors change, and how much do buyers and sellers change what they do because of these factors? We can determine answers to these questions by studying what economists call *elasticity*. Elasticity is a measure of how much supply or demand changes as a result of changes in other factors.

Price elasticity of demand is a measure of how much demand changes in response to changes in price. The answer indicates whether buyers consider a product to be a necessity or a luxury, a need or simply a want. If consumers see a product or service as a necessity, demand will not change much even if the price changes. People still feel a need for the product despite the increased cost. For instance, if the price of insulin changed significantly, people with diabetes would still buy it. The price elasticity of demand for insulin is very small.

In another example, when food prices increase, few people will quit eating. They might change what they eat, or they might eat at restaurants less; but they will still buy food. Demand for food is fairly inelastic; in other words, demand does not change even with increased prices. Generally, the more narrowly we define the market, the more elastic (changeable) is the demand. While the food market is fairly inelastic, a price increase would likely affect the market for steaks; and people would buy something else instead of steaks. Demand for steaks is more elastic than demand for food in general.

Another factor influencing elasticity is whether a product has a close substitute. Demand for name brand macaroni that had a price increase would likely be elastic if generic or store brands were available.

The graphs below illustrate elasticity and inelasticity.

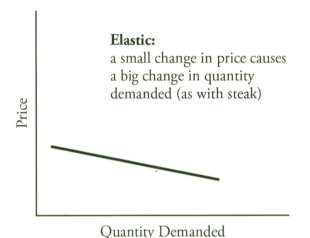

Elastic: a small change in price causes a big change in quantity demanded (as with steak)

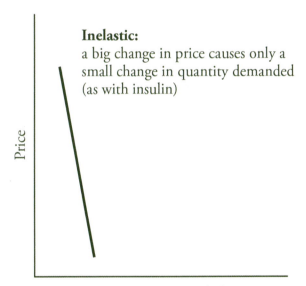

Inelastic: a big change in price causes only a small change in quantity demanded (as with insulin)

Insulin syringe

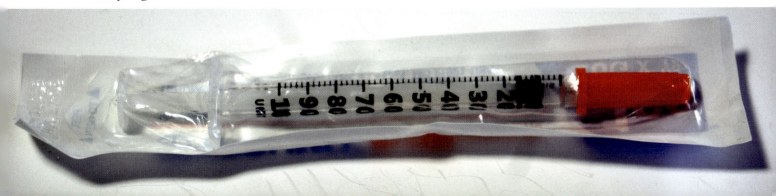

Satellite TV dishes in The Netherlands (2010)

Cross-price elasticity of demand is a measure of how much demand for one product changes because of a price change for another product. When substitutes are available for a product, demand for a substitute will likely increase when the price of a product increases. An increase in cable television rates, for instance, could mean a greater demand for satellite television service. When goods are complements (that is, using one good involves using another), a price increase for one will likely cause demand for both goods to fall. For instance, a rise in the price of printers will likely result in lower demand for printers as well as print toner.

Income elasticity of demand shows how much demand changes with regard to consumers' income. Generally, income elasticity of demand is small for what people believe to be necessities. They will likely buy necessities whether their income goes up or down. Income elasticity of demand is greater for luxuries. People are more likely to buy luxuries if they have greater income and less likely if they have less income.

Price elasticity of supply shows how much the quantity supplied changes because of price. This provides another way to express the general principle that supply increases as price increases.

A formula for each of these principles provides a numerical reading for these indicators of elasticity. For each indicator, the formula is:

$$\frac{\text{percentage change in X (either demand or supply)}}{\text{percentage change in price (or income)}}$$

Lesson 29 - When Markets Change

For instance, if demand for product A goes down 30 percent when the price goes up 10 percent, the price elasticity of demand would be 3 (30 ÷ 10). This is a significant decline in demand because of a relatively small percentage change in price. The rule in economics is that if the absolute value of elasticity shown by the ratio above is less than one, the demand for that product or service is considered to be inelastic (not very changeable). If the absolute value is greater than one, the demand for that product or service is considered to be elastic.

elasticity < 1 = inelastic

elasticity > 1 = elastic

Another statistic related to elasticity is the *impact on total revenue*, which is how changes in price affect total revenue. If demand for a product or service is inelastic, revenue will increase as price increases because consumers will buy the product or service as a necessity, regardless of price. If demand is elastic (that is, if demand can change), an increase in price will lead to lower revenue as consumers choose not to buy the product because of the higher price.

Short-Term and Long-Term Changes

Although the economy is constantly changing, significant changes in supply and demand usually occur gradually instead of dramatically. The supply and demand curves represent long-term trends. People tend to accept changes in price in the short term but then decide to change their behavior in the long term. For instance, if the weather affects the citrus fruit crop in Florida, consumers might pay a higher price for a time; but as the citrus prices remain high consumers will likely decide to buy other farm products.

Some significant changes occur slowly because some elements of the economy are *sticky* or slow to change. For instance, even when prices are increasing due to inflation, wages are usually sticky or slow to change because many workers have contracts that are in force for one or more years or because employers are not likely to adjust wages every few weeks or months. Prices for some resources and for some finished goods are sticky if a signed contract commits a supplier to a certain price for a period of time.

Workers pick up grapefruit after a storm in Florida (1906)

Changing prices have an economic impact on suppliers of goods and services. This impact is called a *menu cost*. This term comes from the practice of restaurants getting menus printed with prices that the owner hopes will be profitable for a long time. It would be expensive for a restaurant to get new menus printed every month or two. If a restaurant faces an increase in prices for the food it buys from a supplier, the restaurant is likely to keep menu prices the same for the short term. Eventually, however, the restaurant will need to adjust its menu prices to reflect the restaurant's increased costs more accurately.

Sometimes significant changes do occur quickly. These are called *supply shocks* or *demand shocks*. A supply shock occurs when the amount of goods or services available for sale increases dramatically (as when a new technology suddenly reduces the amount of time it takes to make a product) or when the amount of goods and services decreases dramatically (as when truckers go on strike and producers cannot obtain the supplies they need).

A demand shock occurs when there are dramatic increases in demand for a product or service (as when stores experience a run on supplies before a hurricane comes ashore) or when there are dramatic decreases in demand for a product or service (as when consumers learn that a product is contaminated and stop buying it). The impact of these shocks is significant, but supply and demand generally return to more normal levels over the long term.

We do not know what changes we might face as we go about our daily business. We are ultimately dependent not on economic principles but on the will of the Lord.

Come now, you who say, "Today or tomorrow we will go to such and such a city, and make a profit and spend a year there and engage in business and make a profit." Yet you do not know what your life will be like tomorrow. You are just a vapor that appears for a little while and then vanishes away. Instead, you ought to say, "If the Lord wills, we will live and also do this or that."
James 4:13-15

Assignments for Lesson 29

Literature   Continue reading *The Rise of Silas Lapham*.

Project   Continue working on your project for this unit.

Student Review   Answer the questions for Lesson 29.

Russian version of the Monopoly board game

30 When Markets Fail

> *The inherent vice of capitalism is the unequal sharing of blessings; the inherent virtue of socialism is the equal sharing of miseries.*
> — Winston Churchill

In this unit, we have discussed how markets that operate on the basis of supply and demand are an efficient way to distribute goods and services. Not only are goods and services available to people who can pay for them, but market economies also make possible the economic productivity and growth that enable more people to have the money to buy goods and services. Price is the key factor that makes supply and demand work. Competition helps keep prices low. In the ideal market, supply and demand cause the market to be cleared of all goods and services that are offered at the equilibrium price.

However, we live in the real world. Not all markets for goods and services are cleared. Supply and demand based on price does not always bring about the most efficient distribution of goods and services. *Market failure* occurs when the market fails to allocate resources efficiently.

The Monopoly

The best-known and probably the most-feared form of market failure is the *monopoly*. If one seller of a product or service controls the entire supply of that product or service in a certain region, without other suppliers or customers having a close substitute, that is called a monopoly. With a monopoly, the single supplier can determine the price for and availability of what it offers.

Having a monopoly might sound like an ideal position for a producer, but a monopoly has many negative attributes for consumers. A monopoly is the enemy of efficiency because the supplier has no motivation to improve production or distribution. Monopolies tend to produce less (and to provide goods and services of lower quality and with higher prices) than when competition exists. A monopoly can be bad for the producer as well. It is possible for public resentment to build toward a monopoly, to the point that many will choose to do without rather than to buy from the monopolist.

Monopolies do not allocate resources efficiently in an economy. Monopolists do not make goods and services available to all who can afford them based on competitive prices. Instead, only those who are able to pay the monopolist's price can obtain the

179

product or service. The actions of the monopolist can result in a scarcity of some products and a surplus of others; but because there is no competition, the monopolist producer does not make those surplus products available as widely as they are available in a competitive market.

An important point about monopolies is that they usually need laws in place that give them special protection. The presence of these laws implies the presence of political conditions that limit individual freedom. In a free market, one or more entrepreneurs will almost always develop substitute goods to compete with a potential monopolist. To protect consumers, monopolies are illegal in the United States.

True monopolies are rare in a market economy. In a sense, every company has a monopoly on the products that it produces; but in most cases other companies have competing or substitute goods that prevent monopoly conditions from existing. For instance, the Coca-Cola company has a monopoly on Coca-Cola. No other company can produce that exact product. However, many other soft drink companies compete successfully with Coca-Cola by offering other soft drinks, so the soft drink market is not monopolistic.

Shades of variation exist with regard to monopolies. *Monopolistic competition* is when several producers offer unique goods and services that, while they are different, still compete with each other. In monopolistic competition there are many buyers and sellers, no one producer controls the market, producers can enter the market freely, consumers can discern non-price differences among the producers, and producers have some degree of control over price. One example of a market with monopolistic competition is the restaurant market. In a sense, Chili's, Applebee's, and Ruby Tuesday each have a monopoly on what they offer; but in another sense they all compete for the same customers who want to dine out.

One company can so dominate a field that it is sometimes said to have a *virtual monopoly*. Some believe that Microsoft has a virtual monopoly on computer operating systems with its Windows product. About 90% of computers sold in the

Coca-Cola products available at a store in Bucharest, Romania (2015)

United States come with the Windows operating system installed. However, Microsoft still develops new and more advanced versions of Windows regularly because the people who run the company know that competing products exist or that another company can produce one. The presence in the computer market of many computer hardware companies that include the Windows operating system along with different features, as well as the presence of Apple computers with its operating system, provide a degree of competition for the Windows products.

Every state has compulsory school attendance laws for children. About 11 percent of children attend private schools, about 2 percent are homeschooled, and the rest attend public schools. Some would say that public schools have a virtual monopoly on education in America. Many indicators suggest that this virtual monopoly has not improved the quality of the service that public schools offer.

Another form of monopoly is called a *natural monopoly*. This is a situation in which economies of scale are such that a single provider can provide and distribute particular goods or services most efficiently. The most common example of a natural monopoly are utilities such as water and electricity service. It would be expensive, unsightly, and probably economically harmful to have two or more sets of electrical transmission wires, water pipes, or sewage disposal lines running throughout a town. What has developed in most places is that one company or one department of government provides a service for a city, but laws regulate the provider in terms of what it can charge, how much and how often it can increase rates, and the quality of service that it provides. A county that grants a license to a utility might also require the utility to extend service to rural areas. No one expects such a provider to lose money, but regulations prevent the provider from charging exorbitant fees since it is the only choice for electricity that people have.

But the economy is always changing, and as a result some natural monopolies do not seem so natural any longer. For instance, many communities have historically contracted with one cable television provider to offer service to residents. In such a situation, the local government regulates the cable company in terms of price and quality of service. The contract is for a set period of time and undergoes a review every few years before the local government renews it. Several national companies offer cable television service, so competition exists among them, even though the residents of a particular community might not have a choice about what cable service they have available. In such a case, the citizens must trust the government to make the choice of cable provider for them. Communities have also traditionally had one provider of telephone service as a public utility.

However, some cities no longer recognize a natural monopoly in such industries and now allow multiple providers to compete for customers of television service and telephone service. Satellite television providers that contract with individual consumers offer direct competition to cable systems. Cellular phone companies also provide competition to what are called landline companies. To make the situation even more complicated, because of advances in digital transmission technology, some companies offer telephone, television, and Internet service directly to consumers either separately or in package deals. As a result of this competition, consumers are able to benefit from lower prices, better quality, and improved service. If a customer is not pleased with one company, he can change to another provider.

Other Forms of Imperfect Competition

A monopoly exists in a market when there is one provider of a particular product or service. An *oligopoly* is where there are only a few large providers, and any one of those providers can have an impact on the market. One example is the passenger jet construction industry. Only a few companies in the world make passenger jets, so any one of them can have a major impact on the market.

A *monopsony* is a market in which there is only one buyer or only one significant buyer. In the United States, the federal government is the primary buyer of military aircraft. Other countries might purchase American-built planes, but domestically there is only one buyer of what the relatively few builders of military planes have to offer. As a result, the government has a large influence on the nature of planes that are produced. Aircraft manufacturers have to listen to what the government wants if they expect to receive a construction contract. Some economists see major sports leagues as monopsonies. The National Football League, for example, is the most significant buyer in the professional football labor market, even though other leagues exist.

An *oligopsony* is a market in which there are only a few major buyers, any of which can exert a significant influence on the market. Large grocery store chains have something of an oligopsony in buying agricultural products. A few national chains buy the vast majority of the food that farmers grow for retail sale in the United States and much of what farmers in several other countries grow as well. Small local farmers have little chance to sell what they produce to large grocery chain stores, unless that chain's local stores make agreements with local farmers. In another example of an oligopsony, only three tobacco product companies buy 90% of the tobacco grown in the United States.

Factors That Cause Market Failure

Market failure can occur for several reasons. Monopolies cause market failure because a company with a monopoly does not have to set its price as a result of competition. The monopolist can charge whatever he wishes. Some customers will be able to buy, and some will not. The goods and services that a monopolist supplies will not be distributed efficiently to the widest possible number of people at the market-clearing price. The position of a monopolist or of oligopolists is sometimes called *market power*. Shortages and surpluses matter less to someone who controls the entire market.

Taxes affect supply and demand equilibrium by increasing the cost of goods and services. This increased cost tends to lower demand. Look at the chart below. Supply Curve 1 shows the ideally efficient supply without taxes. Supply Curve 2 represents the movement of the supply curve after the imposition of a sales tax. Demand decreases because of the higher price. The effect of the tax is to move the market away from greatest efficiency. The imposition of income taxes has the same effect, since consumers have less money to purchase the same offerings of goods and services. Higher taxes that government imposes on businesses leave less money for companies to pay workers. This results in lower employment and lower job creation.

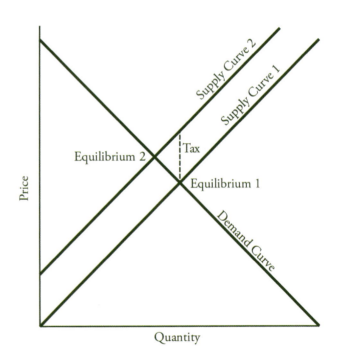

Of course, governments would be hard pressed to operate without some level of taxation. National defense, police protection, and other public goods and services that government provides cost money (we will define public goods shortly). Our society agrees through the decisions of elected officials to fund public goods. Some might say that the public goods which government provides simply replace

Lesson 30 - When Markets Fail

some private goods in the economy. However, governments usually do not provide services as efficiently as private companies do; so there is some effective loss to the economy because taxes tend to interfere with the operation of supply and demand in the market, and higher taxes tend to interfere more.

Price and quantity regulations interfere with market operations. We noted in Lesson 28 how artificial price floors and ceilings that government sets cause inefficiencies in supply and demand. We will see later in this lesson that government orders for the production of certain quantities of goods also prevent the most efficient intersection of supply and demand.

Externalities in the marketplace affect people who are not the actual buyers and sellers in a transaction. Industrial pollution is a commonly-cited externality. A company produces goods to sell to buyers, but in doing so it emits pollution that affects the health of other people who neither make nor buy the products.

In another example, a smoker buys and smokes cigarettes from a store, and a child in the smoker's house develops health problems as a result. Those health problems involve costs that the people affected have to pay, but they are not considered part of the cost of production and the buyers of the products do not pay for them.

When government does not define or enforce property rights well, markets do not allocate resources well. *Property rights* involve the right to exclusive use of property and the right to sell or give the property to others. Supply and demand assume that a producer owns the product and can sell it to a new owner. A lack of protection of property rights discourages people from buying goods or services. If the title of ownership for a piece of property is not clear or if the government can seize the property of individuals at any time without cause, people will be reluctant to purchase a house or a piece of real estate.

Public goods are a reflection of market failure. *Private goods* are goods that one person, household,

Air pollution in Cleveland, Ohio (1973)

or company owns and consumes. They are what we usually think of when we think about goods and services. Public goods, by contrast, are goods and services that more than one person can use at a time. Public roads and public parks are examples of public goods.

Private companies are not likely to make a profit if they offer such goods, so markets generally do not provide them. Instead, the government offers these goods for the public as a whole to use. Taxes all taxpayers pay (and in some cases fees that users pay) fund public goods. However, some people who pay taxes do not use all of these goods; for instance, elderly people do not receive direct benefit from public schools. Children in schools and out-of-town visitors in a park are two kinds of people who use public goods but do not pay for them.

Government can help prevent market failure by keeping markets competitive, by not protecting monopolies, by minimizing public goods and keeping taxes low, by keeping regulations to a minimum, by making sure that the entities which produce externalities bear the costs of them, and by clearly delineating and defending property rights. Government contributes to market failure when it fails to maintain these policies.

Failure to Have a Free Market: What Happened Under Communism

Imagine living in an economy in which supply is determined not by what producers want to make and consumers want to buy but by what bureaucrats decide ought to be produced, where prices are determined not by what the market will bear but by what government officials think ought to be charged, where there is no competition that would lower prices and improve customer service, and where producers and workers are guaranteed that they will keep their positions regardless of productivity, quality of service, or level of sales.

You don't have to imagine it. These were the characteristics of the Communist economies in the Soviet Union and Eastern Europe during much of the 20th century. The Communist party took control of the economies of these countries just as it took control of their governments. And, just as the Communists managed to ruin political life and harm society, they also destroyed the economies of those countries because they did not allow market dynamics to work.

Communist Party officials thought they could guide the economy by top-down decisions instead of by allowing markets to work from the bottom up. They couldn't. Bureaucrats couldn't replicate all of the knowledge diffused throughout millions of producers and consumers that enables markets to work (remember the essay, "I, Pencil").

Government planners feared punishment if they deviated from established rules—even if the rules were ridiculous—so they had no motivation to take risks or to propose changes. Planners decided how to distribute resources and raw materials according to what they wanted or what they thought party leaders wanted, not according to what potential consumers wanted. As a result, some industries had a surplus of materials that sat unused while other industries lacked materials and sat idle.

One story illustrates the dynamics of this kind of command economy. A friend of ours, who spent a year teaching in Communist Poland, told us about another American living in Poland who wanted to buy a large-sized shirt. All this person could find was small-sized shirts. He eventually learned the reason why.

Shirt factories received a quota for the number of shirts the bureaucrats expected them to make, and then the factories received a certain amount of cloth with which they were to make the shirts. As a result, all or nearly all of the shirts they made were small so that they could meet their quota, without regard for the actual market demand for different shirt sizes. This was typical.

Residents of Bucharest, Romania, stand in line to purchase cooking oil (1986)

The Institute of National Remembrance in Poland released a board game in 2011 to educate people about the economic situation in former Communist countries. Called Kolejka (meaning "queue"), players must send family members to stand in line to buy everyday products. If the stores run out, players can turn to the black market. The game became so popular that supply did not keep up with demand.

Stores had piles of some products and shortages of other products because that reflected what government planners had ordered, and subordinates dared not question the orders from higher up. This situation did not occur because the Communist world lacked resources; the Soviet Union had rich resources. It occurred because central planners allocate goods and services poorly while prices in the market allocate goods and services effectively.

Market changes and market failures remind us of the uncertain and fluid nature of economies. During an economic downturn, people in the media often talk about "the uncertain economy." But history has shown that we always have an uncertain economy. We never know for sure what will happen in the coming weeks, months, or years. The periods of prosperity and difficulty that people have experienced have been of varying duration, and the heights and depths to which the economy has moved have been of varying intensity.

The only certainty we have about the economy is that we can't take it with us when we leave this world. Even in this world, wealth is a poor source of security. All markets will eventually fail, so we should be sure that our most important investment—our very self—is in the hands of the One who will never leave us nor forsake us.

*Do not store up for yourselves treasures on earth,
where moth and rust destroy, and where thieves break in and steal.
But store up for yourselves treasures in heaven,
where neither moth nor rust destroys,
and where thieves do not break in or steal;
for where your treasure is, there your heart will be also.
Matthew 6:19-21*

Assignments for Lesson 30

Literature — Continue reading *The Rise of Silas Lapham*.

Project — Finish your project for this unit.

Student Review — Answer the questions for Lesson 30 and take the quiz for Unit 6.

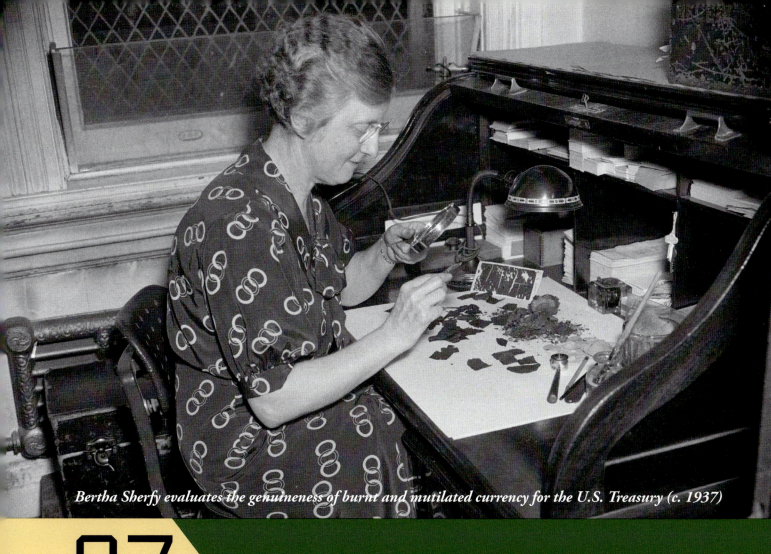

Bertha Sherfy evaluates the genuineness of burnt and mutilated currency for the U.S. Treasury (c. 1937)

07 Money

Money is a medium of exchange that makes the selling and buying of goods and services easier. Money is also a representation of value, a store of value, and a unit of accounting. Governments have moved away from basing their money on the gold standard in favor of issuing fiat currency. Banks and other financial institutions help to create wealth and help an economy function. Investments such as loans, stocks, and bonds that individuals and financial institutions make help the economy grow. Inflation is a general increase in the price of goods and services across the economy. The Federal Reserve System is the central bank of the United States. The Fed oversees the U.S. banking system and has a significant influence on the economy.

Lesson 31 - What Is Money Worth?
Lesson 32 - How Banks Work
Lesson 33 - Wise Investing
Lesson 34 - Inflation (Not Our Friend)
Lesson 35 - What Is the Fed?

Books Used

The Bible
Making Choices
The Rise of Silas Lapham

Project (choose one)

1) Write 300 to 500 words on one of the following topics:

   - How do banks benefit your family? Be specific about the services your family uses and why.

   - Do you think that income from investments should be taxed at a higher rate than other forms of income? Explain why or why not (see Lesson 33).

2) Choose a local bank and call, visit, or use the bank's website to do the following activities:

   Investment: Determine the best long-term option for investment the bank offers. If you put $100 per month in this investment plan, how much would you have at the end of 30 years, assuming the interest on the investment remained the same?

   Mortgage: Find out the average interest rate for home mortgages from the same bank. If you had a $150,000 mortgage, payable over 30 years, how much would you pay per month? What would be your total payout over the 30 years?

3) Memorize 1 Timothy 6:6-10.

Currency exchange kiosk in Moscow, Russia (2010)

31 What Is Money Worth?

Money can't buy happiness.

— *American proverb*

Suppose you were visiting in a foreign country. You wanted to buy some food from a street vendor, but all you had were American dollars. In some countries, the vendor would not sell you anything because American money would not be worth anything to him. He would not know how much to charge you or how much change to give you. If he accepted your money, he would have to take it to a bank or currency exchange; and that might be too much trouble for him. He might make more money staying in his spot and selling to people who had the local currency. In that situation, even though you had money, your money would be worthless because you couldn't buy anything with it.

Or imagine that you are stranded alone on a remote island. Which would be more valuable to you: a suitcase full of money, or a suitcase full of tools to build a shelter and utensils to use in cooking food that you found on the island? Again, given the situation, your money would be worthless.

Money can't buy you salvation, forgiveness, hope, (genuine) friendship, peace of mind, or many other things that we value. For the most important things in life, money is worthless. So why do people spend most of their lives trying to obtain money? It is not just to have little pieces of paper printed with green ink. Money has value only in terms of the goods and services a person can obtain with it.

What Is Money?

Money might seem to be something that does not need defining, but for our purposes we need a clear understanding of it. *Money* includes currency, coins, and deposits in bank accounts—in other words, assets that are immediately available for exchange in a transaction. A common term for money is *liquid* assets; that is, assets that are accessible to use in transactions.

Liquidity refers to the ease with which an asset can be turned into money. Someone might have great wealth in terms of the masterpiece paintings she owns, but only when she sells a painting for money can she use that wealth to buy goods and services because the painting is not a liquid asset. Some assets are more liquid than others. The vegetables that you grow in a garden, for instance, are more liquid than real estate you own. You can sell the vegetables for money more easily than you can sell a house.

The Purposes of Money

Even though money does not have value in and of itself, it has significant value in terms of what it represents and what it can do. First of all, money is a *medium of exchange*, which is a commonly agreed-upon object of value to both parties in an exchange. Having an accepted medium of exchange makes the buying of goods and services easier.

Barter can be a complicated process. If you wanted a table and had only chickens to trade, you might be able to agree with the table-maker on the number of chickens you would have to give for a table. But what could you do if the table-maker did not want chickens? Either you or he would have to take the chickens somewhere else to obtain something of equivalent value that the table-maker wanted. But if you wanted a table and could pay for it with something that you had received for your chickens which had a value that both you and the table-maker recognized, this would simplify the process.

Modern societies have largely replaced barter with the use of money to conclude transactions. Some individuals and families are able to barter their goods and services with others, but in society as a whole the use of money as a medium of exchange has become the way we do business. In addition, because money as a medium of exchange expresses value more precisely than chickens and tables, it makes transactions on the whole less expensive. You can pay a half dollar in a transaction fairly easily, but paying a half chicken would get messy.

Second, money can function as a medium of exchange because money is a *representation of value*, a way to show value to those with whom you are doing business. If you have worked for someone or sold goods or services, you have received money. That money represents the value that your employer or your customers placed on your labor or on your goods or services. Money is also a way to show the comparative value of different goods and services. It demonstrates that a visit to the dentist's office has higher value than a movie ticket and that people value a steak dinner more than a doughnut.

Third, money is a *store of value*, that is, a way to maintain the value of your labor over a long period of time. If you save money, and perhaps even earn interest on it, the amount of money you have will provide you with a way to enjoy the fruit of your labor over many years. Money gives you a way to store up value so that you can make purchases in the future.

Front and back of silver coin from India (c. 500 BC)

Lesson 31 - What Is Money Worth?

Printing plate for making paper currency in China (c. 1000 AD)

If you wanted to buy a car in three years and you wanted to pay for it by growing potatoes, you might try storing up potatoes for three years. However, the car dealer probably would not accept three years' crops of potatoes in payment. Besides, most of the potatoes would have rotted by then. On the other hand, if you grew potatoes, sold them for money year by year, and saved your profits, you could take the money you had saved to the car dealer and buy a car.

Fourth, money is a *unit of accounting*, a way to demonstrate success or failure in a business or other endeavor. The money that a person has (or owes) represents how well that person has worked or has guided a business. It shows how much he has earned, how much debt he has, and in great measure whether the effort has been a success or failure.

Using money as a unit of accounting is a more objective way to determine success or failure than emotions ("I enjoy doing this so much, I can't understand why we're broke") or anecdotes ("We had a lot of sales at the first of the month, and the local paper did a story on our business last week. I thought we had a lot of customers coming in..."). Being happy in your work is important, but that doesn't by itself pay the bills.

The Gold Standard and Fiat Currency

People have used money to purchase goods and services and as a store of value for centuries. Historically, one common medium of exchange was gold. Gold is an example of *commodity money*, or money that is a commodity that has value in itself. Gold has intrinsic value, which means that it has value separate and apart from its use as money. But carrying around large amounts of gold is cumbersome and dangerous. You might lose it or someone might steal it. So people devised gold certificates (sometimes called *representative money*), which were pieces of paper that stood for amounts of gold that were held in a secure place. A person who received these certificates as payment could redeem them for actual gold when it was convenient for him to do so. People also used silver as commodity money to a lesser degree.

When paper money that a government issues represents gold, the currency is said to be on the *gold standard*. For many years the United States and many other countries operated on the gold standard. People could exchange their currency for gold at any time, although few people actually made the exchange. They were satisfied to know that the government held in a safe place the gold that backed the money. (The federal government has historically held much of the United States' gold reserve at Fort Knox, Kentucky.) In some temporary situations, such as wartime, people could not immediately convert currency to gold.

The advantages of the gold standard were that it provided a concrete, reliable, stable basis for the currency that the government issued. It kept the money supply stable without much variation in amount or value, and the exchange rate between national currencies on the gold standard remained fairly stable. The economy did not usually experience significant inflation while on the gold standard.

The downside of the gold standard was that it restricted the money supply in the economy to the amount of gold reserves that the government held. Because of this inflexibility, unemployment tended to be higher on average because businesses could not obtain loans easily to expand. In addition, the gold standard does not reflect other forms of value, such as land or technological ability or productivity. Thus the gold standard tended to limit economic activity and growth and made those who owned the gold or the gold certificates the powerful players in the economy.

A copy of the 1933 executive order instructing U.S. citizens to turn in their gold, printed by the government for display in post offices.

The shock of a new discovery of gold led to short-term instability in prices as people tried to figure out the impact of the new discovery. In addition, the cost of mining gold and producing gold coins and bullion (blocks) was significant, and this drew resources away from its productive use in the economy.

The last part of the nineteenth century and the first part of the twentieth century saw many challenges and disruptions to the gold standard. In the late 1800s, a political debate raged in the U.S. over whether the federal government should expand the money supply by coining silver. The government did this to some degree at different times. Then World War I and the years of world economic instability culminating in the Great Depression affected many parts of the world.

In the early years of the Depression, foreign governments exchanged U.S. dollars for gold. This seriously depleted the country's gold reserves. In 1933 President Franklin Roosevelt issued an executive order that banned the private ownership of gold by Americans with limited exceptions such as jewelry and rare coins. Roosevelt's order also halted the automatic redemption of currency for gold. This removed the United States from the gold standard in practical terms.

In 1946, as part of the Bretton Woods agreements, many countries fixed the exchange rates for their currency to the U.S. dollar; and the United States set the price of gold at $35.00 per ounce. In theory, then, all currencies pegged to the dollar had a fixed value in terms of gold. During the 1960s, France exchanged many of the dollars it held for gold, which again depleted American reserves and lessened American influence in the world economy. In 1971, President Richard Nixon ended the fixed rate system. This allowed the value of gold as a commodity to float to whatever it might bring in the market. Nixon's move also ended the formal link between commodities and world currencies. President Gerald Ford lifted the ban on private ownership of gold in 1974.

The United States Bullion Depository at Fort Knox, Kentucky, opened in 1937, as seen in this postcard from that time. The depository holds about 350,000 gold bars, each worth about half a million dollars in 2016. According to the U.S. Mint website, "No visitors are permitted, and no exceptions are made."

The steps that Roosevelt and Nixon took created what is called *fiat currency*. A fiat is a decree or declaration by a government. Fiat currency is money that has value not based on its relation to a commodity but by a nation's government declaring that its money is legal tender. People can no longer exchange U.S. currency for gold or silver. Even our coins are no longer silver or gold but are alloys that have value by the fiat or declaration of the United States government. All the nations of the world have abandoned the gold standard and now issue fiat currency.

Some people object to fiat currency, saying that it is not as reliable as money backed by gold. But the United States and other countries suffered occasional panics when our money was on the gold standard; so the gold standard in and of itself is no guarantee of stability.

Today's billionaires, such as Bill Gates of Microsoft and the Walton family of Walmart, probably have little of their wealth in the form of gold. Instead, they have wealth in the form of real estate, stocks, and fiat dollars because they have produced goods and services which people have valued and have been willing to pay for. Those billionaires can take those fiat dollars to the store and can buy a real loaf of bread or a (very nice) shirt, or they can purchase a mansion, because those fiat dollars have worth in our economy. What is true for the billionaire is true for the rest of us also.

A major economic disruption could cause those fiat dollars to lose their value, but there is no absolute guarantee that having a stash of gold would help a person make it through the disruption if people did not accept gold as payment. Gold might work in such a situation, but that kind of dramatic scenario would be an enormous crisis unlike anything we have seen. It would likely have many other serious issues that would be hard to predict and prepare for entirely. Trying to prepare for such a doomsday situation by hoarding a large stash of gold seems to be operating on the basis of fear, not faith. How much gold would you need? Wouldn't you always think that you needed more, which dealers in gold would be happy to sell to you? And when would you ever dare to sell it?

The real worth of a currency is not something that a government establishes by decree; instead, a society's acceptance and use of a currency establishes its worth. If people do not trust their nation's money, they will find some other medium of exchange with which they can conduct business. In Europe during World War II, for instance, American soldiers and European citizens found that cigarettes served as a fairly dependable medium of exchange for goods and services in situations where money was scarce and the national currencies of Europe were unreliable because the governments were unstable.

Unlike the illustration at the beginning of this lesson, American dollars actually can be a medium of exchange in a country whose currency is worthless or unstable. People in such a country would rather have American dollars than their own country's currency. In those situations, American dollars have become an accepted medium of exchange, especially on the black market.

Bitcoin

The Internet has opened up new possibilities for financial activities. People have even created a new kind of currency using the Internet. Bitcoin is a digital currency that an anonymous developer announced in 2008 and released for use the next year.

People can obtain bitcoins by doing complicated math work on a computer (a process called "mining") and accepting payment in bitcoins. They can also trade traditional currency, products, and services for bitcoins. They store these coins in digital wallets. The system records transactions for goods and services, and those involved in the transactions do not have to reveal their true identities.

This cafe in Delft, Netherlands, advertises acceptance of Bitcoins (2013)

A slowly growing number of businesses and banks have accepted bitcoin payments. The attractions of bitcoins include anonymity, the fact that the fees are usually lower than typical credit card fees, and the fact that international transactions with bitcoins are easier than those which involve changing currencies.

However, the downsides are many. No government agency insures or guarantees bitcoins, so significant loss is possible and has sometimes taken place. The currency has been subject to wild fluctuations in value because of rumors, scandals, and instability in the bitcoin industry. The anonymity of the system has allowed some people to use it for criminal activity.

Governments have been unclear at times about determining the tax responsibilities of people whose bitcoin accounts have grown. Though some people and institutions have accepted bitcoin as a legitimate medium of exchange, its use still constitutes a tiny fraction of the world economy.

The Meaning of Money

People once understood that money had value because it represented gold. Today our currency does not represent gold, but it represents other forms of value that people in our nation do accept. And remember, money has value not in and of itself but in terms of what it can obtain in the form of goods and services.

Money is neither good nor evil in and of itself. People can use money to accomplish much good, but they can also use it to cause great harm. The difference is in what people do with it and in what they do to obtain it. As Paul pointed out:

*For the love of money is a root of all sorts of evil,
and some by longing for it have wandered away from the faith
and pierced themselves with many griefs.*
1 Timothy 6:10

Assignments for Lesson 31

Making Choices — Read the excerpt from *Principles of Economics* (pages 66-71).

Literature — Continue reading *The Rise of Silas Lapham*. Plan to finish it by the end of this unit.

Project — Choose your project for this unit and start working on it.

Student Review — Answer the questions for Lesson 31.

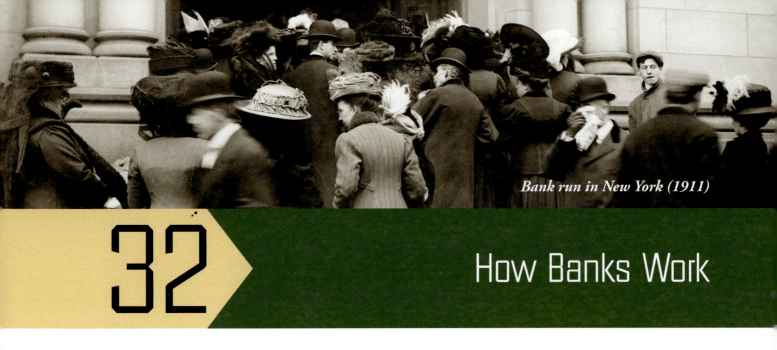
Bank run in New York (1911)

32 How Banks Work

You're thinking of this place all wrong. As if I had the money back in a safe. The money's not here. Your money's in Joe's house . . . right next to yours. And in the Kennedy house, and Mrs. Macklin's house, and a hundred others. Why, you're lending them the money to build, and then they're going to pay it back to you as best they can.

— *The character of George Bailey in the movie* It's a Wonderful Life (1946), *explaining during a run on the bank why everyone can't get his money out of the Bailey Brothers Building and Loan at the same time*

Banks and similar financial organizations are institutions in which people deposit their money. The banks then loan money to individuals and businesses. In this way, banks bring together people who want to save money and people who want to borrow money.

Banks render several services to the public:

Bank are safe places for people to keep their money—safer than in a cookie jar or under a mattress.

Banks enable people to earn money with their money by paying interest on the money that people have deposited there.

Banks encourage the buying of goods and services by allowing depositors to write checks or use a debit card on their deposits instead of their having to carry around cash to pay for purchases.

Banks provide a centralized place for borrowers to obtain loans, instead of potential borrowers having to go around from individual to individual to ask for loans. Consumer credit, which means borrowing by consumers, is a major area of banking activity.

Saving money is a great benefit to individuals and to the economy. When people save money instead of borrowing it, they are not relying on debt.

Lesson 32 - How Banks Work

Saving up for purchases rather than borrowing is a smart decision. Money saved in a bank helps increase productivity because banks use those savings to make loans to businesses so that the businesses can grow.

Experience has shown that people who save have a higher standard of living. They are able to live above the level of just getting by and of having to spend all of their income (and sometimes more than their income) on necessities. People who save are able to wait to make purchases, and thus they can often buy goods of higher quality.

How Banks Create Wealth

Imagine that a new bank opens its doors, and the first customer who comes in opens a saving account and deposits $1,000 in an account that pays 3% annual interest. The bank's assets stand at $1,000 in reserves. However, that $1,000 on deposit is also a liability because the bank is responsible for paying it to the depositor when he demands it.

The next customer is looking for a loan to buy a car. He has found a peach of a used model that only costs $900. The loan officer agrees to lend the man $900 at an interest rate of 6% per year. From the bank's perspective, the loan is an asset because the borrower agrees to pay it back plus the interest. The bank's assets still total $1,000 (now $100 in reserves and $900 in loans). The eager buyer goes to the car dealer and gives him $900. The car dealer then goes to the bank and deposits the $900. Now the bank's assets total $1,900 ($1,000 in reserve deposits and $900 in loans). All of this has happened with the same $1,000 originally deposited. The bank will now want to find a borrower for the latest $900 deposited so it can make a profit on that money as well.

In this way, as the bank repeats the process hundreds and thousands of times, the bank creates wealth by enabling the buying and selling of goods and services. This process is called *multiple-deposit expansion*. A bank's ability to be responsible for funds as well as to make loans with those funds is an example of the *money multiplier*, the rate at which a bank can create money with each dollar of deposits.

We can show a bank's assets and liabilities with what are called T-accounts, the T being the way that the chart displays assets and liabilities:

Assets		Liabilities
Reserves	$1,000	Deposits $1,900
Loans	$ 900	

Farmers State Bank in North Dakota was established in 1911. During the Great Depression, the bank lost many of its depositors and had to reorganize. The bank adopted the new name of McIntosh County Bank in 1940. This branch is located in the town of Zeeland.

A bank's practice of loaning out the majority of money that it has on deposit is called *fractional reserve* banking. Banks are only required by law to have on hand a fraction of the money that people have deposited in them. In the United States, that fraction is about one-tenth (10%) of deposits. Having only a tenth of depositors' money on hand sounds risky; but people are usually happy to leave their money on reserve at the bank, knowing it is safe and knowing that they are able to have access to it by withdrawing small amounts or by writing checks for part of the money they have deposited.

The Federal Deposit Insurance Corporation (FDIC) guarantees that the deposits people have made will be there (up to a certain maximum dollar amount) and that depositors can withdraw it, even though most of the money that customers have deposited is not actually sitting in the bank vault.

Congress established the FDIC in 1933 to protect the money that people deposit in savings accounts, checking accounts, money market accounts, and certificates of deposit in the nation's banks and savings institutions. Congress created the FDIC in response to the thousands of bank failures in the 1920s and 1930s.

This historic FDIC logo shows the original maximum amount covered by deposit insurance: $2,500.

The FDIC receives no tax dollars. Member banks pay insurance premiums, and in return the FDIC insures deposits up to a given amount. Currently the FDIC insures deposits up to $250,000 per depositor, per insured bank, for each kind of deposit. The FDIC also audits financial institutions to insure their soundness and oversees the process if a bank fails and goes into receivership. Since the FDIC came into existence, no depositor has ever lost a penny in FDIC-insured accounts, even when the bank failed that held the accounts.

Kinds of Financial Institutions

The most common kind of banks are *retail banks* and *commercial banks*. Retail banks tend to focus on individual customers, while commercial banks tend to focus on small and medium businesses. In common practice, most banks that you see in your town combine service to both kinds of customers.

Retail banks offer savings accounts, checking accounts, money market accounts, and certificates of deposit. These financial products encourage people to deposit their money so that they can earn interest on their deposits. Banks use deposits to provide mortgages for people buying homes, make loans to small businesses, and offer secured loans for buying cars and other expensive items. These loans carry a higher rate of interest than what the bank pays to depositors.

The difference between the interest charged for loans and the interest paid to depositors is how the bank pays its employees, pays for its own property and other expenses, and makes a profit. These loans are usually secured, which means that the borrower must back the loan with collateral (security or sellable property) that is worth at least as much as the loan.

Usually the collateral for a home mortgage is the house being bought, and the collateral for a car loan is the car itself. The bank is said to have a lien on or title to the collateral that backs the loan until the loan is paid off. The bank wants to be sure that, if the borrower is unable to repay the loan and defaults on his responsibility, it will have an asset that it can sell for at least the amount of the unpaid loan balance. Banks also offer unsecured loans, which usually take the form of personal loans for small amounts that the borrower must pay back in a short period of time (perhaps 90 days).

Credit cards are a form of unsecured loan. *Credit* is the ability to carry debt. Issuing a credit card is a bank's way of saying that it considers that person a good risk for loaning him or her money without requiring any collateral. However, a bank will usually charge a high interest rate on credit card balances that remain unpaid after 30 days. The bank wants to be paid for carrying the risk.

Banks (and the credit card companies that let banks use their well-known credit card brands) also make money on each credit card purchase by charging a fee to the businesses that agree to accept credit cards. These fees are usually about 2% or 3% for each transaction. If a customer uses a credit card to make a $100 purchase at a store, the store might actually receive $97.50. The rest goes to the bank and to the credit card company. The store owner accepts credit cards to encourage consumers to buy his merchandise. The owner is willing to get more sales for $97.50 each instead of having fewer sales at $100 each that customers must pay for by cash or check.

Other financial institutions that do business with the general public include *savings and loan* or *thrift* institutions, which emphasize making mortgage loans to home buyers, and *credit unions*, which operate like banks but are cooperative ventures that depositors own. Credit unions are usually much smaller than banks. However, because they are depositor-owned and do not have the strong motivation for profits that commercial banks do, credit unions sometimes offer higher interest rates on deposits and lower interest rates on loans than banks and thrifts do.

JPMorgan Chase & Co. is the largest commercial bank in the United States with assets of two trillion dollars. Through its subsidiaries, it provides commercial banking, investment banking, asset management, credit cards, and other financial services. The company headquarters in Manhattan is pictured above.

American law used to make clear distinctions between what banks could do and what other kinds of financial companies could do. Deregulation of the financial industry has blurred the distinctions between categories of financial institutions and between traditional banks and insurance companies. Now some insurance companies offer banking services and banks offer some kinds of insurance and investment advisory services. *Mortgage companies* just make home loans. *Investment banks* concentrate on making loans to larger businesses for capital projects. Even with deregulation, financial institutions still often maintain distinct emphases in their business practices.

Interest

Everything has a price, including money. *Interest* is the price of borrowing money. When you deposit money in a bank, the bank pays you interest as its cost for using your money to make more money by loaning your money to others. When you borrow money, say to buy a house, the lender will charge you interest to use their money to pay the builder or the previous owner.

As with any price, the market determines interest rates on the basis of supply and demand. When the supply of money is high and demand is low, interest rates are lower. When supply is low and demand is high, interest rates are higher. A reduction in interest rates means money costs less.

Lower interest rates encourage more borrowing, more investing in economic activity, more consumption, and less saving (because people have less incentive to save). By contrast, higher interest rates lead to less investment because of a lower incentive to borrow. Companies borrow less and, with banks offering higher interest rates, people have the incentive to save more.

Over the centuries, Christians have wrestled with the morality of charging interest. This 14th century Italian picture of bankers is from a discussion of the Seven Vices. It is meant to illustrate avarice.

When interest rates are higher, people make fewer purchases by borrowing, which means fewer purchases made overall. Generally speaking, lower interest rates are better for the economy. Ideally, interest rates move to the point of equilibrium where banks loan all of the money that they have on deposit, except for their fractional reserve.

Interest being the price of money is a simple enough idea, but the way that interest works in real life is not quite that simple. Interest can have a significant impact on an individual, a business, and the economy as a whole.

We can express interest in two ways: nominal and real. *Nominal interest rates* are the stated or advertised rates that a bank charges. The *real (or effective) interest rate* is the difference between the nominal rate and the rate of inflation. For instance, if the nominal interest rate on a savings account is 4% and the inflation rate is 2%, a saver is only really earning 2% real or effective interest because inflation is eating up the other 2% in the increase in the cost of living. If inflation rises dramatically, for short periods of time the real interest rate can be negative; that is, people can actually lose money by saving because they are earning less than the increase in the cost of living. Thus they have no incentive to save.

Interest can be a significant cost and a significant benefit. When a person borrows money to buy a house, the interest on the loan can total as much as or more than the actual cost of the house. A $100,000 loan at 5% interest for thirty years will have an interest charge of over $93,000. This means that if the homeowner keeps the house for thirty years, he will pay the original loan amount almost twice. Thus a borrower should borrow as little as possible, at as low an interest rate as possible, for as short a period of time as possible.

On the other hand, the principle of compound interest is a great benefit of saving. Compound interest means that, when a person saves money, the bank pays interest on that money and also on the interest that the account has already earned.

Lesson 32 - How Banks Work

If you invested $1,000 once at 4% and left it alone for twenty years, because of compound interest, at the end of that period you would have over $2,200, if the interest is compounded or added to the account monthly. Continuous investments over a period of several years bring even more dramatic results. If you invested $100 per month for twenty years at 4% interest, at the end of that period you would have over $36,000.

The Rule of 72 is a way to determine the approximate period of time needed for an investment to double in value. The rule involves dividing 72 by the interest rate to find the number of years. At 4% interest, a one-time investment will double in eighteen years (72/4=18).

More About Money and Banking

The *money supply* in the United States is sometimes expressed as M1 and M2. M1 is the total of currency, traveler's checks, deposits payable upon demand, and other checkable deposits; in other words, very liquid assets. M2 includes the items of M1 plus money market mutual funds, savings, and small time deposits (all of which are somewhat less liquid assets).

The *velocity of money* tells how often the same money is used in transactions during a given period of time. It is expressed as a ratio of the dollar total of transactions in a country compared to the country's money supply.

$$\frac{\text{dollar total of transactions}}{\text{money supply}}$$

If a country has $10,000 in transactions in a year and a money supply of $1,000, the velocity of money would be 10. The velocity of money is an indication of the strength of economic activity.

Jacob "Jack" Lew became U.S. Secretary of the Treasury in 2013. In this photo, he is providing his signature for printing on U.S. currency. Physical currency is only a small part of the total money supply. As of June 2016, the value of Federal Reserve notes in circulation was about $1.4 trillion. At that time M1 was $3.2 trillion and M2 was $12.8 trillion.

The term *credit rating* refers to a determination of a person's credit worthiness in the eyes of the financial system. Credit rating companies give a credit score to people by evaluating such factors as a person's income pattern, his record of paying off debt, and the amount of credit the person has used. A lending institution will use this score in deciding whether to extend the person a loan, how much to loan, and at what interest rate. A bank might not agree to make a loan if the applicant has not worked for very long at his job, if the applicant is requesting a loan to start a new business that seems to have an uncertain future, or if the person has defaulted on a loan in the past.

Sometimes banks borrow from other banks. At the end of a day's transactions, a bank might have a surplus or a deficit in relation to the reserve requirement. Banks with a surplus can loan money overnight to banks that have a deficit at the rate of interest called the federal funds rate.

Non-Bank Banking

A new kind of non-bank banking that has emerged on the Internet is called peer-to-peer or person-to-person lending. Just as ebay.com brings sellers and buyers together for auctions and direct sales, sites such as prosper.com bring together people who want to loan money and people who want to borrow money without a traditional financial institution serving as middle man.

Banks and other financial institutions are efforts to help people handle money wisely in our economy. The Bible describes a clear difference between handling money wisely and handling it foolishly.

> *The crown of the wise is their riches,*
> *But the folly of fools is foolishness.*
> *Proverbs 14:24*

Assignments for Lesson 32

Literature — Continue reading *The Rise of Silas Lapham*.

Project — Continue working on your project for this unit.

Student Review — Answer the questions for Lesson 32.

U.S. Savings Bonds

33 Wise Investing

> *Goodness is the only investment that never fails.*
> *— Henry David Thoreau*

The investments that individuals and financial institutions make in businesses are key factors in economic growth. These investments provide companies with money to buy new machinery and make other capital improvements that increase productivity. As the business grows, investors receive back the money they have invested plus interest or a part of the company's profits. In this way, investors are making money with money.

Remember that the value of money lies in what it can do and what it can obtain. Money that someone invests wisely helps fuel the production of goods and services and helps more people to have jobs and as a result to be able to afford to buy goods and services. This is how investments help the economy grow.

Kinds of Investments

The simplest form of investment is a *loan*. A bank loans money to a business, the business uses that money to produce goods and services, and from its sales the business pays back the loan plus interest. Ideally, businesses should not depend on debt. Most small businesses fail, and when this happens the owner is left with debt to pay and no means to pay it off. But companies do borrow money, and wise operation of a firm can result in a successful business with good sales, wage and salary obligations met, and a profit made. Loans involve risk, but many banks and businesses believe that the possibility of success is worth the risk.

Economists speak of the loanable funds market as a simplified way to envision all of the money saved or invested from all sources that is available for loans. The *equilibrium interest rate* is the real interest rate that exactly balances the supply of loanable funds with the demand.

Another common form of investment are *bonds*. Bonds are certificates of indebtedness. An individual or a financial institution buys bonds for a stated amount called the face value. The issuer of the bond (usually a business or a unit of government) has an obligation to pay back the face value plus the interest stated in the bond. Often the bond issuer pays interest every six or twelve months. Generally speaking, offering higher interest rates encourages more investment. A bond is a kind of loan. It is an asset for the purchaser of the bond and a liability or obligation for the recipient to pay back the purchase price at a specified date.

The person who buys a bond can either keep it until it matures (the time when he can redeem it for full value) or sell it to someone else. If a person buys a bond for $1,000 with four percent annual interest that matures in four years, he might decide to sell the bond after two years to someone else for what the bond is worth at the time. The new bondholder will make his profit for the remaining two years, at which time the bond reaches maturity.

The two most common types of bonds are *corporate bonds*, which corporations offer in order to raise money for capital improvements and thus increase productivity, and *government bonds*, which governments use to fund major projects such as the building of roads, bridges, and schools.

Bonds can be issued for various lengths of time, such as two years, five years, or ten years. Generally, the longer the term, the higher the interest rate. This arrangement rewards investors who agree to tie up their money for longer periods and thus defer being repaid with higher rates of return. The corporation or unit of government hopes that the capital project will have been worthwhile when the bond reaches maturity and has to be paid off. Sometimes things don't go as planned, and the corporation or government either has to issue new bonds to raise money to pay off old indebtedness or face defaulting on the obligation.

Corporate and government debt have become a fact of life in the United States. Businesses and governments face difficult decisions. A city might be growing and need to widen a main road to handle the increased traffic. If government leaders wait until they have enough tax revenue in the bank to pay for the road project outright, traffic might become unbearable, which would discourage further economic growth in the city, both industrial and retail.

If the government borrows the money for the road project by issuing bonds and then pays the bonds off with tax revenues while people use the road, the improvement can help continue the economic growth and (ideally) generate even more tax revenue. Government officials take a more significant risk if they approve a major project while little growth is taking place.

Businesses face the same dilemma. The owner of a business might hope that his or her profits will enable further growth in a few years. However, the owner also risks a decline in sales if he does nothing to grow. The business might borrow money now through a bond issue and purchase improved capital equipment in the hope of maintaining or even increasing its market share, and possibly making even more profit by using the machinery while the bonds are being paid off.

Since bonds produce income, the bondholder has to deal with the question of taxes on that income. Interest earned on corporate bonds is taxable because the investment was made for the purpose of making a profit. Interest on government bonds is sometimes not taxable. However, government bonds usually offer a lower interest rate than corporate bonds. So an investor does not make as much on government bonds, but he usually faces a smaller tax burden by investing in them.

A third way of investing money is through buying *stock*. A person who buys shares of stock in a company is buying a small part of the ownership of the company that issues the stock. The company issuing the stock uses proceeds from the sale of stock to fund business activity.

A company issues shares of stock at a certain price, and the value of each share changes in the market on the basis of supply and demand. If the company does well, the value of the stock goes up because the company is worth more and more people want to buy shares. The stockholder, as an owner of the company, benefits from this increased worth. Stocks do not offer interest, though the company may pay a dividend, which is profit or additional stock distributed proportionately to stockholders.

The value of stock can go down, below what the investor paid for it, even down to zero. Shares of stock in successful companies are generally more profitable than bonds, but stocks carry greater risk.

Lesson 33 - Wise Investing

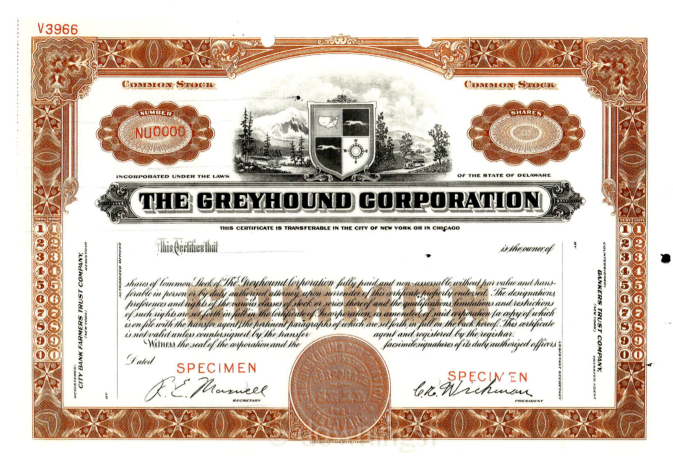

Swedish immigrants Andrew Anderson and Carl Wickman began a transportation service for miners in Minnesota in 1914. The idea took off and by the 1930s, the company carried more passengers by bus between U.S. cities than any other. This stock certificate, issued in 1936, reflects a new company name: The Greyhound Corporation.

Greater risk usually means a greater opportunity for profit and a greater possibility of loss. Bonds offer less profit, but a bondholder generally has the assurance of getting back his initial investment with some interest. Profit from the sale of stock is taxable.

When it comes time for a company to pay its obligations, bondholders get paid before stockholders. A bondholder is a creditor to the company. He has loaned money to the company in what is called *debt financing*, and that loan is an obligation that the company needs to repay. The purchase of shares of stock is called *equity financing*. A stockholder purchases equity in or part ownership of the company, and as such he takes some of the company's risk of profit or loss.

The word *securities* is a broad term that encompasses stocks, bonds, and other financial investments.

Mutual Funds

As you can see, successful investing requires a great deal of knowledge: whether to buy stocks or bonds; which companies are good risks; how much a person should invest and for how long; and when an investor should buy, sell, or hold his stock. Investment banks and full-time investors have the time and expertise to answer these questions well (though even the experts often make mistakes). But how is the average person supposed to know how to invest?

One investment option is the *mutual fund*. Mutual funds are investment companies that offer shares to the public. Many individuals invest in a mutual fund, and the fund pools the money so that all investors in the fund share mutually in its growth or decline. Full-time investment managers use those funds to buy and sell stocks and bonds based on their knowledge of the market. Different kinds of mutual funds focus on different kinds of investments: bonds and other relatively safe investments, growing companies, higher risk new companies with potential for significant profit (sometimes called venture capital investments), and even international funds that seek to take advantage of economic growth in other countries.

Mutual funds enable people who have a relatively small amount of money they want to invest to enter the financial market. Many mutual funds have a good track record of making profits for investors. They also make an enormous amount of money available for businesses to use for growing their activity.

One of the most popular forms of mutual fund investments is a retirement account, often called an IRA (for individual retirement account) or a 401(k) fund (the name comes from the section of the federal tax code that authorized this kind of account). A worker can put part of his or her salary or hourly wage into an IRA or 401(k) account. Many workers agree to have an amount automatically deducted from their paychecks. Some companies also contribute to the 401(k) on behalf of the employee by matching a portion of the employee's investment.

The employee can decide how his or her contribution is invested, and many choose to have the money invested in mutual funds. The investment and any growth in the value of the fund are not subject to being taxed until the money is taken out, which cannot happen without a penalty until the worker is at least 59 1/2 years old.

Most mutual funds are actively-managed, which means that the fund managers try to buy stocks that will perform well and sell stocks that perform poorly. In 1976, John Bogle with The Vanguard Group pioneered the index fund. With an index fund, the managers simply purchase a wide variety of stocks, such as all the stocks on the S&P 500. Index funds outperform most actively-managed funds. While the stock market as a whole tends go up over time, predicting which individual stocks will go up is hard.

Lesson 33 - Wise Investing

Retirement fund investments have enabled many people to save wisely for retirement and have given American companies access to large amounts of money for developing their businesses.

Money market funds are mutual funds that invest in relatively safe and short-term securities such as U.S. Treasury bills. Money market funds usually earn more than bank savings accounts but less than funds that invest in stocks.

Investors do not just buy and sell stocks in companies. The investments themselves have become products to buy and sell. A *hedge fund* takes risks by buying and selling securities in anticipation of what the fund manager thinks the securities are going to be worth in the future. Fund managers use various tactics to sell large amounts of stock quickly and thus make profits. In this way they try to hedge or limit potential losses. Hedge funds are usually available only to wealthy or highly trained investors. *Stock* or *commodity futures* trading also involves buying stock or commodities (such as agricultural products or minerals) in anticipation of what the future price will be.

Leverage buying is a high-risk form of investing in which people buy securities on credit by paying a small amount of money. The term comes from the action of a lever, which can lift a large weight with relatively little work. In the run-up to the 1929 stock market crash, the practice was called buying on margin. The possible benefit is that someone can make a great deal of money with a relatively small investment if the value of the security rises. However, the risk is that the investor can be stuck with a large debt if the value of the security falls and he cannot sell it to pay off his debt.

Should Income from Investments Be Taxed?

A continuing debate in economic and political circles is whether and at what rates profits from investments should be taxed. These taxes are called *capital gains* taxes, which are taxes on the gain or increase in value of capital assets such as stocks and property. The owner receives this gain or profit when he sells those assets.

Some people resent the fact that investors make profits—sometimes large profits—merely by putting money in the hands of others who use that money to buy stocks and other securities. Such activity does not seem to embody the American ideal of working hard to make a living. If anyone can afford to pay higher taxes, the argument goes, surely it is people who have enough money left over from paying the bills to invest in stocks and bonds. They will hardly miss the taxes they have to pay, so why not tax them a little more and make it easier on the average worker?

At first glance, the argument seems to make sense. People who have higher incomes do use a smaller percentage of their income to buy necessities than do people who have lower incomes. But there is another side to the argument. Taxes on savings reduce the return that a saver or investor earns, which lowers the incentive to save. Lower taxes generally lead to more investment.

Investments do not just benefit investors. Investments benefit everyone who gets a job or who pays less for more efficiently-produced goods and services as a result of the investment. Investors accept the risk of loss for the possibility of profit. An investor may not earn any money on a certain investment and may actually lose his initial investment. Investors do not make a profit unless the endeavor in which they are investing is a success. If it is a success, other people benefit also.

And the wealthy are not the only ones who benefit from capital gains. Many average, hard-working people have investments in mutual funds; and those same people work to maintain the value of their homes as a capital asset. Capital gains taxes hit the people in this group harder than people with higher incomes, since those taxes are a greater percentage of their total wealth than they are for wealthier people. Lowering taxes on profits from investments would help the rich, but it would also help everyone else.

What Investments Mean

Making an investment means deciding not to spend money immediately on goods and services and instead use it to focus on long-term goals. This reflects changing one's thinking from "What can I buy with this money now?" to "What can I obtain with this money over time?" and "How can the resources I have help others as well as myself?" As Adam Smith put it, an individual in a free economy pursuing his self-interest helps others as well. You help yourself by purchasing an appliance, and you help others by purchasing an appliance; but you can help others even more by investing in the company that makes appliances so that it can hire more people and develop technology that can lead to better products at lower cost. Then, you can buy a better appliance for less while helping others.

We previously noted the many benefits of saving. Investments are a kind of saving. A principle of economics is that *savings equal investments*. Stocks and bonds are obvious investments, but even simple savings accounts in banks are investments also. A bank cannot generate interest on the money you deposit there without investing it in something that will provide a profit for the bank. Generally speaking, higher rates of savings and investments in a nation make for a stronger economy and more productivity because people are using that money to help businesses grow.

The good stewardship of earning interest on investments even appears in the teaching of Jesus. In the parable of the talents, Jesus describes the master rebuking his slave for burying the master's money instead of investing it.

> *Then you ought to have put my money in the bank, and on my arrival I would have received my money back with interest.*
> *Matthew 25:27*

Assignments for Lesson 33

Literature   Continue reading *The Rise of Silas Lapham*.

Project   Continue working on your project for this unit.

Student Review   Answer the questions for Lesson 33.

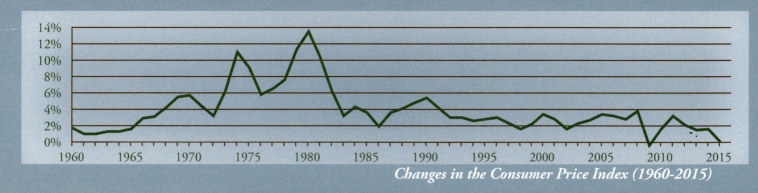

Changes in the Consumer Price Index (1960-2015)

34 > Inflation (Not Our Friend)

*Inflation is when you pay fifteen dollars
for the ten-dollar haircut
you used to get for five dollars
when you had hair.*

— Sam Ewing

Several clues tell you that you're watching an old movie: it is filmed in black and white; the men are wearing double-breasted suits with wide lapels; people are driving huge, funny-looking cars; and one of the characters says something like, "Hey, there's a phone booth. I gotta make a call. Can you gimme a nickel?"

Everyone knows that in the good old days (which are whatever period a person wants to remember fondly), goods and services overall cost less than they do today. If you ask your parents and grandparents what things used to cost, they will likely roll their eyes, shake their heads, and wistfully remember when gasoline cost less than fifty cents a gallon, a call from a pay phone was a dime, and a movie ticket (when there was a movie worth seeing) was a dollar or two. If you really want to get them reminiscing, ask them what they paid for their first car.

In future lessons we will discuss several ways in which economists measure economic activity. For now, consider the chart above, which shows the annual percentage increase in the overall cost of living in the United States between 1960 and 2015.

You can see that the cost of living increased annually by a small percentage until the late 1960s. In the 1970s and early 1980s, the annual increases were dramatic. In some years, the cost of living rose by more than ten percent. The rates of increase slowed during the 1980s and returned to much smaller numbers by the 1990s. Even small increases in the cost of living take a toll. An annual cost of living increase of about 3.4% will cause prices to double in twenty years. With higher rates of increase, prices double more quickly.

Inflation is a general increase in prices for goods and services. Sometimes people say this phenomenon is an increase in the cost of living. Note that economists do not consider higher prices for a few goods and services or in one segment of the economy as inflation. Instead, inflation is a general, across-the-board increase in prices throughout the economy, to the point that it affects almost all people.

When inflation occurs, money loses some of its value. When the cost of living increases by five percent in a year—that is, when the rate of inflation of prices over the period of a year has been five percent—the money you have on December 31 of that year will only buy 95% of what it could have bought on January 1 of that year. Put another way, you must have $105 on December 31 to buy what you could have bought for $100 on January 1.

The inflation that the United States experienced as illustrated in the chart on page 209 was difficult; but it was nothing like the *hyperinflation* (a huge and rapid increase in the cost of living) that people in Germany experienced in the early 1920s. Then the cost of living rose by thousands of percentage points in a matter of months.

People had to carry money to a store in a wheelbarrow to buy a loaf of bread. Such hyperinflation could not last indefinitely. The German economy collapsed, and the fear and turmoil that followed was one factor in the rise of Adolf Hitler. Hitler promised to restore honor to Germany and sanity to German society by taking firm control of the government.

What Causes Inflation?

Inflation is a critical factor in the economy because it affects nearly everyone. It impacts prices, wages, employment, interest rates, the output of goods and services, and the overall standard of living. Inflation is especially hard on people with fixed income, such as those who rely on Social Security or fixed pension payments, because their purchasing power or income does not keep up with the increase in prices.

But what is the root cause of inflation? When prices increase, workers demand to be paid more—or is it that workers demanding higher wages cause companies to raise their prices, which results in inflation? Inflation causes higher interest rates—or do higher interest rates cause inflation?

Inflation became a huge problem in Germany after World War I. The government printed large quantities of money to pay war reparations and avoid unemployment. By 1923 one trillion Marks (the German currency) were worth only one U.S. dollar. At left a banker handles huge stacks of bills. At right a women uses bills to start a fire rather than trying to purchase fuel.

Lesson 34 - Inflation (Not Our Friend)

Nobel prize winning economist Milton Friedman argued convincingly that inflation is "a printing press phenomenon." He said it is "always and everywhere a monetary phenomenon." In other words, the root cause of inflation is the government printing too much money, specifically, when the quantity of money rises more rapidly than the output of goods and services. An old saying about inflation described it as too much money chasing too few goods and services. As it turns out, that old saying had much truth to it.

When the supply of something increases, its price (or value) generally falls. The same is true with money. When the amount of money in circulation increases, its value—expressed in terms of what it can buy—decreases. This perspective is helpful, but it begs another question: why would the government print more money and thus cause inflation? One factor is increased government spending. If the government does not pay for the increase in spending by increasing revenue through higher taxes, it can attempt to pay for the greater spending by printing more money.

The amount of federal spending increased dramatically during the last half of the 1960s and into the 1970s for two main reasons. First, the federal government dramatically expanded social programs such as Medicare, Medicaid, and welfare. In addition, the government spent huge sums on the war in Vietnam. The federal government began running larger and larger deficits. The government borrowed money to cover some of the debt, but it also simply printed more money to pay for the increased spending.

As this increased money supply made its way into the economy, without a corresponding increase in the output of goods and services, too much money started chasing too few goods; and the result was inflation. All of this administered a demand shock to the economy as people began demanding more goods and services with an increasing supply of money. The result was inflation.

Another contributing factor in the early 1970s was the supply shock of Arab oil-producing countries refusing to sell oil to the United States because of this country's support of Israel. This cut the supply of oil, which increased demand, which drove gasoline prices in the United States higher. Higher energy prices led to increases in production costs, which raised prices for goods and services. This caused further inflation.

However, as the prices for goods and services rose, demand fell, which resulted in increased unemployment. The combination of significant inflation along with rising unemployment resulted in a stagnant economy characterized by what became known as *stagflation*.

U.S. economic policy turned the corner in the battle against inflation in 1979, when President Jimmy Carter appointed Paul Volcker to be chairman of the Federal Reserve Board. President Ronald Reagan reappointed Volcker to another four-year term in 1983. Volcker began restricting the money supply. This increased the value of money because the supply fell. Decreased supply leads to higher prices, so a decrease in the money supply resulted in higher interest rates (since interest is the price of money).

Inflation subsided dramatically, but Volcker's policy also contributed to an economic recession in the early 1980s. However, the economy later rebounded as the factors of money supply, interest, and production returned to a more favorable balance with each other. Inflation has been a relatively minor economic issue for many years, in large part because the Federal Reserve has learned how to keep the money supply in pace with output. This is true despite the record federal deficits of the early twenty-first century.

The opposite of inflation is *deflation*, which is an overall decline in prices. Deflation has been rare in recent years. However, an overall lowering of prices, led by prices for farm products, occurred often in the late 1800s. This was a main factor in the rise of the Populist movement and their call for

This 1978 cartoon by Edmund Valtman depicts President Jimmy Carter facing the giant of inflation.

an increase in the money supply by the coining of silver. Farmers believed that with more money in circulation, prices for their products would rise and they would have more money to pay their debts. Several years during the Great Depression of the 1930s witnessed deflation. The U.S. experienced a small rate of deflation in 2009, largely because of the decline in energy prices from 2008.

Other Ideas on the Causes of Inflation

Economists sometimes discuss inflation in terms of demand and supply. For instance, inflation can sometimes be the result of an increase in aggregate demand that is not accompanied by an increase in aggregate supply. This is called *demand-pull inflation* because increased demand without an increase in supply tends to pull prices higher. As we discussed previously, during the 1960s and 1970s demand increased because of a rise in the supply of money which was not accompanied by an increase in aggregate supply.

On the other hand, a decrease in aggregate supply can occur as a result of higher production costs, such as wage increases, higher prices for raw materials, or higher energy costs. This leads to a decrease in productivity, a decrease in supply, and a resulting increase in prices for more scarce resources. This effect is called *cost-push inflation* because higher production costs push prices higher.

Another commonly-cited cause of inflation is the expectation of inflation. This expectation is something like a self-fulfilling prophecy. If you were going to loan someone $100 for a year, all else being equal you might charge him 3% interest for the use

Lesson 34 - Inflation (Not Our Friend)

of your money. However, if you expected inflation to be about 5% over the course of the year, you would charge the borrower 8% interest so that you would make your desired profit and not see inflation eat it away. This expectation of inflation reflected in a higher interest rate can itself contribute to inflation.

The same expectation factor can influence prices. Suppose you own a steel company. As you set the price for your product, you think about the fact that the contract for the union workers you employ will be up for renegotiation this year. The talk is that the union will demand a 6% pay increase. Since labor costs are about half of your production cost, you decide to raise your steel price by 3% to stay even. This increase in your price will mean higher production costs for companies that buy your steel to make the products they make, so those companies will likely raise the prices for their products also.

Workers in your industry as well as in other areas of the economy will cite these higher prices as a reason why they need a pay increase when they negotiate their salaries. But an anticipated demand for a wage increase was the original reason that prices started going up. So which comes first: higher prices or higher wages? This is sometimes called the *wage-price spiral*, as producers and consumers both try to protect themselves from the effects of expected inflation.

The Effects of Inflation

Inflation hurts *purchasing power*, which is the ability of individual consumers to buy goods and services, at least in the short run. Income tends to rise more slowly than prices. A producer of goods and services can raise his price with a company memo or by reprogramming his point of sale computer, but most workers cannot immediately raise their own salary. Inflation also hurts the purchasing power of people on fixed incomes, as mentioned earlier, and of people whose income is rising more slowly than the rate of inflation. As a result, inflation lowers the overall standard of living because it takes more money to buy the same goods and services. However, in the long run income does tend to catch up to price increases.

Inflation can actually help people who have borrowed money at a fixed rate of interest, at least with regard to paying off that debt. Suppose you buy a house by taking out a fifteen-year mortgage at 4% interest. Then four years later, a round of inflation begins that lessens the value of your money. You would then be paying off your mortgage with dollars that aren't worth as much as they were when you took out the mortgage. Assuming your income increases because of inflation, your fixed mortgage payment will be a smaller percentage of your income than when you bought the house. Of course, until your income catches up with inflation, you might be worse off overall because of the general rise in prices. And having less valuable dollars to pay off a mortgage is not usually reason enough to welcome a round of inflation.

Economist William Phillips demonstrated an inverse relationship between inflation and unemployment. In the short run, low inflation (accompanied by low wage increases) is associated with higher unemployment, while higher inflation (which leads to greater wage increases) is associated with lower unemployment. The graphic presentation of this relationship is called the Phillips curve:

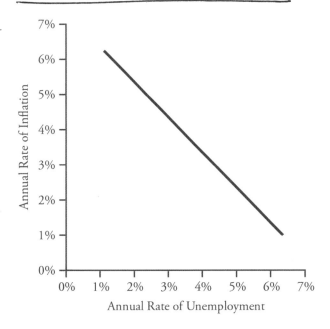

"Now Hiring" sign at a Domino's pizza franchise in Franklin, Tennessee (2015)

Increased aggregate demand, which fuels inflation, leads to less unemployment. People are buying more, so companies hire more people to increase output so that they can keep pace with demand. Companies have to offer higher wages to compete for scarce labor in an inflationary period. By contrast, low inflation is the result of less demand, which lowers prices, which leads to higher unemployment because owners are not able to hire as many people.

This apparent tradeoff between inflation and unemployment makes for difficult policy decisions. Should the government pursue a policy of low inflation, or low unemployment, or should government attempt to maintain a balance between the two? The bottom line is that some degree of inflation helps keep unemployment low, but it is a delicate balancing act to maintain. One goal of the monetary policy that the United States government follows is to maintain this balance.

Lesson 34 - Inflation (Not Our Friend)

Are Interest Rates a Cause or an Effect of Inflation?

A typical government response to inflation is for the Federal Reserve to increase interest rates. When the supply of money increases and inflation occurs, the Federal Reserve can increase interest rates to make money more expensive in order to lessen demand for it. But economists and political commentators often cite higher interest rates as contributing to inflation. When people have to pay more for money, businesses want to charge more for goods and services and people want to make more income, both of which tend to bring about inflation. So do higher interest rates cause inflation, or are higher interest rates an effect of inflation? As we noted earlier about prices, both can be true.

Generally, the Federal Reserve imposes higher interest rates as a response to inflation or to anticipated inflation. But since interest is the price of money, higher interest rates can also be a cause of inflation. The key to halting the spiral appears to be raising interest rates enough to cause the demand for money to subside. This will tend to bring down the rate of inflation, and lower interest rates will follow. The experience of the early 1980s shows that there will be other negative economic effects, such as the slowdown of economic activity in the form of a recession; but the economy does eventually tend to balance out and regain its pattern of growth.

The uncertainties and complexities of inflation remind us that we cannot place our hope in money. Instead, we must depend on the Lord to provide for us.

Instruct those who are rich in this present world not to be conceited or to fix their hope on the uncertainty of riches, but on God, who richly supplies us with all things to enjoy.
1 Timothy 6:17

Assignments for Lesson 34

Literature — Continue reading *The Rise of Silas Lapham*.

Project — Continue working on your project for this unit.

Student Review — Answer the questions for Lesson 34.

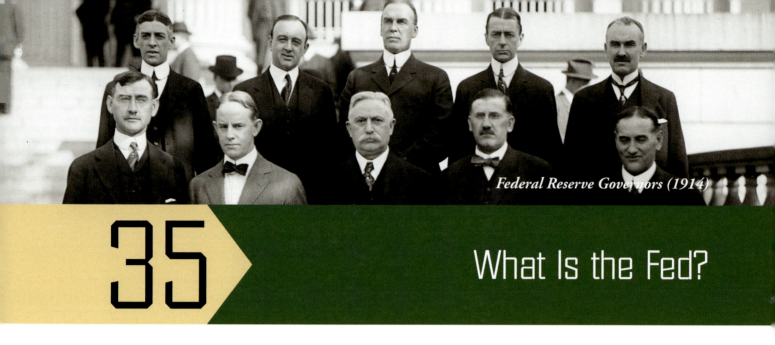
Federal Reserve Governors (1914)

35 What Is the Fed?

The Federal Reserve System is the central bank of the United States. It was founded by Congress in 1913 to provide the nation with a safer, more flexible, and more stable monetary and financial system. Over the years, its role in banking and the economy has expanded.
— The Federal Reserve System: Purposes and Functions
(a publication of the Board of Governors of the
Federal Reserve System, 2005 edition)

The headlines belied the notion that economics was an irrelevant academic subject of no interest to everyday people. Banks closed, manufacturers shut their doors, thousands of people lost their jobs, and financial uncertainty confronted millions of Americans.

This description could apply to many different years in American history. It might have been 1929 or 2008, but it was 1907. The financial panic that struck the U.S. economy that year was especially severe, and it came uncomfortably soon after other panics of the late 1800s. America had tried a central bank twice earlier in its history, but the United States had operated without a central bank for decades.

This time, financial and political leaders decided to work out a plan to help prevent—or at least to lessen the severity of—future periods of economic turmoil. Many elected officials feared and opposed the idea, but in late 1913 Congress established the Federal Reserve System. It began operating the next year. Today the Federal Reserve, or the Fed as it is commonly known, plays an important role in the nation's economic life.

The Structure of the Fed

When political leaders in the early twentieth century debated the idea of a central bank for the United States, some wanted a government-run system while others favored a private institution led by professional bankers. Some wanted a centralized system while others wanted a decentralized approach. The Federal Reserve System created in 1913 is a compromise among these opposing viewpoints.

The federal government created it. The president nominates its leaders and the Senate approves them.

Lesson 35 - What Is the Fed?

The Fed submits regular reports to the Speaker of the U.S. House of Representatives. But despite all these government connections, it is essentially a private bank with headquarters in Washington, D.C.

A seven-member board of governors oversees the Fed. This is the most important element of the Fed's structure. Each member of the board is appointed for one fourteen-year term. Terms are staggered so that one seat on the board comes up for consideration every two years. The president appoints a member of the board to be chairman for a four-year term.

The second element of the Fed's structure is the Federal Open Market Committee (FOMC). This committee oversees the open market operations, which are the Fed's main tool for implementing national monetary policy. The FOMC consists of the seven board members and the presidents of the twelve Federal Reserve regional banks; however, only five of the regional presidents have voting privileges at any one time. The president of the New York Federal Reserve Bank has a permanent vote, and the other four votes rotate among the other presidents every two or three years.

The third part of the Fed's structure consists of the twelve regional Federal Reserve Banks located in major cities across the country. Each of these regional banks serves a Federal Reserve district and has a nine-member board of directors. Most regional banks have branches in other cities as well.

The fourth element involves private U.S. member banks which maintain accounts in the regional Reserve Banks. All federally-chartered banks and some state-chartered banks are members of the system. Most banks in the United States are not member banks of the Federal Reserve System, but member banks tend to be much larger than non-member banks.

Map of the Federal Reserve regions

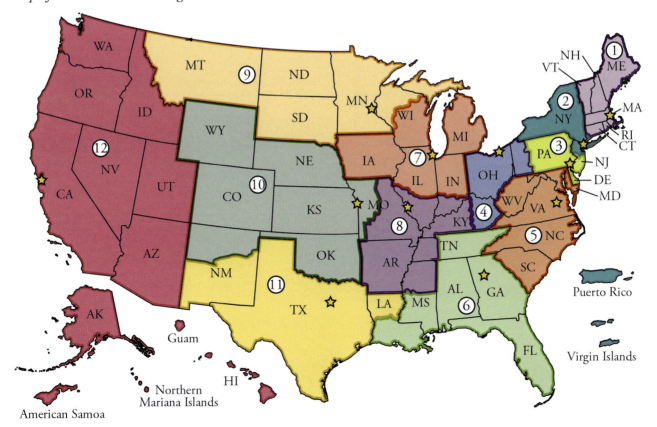

Finally, the fifth element of the Fed's structure is made up of advisory councils and committees that offer their input to the Fed Board or to the directors of the regional banks. The four groups that advise the Federal Board of Governors are:

- The Federal Advisory Council, which consists of representatives of the banking industry;

Many of the Federal Reserve banks feature museums about the Fed and the U.S. financial system.

- The Model Validation Council, on which sit university professors and which advises the Board of Governors about their method of testing the soundness of major banks;

- The Community Advisory Council, a diverse group that advises the Board of Governors on their policies, especially regarding policies that affect low- and moderate-income Americans; and

- The Community Depository Institutions Advisory Council, which is made up of representatives from banks, thrift institutions, and credit unions and provides the Board of Governors with input from the perspective of those financial institutions. The Board of Governors, as opposed to an act of Congress, created this last advisory council.

Committees that provide their perspectives to the regional boards focus on agriculture, small business, labor, and other specific economic issues.

Responsibilities of the Fed

The Federal Reserve System has four areas of responsibility:

- To implement federal monetary policy, primarily through managing the money supply and the interest rates it charges for lending money to banks;

- To supervise and regulate the banking industry;

- To maintain stability in financial markets (one way the Fed does this is by being the lender of last resort in

The William McChesney Martin Jr. Federal Reserve Board Building in Washington, D.C., is commonly called the Federal Reserve Annex. It is named after the longest-serving Chairman of the Federal Reserve. William Martin was appointed by President Truman in 1951 and served until 1970 under four additional presidents.

extraordinary circumstances, such as its approval in September of 2008 of an $85 billion loan to prevent the bankruptcy of the insurance company American International Group [AIG]);

- To provide financial services to banks, the United States government, and foreign entities.

The Fed is a bankers' bank and the government's bank. Individual citizens do not have accounts at the Fed, but banks do. The United States government maintains an account at the Federal Reserve Bank, into which it deposits tax receipts and from which it makes payments for government obligations.

One service that the Fed provides to banks is a national check clearing system. During the Great Depression, some banks refused to clear checks written on accounts at some other banks, even solvent ones. This contributed to the disruption of the economy. The national check clearing system eliminated this problem. Also, the Fed officially issues the coins and currency that the United States Treasury Department produces. The Fed buys the currency essentially at cost from the Treasury to use in its transactions.

Oversight of Monetary Policy

Monetary policy involves overseeing the availability and cost of money to accomplish the economic goals of the national government. In other words, the Fed seeks to guide the amount of money that is available in the economy. Since this amount can rise or fall depending on conditions, the money supply is said to be *elastic*. The nation's economic goals include:

- Stable prices (avoiding significant inflation or deflation),
- Maximum employment,
- Moderate long-term interest rates, and
- Promotion of healthy and sustainable economic growth.

The Fed uses three primary tools to manage the money supply and accomplish these goals. First, the Fed can adjust the *reserve requirements* for how much cash banks must have on hand to satisfy depositors' demands. The Fed rarely uses this tool because banks would find frequent changes in the reserve requirement to be unsettling. A bank that closed its business day within the reserve requirement might open its doors the next day below the new requirement and have to scramble to obtain the funds it needed.

Second, the Fed adjusts the *discount rate* that it charges banks for loans of its funds. Lower rates encourage banks to borrow more from the Fed, which makes more money available to individuals and businesses. Higher rates discourage borrowing, which lessens the amount of money available in the economy.

Third, the tool that the Fed uses most is its *open market operations*. In these operations, the Fed buys and sells U.S. Treasury bonds and other federally-issued securities to inject money into or to withdraw money from the economy. The purpose of these transactions is to affect the *federal funds rate*,

A meeting of the Federal Open Market Committee (2016)

Protesters at the Federal Reserve branch bank in Charlotte, North Carolina (2008)

which is the interest that banks charge each other for overnight loans, usually to maintain the reserve requirements. Banks often cut it close in maintaining the reserve requirement because money sitting in the bank is not making any money.

If a bank has had an unusually high number of withdrawals or has issued a number of loans in a day, it might fall below the reserve requirement and need a short-term injection of cash. Another bank might have a surplus of funds that it would be willing to lend and thus make a profit from the transaction. Banks that maintain accounts with the Fed often simply shift money between their accounts to accomplish these transactions. The banks often reverse the transactions a day or two later in what are called *repurchase agreements* or repos.

The Federal Open Market Committee meets about every six weeks and sets a target federal funds rate. In pursuit of that target, the Fed then buys or sells government securities from dealers in the open securities market. If the Fed wants to inject more money into the economy, it buys bonds; and that money enters the economy. If the Fed wants to lessen the amount of money in the economy, it sells bonds and deposits the money it receives in a Federal Reserve Bank. This reduces the amount of money available in the economy. The Fed requires investment companies that deal in securities to participate in these sales. These firms then often resell the bonds they buy to others, including foreign investors. Securities dealers involved include Bank of America and Citibank, but also Deutsche Bank of Germany and some Japanese banks.

Open market operations do not directly set interest rates. Instead, they are an indirect way to influence interest rates because the amount of money available in the economy influences the rates of interest that banks charge. Usually the discount rate (what the Fed charges member banks for loans) is about 1% above the federal funds rate, and the prime rate (the rate banks charge their best customers for loans) is about 3% above the federal funds rate. Other rates, for home mortgages and other kinds of loans, adjust accordingly in the marketplace.

The Federal Reserve Board in Washington and each of the twelve regional banks maintain websites that describe their operations and offer varying amounts of economic and educational information.

An Imperfect Process

The Fed oversees the nation's monetary policy. The other main part of American economic policy is fiscal policy, which the president, other officials in the executive branch, and Congress guide. We will discuss how these branches of government implement fiscal policy in the unit on government.

The work of the Fed is not perfect. The Fed cannot know what events and trends will take place in the future. The Federal Reserve Board of Governors can only attempt to guide the overall economy in the way that they think is best. The interplay between what people do and how the Fed responds to their actions, and what the Fed does and how people respond to its actions, helps economics remain a dynamic, always-moving process.

Jesus once described a situation in which one friend asked another for a nighttime loan—of bread.

> *Then He said to them, "Suppose one of you has a friend, and goes to him at midnight and says to him, 'Friend, lend me three loaves; for a friend of mine has come to me from a journey, and I have nothing to set before him.'"*
> *Luke 11:5-6*

Assignments for Lesson 35

Making Choices — Read "Finance and Society" (pages 72-77).

Literature — Finish reading *The Rise of Silas Lapham*. Read the literary analysis of the book beginning on page 29 in the *Student Review* and answer the questions over the book.

Project — Finish your project for this unit.

Student Review — Answer the questions for Lesson 35 and take the quiz for Unit 7.

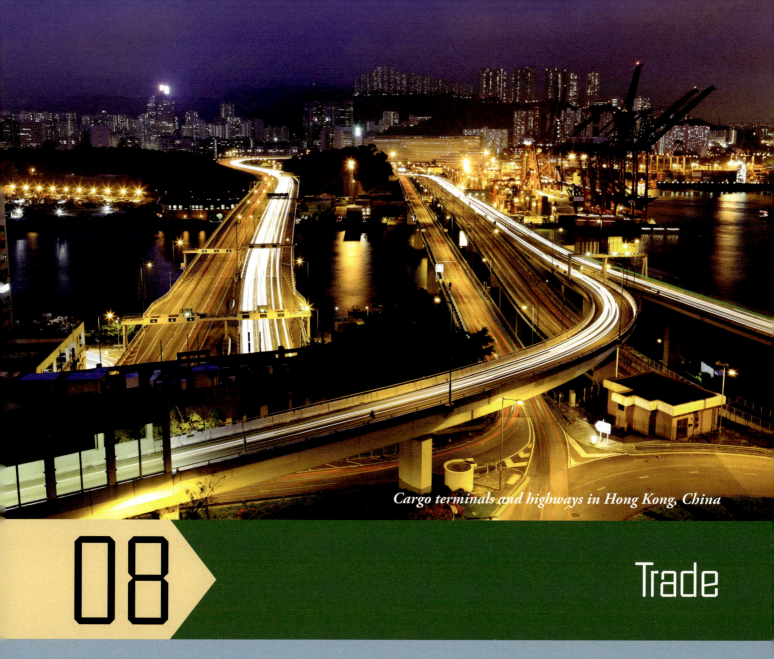

Cargo terminals and highways in Hong Kong, China

08 Trade

The goal of international trade is to create a win-win situation for the countries involved. International trade has provided many benefits to trading countries. The basis of trade are the principles of specialization and comparative advantage. Government policies such as tariffs, quotas, sanctions, and subsidies restrict trade. Free trade encourages and enables economic growth. Foreign trade, foreign investment in the United States, and U.S. companies moving production to other countries are subjects of considerable debate. The exchange of currency is one aspect of international trade.

Lesson 36 - Trade Is Good
Lesson 37 - Restrictions on Trade
Lesson 38 - The Case for Free Trade
Lesson 39 - Have We Been Exported?
Lesson 40 - Money Changes Clothes

Books Used

The Bible
Making Choices
The Travels of a T-Shirt in the Global Economy

Project (choose one)

1) Write 300 to 500 words on one of the following topics:

- Write a speech outlining your views on trade. Should U.S. corporations or agriculture receive subsidies to provide jobs? Should the U.S. rely on tariffs to regulate imports? Should the U.S. limit goods imported from other nations? Answer these questions and include other points that express your views.

- Imagine that a major manufacturing industry in your town causes a local controversy by announcing it is relocating to another country to reduce labor costs. Write a letter to the editor of the local newspaper expressing your thoughts.

2) Plan a meal that uses mostly foods imported from other countries. Browsing in the international section of a large grocery store will provide inspiration. Prepare this meal for your family.

3) Write and illustrate a children's book that explains how an everyday item is made (including the necessary raw materials), transported, stored, sold, and finally ends up in a child's possession (such as a bicycle for a birthday present, or a pair of shoes). Create a cover and at least 20 pages.

Literature

Pietra Rivoli, born in 1957, is a professor of finance and international business at Georgetown University in Washington, D.C., where she has served since 1983. Her special interests are social justice issues in international business and China, where she regularly leads graduate students for special study.

Her book *The Travels of a T-Shirt in the Global Economy* has garnered both popular and scholarly acclaim. Rivoli creatively and effectively uses the life-story of a single common product, the T-shirt, to explore the many facets of globalization. She keeps the story on a personal level, interacting with people as diverse as Texas cotton farmers, Chinese factory workers, Washington lobbyists, and African used clothing merchants.

It is a story in which practically every person in the world is involved. She effectively conveys the complexity of the issues at stake, requiring the reader to grapple with many compelling questions. *The Travels of a T-Shirt in the Global Economy* has been published in three editions (2005, 2009, 2014) and is available in fourteen languages.

A ship from South Korean company Hanjin prepares to unload in Oakland, California (2015)

36 Trade Is Good

It is the maxim of every prudent master of a family, never to attempt to make at home what it will cost him more to make than to buy. The tailor does not attempt to make his own shoes, but buys them of a shoemaker. The shoemaker does not attempt to make his own clothes, but employs a tailor. The farmer attempts to make neither the one nor the other, but employs those different artificers. All of them find it in their interests to employ their whole industry in a way in which they have some advantage over their neighbors, and to purchase with a part of its produce, or what is the same thing, with the price of a part of it, whatever else they have occasion for.

— Adam Smith

As Portuguese ships venture into unknown waters, they press ever further down the African coast. Finally they cross the Indian Ocean to the Far East.

Christopher Columbus embarks on a daring journey west.

What was the motivation behind these adventures? Trade. Asia produced spices and other commodities that Europeans wanted.

The American colonies of Great Britain grow increasingly restless under British rule. Eventually the colonies break the political bonds they have with Britain and create a new nation.

What motivated this bold move? One reason was trade. The London government maintained strict oversight of colonial trade, and many Americans wanted to determine their own political and economic destiny.

The Communist government of China, which for decades fiercely maintained a command economy, welcomes foreign businesses and allows private ownership by Chinese citizens of enterprises within China. This changes the economic landscape of the most populous nation in the world, and it changes how the rest of the world relates to China.

What is the motivation for these changes? Trade. The Chinese government has seen the economic development that comes about through trade, and companies in other countries are eager to do business with the Chinese.

The European Union is made up of trading partner countries that were once bitter enemies.

India is an ever-larger player in the world market. Globalization in economic activity is a fact of life.

All of these developments involve trade. In today's world, the United States is a major player in the world economy through its policies and practices related to international trade, and trade is a big part of economics.

What Is Trade?

We sometimes use the word *trade* to refer to any exchange or purchase of goods and services. For example, we might talk about two boys who trade baseball cards or a professional who works at his trade. In economics, however, the term most often describes purchases between countries.

Trade consists of exports and imports. *Exports* are goods and services that producers create within a country and then sell and send to people, companies, or governments in other countries. *Imports* are goods and services that producers in other countries make and then people, companies, and governments purchase and bring into their own country.

Trade is *voluntary exchange*, which means it involves decisions that people make freely and that no one forces onto someone else. Two partners participate in voluntary exchange when both of them believe that they will be better off by engaging in trade. The purpose of trade is not to establish a win-lose relationship, in which one party gets a great deal while the other side gets hammered. Instead, the purpose is to create a win-win arrangement, in which both parties receive advantages from the deal.

For instance, companies in the United States buy bananas from Honduras, and companies in the United States sell medical supplies to companies, individuals, or the government in Honduras. Americans have bananas to enhance their diet, and Hondurans have greater access to medical supplies. Both countries believe that they are better off by engaging in this trade.

The cargo ship Dole Honduras *unloads fruit from Central America at the Port of San Diego (2008)*

Lesson 36 - Trade Is Good

Why People Engage in Trade

Throughout human history, people have engaged in trade because they believe that they benefit from it. Traders profit from it, of course, but so do producers and consumers. Looking at what life would be like without trade helps us see this benefit more clearly.

Imagine a country that does not trade with other nations. The people of that country have to produce within its borders all of the goods and services that they want and need. If a particular food doesn't grow there, the people do not have it to eat. People within the country have to design and build whatever machinery that companies use in the production of goods, with whatever materials, skills, and technology the country has available. The country hires no experts from other countries and uses no technology that people in other countries develop. If a product made within the country is poorly made or takes a long time to produce, consumers have no choices about the product unless another domestic company (company within the country) develops a superior substitute.

National governments control what comes into a country and what goes out from it. Therefore the practice described above of not trading with other countries would be a policy decision that the country's government made. In this imaginary non-trading country, the government would be limiting choices for its people. The citizens of that country would likely have to settle for inferior goods and services that are relatively more expensive. In such a country, the government would be protecting the status quo, resulting in a sort of monopoly. Their consumers would not be free to seek better goods and their producers would not be free to seek more promising markets in other countries. Government leaders who refused to allow trade with other countries would likely just be concerned about getting what they wanted and not about the well-being of the population or about the economic growth of the nation as a whole.

International trade, on the other hand, makes more goods and services available to the people of a nation and at prices that they can afford. Increased foreign markets for goods and services that workers in a country produce means economic growth for that country in the form of more jobs and a higher standard of living. Entrepreneurs develop new industries to meet ever greater needs within the country and in other countries. Trading nations become interdependent and thus are less likely to be at odds with each other to the point of going to war. It is in the self-interest of trading nations to cooperate and act as partners.

All else being equal, exporting goods and services helps producers who export because they have a larger market; but it can hurt consumers in the exporting country who as a result of the trade have that much less to buy. All else being equal, importing helps consumers because they have more to buy; but it can hurt domestic producers who have more competition. As the market works, however, these factors balance out and the economy grows.

Specialization

The principles of specialization and comparative advantage are the basis of trade that benefits all countries.

Think about an individual who does not trade with others. Everything he has, he has to make himself. He might not be a particularly good tailor, but he must make his own clothes. It might take him a long time to make a gun, but if he wants meat he has to make one. This man might be an excellent shepherd, home builder, or writer; but he has little time to do what he does well because he has to spend so much time doing the things he doesn't do well. He might be able to raise a large flock of sheep, build several houses, or write a best seller and use the profit to buy good clothes and an excellent rifle, but he doesn't have the chance to do so because he is busy doing other things. This does not seem to be the best use of his time and resources.

Carpets, yarn, and other textile products account for one-third of exports from the country of Nepal.

When a person concentrates on one kind of work and uses the profits from that work to buy the other things he needs, this is called *specialization*. Evidence has shown convincingly that a person is more productive and thus more economically successful when he or she specializes in a particular occupation.

The same is true of companies. The first successful automobile companies in America illustrated this. They could produce more cars when many workers performed distinct tasks along an assembly line than they could if each worker tried to build an entire car by himself. In turn, a nation's economy is more productive and successful when workers in general practice specialization.

The same is true in international trade. When countries specialize in certain kinds of work and then trade for the products of workers in other countries who have specialized in other kinds of work, all countries are better off. Of course, not all workers in a country will work in just one kind of job. Some people in every country will work in grocery stores, some will be nurses or lawyers or teachers, and so forth; but the economy as a whole in each country will benefit if the country's industries pursue a level of specialization.

Some people choose to go against the tide of specialization by trying to be self-sustaining. This means that they produce as many goods and services themselves as they can. We can applaud and admire a person's decision to develop several skills and to be primarily dependent on his or her own efforts. Indeed, workers have understandably resisted being treated as machines when they have had to do the same mind-numbing jobs over and over, day after day, year after year. Companies have sometimes formed teams of workers who share responsibilities for certain products.

Nevertheless, a country enjoys greater economic growth when people pursue some degree of specialization. Even the most self-sustaining people are dependent on others to provide some goods and services. For example, someone may build his own home from timber off his own land, but he will likely purchase nails and screws. The self-sustainer also needs other people to be a market for what the self-sustainer produces.

Lesson 36 - Trade Is Good

Comparative Advantage and Absolute Advantage

Specialization helps economic activity and growth by the principle of comparative advantage. Remember that opportunity cost is the greatest alternative good that one gives up to engage in a particular activity (see Lesson 2). A young man who chooses to mow lawns for pay in the summer is choosing not to work in a grocery store or start an online business. His opportunity cost for mowing lawns is the most he could earn doing some other profitable work.

Consider chores in a family. Through her training and experience, Mom is better at cooking than her son Billy is. Mom is also better at sweeping the porch than Billy is, but for Mom to sweep the porch she would have to give up valuable time cooking (that is, she would pay a greater opportunity cost compared to what Billy would have to give up to sweep the porch). Billy does not have as many housekeeping skills yet, so he gives up less (that is, he has a lower opportunity cost) sweeping the porch than Mom does. Therefore it is better for the family for Mom to specialize in cooking and for Billy to specialize in sweeping the porch.

When one producer has a smaller opportunity cost of producing a good or service compared to another producer, that is a *comparative advantage*. This can apply to individuals within a country or to countries as a whole. Nations of the world have different endowments of land, labor, capital, technology, and natural resources. A wise use of these endowments gives a nation a comparative advantage over other nations, and this results in economic activity and trade that benefit many countries.

For instance, Switzerland is not likely ever to become a major sea power because it is landlocked. The Swiss would pay a large opportunity cost by giving up their many advantages (tourism, banking, and so forth) if they tried to become a sea power. By contrast, a coastal country such as Spain, Portugal, or France would give up little to develop its seafaring strength. So Switzerland has a comparative advantage over Spain in banking and Spain has a comparative advantage over Switzerland in maritime business.

Japan is never going to be a major oil producing country, as far as anyone knows today. Japan has other strengths, such as technological development and skills in carmaking. Japan would pay a great opportunity cost to become a major oil refining country. Saudi Arabia, on the other hand, is rich in oil reserves. The Saudis would pay a large opportunity cost to ignore developing their oil reserves to try to develop an automobile manufacturing industry. Japan has a comparative advantage over Saudi Arabia in automaking, and Saudi Arabia has a comparative advantage over Japan in oil production. Both countries have a lower opportunity cost and thus a comparative advantage when they develop their respective strengths and take advantage of their natural endowments.

The United States has a skilled workforce, access to job retraining programs, impressive technology, and abundant natural resources. China has an abundance of labor that is not as highly trained. For the United States to concentrate on producing consumer goods would mean a great opportunity cost because U.S. workers would not be taking advantage of their situation. On the other hand, Chinese workers have a lower opportunity cost for making consumer goods because to make them involves giving up less valuable alternatives.

However, as we have noted, the economy is always changing. Chinese workers are gaining skills and their income is rising. A significant amount of production has moved from China to Vietnam, where workers are less skilled and pay is generally lower. Vietnamese workers give up less valuable alternative uses of their labor, so they have a lower opportunity cost than workers in China. Eventually, Vietnamese workers may gain skills and receive higher pay; and low-cost production may move to yet another country. Other factors, such as political stability within a country, can change the parameters for production and trade also.

A related but somewhat different measure of economic activity is absolute advantage. *Absolute advantage* exists when one person or country can produce goods with a smaller input of resources than another. Canada has an absolute advantage over Honduras in the production of maple syrup. Honduras has an absolute advantage over Canada in the production of bananas. In each case, the country with the absolute advantage can produce the goods with less per-unit cost than the other country can.

Comparative advantage and absolute advantage are similar, but they measure economic activity from different perspectives. Comparative advantage compares what producers *give up* to produce something, while absolute advantage compares what producers *use* to produce something.

A country might not have an absolute advantage over other countries in any product, but every country has a comparative advantage over some other countries with whom it might engage in trade. If a country produces goods and services based on the comparative advantages of its resources and trades with other countries that have comparative advantages in producing other goods and services, all the countries will be better off economically.

Do countries actually consider opportunity cost, comparative advantage, and absolute advantage when developing their industries? Yes and no. No world planning committee assigns industries to various countries based on objective analysis of opportunity cost. Nations are free to develop whatever industries they wish. However, government officials and business entrepreneurs do consider the resources that nations have, what producers might give up to devote themselves to a particular industry, and other related issues in making economic plans.

Jesus spoke of a trade that people decide to make with their lives. He taught that when you pursue one of the options, you give up the other.

For what will it profit a man if he gains the whole world and forfeits his soul? Or what will a man give in exchange for his soul?
Matthew 16:26

Assignments for Lesson 36

Literature — Read "What Do You Think About What He Thinks? A Primer for Analysis of Non-Fiction," available on page 10 of the *Student Review* or on our website.

Begin reading *The Travels of a T-Shirt in the Global Economy*. Plan to finish it by the end of Unit 11.

Project — Choose your project for this unit and start working on it.

Student Review — Answer the questions for Lesson 36.

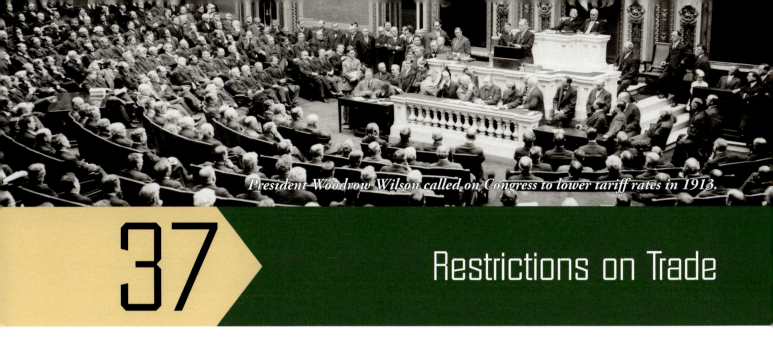
President Woodrow Wilson called on Congress to lower tariff rates in 1913.

37 Restrictions on Trade

Does anyone seriously believe that, if we begin creating international trade restrictions to limit the outsourcing of American jobs, other countries will not pass similar restrictions on the outsourcing of their jobs to America?
— *Thomas Sowell*

Countries engage in trade for many reasons: greater productivity of industry, a higher standard of living for citizens, more choices for consumers, wise use of a nation's productive resources, and an interdependence among nations that can lead to better relations.

However, countries do not always happily engage in trade with each other. Sometimes governments establish policies that limit trade. Government policies on trade are a major influence in the economy. *Trade restrictions* are government policies that hinder, complicate, or eliminate trade between nations.

Trade restrictions can focus on either conditions within the country establishing the restrictions, or conditions in another country against which a government targets restrictions. Conditions within a country sometimes lead the government to establish a policy of *protectionism*. The purpose of protectionist laws is to protect domestic industries from what the government in that country sees as unfair competition from foreign industries. Conditions in other countries sometimes cause governments to establish trade sanctions that affect trade with the other country.

Tariffs

The most common way a country restricts international trade is by enacting *import tariffs*. An import tariff is a tax placed on goods that businesses import into a country. One purpose for tariffs is to raise revenue for a government, but a common motivation for imposing tariffs is to protect domestic industry.

If a foreign country develops an industry that produces certain goods at lower cost than the cost of production is for those same goods or close substitutes, leaders in that industry in the United States might lobby Congress to impose tariffs on those imported goods either to prevent their importation or to raise their price to the consumer to a level that would make domestically-produced goods competitive with regard to price.

231

Importing companies usually pass on the cost of tariffs to the consumer in the form of higher prices.

For example, if basket weavers in Portugal can make baskets at a cost that enables importers to sell them in the United States for $1 each, whereas American-made baskets sell for $2 each, the American basket industry might pressure Congress to impose a tariff of $1 or more per basket on Portuguese imports. This would keep American baskets competitive in terms of price.

Although import tariffs provide protection to American industries, such tariffs have several negative consequences. First, they lead to higher prices for U.S. consumers. Americans will either have to pay higher prices for imports that include the tariff charges, or they will have to pay the higher protected price for domestically-produced goods. In the example of Portuguese baskets, instead of being able to buy baskets for $1 each, Americans will have to pay $2 or more each for baskets.

Second, higher prices lead to decreased consumption, which lowers production, which can lead to fewer jobs. Tariffs prevent a country from fully enjoying the benefits of trade. They can also lead to an inefficient use of a nation's resources because the $1 extra American consumers pay for an imported basket goes to the government rather than to the private sector, i.e. the domestic basket maker. Import tariffs often hurt families with lower incomes, since wealthier consumers can more often afford to pay higher prices for the goods they want.

President Theodore Roosevelt proposed tariff reform in 1905, but he was opposed by Speaker of the House Joseph Cannon. This cartoon from Puck *by John S. Pughe depicts various American industries (such as clothing, tobacco, sugar, paper, coal, and beef) as children who claim to need protection from the government in the form of tariffs. Meanwhile the children are abusing dolls who represent independent producers, small dealers, consumers, and the public. In the magazine caption, Cannon asks Roosevelt, "Oh, Sir, you would not turn these helpless, half-grown babes out into a cruel world, would you?"*

Lesson 37 - Restrictions on Trade

Finally, if the United States imports less, other countries will be less likely to buy the goods and services of American companies. Those other countries will not have revenue from sales to the United States with which to buy our goods and services. Sometimes other countries will establish tariffs in retaliation against tariffs their exporters have to face. When imports fall, exports fall also, which can lead to domestic job loss. History has shown that, on the whole, countries that have lower tariffs experience greater economic growth.

Quotas

Another way that governments can restrict imports is by establishing *import quotas*. Import quotas only allow a certain amount of goods to be brought into the country for sale. This avoids imposing tariffs; but it still limits supply, which tends to drive up prices.

In the 1980s, cars imported from Japan gained popularity in the United States, and American-made cars were not selling well. The Reagan administration asked Japanese automakers to limit voluntarily the number of cars they exported to the United States (with the threat of Congress imposing even lower quotas by law if they did not act voluntarily). This allowed Japanese cars to remain on the market in the U.S., but it gave American automakers a chance to maintain or increase their market share of new cars sold in America.

Japanese automakers did limit exports to the U.S. for a period of time, but American automakers did not use the protection to change their products enough to make American car buyers want to buy American models instead of Japanese models. Over time, the Japanese companies dropped the quotas, the market share of Japanese companies continued to increase, and the market share of American companies continued to decline.

A different form of import quota is the requirement that a certain percentage of a product has to consist of parts made in the United States. For example, Congress might require that 30% or 60% of the parts in a car, stereo system, or other product that is sold in this country be made in this country or that American workers must assemble the finished product in this country. This maintains American involvement in the industry but allows for some level of importation from other countries.

China became the world's leading automaker in 2009. It now produces more cars than the United States and Japan combined. This 2011 photo is of a plant run by Geely, a Chinese car company. Most Chinese cars are sold in China, but exports have been growing to countries such as Iran, Vietnam, and Brazil.

Trade Sanctions

The other focus for a government imposing trade restrictions involves addressing conditions in another country. A *sanction* is an order forbidding citizens from trading with another country. A foreign country might be experiencing a blight on an agricultural product, and the American government might impose a sanction on importing that product, not wanting that blight to be brought into this country. In another situation, a manufacturer in another country might be found to be using lead paint on its goods. The United States might consider this a threat to the health of Americans and impose a sanction on those goods, refusing to let them be imported. Trade sanctions might also include a ban on exporting goods from the U.S. to another country.

Another motivation for imposing sanctions is to protest the policies of another government. Many countries refused to do business with the Republic of South Africa when it followed the policy of segregation called apartheid. The United Nations Security Council imposed trade sanctions on Iraq after its invasion of Kuwait in 1990. The sanctions were intended to compel Iraq's withdrawal from Kuwait and to reveal and destroy any weapons of mass destruction. The UN kept the sanctions in place until the Iraqi leader, Saddam Hussein, fell from power in 2003. The UN Security Council has imposed trade sanctions against North Korea because of North Korea's development of a nuclear weapons program.

Sanctions can sometimes cause a country to correct economic conditions in order to restore trade. Suppose that the United States government determined that working conditions in Bangladeshi clothing factories were unsafe and therefore the U.S. would no longer import clothing from Bangladesh. The Bengali government could then require companies making clothing in that country to improve worker safety conditions in its factories. While this is a humanitarian issue, it is also an economic one because such safety measures cost money and therefore increase the cost of producing clothing in Bangladesh.

On the other hand, sanctions designed to put pressure on a foreign government to change political or social policies have a less consistent record. The offending government can demonize the United States and other countries in the eyes of its citizens, portray itself as an innocent victim, and sometimes find other trading partners who are willing to do business with the country. Experience has shown that a policy of engagement (working with another country) rather than sanctions has sometimes been the better course for helping bring about change in other countries.

Here are some practical questions that demonstrate the difficulty of determining when imposing sanctions is the better course and when engagement is the better course:

Should the United States have engaged in trade with Nazi Germany while that country pursued a policy of exterminating Jews?

Should the U.S. have traded with the Soviet Union while that country kept thousands of political prisoners incarcerated?

Was the U.S. able to influence Cuba's regime to expand political and personal liberty while it did not trade with the island nation, or will recent diplomatic recognition and greater trade with Cuba lead to greater freedom for Cubans?

Would refusing to trade with Communist China move the Chinese government to grant greater religious and political liberties to its citizens, or will trading with China be more likely to accomplish this goal?

Workers at the Rana Plaza building in Dhaka, Bangladesh, produced clothing for several major international retailers. Because of unsafe construction and improper use, the building collapsed in 2013. The collapse killed 1,100 people and injured 2,500.

Sugar producers in the United States receive extensive subsidies. This makes the cost of sugar in the U.S. roughly twice the average cost elsewhere in the world. This sugar refinery is in Chalmette, Louisiana.

Subsidies

Another government policy that affects trade is the practice of *subsidies*. Subsidies are government payments to industries that have to compete in a world market where prices are lower than they are in the producing country. The net effect is similar to that of a tariff, but the government receives money from a tariff and pays money with a subsidy.

If American widget makers found themselves competing in the world market where the going price was $1 per widget but it cost an American manufacturer $2 a widget to produce them, the United States government might enact a $1 per widget subsidy. The government would pay this subsidy to the manufacturer, who could then sell its widgets for $1 each but actually receive $2 each ($1 in sales plus $1 from the subsidy). This would enable American widgets to compete in the world market and would enable the American manufacturer to stay in business.

Many governments provide subsidies for agricultural products. Exports of American farm products are an important part of the domestic farm economy, but American growers face a world market in which prices are lower than they are in the United States. The American government subsidizes American farmers so that they can sell their goods in the world market at competitive prices and still show a profit.

One defense for subsidies is that producers can't compete when prices are low. On the other hand, growers in developing nations say that they can't compete in a world market dominated by subsidies. Subsidies are an artificial support for higher prices that prevent the forces of supply and demand from arriving at the market clearing or equilibrium price. As a result, subsidies hurt the economy to some degree, even as they help some segments of the economy and as elected officials receive support from people in subsidized industries.

All of the trade restrictions that this lesson describes make trade between nations more expensive or more difficult for consumers. The next lesson presents the case for free trade as the better way for international commerce to take place.

In the book of Genesis, Hamor wanted the sons of Jacob to live in the land and trade without restrictions as part of the arrangement he offered the family of Jacob.

---

*Thus you shall live with us, and the land shall be open before you;
live and trade in it and acquire property in it.*
Genesis 34:10

Assignments for Lesson 37

Making Choices — Read "The Candlemakers' Petition" (pages 78-81).

Literature — Continue reading *The Travels of a T-Shirt in the Global Economy*.

Project — Continue working on your project for this unit.

Student Review — Answer the questions for Lesson 37.

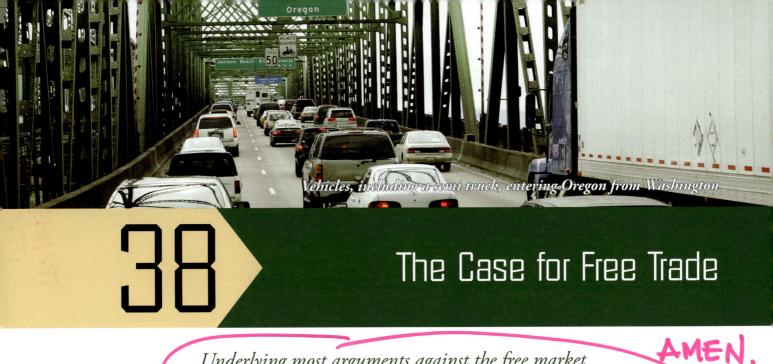

Vehicles, including a semi truck, entering Oregon from Washington

38 The Case for Free Trade

> *Underlying most arguments against the free market is a lack of belief in freedom itself.*
> — Milton Friedman

We have outlined the nature and benefits of international trade and described restrictions that governments sometimes place on trade. In this lesson we present the case for free trade, which is trade that takes place as much as possible without the restrictions that the previous lesson described.

Practical Benefits

Policies that limit free trade impede economic growth and opportunity. Trade restrictions reduce the selection of goods and services that the public has available to them and artificially raise the prices that businesses charge for goods and services. The higher prices that are a result of tariffs and the money a government spends on subsidies are funds that could go toward developing other parts of the economy but do not because of those trade restrictions.

Free trade is more than just insistence on an ideological principle. Trade provides concrete benefits to a nation's people. International markets for a nation's output of goods and services mean more jobs, greater economic opportunity, and a higher standard of living for its citizens. Free trade means more goods and services available to people at prices they can afford. Trade also increases the opportunity for interdependence and mutual understanding among trading nations.

One historical example that demonstrates these impacts is the decline of feudalism in medieval Europe as new possibilities for work and sources of wealth opened up for Europeans through trade. The experience of free trade among the fifty United States is another example of how free trade provides economic benefits.

The U.S. economy would not be as strong as it is if state governments had spent economic and political resources on trade wars, erected tariff walls, negotiated trade treaties, and dealt with other trade issues among the several states. All Americans have benefited from free trade within our country. Free trade between countries can produce those same benefits for people around the world.

237

The Historical Pattern

The economic program that the first Secretary of the Treasury, Alexander Hamilton, proposed and that Congress adopted included a system of tariffs on imported goods. Hamilton hoped that, with imports costing American consumers more because of tariffs, American industries would be able to develop without competition from mature industries in other countries. The American economy did grow, although we cannot know how much more or less it might have grown without import tariffs. At the time, such tariffs were a common part of international trade.

During the 1800s and early 1900s, the Whigs and later the Republicans tended to support higher tariffs while Democrats tended to support lower tariffs. The last gasp of classic protectionism in America was the Smoot-Hawley Tariff of 1930, which raised tariffs significantly on thousands of imported goods. Other countries retaliated with tariffs on American goods, and as a result America's foreign trade fell by more than half. The law cost American jobs and probably contributed to the severity of the Great Depression.

President Franklin Roosevelt began a pattern of negotiating reciprocal trade agreements with individual nations. Congress and the executive branch worked together to establish tariff rates. Following World War II, representatives from a number of nations developed the General Agreement on Tariffs and Trade (GATT). The United States adopted the GATT treaty in 1947. This treaty created a forum for international trade negotiations and was the forerunner of the current World Trade Organization (WTO).

Cooperation between nations such as the North American Free Trade Agreement (NAFTA) was a further step toward free trade. The Trans-Pacific Partnership (TPP), awaiting ratification at the time this book was published, is a proposed agreement to reduce tariffs between the U.S. and eleven other countries touching the Pacific Ocean. The TPP has provisions about labor standards, environmental protection, and other issues related to trade.

Another trend has been the extension of Most Favored Nation (MFN) status to an increasing number of trading partners with the United States. This status means that a nation receives the best trade arrangements that the United States gives any country. These arrangements include no or low tariffs, depending on the item in question and other factors. The U.S. government has replaced the MFN term with the term permanent Normal Trade Relations (NTR). The United States has extended NTR status to all countries except Cuba and North Korea.

Though modern agreements still involve significant government oversight of trade, the historical trend among the countries of the world has been toward freer trade.

Protesting the Trans-Pacific Partnership Agreement in Wellington, New Zealand (2014)

Lesson 38 - The Case for Free Trade

Top Ten Countries Receiving U.S. Exports of Goods

Canada	281 (billion US$)
Mexico	236
China	116
Japan	62
United Kingdom	56
Germany	50
South Korea	43
Netherlands	40
Hong Kong	37
Belgium	34

Top Ten Goods Exported

1. Civilian aircraft
2. Pharmaceutical preparations
3. Industrial machines
4. Petroleum products
5. Electric apparatus
6. Semiconductors
7. Telecommunications equipment
8. Fuel oil
9. Medicinal equipment
10. Engines for civilian aircraft

Top Ten Countries Supplying U.S. Imports of Goods

China	483 (billion US$)
Mexico	296
Canada	296
Japan	131
Germany	125
South Korea	72
United Kingdom	58
France	48
India	45
Italy	44

Top Ten Goods Imported

1. Crude oil
2. Pharmaceutical preparations
3. Cell phones and other household goods
4. Telecommunications equipment
5. Computers
6. Computer accessories
7. Industrial machines
8. Textiles
9. Electric apparatus
10. Apparel/household goods (cotton)

*Based on 2015 data from the U.S. Census Bureau

Factors That Increase Trade

In addition to supporting freer trade, nations can implement specific policies that enable them to increase their participation in the global economy. Experience has shown that the following policies provide benefits for countries that put these policies in place.

Better communication. Producers need to know what consumers and potential consumers want. At the same time, potential consumers need to know about the goods and services that producers offer. Clearer and more complete communication helps in both directions. The Internet has been a major factor in expanding the knowledge base of the world's consumers and thus increasing international trade. The freer exchange of information helps everyone.

Better transportation. Producers and consumers want shippers to transport goods and services as quickly and as inexpensively as possible. Improvements in maritime shipping, truck and rail delivery, and air transportation lead to increased trade. This applies to a producing country, in getting goods from the point of production to the point of export, and to a receiving country, in getting goods from the point of import to where consumers live. Better transportation requires government investment in the transportation infrastructure of a country. As with the other factors, better transportation helps not only trade but also other aspects of a nation's life.

Lower transaction costs. Transaction costs are costs other than the cost of the goods and services themselves that are related to the purchase of goods and services. Sellers usually pass on transaction costs to consumers in the form of higher prices. Import tariffs are an example of transaction costs. Such costs can also include fuel expenses for truckers and costs that retailers bear such as business taxes and the costs of complying with regulations. Generally speaking, lower transaction costs will mean an increase in trade.

Fair Trade

Free trade is not the same thing as fair trade. Fair trade is an economic movement intended to help families and small companies in less-developed countries compete in the world economy. The goal of fair trade is to help workers move toward economic stability by giving them a good price for their products. Several religious organizations are involved in the fair trade movement.

Organizations that support the fair trade movement buy handcrafts and agricultural products from small producers, usually at prices somewhat higher than the market equilibrium, and then sell the products in catalogs; on websites; in fair trade stores such as Ten Thousand Villages; and also in some traditional stores, mostly in the United States, Canada, and Europe.

The fair trade movement developed in the 1940s and 1950s to support people with limited economic opportunities and in response to what some saw as exploitation of third-world countries by large multinational corporations in their typical production practices. At the time, the United States and its allies and the Soviet Union and its allies were the two main political spheres in the world. Observers said that other countries, most of which were economically underdeveloped and that were not aligned with either the U.S. or the Soviet Union, were considered the third world.

The fair trade movement makes locally- and uniquely-made crafts available to consumers in other parts of the world and allows people to do what is called conscience shopping for what they buy. Customers for these products usually don't mind

Edna Ruth Byler of Pennsylvania visited Puerto Rico in 1946. She met women there who could create beautiful pieces of embroidery but did not have access to a market to sell them. Byler purchased some items and took them home to sell to friends and neighbors. Working with the Mennonite Central Committee, Byler visited other countries such as India and Jordan to make purchases. Her pioneering work eventually became Ten Thousand Villages, which now partners with thousands of artists in thirty countries to bring goods to stores in the United States and Canada. This store is located in New Hamburg, Ontario.

paying more for these items since they understand the purpose of the sales.

Technically, since the movement relies on assistance from concerned organizations, fair trade prices are price floors that sellers set above the market equilibrium price. This generally results in a surplus of goods and interferes with simple market supply and demand. However, this is a voluntary exchange between producers and consumers rather than a government mandate. The good that fair traders accomplish by helping poor families and by providing the enjoyment that comes from owning these unique items has a value beyond dollars and cents.

Not a Level Field

Since trade offers many benefits to the countries that take part in it, trade that is free of restrictions offers these benefits more widely. However, not all nations are at the same place with regard to their national economy and their participation in the global economy. The world is not a completely level playing field economically, just as it is not a level field politically, educationally, or socially.

Countries are different sizes and have different resources. Different countries have developed different attitudes toward productive work.

Corrupt leaders have run some countries into the ground economically. Some countries are trying to move forward in a global economy that a few major players already dominate.

Not all countries are willing to embrace free trade at the same time and to the same extent. Some still want tariff protection for their domestic industries. Some fear that they will be dumping grounds for cheap goods that companies import from large industrial nations. The world will not become a completely level playing field economically overnight, if ever. The United States can use its influence to help the people of other countries have a better quality of life and enjoy the benefits of economic growth. The best way to accomplish these goals is through the pursuit of free trade.

Free trade is good because freedom is good. Economic freedom is tied to political freedom. The right to vote, the right to free speech, and the right to pursue economic possibilities create a setting in which people can utilize their God-given abilities and become more of what God can enable them to be. Political and economic restrictions mean that someone is imposing their view of what others should and should not be doing. This kind of personal, political, and economic coercion carries a cost; and the people who live under it must pay the cost of that coercion.

Christ offers us a different kind of freedom, one that we can know regardless of the political and economic system under which we live. We can be thankful for freedom in Christ and refuse to submit to sinful spiritual coercion from other humans, as Paul encouraged the Galatians to do.

It was for freedom that Christ set us free; therefore keep standing firm and do not be subject again to a yoke of slavery.
Galatians 5:1

Assignments for Lesson 38

Literature — Continue reading *The Travels of a T-Shirt in the Global Economy*.

Project — Continue working on your project for this unit.

Student Review — Answer the questions for Lesson 38.

Volkswagen

German automaker Volkswagen opened an assembly plant in Chattanooga, Tennessee, in 2011.

39 — Have We Been Exported?

> "Made in China"
> — Seen on many items sold in the United States

Despite the benefits of trade and the advantages of free trade, many people still have serious questions about the nature of America's engagement with the global economy. This lesson examines some of those questions.

Foreign Investments

American economic involvement with the rest of the world does not only take the form of exporting and importing typical goods and services. Sometimes it takes the form of money. For example, Americans invest in foreign business; and they do this primarily in two ways. First, American companies invest money to build factories or set up businesses in other countries. Second, Americans buy stocks or bonds in foreign companies. Americans invest in the economies of other countries in these ways because they hope to make a profit on their investment.

American investments in other countries provide the financial capital to help those nations grow economically. Critics sometimes say that American companies take advantage of other countries by paying relatively low wages to obtain products cheaply. It is true that the wages which American companies pay to workers in other countries are usually lower than wages that those companies pay American workers, but the wages that those foreign workers earn are usually higher than what they had been earning. This is why people are eager to apply for each job that an American-owned company offers in a foreign factory.

At the same time, people and businesses in other countries make investments in the United States. Foreign businesses build factories in the United States; a prime example today are foreign car manufacturers. In addition, foreign investors buy stocks and bonds of American companies. Foreign banks and investors buy U.S. government bonds. The people who make these investments hope to make a profit. Foreign investors in the United States believe that, even when America is going through difficult economic times, the U.S. is still a good investment that will pay off.

Foreign investments in the United States help our economy grow. These investments are also a way for foreign companies to avoid possible tariffs and

243

import quotas. Some of the profits that a foreign-owned company makes in the United States return to the investor's home country; but some investors re-invest in the United States by using profits to expand American operations.

Foreign investors (both governments and private entities) also hold a significant percentage of the debt that the United States government owes. As of June 2016, foreign investors held over $6 trillion worth of U.S. Treasury Securities. For comparison, individuals and institutions in the United States owned twice as much about $13 trillion.

Increasing debt for growing government expenditures makes the American people more dependent on foreign-held debt. If foreign investors were not investing in government debt, they might well be investing in private American companies. This could mean growth in productive industries rather than paying the salaries of government workers. Workers get paid either way, whether they are government employees or employees in the private sector. However, investment in business brings better results in terms of creating more economic growth.

Top Fifteen Foreign Holders of U.S. Treasury Securities (2016)

Country	Amount (billion US$)
China	1,241
Japan	1,148
Ireland	271
Cayman Islands	269
Brazil	252
Switzerland	237
United Kingdom	232
Luxembourg	225
Taiwan	188
Hong Kong	185
Belgium	156
India	117
Singapore	107
Germany	99
Saudi Arabia	98

Tokyo (shown above) is Japan's capital and largest city. Japan's national Government Pension Investment Fund is the largest pension fund in the world with over $1 trillion in assets. It holds a large quantity of foreign bonds, including U.S. Treasury notes.

Balance of Trade, Balance of Payments

One way to measure a nation's trading activity is by its *trade balance,* also called the *balance of trade.* The balance of trade is the difference between a country's imports and exports. When a country imports more than it exports, it is said to have a *trade deficit.* When a nation exports more than it imports, this is called a *trade surplus.*

The trade balance is not the only aspect of a country's economic interaction with other countries. The *balance of payments* is the record of all transactions between the people of one country and the rest of the world. We can break down the balance of payments into the *current account* and the *capital account.*

Current Account. The current account is also called net foreign assets. Using the U.S. as an example, this account includes the sum of the U.S. trade balance, the net factor income (interest and dividends Americans receive from foreign investments plus money Americans living in another country send back to their families in this country), and net transfer payments such as direct foreign aid. The term current means that these are the goods and services that are immediately or currently consumed.

Capital Account. The capital account reflects any exchange involving a change of ownership of an asset, such as if a domestic party buys a foreign asset or a foreign party buys a domestic asset. It reflects the result of purchasing a capital investment. Some economists refer to this as the *financial account* and use *capital account* to refer to a subset of capital transfers.

The net measurement of the current account and the capital account can influence the foreign exchange market, as we will see in the next lesson.

Many Apple technology products are marketed as "Designed by Apple in California Assembled in China."

Is a Trade Deficit Bad?

As we mentioned earlier, if a nation imports more than it exports, it has a trade deficit or a negative balance of trade. For many years the United States had a trade surplus. Then the U.S. developed a trade deficit for two main reasons. First, foreign banks and private foreign investors purchased U.S. government bonds issued to cover government debt. Second, Americans became increasingly dependent on foreign products such as oil and consumer goods. Now the U.S. buys much more from other countries than it sells to other countries.

Foreign buyers pay American suppliers for the exports that leave this country. This brings money from other countries into the United States, which in accounting terms is called an investment in the U.S. In other words, the money we bring in pays for the exports we ship out. On the other hand, American buyers who bring imports into the country pay foreign suppliers for those imports. These payments are foreign investments by American companies.

If the United States did not import goods, it would probably not be able to export goods. If we do not provide a market for foreign goods, other countries will not want to provide a market for our goods. So, we must have imports in order to have exports. In a sense, we pay for our imports with our exports. If in the exchange the U.S. has a trade deficit, we make it up by borrowing. Domestic investors provide much of this money, while foreign investors also provide a significant share.

A trade deficit is not in and of itself a bad thing. The more important question to answer is what we do with the goods that we import. If we use those imports to improve our standard of living, concentrate more on our comparative advantage, and utilize our resources well, those imports will be a benefit.

However, a trade deficit does have its disadvantages. Any country that trades with another country is dependent to some degree on what happens in that other country. For instance, our dependence on foreign oil has led to major problems because of events and policies in oil-exporting countries. A trade deficit indicates a relatively greater dependence on foreign suppliers, while a trade surplus indicates a relatively greater dependence on foreign buyers. A country with a negative balance of payments would seem especially dependent on other countries and on debt to fund the import imbalance.

If political instability in a foreign country affects a foreign producer or buyer, or if American relations with the host country of a foreign trading partner turn sour, this might reduce or eliminate the supply of foreign goods and services we enjoy and reduce or eliminate the market there for our goods and services. If, for example, Communist China ever decided to make a military move to assert its claim on the island of Taiwan, American economic dependence on China might leave the U.S. in a difficult diplomatic situation.

The fact that what happens elsewhere can affect the United States is the downside to globalization and interdependence. Since we cannot assume that foreign events will never affect the United States, American trade policies should help limit the impact those events have.

Moving Production Offshore

American businesses have increasingly moved the production of certain goods to other countries. One motivation for this has been to reduce labor costs. For some companies, it is economically advantageous to build a factory in another country, send raw materials or parts there, hire and train workers there, and send the finished products back to the United States. This is cheaper for many companies than paying American workers and carrying out production here, even in U.S. factories that the company already owns.

When a company moves production to another country (often called moving production offshore, even if it is to Mexico or Canada), it changes the competitive dynamics in that industry with regard to price. The price for which that company can offer the product becomes the standard against which other companies must compete in terms of price. Competing companies then have some choices to make. They can move production offshore also, or they can keep production in the United States and try to compete on factors other than price. They might advertise their products as "American Made with American Quality," or they might aim for a different share of the market, such as selling their products in higher-priced stores.

A company considering moving production offshore will need to do a cost-benefit analysis of such a move. There are costs and benefits other than price. The company will become dependent on the trade and commerce policies of another government and will have to deal with another layer of logistics in order to get their products back to the United States. Customer satisfaction is another issue. Some companies have moved their customer service departments offshore. As a result, customer calls are routed to representatives in India, the Philippines, or some other country. This might save the company money, but it can frustrate customers who cannot understand the representatives. Those customers might decide to take their business to another company.

Offshore production reflects the principle of opportunity cost. Remember that opportunity cost is the alternative of greatest value that someone gives up to do what he is doing. Workers in other countries give up less to work in American-owned factories than American workers do by working in a factory in America. If a worker in another country is able to get a job in an American-owned factory there for $3.00 per hour, he will have to give up another job at which he might only make $2.00 an hour. If an American worker in the U.S. gets a job in a factory making $15.00 per hour, he might give up a job making $12.00 per hour somewhere else.

Since the worker in the other country gives up less, he has a lower opportunity cost. This tradeoff makes the operation of an American-owned factory in that other country a more profitable choice for the company and for the worker from that country. The American worker will not have a job with that company because the company will not build a factory in the U.S.; but with specialization in the U.S. focusing on higher-skill work, the American worker might be able to get a job with another company making $15.00 or $18.00 per hour.

In addition, building industries in other countries can increase the world market for American products as wages rise in those other countries. Moving production offshore challenges American workers to retrain for new and ideally higher-paying skills in the ever-changing economy.

TeleTech, headquartered in Englewood, Colorado, partners with clients around the world to provide customer service to endusers. TeleTech has offices on six continents. Several are in the Philippines, including this one in Dumaguete City.

Sign on a general store in Arizona (2015)

On the other hand, American workers are hurt by losing their jobs, certainly in the short-run and sometimes in the long-run also. Communities are hurt by the closing of factories, and local business and political leaders have to work on new goals and seek out new possibilities for local residents to find work. No doubt a certain level of resentment toward the company can remain. These are reasons why the company has to determine if the benefits of such a move outweigh the costs.

Sometimes moving production off shore has ironic results. As of 2016, the largest printer of Bibles in the world was Amity Printing, located in Nanjing, China. The Communist Chinese government places strict limits on Christians and sometimes persecutes them. It also restricts the sale of Bibles within China to the officially-sanctioned Three Self Patriotic Movement churches. But the Chinese government is glad for American and other publishers to print Bibles in China for export to other countries.

Balancing the Pros and Cons

Sometimes we Americans grumble about all of the imported goods we see on American store shelves. We see bumper stickers telling us to "Buy American." I have done my share of grumbling, and I admit that I usually prefer to buy American-made goods. On the whole, I trust American quality more that I do the quality of goods made in other countries. Stories regarding lower food production standards and the use of lead paint in other countries concern me.

I am also concerned about the increasing economic dependence that the United States has on production in other countries. Some of those countries are subject to political unrest. The United States could face a difficult situation if an important trading partner became a political enemy. National security questions can arise, as we have seen in our dependence on oil imported from the Middle East. A company or a nation should not focus on short-term improvement in the bottom line while failing to consider possible long-term negative consequences.

But trade is a two-way street. Eliminating imports means that other countries will not want to buy what we produce. This happened as a result of the Smoot-Hawley Tariff in 1930, and it significantly hurt the American economy. Companies export much of what American workers produce. If we don't trade with other countries, those other countries will find other sources for what they want or they will develop the skills and technology necessary for them to produce the goods themselves. The warning against a decision based on short-term thinking applies here also. We don't need to implement policies based on a short-sighted "America First" reaction without considering the long-term consequences of such decisions for America.

Trade decisions do not just affect us. As they do affect us, trade means more American jobs and increases our standard of living. But we cannot base our trade policy solely on the advantages Americans gain from it. Trade must be win-win if other countries are going to agree to it. As we consider what is the best trade policy for the United States to pursue in a world that is an uneven playing field, we also have to consider how others will be better off through trade with the United States.

Voluntary trade is a win-win transaction overall or countries would not engage in it. Both countries that engage in trade are better off in the big picture. Many workers who are laid off find other jobs or retrain and then find work, while other former workers go into business for themselves and see their job loss as a blessing and an open door for personal and economic growth.

We cannot keep the same number of people doing the same jobs in the same industries forever. If that were a good thing, we would still have thriving typewriter and corded telephone industries. The economy changes, and people have to change with it. Through innovation, companies offer more goods and services, a larger economic pie develops, and more people have bigger pieces of the pie. This trend is called *creative destruction*: through the creation of new industries and better technology, some jobs are lost, but more jobs are created and the overall economy grows. If nothing else, the economy has to change for more and more people to find jobs simply because the population is growing.

However, there are some losers at the smaller microeconomic level. As we have said, when a company moves production offshore, or when cheaper imports cause an American business to close, some people lose their jobs and cannot find other work. The gains outweigh the losses overall, but individuals are sometimes hurt while company owners make a profit. Protectionism is not the answer either. We have seen how protectionism has the unintended consequence of hurting the American consumer.

One major political issue involves determining compensation for those whom trade hurts and what form that compensation takes. In *In His Steps* (see Lesson 29), the government offered no unemployment benefits to the typesetter who had lost his job. Today, many workers who lose their jobs can receive unemployment assistance for several months, help in finding another job, and retraining to learn new skills, all through government programs. In some ways, the government has taken over giving out the assistance that private sources used to provide.

Retraining of unemployed workers in Hagerstown, Maryland (1962)

We are not exporting America. The U.S. actually loses more jobs to innovation than it does to production going to other countries, but the economy continues to grow. U.S. manufacturing output is higher than ever. However, manufacturing employment is lower than it has been in the past. The U.S. is producing greater manufacturing value with fewer manufacturing workers. More people are working at other kinds of jobs.

Change is difficult, but in the long run change can produce growth. Some trade policy decisions do seem short-sighted, but in the long run we have to participate in and lead in the world economy as it is.

King Solomon exported wheat and oil and imported lumber from King Hiram of Tyre to build the temple.

So Hiram sent word to Solomon, saying, "I have heard the message which you have sent me; I will do what you desire concerning the cedar and cypress timber. My servants will bring them down from Lebanon to the sea; and I will make them into rafts to go by sea to the place where you direct me, and I will have them broken up there, and you shall carry them away. Then you shall accomplish my desire by giving food to my household."
1 Kings 5:8-9

Assignments for Lesson 39

Making Choices — Read the press releases from U.S. Customs and Border Protection (pages 82-84).

Literature — Continue reading *The Travels of a T-Shirt in the Global Economy*.

Project — Continue working on your project for this unit.

Student Review — Answer the questions for Lesson 39.

Currency Exchange Rate Display

40 Money Changes Clothes

When preparing to travel, lay out all your clothes and all your money. Then take half the clothes and twice the money.

— Susan Heller

When you buy a T-shirt in a store, you pay the clerk with American dollars. But when you are in another country and buy something from a vendor, you have to add a step. At some point, you or the vendor must exchange your American dollars for the currency that people use in that other country. We discussed money in the previous unit, and in this unit we have talked about trade. In this lesson we deal with the trading of money between countries.

Exchange Rate

A *currency exchange rate* is the price of one country's currency expressed in terms of another country's currency. For example, on the day I wrote this lesson, one U.S. dollar could buy .73 British pounds, .85 euros, or 132.94 Japanese yen. To think of the prices in the opposite direction, one British pound was worth $1.32, one euro was worth $1.17, and one yen was worth 1.3 cents.

The forces of supply and demand determine the prices for money, just as they do with other prices. When the supply of a currency in currency exchange markets is greater, its value is less. When demand increases for a currency, its value increases. Usually, currency exchange rates do not fluctuate widely from day to day. Significant changes occur gradually over a long period of time, and they will vary from year to year. The *equilibrium exchange rate* is the exchange rate at which currency demand equals currency supply.

Sometimes we see exchange rates expressed in the form of a ratio: € .85/$1.00 (one hundred American dollars buys 85 euros). If the ratio changes to € .95/$1.00, the dollar is said to have appreciated or strengthened in relation to the euro because the same dollar will buy more of the foreign currency (100 American dollars would buy 95 euros). At the same time, the euro is said to have depreciated or weakened with reference to the dollar.

If the ratio moves to € .75/$1.00, the dollar has gotten weaker in relation to the euro and the euro has strengthened in relation to the dollar (one hundred American dollars would buy only 75 euros). Weaker dollars encourage foreigners to buy more American goods (75 euros would buy 100 American dollars, whereas before it took 85 or 95 euros to buy 100

251

American dollars), while stronger or more expensive dollars mean that foreigners are less likely to buy American goods because they cost more in terms of their own currency.

Currency Exchange for Travel

Suppose you want to travel to Germany. You know that while you are there you will want to eat at restaurants and buy souvenirs. You will also want to buy a Eurorail pass to go to different parts of the country. You establish a budget for how much you can spend. You now need euros to carry out all of your exciting plans.

You can take your U.S. dollars to your own bank to buy euros, or you can purchase them at an ATM or other location when you arrive in Germany. Your purchase will be on the basis of the *nominal exchange rate*, which is the rate at which you can exchange one currency for another. You can also use a credit card and let the credit card company figure what your purchases in euros cost in the U.S. dollars you will use to pay your bill. By the way, it is always important to let your bank and credit card company know of your travel plans, so they will know that you are the actual person making foreign purchases.

Currency Exchange in Trade

As important as tourism is, your buying of euros is (pardon the expression) small change compared to the amounts of currencies that change hands in international trade. More people buy goods from other countries than actually visit other countries. A tourist visiting China will probably not buy a large-screen television made in China while visiting that county. But that person might buy one from a store in the United States that imports televisions from China. How those televisions get to American store shelves involves currency exchange.

Electronics display at a Costco Wholesale store (2014)

Acme Department Store decides that it wants to carry Chinese-made televisions. Acme's buyers make deals with producers to buy them (in reality, there may be several layers of middlemen, but let's keep it simple). To obtain these items, Acme will need to do what tourists do: use its dollars in a U.S. bank to buy Chinese yuan. Acme will then use that currency to buy televisions from the Chinese company and import them to sell to American consumers.

Currency Exchange in Investments

Foreign banks commonly buy U.S. government bonds as investments. Foreign investors believe that the bonds will keep their value. They might also invest in bonds that American companies issue.

These investors will follow the same procedure that people used in the previous illustrations, except that in this case buyers are purchasing securities and stocks. The investors buy dollars in a currency exchange with their national currency, then they make the investment with dollars that they pay to the Treasury Department, American investment bank, or private company. Several foreign car makers have built factories in the United States. To do so, they had to buy dollars in a currency market in order to buy land from its American owner and pay an American construction company to build the factory.

The level of ease and the cost with which people can make international payments, whether for travel or trade or investment, will either encourage or hinder international trade and finance.

Factors Affecting Exchange Rates

As we mentioned earlier, supply and demand in the exchange market determine currency exchange rates. When an American company buys products from abroad, the transaction puts dollars into the exchange market. This greater supply makes dollars worth less in the exchange market. This in turn encourages people in foreign countries to buy more from the United States because dollars are cheaper in terms of their own currency.

The reverse occurs when an American company exports goods and services to other countries. Buyers in other countries buy dollars in exchange markets to pay for the goods. This lessens the supply of dollars, which causes the value of dollars to increase. This leads to foreign entities buying fewer U.S. goods because dollars are more expensive. This buying and selling are the ebb and flow that make currency values in exchange markets fluctuate mildly from day to day.

Foreign investment in the United States has the same effect as American exports. The transaction takes dollars out of the market, which makes dollars worth more. When Americans invest in a foreign country, it has the same effect as buying products to import into the United States. Americans put dollars into the exchange market for buying foreign currency, and the greater supply lessens the value of the dollar.

The actions of the Federal Reserve's Federal Open Market Committee that affect interest rates, which we discussed in Lesson 35, also affect foreign investment. If U.S. interest rates move higher, this encourages more foreign investment in the United States. After all, who wouldn't want to get more for his money? If interest rates are lower, this discourages foreign investment.

Changes in the interest rate might seem small, but because of the amounts of money involved the change can make a big difference. For example, a change in the interest rate from 2% to 2.25% would mean, on $10 billion dollars, a difference of $25 million dollars!

Factors within a country that are not directly economic affect the demand and thus the price for currency in international markets. These factors can include weather disasters that affect farm crops, other natural disasters such as an earthquake, or uncertainty over the outcome of an election.

Suppose a revolution erupts in another country. People outside of that country probably will not want to buy the national currency, since it might not be worth anything in a few weeks. Wealthy citizens in the country experiencing the revolution might want to buy the currency of a more stable country so their wealth won't lose its value. This action further decreases the value of the currency as more of it moves into the currency market.

Or suppose that a country is going through an economic recession. The value of its currency will be lower. This might encourage travelers who can buy the currency relatively cheaply to enjoy a relatively inexpensive vacation there. On the other hand, if a country is enjoying economic growth, its currency will be in greater demand and thus worth more, the exchange rate will be higher, and a trip there or an investment there will be more expensive in terms of another nation's currency.

Real Exchange Rate

Suppose that during your trip to Germany you go into a music store and find a wonderful CD of your favorite Beethoven symphony. You think it would be neat to buy it in Germany, Beethoven's home country. You notice the price, do some quick calculations, and are shocked to realize that it costs 25% more in terms of dollars (the real cost to you) than it likely would in the United States. You could buy five CDs in the United States for what you would have to pay for four in Germany.

You have just been introduced to the *real exchange rate*, which is the rate of exchange for goods and services between one country and another. In this case, the real exchange rate is 1.20 US CDs to 1 German CD. For any number of reasons, the same goods might have different values in different countries. CDs might be more expensive in Germany than in the United States because there is less selection, or because manufacturers have to include a higher import cost, or because performers receive a greater royalty. This kind of difference in value might apply to a ton of wheat, an MP3 player, or any specific product.

The real exchange rate affects both imports and exports. Traders need to know not just what a product will cost in terms of dollars but what the same product will cost when they purchase it from different providers. If a storm damages the banana crop in Honduras, the bananas available from Honduras might be more expensive compared to bananas from Colombia. For example, five tons of Honduran bananas might cost as much as eight tons of Colombian bananas. Traders, investors, and consumers always seek the best deal, and knowing the real exchange rate helps buyers understand their options.

Arbitrage is the term used for taking advantage of price differences. Less expensive domestic goods in terms of the real exchange rate encourage domestic buyers as well as importers in other countries to buy those less expensive goods. This arbitrage exerts pressure on both currencies to make the real exchange rate closer to 1 to 1.

Sometimes reality gets unusual. Our friends who lived in Communist Poland in the 1970s (see Lesson 30) described to us getting paid in cash in Polish currency. They had few things they needed to buy, there was not much in stores available to buy, and there was no exchange rate because they were not allowed to exchange the Polish currency

Record store in Leipzig, Germany (2008)

People's Bank of China, Beijing (2015)

for American dollars. There was not a great demand for Polish currency in exchange markets, even though the Polish people would have been eager to exchange it for other currencies if they could. Our friends just stacked the cash in a cupboard. Before they left the country, they were allowed to buy a few relatively small items to take back to America with them. They had a rich cultural experience, but the Polish currency in which they were paid was almost worthless.

China's Currency Tactic

Currency exchange rates can have an impact on international trade. Many observers have accused China of manipulating the value of its currency to its own advantage. Until 2005 the Chinese government pegged the value of the yuan artificially low, cheaper than the yuan would have been if traded freely in currency exchange markets. It sought to maintain this rate by buying huge amounts of American currency, which it then used to buy American government debt.

These actions put a large amount of the yuan into exchange markets, which kept its value depressed. In recent years, the People's Bank of China has allowed the value of the yuan on currency markets to fluctuate more, but it still maintains some control over the relative value of the currency.

The effect of the former policy was to encourage other countries to buy Chinese goods because those other countries could buy the yuan cheaply to pay for Chinese products. It also made imports into China relatively expensive, which kept other countries from benefiting from the growing domestic market in China. This policy protected Chinese industries from foreign competition without the imposition of a tariff or subsidy.

Encouraging exports and discouraging imports in this way seemed to be an unfair trading practice. Many people believed that trade with China would remain out of balance unless China allowed the value of the yuan to rise to its real competitive level, or unless other countries took actions such as filing complaints with the World Trade Organization or imposing tariffs on goods imported from China.

As we have said, money is a medium of exchange. It conveys value and worth. But in conveying value and worth in international trade, money is itself subject to the same factors of supply and demand.

In Jesus' day, the Jewish leaders required people to make contributions to the temple in Jewish money. This meant that people from other lands had to exchange their currency for Jewish currency. The money changers in the temple provided this service—for a fee. The people had the demand, while the money changers had the supply. Merchants in the temple also sold kosher or clean animals for people to sacrifice.

Supply and demand was at work in those exchanges because of the rules that the Jewish leaders had established regarding temple worship. Jesus objected to the Jewish leaders imposing these rules and then allowing sellers to make a profit from this controlled, enforced trade that sellers carried on in the name of being faithful to God.

And Jesus entered the temple and drove out all those who were buying and selling in the temple, and overturned the tables of the money changers and the seats of those who were selling doves.
Matthew 21:12

Assignments for Lesson 40

Literature Continue reading *The Travels of a T-Shirt in the Global Economy*.

Project Finish your project for this unit.

Student Review Answer the questions for Lesson 40 and take the quiz for Unit 8.

Business District, Newkirk, Oklahoma (2013)

09 Business

Businesses offer goods and services in a market. United States law provides for specific ways for businesses to organize. Small businesses are a vital element of economic growth in the United States. People who start businesses must consider many issues in order to build successful enterprises. Profit and loss are powerful motivations for businesses to offer quality goods and services at reasonable prices. Marginal analysis helps a business owner know how best to expand his business. The business cycle is a series of expansions and contractions in an economy.

Lesson 41 - Building Blocks of Business
Lesson 42 - Small Business, Big Dream
Lesson 43 - So You Want to Start a Business?
Lesson 44 - It Comes Down to Profit and Loss
Lesson 45 - The Economy-Go-Round

Books Used

The Bible
Making Choices
The Travels of a T-Shirt in the Global Economy

Project (choose one)

1) Write 300 to 500 words on one of the following topics:

- Think about a business that you could start. Make a detailed business plan. Determine how many people you would need to hire (if any), and what their responsibilities and pay level would be. Determine what you would need to purchase or rent to run your business (a car, signs, office space, etc.). Make an educated estimate of the amount of capital required to start your business. List ways that you could market your business. Write a mission statement for your proposed business (see Lesson 43).

- Write a short story about a small or large business.

2) Design a full-page magazine ad for one of the companies listed in the chart on page 262. You can design it on a computer or by hand using the medium of your choice (paint, pastels, pencil, colored pencil, marker, ink, chalk, etc.).

3) Design a brochure that features at least ten small, locally-owned, independent (non-chain) restaurants and shops in your area with the purpose of encouraging local residents to patronize them.

Walmart Shareholders' Meeting, Fayetteville, Arkansas (2010)

41 Building Blocks of Business

There is one rule for industrialists and that is: make the best quality goods possible at the lowest cost possible, paying the highest wages possible.

— Henry Ford

We have said that economics involves a study of the production, distribution, and consumption of goods and services. In a free market, anyone can carry out one or more of these functions. In the United States, we usually refer to the producers and distributors of these goods and services as businesses, companies, or firms. Most economic information that we can track centers in what these businesses do.

Why People Start Businesses

People begin businesses for several reasons. One reason is simply to make a living. Most people learn that working and being productive is a good way to spend your life. They learn that people need to be responsible and provide for themselves so others don't have to. The typical person prefers eating to not eating and having a roof over his head to sleeping on a park bench. He doesn't expect the government, his church, his family, or some friends to support him, so he goes to work for a producer or he begins a company to provide a product or service. He hopes to make a profit from his work that will support him and his family. The combined efforts of the millions of people who work for others or start their own businesses make up the economic activity of a nation.

Making a living might not sound like the embodiment of a noble ideal, but what this person is doing is worthwhile. Supporting yourself is better than expecting others to support you. When a person supports himself and makes a profit, he generates money with which he can help others.

Another reason to start a company is to fulfill a dream, perhaps to accomplish a lifelong ambition to do a particular work. Someone notices a need that is not met, or he or she has a goal of doing something that he or she finds fulfilling. This kind of dream is often the starting point for a great endeavor. Of course, making that great endeavor generate income is necessary to keep it going. A person won't be able to accomplish his or her dream for very long if doing so doesn't pay the bills.

Other reasons for running a business include providing a way for others to receive training in a skill or trade, continuing a business that has been in the family for years, or providing employment so others can achieve a higher standard of living. These reasons do not have to be mutually exclusive. A business can accomplish several of these goals.

A common question about business is whether a business should focus on its mission or its profits. Focusing on the mission can be so idealistic that the business closes. On the other hand, focusing on profits can tempt the businessperson to compromise fundamental principles such as honesty and quality. Principles have to come first, and people who want to do what is right cannot compromise them.

If they do compromise on what is right, the financial return will not be worth it. Often, the person who is just out to make a profit will wind up failing in business because consumers can tell that the businessperson's focus is on money instead of people. A clear commitment to God and His principles will give a person the reassurance of doing what is right, and God says that He will honor that kind of commitment (see Matthew 6:33).

Ways of Setting Up a Business

When a person has decided what he or she wants to do in a business, the next step is to decide how to go about it. In the United States, the law provides four basic options for organizing a business. Each option has pros and cons depending on the mission, scope, and personnel involved.

Sole proprietorship. By far the most common type of business organization in the U.S. is the sole proprietorship. If Sam Smith wants to set up a plumbing business, he can buy some tools, get some business cards printed, and have "Smith Plumbing" painted on the side of his truck. If Judy Jones wants to start a bookkeeping business, she can furnish a home office, build a website, and knock on the doors of some businesses in town. The process for setting up a sole proprietorship is fairly easy; usually registering with the county and state is all that is necessary. A sole proprietorship faces fewer government regulations than other forms of business.

The owner of this kind of business has complete control over what the business does. A sole proprietorship can have employees, such as a plumber's assistant or a receptionist. The proprietor pays his or her employees out of the sales or receipts of the business; remember that labor is a cost of production. Only whatever is left after all the bills are paid—including wages for labor—is considered profit. A sole proprietor receives the profit from the business and pays taxes on that profit.

On the other hand, the sole proprietor is legally responsible (liable) for all financial responsibilities that the business has. Finding financial backing for a sole proprietorship is sometimes difficult, and going into debt greatly increases one's risk and obligations. Moreover, anyone who works for the business will want to be assured that he or she will get paid.

The sole proprietor is responsible for every aspect of the business: maintenance of equipment, maintaining financial records, advertising and sales, hiring and managing workers, and overseeing the work itself. The proprietor can give some of these jobs to employees, but the owner of the business still carries the responsibility for it all. When the owner retires or dies, unless the owner has made arrangements to sell the business or for an heir to receive it, the business ends.

In the United States, almost three out of four businesses are sole proprietorships. Although these businesses are numerous, they are usually small. They account for about 4% of sales in the American economy.

Partnership. The next most complicated form of business organization is the partnership, in which two or more people agree to start a business

Horst and Gerda Hofer emigrated from West Germany to Atlanta in the late 1950s in response to an advertisement for a baker and pastry chef. After working several years for others, they opened their own German-style bakery in 1973. In 1991 the Hofers opened this location in Helen, Georgia. Their son Ralph now owns and operates it.

---

and share in the profit or the loss. Sometimes one partner agrees to be the day-to-day manager while the other is called a silent partner and just provides the funding and perhaps some advice. Partners can divide up the ownership and the percentage of profits however they wish.

A partnership is relatively easy to set up and faces few legal regulations. Such an arrangement can allow partners to utilize their different strengths to help the business grow. Often a partnership has access to greater financial resources and can employ more skilled workers than a sole proprietorship. Although the partners share in the profits, each partner is completely liable for all of the debts and obligations of the business. When one partner leaves or dies, the partnership must be reorganized or dissolved. Sometimes partners have differing ideas about what to do or how to grow, and conflicts can arise even among well-meaning people.

Partnerships comprise about ten percent of American businesses, and they are responsible for about 12% of the nation's sales activity. Accountants, architects, and attorneys often form partnerships. Some partners organize their business as an LLP, or limited liability partnership. This form of organization limits the financial liability or responsibility of the individual partners.

LLC. A limited liability company, or LLC, is a flexible form of organization that combines some features of a sole proprietorship or partnership with those of a corporation. It is a distinct legal entity, but it does not have to follow all of the rules that apply to corporations.

Corporation. The most complex form of business organization is the corporation. The business owner or owners must charter and set up the corporation according to the laws of the state where the corporate headquarters are located. A corporation has a board of directors that meets regularly. It also has officers (chief executive officer, chief financial officer, and so forth) that oversee the daily operation of the company.

A corporation is a separate entity from its owners and directors. This limits the legal liability of each individual owner, director, and officer. The corporation continues to exist even if an owner or director leaves the company.

Most very large companies are corporations. About 18% of U.S. businesses are organized in this way, and they produce 84% of sales in the American economy.

Twenty Largest Companies in the United States (based on revenue, as of 2016)

Company	Headquarters	Industry	Revenue	Employees
Walmart	Bentonville, AR	Retail	$482 billion	2,300,000
ExxonMobil	Irving, TX	Energy	$246 billion	76,000
Apple	Cupertino, CA	Electronics	$234 billion	110,000
Berkshire Hathaway	Omaha, NE	Holding company	$211 billion	331,000
McKesson	San Francisco, CA	Pharmaceuticals	$181 billion	70,000
UnitedHealth Group	Minnetonka, MN	Health insurance	$157 billion	200,000
CVS Health	Woonsocket, RI	Food and drug store	$153 billion	199,000
General Motors	Detroit, MI	Motor vehicles	$152 billion	215,000
Ford Motor	Dearborn, MI	Motor vehicles	$150 billion	199,000
AT&T	Dallas, TX	Telecommunications	$147 billion	281,000
General Electric	Fairfield, CT	Industrials	$140 billion	333,000
AmerisourceBergen	Chesterbrook, PA	Pharmaceuticals	$136 billion	17,000
Verizon	New York, NY	Telecommunications	$132 billion	178,000
Chevron	San Ramon, CA	Energy	$131 billion	62,000
Cargill	Wayzata, MN	Food production	$120 billion	153,000
Costco	Issaquah, WA	Retail	$116 billion	161,000
Fannie Mae	Washington, DC	Financial services	$110 billion	7,300
Kroger	Cincinnati, OH	Food and drug stores	$110 billion	431,000
Amazon.com	Seattle, WA	Retail and technology	$107 billion	231,000
Walgreens Boots Alliance	Deerfield, IL	Food and drug stores	$103 billion	303,000

Lesson 41 - Building Blocks of Business

The owners of a corporation receive shares of stock, which represent the small parts of the company that they own. Owners can influence the management of the corporation based on their percentage of ownership. Corporations usually find raising money for their operation and growth easier than it is for sole proprietorships and partnerships because they are larger, more organized business ventures that have more of the skills and resources businesses need to be successful.

On the other hand, setting up a corporation is difficult and relatively expensive. Numerous laws regulate the operations of a corporation. Owners have less control over decisions related to the business since usually they each own only a small percentage of the business. A corporation has to pay taxes on its profits as an income-producing entity, in addition to the taxes that the owners have to pay on what they earn from the corporation individually.

Corporations can be private or public. A private corporation is a company that a relatively few people, sometimes just family members, own. This kind of corporation rarely sells its stock to anyone else. A public corporation usually has many shareholders who buy and sell shares of stock in the stock market. In the chart at left of the twenty largest companies in America, all of them are public except for Cargill.

A PC is a professional corporation, which physicians, attorneys, or other professionals form to separate their professional liabilities from their personal finances.

One special kind of corporation is the non-profit corporation. Whereas a for-profit corporation exists to make money for its owners, a non-profit corporation exists to provide or promote services for the public good. A non-profit corporation can take in more than it spends in a year; but the corporation must retain that surplus to use in its programs, and the corporation cannot give that surplus to individuals. The non-profit organization can hire executives and employees and own property.

Warren Buffet, CEO of Berkshire Hathaway, meets with President Obama in 2010.

Most non-profit organizations apply for an exemption from the federal government to avoid paying corporate taxes, although employees of the organization do have to pay income tax on their wages or salaries. Contributions to a federally-recognized charitable organization (often called a 501(c)(3) organization for the provision in the tax code that regulates them) can be deducted from the contributor's taxable income. Non-profit corporations have to file regular reports and follow certain accounting guidelines to keep their tax-exempt status.

About two million non-profit organizations exist in the United States. They employ about ten million people. Hospitals, charities, museums, and other artistic and educational institutions are often set up as non-profit corporations.

Getting a business organized is one step in the production of goods and services. In the next lesson, we will consider the importance of small businesses in the American economy; and we will think about one kind of business leader, the entrepreneur.

Regardless of the form that a businessperson uses to establish his or her business, that person must operate the business on godly principles to be truly successful.

*The reward of humility and the fear of the Lord
Are riches, honor and life.*
Proverbs 22:4

Assignments for Lesson 41

Making Choices — Read "Market Entrepreneurs: Building Empires of Service" (pages 85-93).

Literature — Continue reading *The Travels of a T-Shirt in the Global Economy*. Plan to finish it by the end of Unit 11.

Project — Choose your project for this unit and start working on it.

Student Review — Answer the questions for Lesson 41.

Dry goods store, Kansas (c. 1890)

42 Small Business, Big Dream

You see things; and you say, "Why?"
But I dream things that never were; and I say, "Why not?"
— George Bernard Shaw

The story of the American economy involves much more than just huge corporations such as Exxon and Apple. Small businesses fill a large and vital role in the American economy.

What are Small Businesses?

A small business is privately owned, generally has under 500 employees, and is not dominant in its field. It may have any of the available legal business structures. The smallest businesses are those based in homes and are sometimes called microbusinesses. A "mom and pop operation" is a colloquial term that describes a family-owned business, usually with no more than ten employees.

The list of the kinds of small businesses that exist is almost endless. Restaurants, print shops, photographers, accountants, convenience stores, attorneys, doctors, and small-scale manufacturers are a few examples. Companies that hire between 100 and 500 employees are usually considered mid-sized small businesses.

Small business owners enjoy being their own boss. They like having the responsibility for making the decisions about their business, and they like receiving the benefits of their work directly. A small business can begin with relatively little money and can operate even on a part-time basis. This kind of business can fill a specialized niche that is passed over by larger companies, which are committed to supplying particular kinds of goods in large quantities. Small businesses often know their customers personally, and they can adapt quickly to changes in the marketplace.

Small business owners are responsible for hiring and training workers, ordering supplies, doing the paperwork involved in keeping records and filing tax forms, and—primarily—serving their customers. People who run small businesses often have to work long hours and usually realize that they actually answer to many bosses, namely their customers.

Money is almost always a big issue for small business owners. Many times someone will use his savings to start a business. He might also borrow money from a friend, family member, or bank, or he might use a credit card. Controlling costs is a major

265

issue for these companies. Typical costs in addition to the costs of production are insurance, energy, facility rental, and taxes.

Small businesses advertise on the Internet, through local media, and in many other ways. Sometimes a business owner will take the trouble and expense to obtain certification in his or her field, and the owner will likely use that certification in his advertising. However, the most effective form of advertising are word of mouth recommendations from satisfied customers who tell their friends.

One way that businesses combine the power and name recognition of a big company with the local service of a small company is through franchising. A large company, such as McDonald's, Comfort Inn, or Ace Hardware, will sell the right to use its name and business model to a local person in the form of a franchise. The local owner has the advantage of national advertising and big-company purchasing power, but he can own his business locally.

Though owning a franchise has benefits, the franchisee must usually pay a significant upfront fee; and she may be limited in what she can do by the national company's standards of practice. Another way that small business owners try to have more economic strength is through organizations such as a Chamber of Commerce or a national industry-based advocacy group.

The Economic Impact of Small Business

American companies that employ fewer than 500 people account for 99.7% of all firms with employees. They produce just over half of the nation's non-farm private gross domestic product and employ about half of the country's private employees. About half of these businesses are based in homes while only 2% are franchises. Each year on average, small businesses create 60 to 80 percent of the new jobs created in the American economy.

Maine Stay Inn, Camden, Maine (2014)

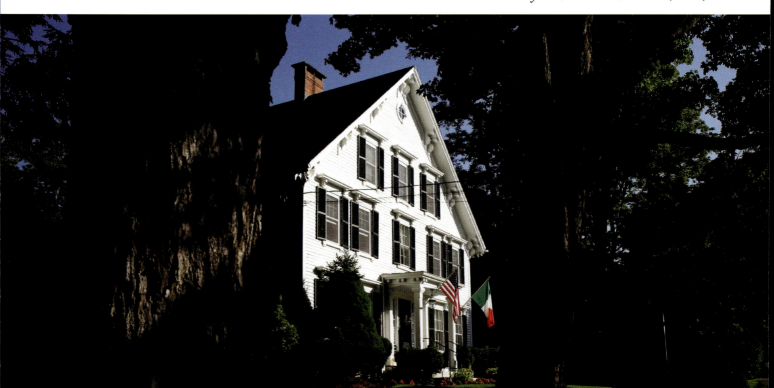

Northern Lights Pizzeria, Skagway, Alaska (2009)

As of 2013, 27.9 million small businesses were in operation in the United States. Companies that had 500 or more employees totaled 18,500. Over 22 million firms did not have employees, while the rest hired at least one worker. Of those that had employees, about 80% had fewer than ten workers.

About a third of the money that the federal government budgets for work by private contractors must go to small businesses. The guidelines for what constitutes a small business for these contracts runs to over forty pages and varies according to the industry. Some of the companies that qualify to bid on these projects have millions of dollars in annual sales.

Success and Failure

About half of all new companies survive at least five years, and about one-third last ten years or longer. In a typical year, around 600,000 companies begin and a slightly smaller number close.

Millions of Americans depend on the management skills of small business owners by either working for a small business or buying from small businesses. Even though many businesses fail, the owners often see these failures as learning experiences that will help them do better next time. We will look at common reasons for business success and failure in the next lesson.

Entrepreneurs

A person who starts a small businesses is often called an *entrepreneur*. The word is from the French and means one who begins or undertakes something. Most students of business and economics credit nineteenth-century economist Jean-Baptiste Say with coining the term. Entrepreneurs are business persons who organize a new firm or develop a new product or technology. They often risk their personal resources to be able to make a profit. They are often creative and visionary in their approach to what their company offers to the public.

An entrepreneur might be an inventor who develops a new product, an innovator who brings an invention to the marketplace in a distinctive way, or someone who simply believes deeply in what he is doing and works hard to serve the public. They are successful when their companies produce goods and services that customers value highly.

The entrepreneurial spirit can be present in a small business owner who is willing to look at things in a new way, and it can also be alive in the research and development department of a large corporation. If an idea catches on, today's entrepreneur can become tomorrow's business leader who inspires others to envision a new idea or approach and to take the risk of offering it to the public.

In the book of Acts, Lydia was a businesswoman who responded to the gospel and began using her life to serve the Lord.

A woman named Lydia, from the city of Thyatira, a seller of purple fabrics, a worshiper of God, was listening; and the Lord opened her heart to respond to the things spoken by Paul. And when she and her household had been baptized, she urged us, saying, "If you have judged me to be faithful to the Lord, come into my house and stay." And she prevailed upon us.
Acts 16:14-15

Assignments for Lesson 42

Making Choices — Read "What Makes for Success?" (pages 94-97).

Literature — Continue reading *The Travels of a T-Shirt in the Global Economy*.

Project — Continue working on your project for this unit.

Student Review — Answer the questions for Lesson 42.

Idea #1: Lawn Care

43   So You Want to Start a Business?

Greater than the tread of mighty armies is an idea whose time has come.
— *Victor Hugo*

On average in the United States, over 1,700 businesses start every day of the year and about 1,500 close every day of the year. If you want to go into business for yourself, you need to know how you can be one of those that make it—those who correctly appraise the demand for a product or service and are able to supply it in the market at a competitive price. In this lesson we discuss some of the issues that businesses must address if they are going to be able to contribute to the economy of a locality, the nation, and perhaps the world.

How Do I Begin?

Your first act should be to take your dreams and ideas to God in prayer. Of course, praying about it is no guarantee of success in financial terms. Many businesses that are not the subject of prayer are financial successes, and many businesses that people have prayed about fail. God's wisdom is perfect and He shapes us through both success and failure. But prayer is an essential first step. You might realize how you need to refine your dream or even that you need to change it. Without a doubt, the process of prayer will change you.

You need to decide that you are going to be a servant. Jesus wants His followers to be servants. Successful businesses provide a service in some way. You want your business to be a blessing to others. This means that you will need to listen to people, respond to their needs, and do more for them than they expect.

You need to have a goal of achieving sales. It should be obvious that sales are the main source of revenue for a company. You might be excited about going into business with a friend, but that won't bring you sales. You might want to have a slick website, nifty business cards, a catchy logo and motto, and a state of the art computer system to keep track of customers, sales, expenses, and inventory; but none of that will automatically generate sales. If you are going to have a business, you will need to do some selling. If you don't see yourself as someone who can sell things sincerely, something needs to change: either you need to develop your willingness and ability to sell, or you need to choose another way to support yourself besides starting a business.

269

Idea #2: Handmade Crafts

Selling is not a worldly compromise that some people make while others pursue truly worthwhile work such as being a missionary. Most of the people who are missionaries receive support from people who sell goods and services or from people who work for companies that sell goods and services. Selling helps people obtain the goods and services they want and need. Selling also enables business owners to bless others with their profits.

What Am I Going to Do?

You should make an appraisal of your talents and interests. People who have a passion for what they do and are good at it generally have the most successful businesses. You might want to get advice from your family and friends. They might be more objective about where your strengths lie than you are. You might want to start a business for which you have no training or experience, but if that is the case you need to admit it and go about getting the training and experience you need.

Do you want to sell goods, or services, or both? You might want to provide replacement parts as well as offer repair service. You might decide to have a business that offers home medical equipment in addition to offering home health care.

Do you want to sell goods that others make, do you want to create your own products, or do you want to do both? Perhaps you are good at creating one particular kind of item, and you want to sell those along with different items that others make.

Do you want to sell to individual customers at retail, to other retailers at wholesale, or both? Selling at retail provides greater profit per sale, but it also requires more work to make each sale.

What Is the Market?

You must find out what people want and what they need, which can be two different things. In other words, what is the demand for your goods and services? You might have to apply your talents in a slightly different way from what you think at first in order to supply what people are demanding. What is a niche that you can fill? What new product or new way of providing a product or service can you offer?

You must determine the current supply. If you want to mow lawns but your town is crawling with lawn care companies, perhaps you can find another niche to fill, such as landscaping, gutter cleaning, or driveway sealing. Once you determine the demand, you will need to decide if you can meet the demand. Perhaps the need is not where your interests or talents lie. Perhaps you will need to collaborate with someone else so that the two of you together can accomplish what neither of you could individually. You will want to assess the level of competition now, but you will also want to consider how the market might change in the future.

What Will Be My Costs?

You must decide what facilities you will need. Should you build a store or office, rent a facility, buy an existing location, or work out of your home? What will you need to invest in capital goods, such as machinery? What other equipment, such as computers and phones, will you need?

Do you want to do the work yourself or do you want to hire others? If you hire others, what pay and benefits will you want and need to offer? Are you willing to interview, train, and manage other people? Labor will probably be your single biggest expense.

Lesson 43 - So You Want to Start a Business?

What will be your cost of production? Will you be able to order the materials and other resources you need? Can you afford the technology you need to make your firm competitive? Will you be able to offer the product or service at a price that will enable you to make a profit?

What will be the optimal level of production? The answer is not necessarily "as much as possible." The costs for a high level of production might make it less profitable than a lower figure. You will have to keep track of sales to know if and when you need to increase or cut production.

A *sunk cost* is a cost you have paid and cannot recover. Paying too much for a new computer is a sunk cost. Most economists believe that a business owner should simply ignore sunk costs and focus on costs and profits from now on. Many people want to recover such a cost and will let it influence future decisions, such as deciding to cut back on advertising expense to try to make up for the high price paid for the computer. Doing this might hurt his business when he should simply put a sunk cost behind him and move on.

How Can I Reach Customers?

You will want to determine the best way to get your goods and services in front of potential buyers. This involves finding the market, real or virtual, in which you want to do business and where you can most effectively sell your product or service to potential customers. What will persuade people to buy from you? This persuasion does not mean slick talk and fooling people. Instead, you will want to educate them about you and your product or service. You will want to identify and promote your Unique Selling Proposition (USP), which is what makes your business stand out. A USP is something a business can advertise to potential buyers to help them know how a product is different from and better than products competitors offer.

As you inform people about your business, you will want to emphasize benefits instead of features. You might be tempted to list ten things that your product has, but that does not necessarily communicate why a customer should buy your product. Instead, you need to explain how your product will solve a problem for your customers.

The Internet has transformed the way Americans learn about new products and services. A company website is practically essential to succeed in business today, and social media offers direct ways to connect with potential customers. Internet advertising allows business owners to connect with a highly-targeted audience to identify their ideal clients.

As we mentioned earlier, your business will be more successful when you present it as a service to people. Ideally, you will not just want to serve someone once. You will want to keep customers who return to make purchases in the future. The best and most important customers for your business are the ones you already have. Not only do you want them to buy from you again; you want them to recommend your business to others.

Idea #3: Music Lessons

Unit 9: Business

Idea #4: Cleaning Service

How Will I Need to Manage My Business?

You will have to set a price for what you provide that will both attract customers and generate sufficient revenue for you to stay in business. What others charge for similar goods or services is a good guideline, but your product and your situation will probably not be exactly the same as those of your competitor.

You will need to be able to adapt to changes. You will have to put your product or service on the market, gauge customer reaction as best you can, and then change what you offer slightly to meet actual customer reaction. If you have a storefront location, you will have to handle changes in traffic flow. You will need to adapt to changes in buying habits, such as if people begin buying more of your category of product on the Internet.

Good management involves handling the unexpected: your equipment breaks at 4:55 p.m., a worker calls in sick at your busiest period, or your outside trash bin is overflowing because the garbage service has a new driver who forgot to stop at your location. All of your planning will not prevent crises from occurring, but you will be a better manager by learning from your experiences and the experiences of others.

What Risks Do I Face?

Do you have the time it will take to succeed? You might like to see everything come together immediately, but most companies take several years to become successful. Make a long-range plan and decide to work hard.

You will probably have some financial costs before you ever make a sale. You might have to print some flyers advertising your babysitting service, or you might have to purchase a large piece of equipment to be able to provide the service you advertise. Can you handle this without going into debt?

All businesses have the significant risk of financial loss. You do not have a guarantee of a profit in any endeavor. We will talk more about profit and loss in the next lesson.

Why Do Businesses Succeed—and Fail?

Business experts have identified several key factors that usually determine whether a business will succeed or fail.

Management. A successful leader has a positive attitude, is willing to work hard, develops the talents of others, and is patient and persistent. He or she has a passion to serve others and is not afraid to fail. A manufacturer might have a great product, or a restaurant might have great food, but if management doesn't lead those businesses in the right way, success will be difficult.

Planning. Successful business leaders have a clear idea about where they want to go in terms of marketing, organization, and operations. They are not just at the mercy of whatever happens, but instead they take the time to look past the present crisis.

Lesson 43 - So You Want to Start a Business?

If they don't, they will find crises consuming them until the pressure becomes too much to handle.

Money. Businesses fail because they have too much debt, and businesses fail because they do not have enough cash. Managing money well is a key to business success.

Location. A brilliant business person might set up an office, hang out a sign—and watch nothing happen. A business has to go where its customers are, whether that is a physical location or on the Internet.

Overexpansion. Good business owners are optimistic. Wise business owners know how optimistic to be. Money spent is hard to recover.

Here is some advice from people who have had experience in starting and running a business:

Don't be afraid to fail. If your business fails, see it as part of God's plan to take you to a better place.

Be willing to change. Recognize how and when change needs to happen. Don't change just for the sake of change, but don't resist change just for the sake of doing things the way you have always done them.

Learn from others. Be humble and ask for advice. Many business owners are happy to share what they have learned from their successes and mistakes. Pride goes before a fall, and it would be a shame to have to deal with a problem just because you were too proud to learn from someone else who had already faced a similar situation.

Welcome talent, and seek to grow it. Your business does not have to revolve around you. It will probably be more successful if it doesn't. You will be blessed by recognizing what others have to offer. You will bless others by encouraging and training them in developing their skills.

Don't try to do everything yourself. As your business grows, realize that you cannot do everything yourself. Resisting this change is a common failing that keeps businesses from growing as much as they could. See the changes as an opportunity for you to move on to new heights while you open up opportunities for others.

Just because someone is good at one aspect of business, that does not mean he or she will be good at all areas of business. Someone might be great at seeing the big picture and developing a vision for what a business should do, but he could struggle with being able to manage the details of daily operation. Someone else could have considerable talent at handling technical aspects of a business but not handle customer relations well. Different people can provide different kinds of leadership. No one is able to do well at everything a successful business needs.

Idea #5: Website and Graphic Design

Unit 9: Business

Businesses fail for a number of reasons. The owner can work hard and do the right things and the business still close because of a downturn in the general economy. But the owner working hard and doing the right things increase the likelihood that the business will succeed.

After reading all of this, are you exhausted—or energized? You can find many excellent resources for starting and running a business that will give you much more detailed direction. Economics is about supply, demand, and prices; but this lesson illustrates how intricate those seemingly simple concepts are.

Jesus once spoke to a large crowd of people who appeared to want to become His disciples. He used an illustration to teach how important it is for a person to think carefully about what he or she is getting into.

Idea #6: Photography

For which one of you, when he wants to build a tower, does not first sit down and calculate the cost to see if he has enough to complete it? Otherwise, when he has laid a foundation and is not able to finish, all who observe it begin to ridicule him, saying, "This man began to build and was not able to finish."
Luke 14:28-30

Assignments for Lesson 43

Making Choices — Read "Lilian's Business Venture" (pages 98-101).

Literature — Continue reading *The Travels of a T-Shirt in the Global Economy*.

Project — Continue working on your project for this unit.

Student Review — Answer the questions for Lesson 43.

44 — It Comes Down to Profit and Loss

> *A business absolutely devoted to service will have only one worry about profits. They will be embarrassingly large.*
>
> — Henry Ford

Profit is the money that a business makes by selling goods and services. A businessperson determines his profit by calculating total revenue and subtracting total cost. The difference is profit. Profit is the amount of money the businessperson has left after he pays for production resources, pays his workers, and meets all other business costs.

Profit is a powerful motivation for suppliers to produce as efficiently as possible quality goods and services that consumers want to buy. The possibility of profit encourages people to take risks. It encourages product quality, lower prices, consistent maintenance of equipment, the offering of competitive wages to attract skilled and productive workers, and the offering of rewards for work well done. The profit motive is the driving force of the free market economy.

Most American businesses earn a profit of less than 10% of sales after they pay all expenses and salaries. To many people this is surprisingly small. However, that 10% motivates efficiency in the other 90% of sales. Without some profit, salaries would be lower or owners would have to pay workers out of the company's net worth. Having no profit would mean that the company would not have money to invest in growing the business.

The possibility of loss, which happens when expenses are greater than sales revenue, is another real motivation for businesses. Businesses that experience a loss and survive use the experience to change and improve. Of course, when a company loses money or has to close, it is a hurtful experience for owners, workers, and customers. An entity (such as government) that does not have to face the effects of inefficiency and overspending is usually more expensive to run and operates less efficiently.

Determining Profit

The illustrations we use in this lesson are examples of microeconomics, looking at the economics of an individual business.

Profit equals revenue (or sales) minus costs.

Profit = Revenue − Costs

Revenue equals the selling price of the goods times the quantity sold.

> **Revenue = Price of goods sold × quantity sold**

The market usually dictates the price that a company charges for a product or service, unless the company is a price maker. A producer usually cannot charge whatever price he chooses. If competing goods have significantly lower prices than his, the producer will likely sell fewer goods and as a result have less revenue and thus less profit.

Since this is the case, the revenue factor over which the producer has most control is the quantity sold. If a producer wants to increase his revenue, he needs to find ways to increase the number of units he sells. This might mean lowering the price to increase sales, finding additional methods to advertise his product or service, or promoting the product or service more effectively by showing how it meets needs or solves problems.

Economists talk about two kinds of profit. *Accounting profit* is the profit that an accountant determines and that shows up on the books: revenue minus the costs (rent, utilities, price of materials, labor, and so forth), which he can enter into a ledger. *Economic profit* is what an economist sees. An economist determines this by subtracting the opportunity cost as well as the ledger costs from the revenue. Opportunity cost, what a person gives up to engage in a particular activity, is real. It has an economic impact, even though it might not show up in the books.

Suppose you leave your $60,000-a-year salaried job and start a sole proprietorship business. The first year, you have sales of $110,000 and ledger costs (sometimes called explicit costs) of $100,000, including your personal salary of $40,000. This means that you paid all of your bills, paid yourself $40,000, and had $10,000 left over that you can use to invest in the business, take a trip, or buy a new computer.

Then you stop and think. You left a job making $60,000 in order to fulfill your dream of running your own business. You had been scrimping and saving, putting away $5,000 a year for five years to start the business. If you had kept your job, you could have walked away with $25,000 in the bank and had fewer sleepless nights, but instead you walked away with $10,000, lived on less income, and had more gray hair. Was your business a success?

On the books, your business was a success. In the eyes of an economist, you paid a heavy price. Of course, you need to remember several intangible factors. You fulfilled your dream. Your prospects for growing your business are good. The $40,000 you paid yourself plus the $10,000 in profit got you pretty close to what you had been making, not bad for the first year. Still, you will need to examine carefully the possibilities of growing the business over the next few years before you can call the business a success.

Determining Costs

Besides the quantity sold, the other factor over which a business owner has some degree of control are his costs of production. Costs for a business include the price of inputs or factors of production (land, labor, capital, and technology). Sometimes the costs for such things as utilities, telephone service, getting business cards printed, and buying office furniture are called the cost of doing business. This means that, if you are going to operate a business, you are going to have some expenses; but you hope that the expenses you incur will help you to make a profit. Responsible businesses try to keep their expenses to a minimum. Irresponsible businesses that spend freely on lavish buildings and expensive furniture often wind up in debt and have to live on loans or go out of business.

Business owners can break down costs into short-run costs and long-run costs. Short-run costs are expenses required for things that the business uses quickly. Wood for a yo-yo factory or sponges for a car wash are examples of short-run costs. Long-

Lesson 44 - It Comes Down to Profit and Loss

run (or capital) costs are for things that the company expects to have for a long time. Building a factory and putting machinery in it are examples of long-run costs.

A business can also separate fixed costs from variable costs. *Fixed costs* are expenses that have to be paid regardless of the rate of production. Rent payments and insurance are examples of fixed costs. *Variable costs* are expenses that change depending on the amount of production taking place. The cost of raw materials can vary from time to time, and the amount of goods produced will influence how much raw material the company needs. More production will probably mean higher utility costs also. Another variable cost is labor. A company's labor expense will also depend on how much the company is producing.

Businesses want to know the total costs and the average cost per unit produced. The company owner might learn that his long-term costs are raising the cost of production unnecessarily. He might also realize that he can lessen the impact of his variable costs by increased productivity.

A business is always looking for ways to cut costs in order to increase profits. A business owner cannot control how many people buy his product, but he can have some influence over what it costs to produce it. One way is to lower the price of inputs, such as materials or labor. Another way to cut costs is to increase the productivity of workers. When raw materials cost less, or when workers can produce more while working the same number of hours, the cost per unit produced goes down.

Marginal Analysis

Most companies are not satisfied with the status quo. They want to grow in order to generate more profit. This growth necessitates dealing with costs. Businesses want to know what changes will increase profits, and what changes will hurt profits. Examining this issue is called *marginal analysis*, a study of factors that lead to a change in business behavior.

For an example of marginal analysis, let's look in on Ron's Repair Shop. The shop charges $100 per repair. He pays each worker he hires $100 per day, and his fixed costs for rent and utilities are $100 per day. The chart on the next page tells the story.

Marginal Analysis of Ron's Repair Shop

Workers Hired	Units Repaired	Variable Costs (Wages)	Fixed Costs	Total Costs	Revenue Per Unit	Total Revenue	Profit (Revenue - Costs)
0	0	0	100	100	100	0	-100
1	2	100	100	200	100	200	0
2	5	200	100	300	100	500	200
3	9	300	100	400	100	900	500
4	12	400	100	500	100	1200	700
5	13	500	100	600	100	1300	700
6	12	600	100	700	100	1200	500
7	12	700	100	800	100	1200	400

If Ron hired no one and performed no repairs, he would lose $100 per day because of his fixed costs. Ron hired his first worker, who repaired two units in one day. This paid for the worker's salary and the fixed costs, so Ron's profit was zero. But Ron was hopeful. He hired a second worker, and the two workers combined to crank out five units in one day.

This gave Ron his first profit of $200 per day ($500 revenue minus $300 in costs), and the owner and his two workers shared a pizza to celebrate. Ron then hired a third worker, and the three workers worked so well together that they repaired nine units in one day. Ron's profit jumped to $500, and he began shopping for a new car.

The fourth worker he hired maintained the average: the shop repaired twelve units, giving Ron $700 profit for one day. The men were able to help each other do a better job on each repair. Ron thought he had found the ticket to wealth and began looking at boats. Ron hired another worker, but now something was different.

The five workers repaired thirteen units, but the fifth worker only paid for himself and did not add to the profit. The men in the shop had to share some of the equipment, and their focus was not as sharp now with so many people in the limited space.

Ron hired a sixth man and then a seventh, and his profit actually began to go down. The two new men he brought on didn't repair anything; they just ran among the other workers taking tools from one man to the other. The new guys stepped on the air hoses that the experienced workers were using. With the confusion and frustration in the shop, production actually went down. What was happening?

For any number of reasons, more is not always better. The *law of diminishing marginal returns* states that the productivity of an input decreases as the quantity of the input increases. More workers or more raw materials do not necessarily mean more profit. To make more profits possible, Ron would have had to expand his shop, which would have meant significant additional expense. Higher revenue does not necessarily mean more profit if more sales incur higher costs. With four or five workers, Ron reached the *profit maximizing level of output*, the level of production that produces the greatest net profit. Ron learned to be happy with what he had, he let the last two men he hired go, and he began shopping for a nice used car.

Lesson 44 - It Comes Down to Profit and Loss

Graphing Marginal Analysis

We can show on a graph the marginal analysis that Ron did on his business.

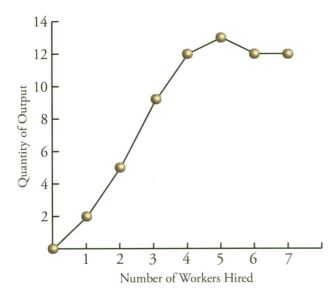

Notice how the output grew with the number of workers to a point, then increased less, and finally decreased with the last two workers hired. This is called the *production function*, a comparison of the quantity of inputs to the quantity of outputs.

Another analysis involves comparing the average cost per unit produced with the average marginal cost. The average marginal cost is determined by dividing the change in total cost by the change in quantity produced.

Ron still wasn't sure, however, whether having a four-man crew or a five-man crew was best; so he did some further marginal analysis. When the units repaired went from 12 to 13, the average cost per unit began to increase. This was the same point (going from 4 workers to 5) when the average marginal cost began to exceed the average cost per unit. This is because the fifth worker did not increase productivity; he only paid for his own salary.

The general rule is this: when average marginal cost is less than average total cost, average total cost is falling. In other words, the added average marginal cost is bringing down the average total cost, so the business growth is producing more profit. However, when average marginal cost is greater than average total cost, average total cost is rising. The additional expense is driving up the average cost, and the change is not producing more profit. So Ron decided to let the fifth man go also.

Average Cost Per Unit	
Units Repaired	Average Cost
2	100
5	60
9	44.44
12	41.67
13	46.15
12	58.33
12	66.67

Average Marginal Cost			
Change in Number of Workers	Marginal Change in Total Cost	Change in Quantity Produced	Average Marginal Cost
0-1	100	2	100 / 2 = 50
1-2	100	3	100 / 3 = 33
2-3	100	4	100 / 4 = 25
3-4	100	3	100 / 3 = 33
4-5	100	1	100 / 1 = 100
5-6	100	-1	100 / -1 = -100
6-7	100	0	undefined

Deadweight Loss

Producers accept costs that are related to production. What is difficult for a producer to take is a deadweight loss, which is a reduction in efficiency that leads to a loss in profit or a loss to society.

Imagine an economy in which doughnut supply and doughnut demand have reached equilibrium. People purchase the doughnuts supplied at the price the doughnut shops charge for them. But then the government, always on the lookout for additional revenue and concerned about the impact of doughnut consumption on public health, enacts a 20% tax on each and every doughnut. The graph below illustrates what happens.

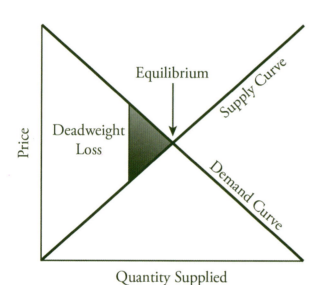

The increased price because of the tax lowers demand. Lower demand results in decreased quantity supplied. The shaded area to the left of the equilibrium point is the deadweight loss to the doughnut market. What will also happen is that revenue from the tax will not be what the government hoped, since doughnut sales will decline. The doughnut market has become inefficient to some degree because of the tax.

Monopoly pricing can also result in a deadweight loss. If a monopolist charges a price above the equilibrium, some who cannot pay the higher price will not be able to derive the benefit from the product. This results in a poor allocation of resources and a deadweight loss to society.

Another example of a deadweight loss is decreased production due to an inaccurate prediction of labor needs. Suppose a producer plans his production for the year and hires accordingly, but then he finds that he could actually profitably employ 10% more workers. However, all of the potential employees are now working for someone else. The producer has production capacity standing idle, and this is a deadweight loss to him and to the market.

Are Some Profits Excessive?

Sometimes people accuse companies of making excessive profits or enjoying windfall profits. We hear this from time to time about oil companies and pharmaceutical companies, for instance. A sole proprietor who owns a lawn care business and who sees his profit cut because of rising gasoline prices can be discouraged by reading news stories about the record profits oil companies make because of those same high gas prices.

But is there such a thing as an unjust level of profit, assuming that the business is obeying all laws? Is limiting profit by law a good idea? What about imposing a high tax on profits above a certain level? What would that level be, and who would decide it? Should we have a law that limits the size of house that someone can own or buy?

A law that limited profit would place additional costs on the economy beyond the amount of the tax collected on business profit. Such a law would discourage people from taking the risk of starting or growing a business, since that business owner would have to take that step with the knowledge that if he is successful, his profit will be limited.

Imagine a law that limited the amount of income an individual—that same lawn care owner, for instance—could earn. Such a law would discourage work that would earn someone more than the maximum allowable amount. Would you want to live in a society that placed limits on people's hard work and creativity?

Although people might have definite opinions about what is a proper level of profit morally and spiritually, setting a legal limit on profits or imposing an excess profits tax would be a way of saying that government bureaucrats or members of Congress know how to distribute the wealth that you earn better than you do. How can they know, after all you have done to make your business work, what is an appropriate profit? Such a law would be an artificial and politically-motivated encroachment into the market.

Unfortunately, the quest for profit can motivate greed and unethical or even illegal activities. Some people use economic freedom to take wrongful advantage of others. But socialist systems and non-profit organizations experience greed and illegal activity also. On the plus side, profits have motivated many advances in products and services that companies have made available to the public. Profits have also been the source for significant charitable donations that have blessed many people.

Profit is vital to the success of a business and to the functioning of our economy; but Paul understood that making a profit is not the key to a successful life.

I know how to get along with humble means,
and I also know how to live in prosperity;
in any and every circumstance I have learned the secret
of being filled and going hungry, both of having abundance
and suffering need. I can do all things through Him who strengthens me.
Philippians 4:12-13

Assignments for Lesson 44

Literature — Continue reading *The Travels of a T-Shirt in the Global Economy*.

Project — Continue working on your project for this unit.

Student Review — Answer the questions for Lesson 44.

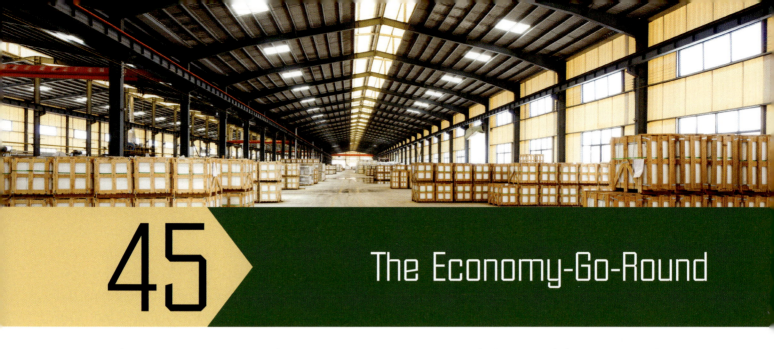

45   The Economy-Go-Round

This crisis is not simply a more severe version of the usual business cycle recession, the typical downturn in which economies ultimately adjust and stabilize.

— Timothy Geithner, Secretary of the Treasury (2009)

In the last lesson we talked about the microeconomics of particular businesses. In this lesson we shift back to macroeconomics and look at trends in the economy as a whole. Of course, individual businesses make up the general economy; so the two specialities relate to each other.

Every business has busy periods and slack times. Business owners know that they will be busier at certain periods of the year than at others. Many retail shops, for instance, are often busiest in November and December and slowest in January and February. Outdoor shops, on the other hand, have their best sales in the spring and early summer. A homeschool curriculum vendor will have peak sales in July and August as the school year approaches.

In the same way, an economy does not experience an endless smooth ride along a constant, upwardly-sloping line. The overall output of an economy might move upward in general over a long period of time, but during that long upward movement shorter periods of instability occur. A surge of economic growth can push the economy above the trend line, while a decline will take it below the line.

A series of expansions and contractions (or surges and declines) make up the *business cycle*. Expansions and contractions might be short-term, or they might occur over many months. These changes in the economy have consequences for employment, levels of income, business success or failure, interest rates, consumer purchasing, and prices.

Economists see the typical business cycle as having two phases and two turning points. See the chart on the next page.

The first phase is an expansion (E). This phase is characterized by increases in the real gross domestic product (GDP, a term for economic output we will define later), growth in the number of jobs, higher average household income, greater business profits, numerous business expansions, and the formation of many new businesses.

A peak (P) is the turning point at which GDP, household income, and profits have reached their highest level and unemployment is at a relatively low level.

Lesson 45 - The Economy-Go-Round

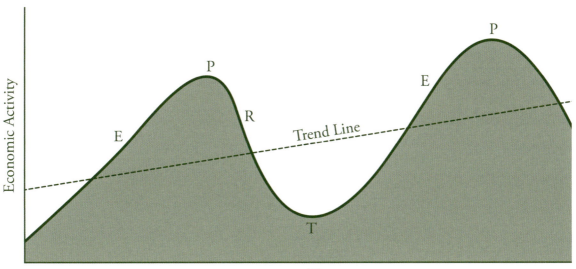

A recession (R) is a phase of significant decline in real GDP, income, and profits while unemployment is rising. Average hours worked and the length of the work week generally decline. Consumers cut back on spending and sales decrease. This usually results in job loss and a decline in household income, which can depress consumer spending even more. The economic curtailment also leads to lower prices for shares of corporate stock, since the supply exceeds demand. In a later lesson, we will discuss in more detail how economists measure recessions.

A trough (T) is the opposite of a peak. A trough is the turning point in the cycle at which economic activity reaches a low ebb and from which an expansion follows.

Fisher Body was an early maker of auto bodies, the exterior frame of a vehicle. After building this factory in Detroit in 1919, the company merged with General Motors. This plant closed in 1984 and has been largely unused since.

This is Pittsburgh, Pennsylvania, in 1974. During the 1970s and 80s, the city experienced economic hardships as the steel industry declined. This affected other related industries such as railroads and mining.

A complete business cycle encompasses the calendar time between two peaks or two troughs. Unlike the anticipated slow seasons during a calendar year, business cycles do not occur in true cyclical or regular fashion. They occur erratically and last for varying lengths of time. Thus, some economists prefer the term *economic fluctuations*.

Causes of Business Cycles

Most economists describe the reason that business cycles occur using the aggregate supply/aggregate demand model we discussed in Unit 6. Economic declines can begin with demand shocks such as a cutback in consumption. Also, a period in which lending institutions are more reluctant to make loans will lead to reduced demand and can bring about a recession. Supply shocks, such as a reduction in the availability of oil or a sharp increase in oil prices, can lead to a recession. A natural disaster, such as a hurricane or earthquake, can interrupt supply and lead to a contraction or a slowing down of the economy.

On the other hand, some demand shocks move the economy toward recovery. An increase in government spending or a greater availability of credit are positive demand shocks that increase demand and lead to more economic activity. Supply shocks that can cause recovery and growth include trends such as the development of the Internet and the rapid growth of Internet-based businesses. Such activity opens new markets, creates new jobs, and offers the opportunity for greater rates of spending.

Milton Friedman believed that the money supply not keeping pace with output causes economic fluctuations. The Austrian School of Economics holds that a central government's intervention in the money and credit markets brings on a recession.

This is Pittsburgh thirty years later. New technologies opened up new opportunities for workers, and residents of the city adjusted to a new economic situation.

Some economists believe that business cycles (or economic fluctuations) are not inevitable in the capitalist system. However, since a market economy gives individuals, businesses, and government leaders freedom to make decisions, sometimes those decisions will have negative consequences for segments of the economy or the economy as a whole.

While fluctuations might not be predictable, they do definitely occur. An economy is not a completely controllable machine. However, since World War II, economic growth in the United States has been more steady and fluctuations have been less dramatic. The general trend of economic growth will likely continue to involve taking a few steps forward and, from time to time, a step back.

In Lessons 69 and 70, we will discuss the Great Depression of the 1930s and the Great Recession of 2007-2009.

Growing Through Hard Times

Economic slowdowns can bring pain to individuals, families, and groups. However, recessions can provide businesses with the incentive to reorganize and to trim their costs in order to regain profits. Sometimes, however, this trimming can include cutting back on the number of employees. These changes over the long run can mean greater efficiency and more job opportunities as new fields of business grow and develop. And, as we have noted, someone who loses his job can take it as an opportunity to seek additional training, look for a more fulfilling job, or start his own business.

No one likes to go through difficult times, but James speaks of the attitude that will help a Christian grow through a trial. Experiencing a test can help a person grow in endurance, which can help that person grow in maturity.

*Consider it all joy, my brethren, when you encounter various trials,
knowing that the testing of your faith produces endurance.
And let endurance have its perfect result,
so that you may be perfect and complete, lacking in nothing.
James 1:2-4*

Assignments for Lesson 45

Literature — Continue reading *The Travels of a T-Shirt in the Global Economy*.

Project — Finish your project for this unit.

Student Review — Answer the questions for Lesson 45 and take the quiz for Unit 9.

Window washers at the Central Library, Seattle, Washington (2007)

10 Labor

Human labor is a factor in the production and distribution of goods and services. Rather than being enemies, business owners and employees depend on each other for success. People offer different kinds of labor in the labor market, which experiences supply and demand just as any market does. The price of labor is the pay that workers earn, usually in the form of either wages or salary. Unions are labor organizations that use the power of large numbers of workers to increase pay and improve working conditions. The level of employment (and unemployment) in an economy is an indication of the level of productivity in that economy.

Lesson 46 - Now Hiring
Lesson 47 - Workers and Their Jobs
Lesson 48 - Unions
Lesson 49 - Income
Lesson 50 - Out of Work

Books Used

The Bible
Making Choices
The Travels of a T-Shirt in the Global Economy

Project (choose one)

1) Write 300 to 500 words on one of the following topics:

   - What is the value of work for the individual and society? How is work an important part of business and the economy? How can work honor God?

   - Write the work/employment biography of one of your parents or grandparents. Do preliminary research by learning the answers to these questions: What jobs have they held? What did they earn at those jobs? Were they satisfied with their pay? Did they feel employers and managers treated them fairly? Why did they move from one job to the next? Were they ever unemployed?

2) Make a mini-documentary (three to five minutes) that champions the value of labor.

3) Design a board game with a theme of labor. Include various types of work, training for specific jobs, wages, unions, and unemployment as elements of the game. Create and play the game with your family.

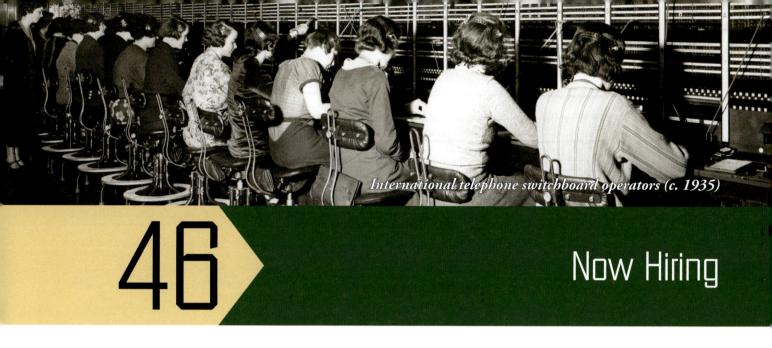
International telephone switchboard operators (c. 1935)

46 Now Hiring

Labor disgraces no man.
— Ulysses S. Grant

Labor, the work that men and women perform, is a human resource that is a factor in the production of goods and services in the economy. Employers pay workers to produce goods and services that the employers can sell to cover their expenses and make a profit. People earn income by exchanging their time, knowledge, and skill for pay.

Saying that labor is a factor of production does not mean that labor is merely a factor of production. Human beings made in the image of God perform labor. This fact makes the people doing the work and the labor they do valuable. This is another reminder that, behind the principles and figures in economics, are real people.

The idea that Karl Marx promoted, that workers create wealth while owners simply take advantage of workers and skim off profits, is false and simplistic. Owners take risks in financing businesses and in providing technology, advertising, and everything else a business needs. They also provide labor themselves. In many businesses, the owner works harder than anyone else.

Some business owners have treated workers unjustly; but that is the exception and not the rule. If owners did not provide places of work and work to do, laborers could not earn money for their work. At the same time, if laborers did not provide this critical human resource, all the great business ideas of the world would come to nothing. Business and labor depend on each other.

The interdependence of business and labor, as well as the interdependence of many different kinds of labor, are essential aspects of economic activity. As the essay "I, Pencil" illustrates, many different individuals work to produce one product. Think about the interaction of work in making a recorded song. Someone writes the song. The singer and musicians perform the song. Others produce the recording, transfer it to formats that customers can use, promote the product to customers, and perform other necessary tasks. The recording company provides the studio, the equipment, and the means of production and distribution. All of the steps are essential, and everyone working together produces income for each person who worked on the project. The same kind of interaction takes place with almost every product and service that an economy offers.

Supply and Demand in the Labor Market

Labor is a commodity that people offer in a market. As with any commodity, labor has a price. The price for labor is called wages or salary (we'll explain the difference in Lesson 49). Supply and demand determine the price that buyers of the commodity (namely, employers) pay for labor. The aggregate demand for labor by all firms in an economy provides the *total labor demand*. The aggregate of choices that individuals make to enter the labor market results in the *total labor supply*.

The price of this commodity determines its supply and demand. Firms generally hire more workers at lower wages and fewer workers at higher wages. At the same time, relatively fewer workers will offer their services at lower wages, while more workers will want to work for higher wages. The intersection of the supply curve and the demand curve (point W-L on the graph below) is the equilibrium wage rate and the equilibrium level of employment or quantity of workers hired.

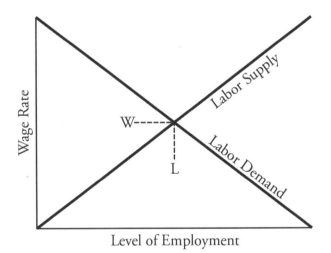

Changes in labor supply or labor demand will change the incentives people have to offer their labor for pay. This will move the equilibrium wage and employment level. For instance, a decrease consumer demand for a particular product or or new government regulations or taxes that increase the cost of labor, will reduce the quantity of labor that business owners demand. This will cause the demand curve to shift to the left. The decrease in demand exerts downward pressure on wage rates and also leads employers to hire fewer workers. When this happens in one labor market, some workers will likely move to another market where their skills will be in greater demand.

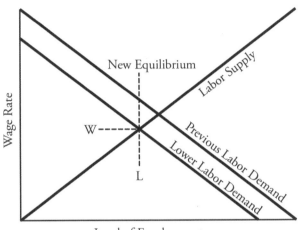

Changes in wages and benefits and in job creation also affect labor demand and supply (We'll discuss the meaning of benefits in Lesson 49). Higher wage rates tend to cause lower demand for labor. An increase in jobs that owners offer (labor demand) increases the wage rate as employers look for more workers and are willing to pay more to get them.

Changes in the labor supply can take place as a result of population growth or decline (involving rates of birth and immigration), the ages of workers in the labor force, changes in training possibilities, changes in benefits, or changes in the nature of the work force.

These are ideal characteristics of a perfectly competitive labor market. Factors that cause deviations from this ideal include wage restrictions (such as minimum wage laws), unions that dictate the price of labor, monopsonies (a single buyer for labor that can dictate wages), and product monopolies (a single supplier that can set wage rates).

The California Conservation Corps (CCC) was established in 1976 and modeled after the Civilian Conservation Corps of the 1930s. It employs and trains young adults to provide an emergency response to fires, floods, earthquakes, oil spills, and pest infestations. These CCC members are military veterans who are learning forestry and firefighting in South Dakota in 2012.

The U.S. Department of Labor defines the labor force in the United States as all people sixteen or older who are employed or actively seeking work. In July 2016, the United States civilian labor force totaled 159.3 million people. Of that number, 151.5 million were employed and 7.8 million (4.9% of the labor force) were unemployed.

Reasons for Labor Demand and Supply

Firms want workers with certain skills that they believe will maximize profit. This creates the labor demand for a given occupation. When adding workers is profitable, companies will add workers because of the incentive of higher profits. Increasing demand for goods and services leads to companies wanting to increase output, which spurs job creation. However, a firm will need to do marginal analysis to determine when hiring additional workers becomes unprofitable (as we saw with Ron's repair shop in Lesson 44).

People who can offer the skills companies want create the labor supply. People make decisions about whether to enter the work force, how many hours per week they want to work (that is, full-time or part-time work), and whether they want to invest the time and money to develop certain skills. The decisions that both companies and individuals make involve opportunity costs. The company could use the money they will pay in wages for other purposes, and the individuals can choose to do other things instead of working at a particular job or acquiring training.

People decide to become workers for a number of reasons, such as a desire for income, seeking personal fulfillment by using talents, or wanting to serve others. Any of these motivations can be a part of wanting to serve God. The decision involves determining what that person can earn, whether he or she has a greater desire or need to work in a non-paying context (such as caring for children or an elderly parent), the need for schooling or specific training, leisure time the person might want, and what if any non-labor income the person might have (such as income from investments, an inheritance, pensions, or welfare).

Investment in training and education generally improves the labor capital (that is, the worth, value, or quality of labor) that a person can offer. Training increases productivity, which increases income potential and raises one's standard of living. A commitment to such systematic training is more likely if a person has received encouragement in the value of education, if he or she has developed a sense of personal responsibility and a sense of pride in working, and if the person has learned the value of delayed gratification.

Ideally, the work that people do gives them a sense of purpose, blesses other people, and provides the worker, the employer, and the buyer of the goods and services with what they want and need. The highest purpose of work is to glorify God. Accomplishing these goals with the work a person does is a great use of one's life.

Labor has been part of human life since the Garden of Eden. The Lord told Adam to subdue and rule over the earth (Genesis 1:26-30). However, the difficulty in labor came as a result of Adam's sin:

Then to Adam He said, "Because you have listened to the voice of your wife, and have eaten from the tree about which I commanded you, saying, 'You shall not eat from it'; cursed is the ground because of you; in toil you will eat of it all the days of your life. Both thorns and thistles it shall grow for you; and you will eat the plants of the field; by the sweat of your face you will eat bread, till you return to the ground, Because from it you were taken; for you are dust, and to dust you shall return."
Genesis 3:17-19

Assignments for Lesson 46

Making Choices — Read the excerpt from *Mind Amongst the Spindles* (pages 102-105).

Literature — Continue reading *The Travels of a T-Shirt in the Global Economy*. Plan to finish it by the end of Unit 11.

Project — Choose your project for this unit and start working on it.

Student Review — Answer the questions for Lesson 46.

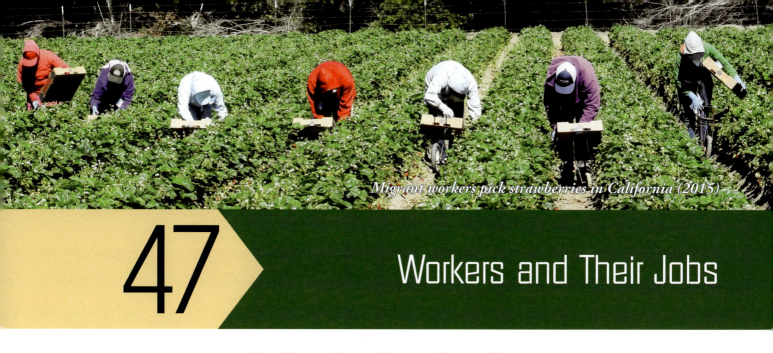
Migrant workers pick strawberries in California (2015)

47 Workers and Their Jobs

By the work one knows the workman.
— *Jean de la Fontaine*

Not all work is the same. Owning your own business is different from working for someone else. Some jobs require specific education and training, while others do not. Some workers operate big machinery outside in the cold and heat, while others write computer software inside an office or at home. Controversial issues such as the practice of discrimination in the work force arise at times. This lesson discusses the categories of labor that many people use and some of the issues regarding labor. The other lessons in this unit deal with other labor issues in our society.

White Collar, Blue Collar

For much of the twentieth century, many people referred to jobs as either white collar or blue collar. These descriptions came from the color of shirts that people who held these jobs usually wore at work. White collar positions were usually professional occupations in which people received an annual salary, worked in an office, and had an administrative or oversight role. The men who worked in these jobs usually wore white dress shirts. Blue collar jobs involved manual labor, often performed in a factory setting or outdoors. Blue collar workers generally received an hourly wage. These workers came to be called blue collar because many wore uniforms with blue shirts. Around the middle of the twentieth century, about 20% of workers were white collar and the rest were blue collar.

The labor market has changed considerably since then. The increasing use of technology in the workplace has diminished the number of blue collar jobs while the need for highly trained managers has increased. Economists today consider about 60% of jobs to be white collar.

However, this traditional way of categorizing jobs is not really accurate any longer. For one thing, the trend toward more casual business attire has blurred the distinction between kinds of jobs. Office and administrative personnel do not necessarily wear white collars, and laborers in the factory might not wear a collared shirt at all. Some white collar workers, such as restaurant managers, at times have to do work that most people would consider to be blue collar labor. White collar workers have traditionally been seen as earning more money, but some people in blue collar positions earn more than people who fill some white collar jobs. Moreover,

293

the white collar-blue collar distinction assumed that men made up the vast majority of the work force, which is no longer true.

Other collar colors have entered the discussion of work categories. Positions such as secretaries and teachers, which women traditionally filled in the 20th century, were sometimes called pink collar jobs. That categorization is also outdated. More recently, positions involved with producing goods and services that are environmentally friendly, especially those that relate to developing renewable energy sources, have been called green collar jobs.

Contemporary Job Classifications

The federal government has identified 23 major groups of jobs, termed the Standard Occupational Classifications. Within these major headings are literally hundreds of more specific job titles and job descriptions.

- Management
- Business and Financial Operations
- Computer and Mathematical
- Architecture and Engineering
- Life, Physical, and Social Science
- Community and Social Services
- Legal
- Education, Training, and Library
- Arts, Design, Entertainment, Sports, and Media
- Healthcare Practitioners and Technical
- Healthcare Support
- Protective Service
- Food Preparation and Serving Related
- Building and Grounds Cleaning and Maintenance
- Personal Care and Service
- Sales and Related
- Office and Administrative Support
- Farming, Fishing, and Forestry
- Construction and Extraction
- Installation, Maintenance, and Repair
- Production
- Transportation and Material Moving
- Military Specific

Road construction workers, Denver, Colorado (2011)

After working as a vice president at Google, Sheryl Sandberg became chief operating officer of Facebook in 2008. As a high profile business leader, she has encouraged women and men to work together to create more opportunities for everyone to find fulfillment at work and at home.

A Changing Work Place

A growing number of workers are self-employed. A self-employed person may run a business that directly serves individuals or a self-employed person may work for other companies as a consultant or contract worker. With the latter arrangement, firms can get the work done that they need but do not have to provide employee benefits to the consultant. The Bureau of Labor Statistics in the Department of Labor says that about 11% of the total working population considers itself to be self-employed. Self-employed persons perform many different tasks, including some that most people would traditionally have classified as either white collar (such as a computer programmer) or blue collar (a plumber).

American workers change jobs more frequently than their counterparts did several decades ago. The image of someone going to work for a company as a young person and retiring from that same company forty or so years later does not characterize the American work place today. Hard data is scarce, but a common estimate is that the average American worker changes jobs about seven times during his working career. At the same time, while workers have less loyalty to their employers, many employers have less loyalty to their workers as well. Outsourcing (having a private contractor outside the company perform certain tasks) and downsizing are common ways that companies eliminate positions on their payrolls. Sometimes these cuts involve employees who have put in many years of service.

Women in the Work Force

Female workers make up a greater percentage of the labor force than was the case in the middle of the twentieth century and earlier. A number of factors have influenced this trend. More women have gone to college and thus have received the training that employers seek. Increasing wage rates, especially for women, have made employment more attractive.

On average, American women are older when they begin having children, so they often spend several years without facing the need to decide between working and rearing children. In addition, the number of working mothers has increased. Social attitudes about women in the working world have become more accepting.

Other changes have accompanied the greater female presence in the work force, but it is difficult to determine if these changes are causes or effects of more women working, or if they are both causes and effects to some degree. For instance, the demand for daycare services has increased as mothers have joined the work force. Many daycare businesses began in response to the need for child care that working mothers had, but the presence of daycare services has probably also encouraged some mothers to choose to work outside of the home. Our economy has also seen a significant increase in fast food restaurants and processed food products in grocery stores. These changes are also probably partly an effect of and partly a cause for women working outside the home.

Immigration

The coming of people born in other countries to the United States has long been controversial, but it has always been an integral part of our history and our economic development. British, French, and Spanish immigrants established colonies in North America. Traders brought millions of Africans by force to serve as slaves. Millions of people from Ireland, Germany, and other European countries came in the first half of the nineteenth century and again in the late nineteenth century and early twentieth century to find work, religious freedom, a new start, and, as with the Irish, to survive. Many Asian immigrants arrived in the latter part of the nineteenth century, and more arrived during the 1900s. Migrant workers have long provided farm labor in the American Southwest and Far West. From the late twentieth century into the twenty-first, Hispanic immigration was the dominant people movement into the United States.

These immigrants have added a significant number of workers to the labor force, and this increase has helped the growth of American industry. Many of these people left their families and just about all of their worldly possessions to risk coming to America in the hope of building a better life. A large number became economically successful, a few extremely so.

In recent years, about one million people per year have become legal permanent residents of the United States. Hundreds of thousands of legal visitors overstay their visas, and an unknown number of people enter the country illegally. The immigration issue involves numerous questions:

Some immigrants come to the United States with college degrees and high tech skills but are unable to find work in their field of expertise, while others (probably numerically the majority) come with relatively low work skills and have few opportunities to develop better skills. What is the best way for the immigrant labor force to contribute to the U.S. economy?

What economic impact do immigrants, especially undocumented workers and their families, have on the American social infrastructure such as health care and education?

Are the immigrants doing the work that Americans won't do, as some claim, or is that just an excuse for hiring the immigrants and paying them low wages?

Ironically, American companies are moving jobs to other countries while people from other countries are moving here for work. Is it possible—or wise—to blend these two trends together for the good of everyone?

Portuguese immigrants working at the Royal Mill in River Point, Rhode Island (1909)

Does the relatively low pay that immigrants receive have a downward pull on wage rates and work opportunities for citizens already living here? Another way to phrase this question is to ask whether these workers are substitute labor or complementary labor. To illustrate, imagine worker A, an American-born physician, worker B, an American-born worker with limited skills, and worker C, a foreign-born worker also with limited skills. Workers B and C utilize the skills of worker A and so are said to complement the physician's work. They are not an employment threat to A. However, B and C have similar skill levels, so they are an employment threat to each other and are considered substitute labor. If there is only one job opening, one will be hired and the other will not be hired. Because many immigrant workers are willing to accept lower wages, they will tend to pull down wages for low-skill native-born workers.

What role in immigration should the companies that hire undocumented workers have? These companies profit from the immigrants' labor. Should the companies be responsible for their documentation?

Discrimination   *age too*

We can be thankful for the progress in the United States toward all people having equal rights and opportunities regardless of their gender, race, or national background. However, discrimination against certain groups has been and to some extent continues to be present in our society. This practice has a negative effect on all of society, including our economic lives.

First, erroneous assumptions lead to erroneous conclusions. To assume that certain people do not deserve the same pay or the same opportunities is to introduce inequity in the labor market. In addition to this practice being morally wrong, it hurts the American economy. Disruption of the labor market disrupts the economy.

Second, a work force that is based on prejudice—whether by an employer, a fellow worker, or customers—denies by law or by custom the right and freedom of individuals to achieve all that they can on the basis of their individual talent. This leads to a misallocation of resources, which results in an economy that is less than optimally efficient. It also dishonors God and dishonors people made in God's image.

Discrimination says that people in a certain part of the market can only participate the way that people in another part of the market say they can. The group that is discriminated against will probably have to accept lower wages, higher prices, and a lower standard of living. Such an arrangement is not a free market economy because a part of the population does not have free and equal access to the market.

Third, while discrimination limits the options of one group, it reinforces the economic position of the group in power. Such a group in power will base at least part of its dominant position on keeping persons in the other group "in their place." Those in power do this at least partly out of fear of what might happen if all people had the same opportunities. Artificial limitations such as discrimination prevent the economy from growing as fully as it could without those limitations. Those in power hurt themselves by imposing such limitations. Freedom is a better tool than fear for bringing about growth in the market.

Paul taught Christians to work as though they were working for the Lord and not for men. Workers may come up with many excuses for not doing their best at work ("The boss doesn't pay me enough," "She doesn't treat me fairly," "He doesn't work hard himself," and so forth), but we have no excuses for not giving our best for the One who gave His all for us.

Whatever you do, do your work heartily, as for the Lord rather than for men, knowing that from the Lord you will receive the reward of the inheritance. It is the Lord Christ whom you serve.
Colossians 3:23-24

Assignments for Lesson 47

Literature — Continue reading *The Travels of a T-Shirt in the Global Economy*.

Project — Continue working on your project for this unit.

Student Review — Answer the questions for Lesson 47.

American Federation of Labor Convention, El Paso, Texas (1924)

48 Unions

*When school children start paying union dues,
that's when I'll start representing the interests of school children.*
— Albert Shanker (1928-1997),
president of the American Federation of Teachers

People have always labored for other people. These roles have included farmhands, store clerks, factory workers, miners, and many others. For much of history, business owners had significant power over the pay and working conditions of those who worked for them. The workers had one main asset, which was the work they performed. Workers began to organize themselves into unions to seek better pay and better working conditions, and unions became a significant factor in the American economy. Workers needed employers to provide jobs, and employers needed workers to produce what they wanted to sell; but often the relationship between labor and management was adversarial instead of mutually supportive.

In the nineteenth century, laborers often worked for low wages in poor conditions because higher wages and better conditions would have cost the business owners money. Work-related injuries and deaths were frequent, and most employees had no worker's compensation program. Companies could secretly engage in practices that restrained trade, but workers were generally not legally able to join together to make their position stronger in dealing with employers. Socialists were involved with some union activities, and many Americans feared unions as a socialist movement. Business owners appeared to have total control over their workers.

Despite the difficulties, workers organized unions to bargain collectively with industry owners. In collective bargaining an employer and a labor union negotiate about issues such as wages, hours, and working conditions. When owners resisted union demands, workers went on strike and stopped working. Owners sometimes locked workers out and sometimes hired replacement workers. Violence occasionally erupted, caused at various times by union members, by security guards hired by owners, or by others who wanted to stir up trouble.

In the twentieth century, businesses recognized the right of labor unions to exist and to represent their workers in collective bargaining. As their power grew, unions gained the ability to shut down a factory, sometimes an industry, and at times they even threatened to shut down the greater part of the American economy.

Around the middle of the twentieth century, about one-third of all American workers were members of unions. Some states passed laws that said in certain industries, workers have to be members of a labor union. These laws are called closed shop laws. States that do not require union membership are called open shop or right to work states.

When unions negotiated contracts, they did not just bargain for increased pay. Sometimes they demanded other provisions, such as requiring a certain number of workers for a particular task or location, even if the job did not require that many workers. This was called featherbedding. Also, it became common for union members to refuse to assist in sometimes simple tasks that were not part of their specific job description. Management would have to hire or call in another union worker whose job description included that task, even if the first worker sat idle.

In some situations, when a union was the official bargaining agent for workers, the union could collect membership dues even from workers who were not members of the union. Sometimes owners hired replacement workers to do the work that striking union members were not doing. The union members sometimes attacked the replacement workers (whom the union members called scabs). In other cases, striking workers refused to allow replacements to cross picket lines. The power of labor unions grew significantly.

Laws passed by Congress sometimes expanded and sometimes limited the power of unions. The National Labor Relations Act (sometimes called the Wagner Act) of 1935 codified and expanded many rights for unions. The Labor-Management Relations Act (the Taft-Hartley Act) of 1947 limited the powers of both unions and management.

Later in the twentieth century, business owners began using new strategies. They sometimes moved production to states that allowed non-union labor. The building of automobile manufacturing plants in the South instead of in Michigan, where they had traditionally built them, is a notable example of this. Companies also began paying non-union workers about the same as what union workers received, which owners hoped would discourage workers from forming or joining unions.

Business conditions also changed. As blue collar jobs declined, many of the people hired to fill white collar jobs wanted business owners to deal with them individually and not as members of a union. The government did more to protect worker rights and worker safety. As a result, the need for unions and the desire for unions declined. Beginning in the late twentieth century, companies negotiating new contracts with unions often insisted on wage and benefit concessions from the unions in order to cut production costs. Unions had to go along or risk having many of their members lose their jobs.

The nature and extent of unionized labor has changed from what it once was, but unions continue to be a major factor in the economy. In the early twenty-first century, about one-sixth of American workers were members of unions, about half the percentage of a few decades earlier.

The Industrial Workers of the World (IWW) was founded in 1905. One of the policies they and other unions advocated was an eight-hour workday. At the time, workers at some jobs could be on duty up to sixteen hours per day, six or even seven days a week.

Members of the Chicago Teachers Union went on strike for seven days in September 2012. Their dispute with the city focused on pay, benefits, and how to evaluate teacher performance.

Whereas the largest and most powerful unions were once those for industrial workers, in more recent times the largest and strongest unions have been those organized by government workers, such as the National Education Association (NEA) and the American Federation of State, County, and Municipal Employees (AFSCME). The Service Employees International Union (SEIU) has many members who are government employees. In 2015 unionized workers made up 11.5% of the American work force. This figure includes 6.7% of the private work force and 35.2% of government employees.

Economic Impact of Unions

Are labor unions helpful or harmful? They have been both. Unions have helped American workers to obtain better pay and to be able to enjoy better working conditions. In other words, they have helped laborers enjoy a larger piece of the economic pie. This progress did not come cheaply or easily. Some workers paid with their lives, at the hands of other Americans, for more people to be able to enjoy life, liberty, and the pursuit of happiness.

At other times, the power of unions has gone too far. Unions have cost American businesses unnecessary expense, which raised the price of goods and services that those companies produced. Their ability to collect union dues from non-union workers cost those workers some of their income. Just as unrestrained management hurt business and the good of society, unrestrained labor unions hurt business and were counterproductive to the economic well-being of the country.

Workers at the Clinton Marine Terminal in Maryland load coal and repair railroad track (1973)

Most economists agree that unions are a cartel, an organization that limits the supply of a commodity—in this case, labor—in the market. As a result of this limited supply, the price for the commodity—in other words, the cost of labor—rises above the market equilibrium. Several studies estimate that union workers receive 15-20% higher pay than non-union workers doing approximately the same job.

Because unions have raised wage rates, prices for union-made goods have risen. At the same time, the demand for workers in those industries has declined. Companies that have to pay higher wages often hire fewer workers and use machinery more.

In the first half of the twentieth century, for instance, pay for unionized coal miners rose significantly. At the same time many industries switched from using coal to using oil for their energy needs because higher pay for unionized coal miners increased the price of coal. This change, along with an increased use of machinery in mines, caused a decline in the number of mine workers.

In the railroad industry, between 1973 and 1987 union members' pay rose from an average of 32% above non-union rates to 50% above non-union rates. During that period, however, railroad employment fell from 520,000 to 249,000 workers. By the early twenty-first century, railroad employment had fallen another 13% while total non-farm employment rose 26% during the period.

In other words, rail workers received higher pay, but rail companies employed fewer people.

Demand declines when prices increase. Changes in the coal mining and railroading industries were the result of several factors, but unions played a role in those changes.

Unions have also had an impact on non-union wages. Workers who have not been able to find or keep union jobs take non-union positions, and the increased supply of workers for these jobs has tended to exert a downward pressure on the wages offered for these positions as companies find people willing to work for less pay.

In closed shop situations, unions have a monopoly on the supply of labor. Monopolies must have the support of laws in order to exist, and this is true with unions. Labor unions are exempt from antitrust laws, and they are considered non-profit organizations and thus are exempt from having to pay taxes on union income (although union members pay income tax on their wages).

In their early history, craft unions, organized to represent persons who held similar jobs across the economy, tended to discriminate against minorities. Craft unions generally did not allow African Americans to become members of those unions in the 1930s and 1940s. Union leaders used their power to restrict access to jobs to only the people they wanted to have them. Black workers were more likely to be members of industrial unions, which included people performing a variety of specific jobs within a particular industry.

Civil rights leaders Booker T. Washington and W. E. B. DuBois disagreed with each other over the best way to achieve equal rights for African Americans; but they both opposed unions. In more recent years, labor unions like the rest of American society have moved toward greater acceptance of racial minorities.

Members of labor unions at the March on Washington (1963)

Two results of union activity are examples of tradeoffs. Certain unions have enabled their workers to earn a higher income, but at the price of fewer people working in those industries and crafts. The higher pay for union workers has led to higher prices that everyone, union workers and non-union workers, have had to pay for goods and services.

Unions have created advantages for some people in the American economy along with disadvantages for others. We cannot know what would have happened if unions had not been formed or if labor history had gone in another direction. We can say that the general trend has been toward higher wages and better working conditions for American workers and that unions have played a part in bringing these about. Workers who barely got by and who risked injury and death in their jobs understandably welcomed the help offered by unions in getting better conditions. At the same time, unions have had a detrimental effect in some ways. Some people have lost their jobs because of union activity or have suffered as a result of strong-arm union tactics.

The possibility of difficulties in the relationship between owners and laborers has existed for a long time. Both employers and workers have a responsibility to do what is right. James warned the wealthy not to withhold the pay of those who worked for them.

---

*Behold, the pay of the laborers who mowed your fields,
and which has been withheld by you, cries out against you;
and the outcry of those who did the harvesting
has reached the ears of the Lord of Sabaoth.*

James 5:4

Assignments for Lesson 48

Making Choices — Read "Labor Unions in a Free Market" (pages 106-115).

Literature — Continue reading *The Travels of a T-Shirt in the Global Economy*.

Project — Continue working on your project for this unit.

Student Review — Answer the questions for Lesson 48.

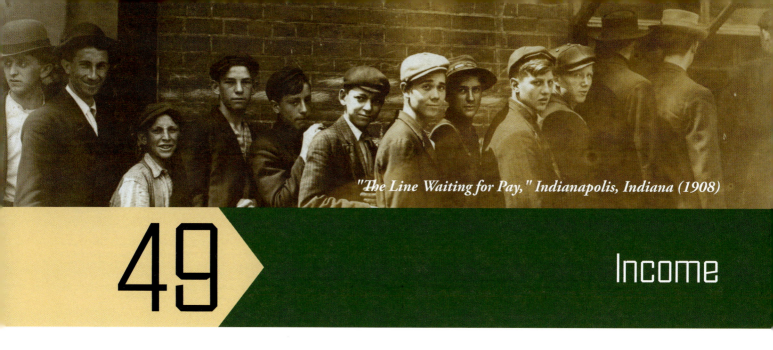

"The Line Waiting for Pay," Indianapolis, Indiana (1908)

49 Income

In the arena of human life the honors and rewards fall to those who show their good qualities in action.

— *Aristotle*

The trend in American economic history has been for the income of workers to increase relative to the cost of living. This rising wealth of workers has meant economic success for millions of families. Jobs that pay well can lift people out of poverty and put them on the road to a better life in economic terms. Workers who receive better pay also strengthen the economy as they can be consumers of the goods and services that our economy produces.

When workers provide their labor to producers for the purpose of turning out goods and services that producers can sell to consumers, the workers get paid. They typically get paid by means of wages or a salary. Often laborers receive wages by the hour while managers and employed professionals receive a salary. A wage is an hourly rate paid for labor rendered. Traditionally, a salary is pay for a job performed regardless of how long it takes to do the work. However, in 2016 the U.S. Department of Labor announced new rules requiring employers to pay overtime to certain salaried workers.

Each method of payment has advantages and disadvantages. The hourly wage earner knows that at the end of his shift he is usually free to go home. If the hourly worker has to work additional time, he or she usually receives overtime pay, often 1 1/2 to 2 times his hourly wage, for every hour over a set number of hours (usually forty) that he or she works in a week. A salary, meanwhile, is usually higher than what that person would earn at an hourly rate; but company management often expects the salaried employee to work more than forty hours a week. Management expects the salaried employee to work until the job is done. Sometimes a salaried worker has to take work home to complete it.

Income from a job includes wages or salary plus benefits. Benefits are things of value that employers provide which are usually not taxable, such as employer contributions toward health insurance coverage or contributions to a retirement fund. During World War II, employers throughout the economy began to offer their employees benefits. The federal government did not allow pay increases during the war, so (under the threat of worker strikes) employers began providing benefits which the government said did not have to be taxed.

305

Employers automatically withhold from the paychecks of hourly and salaried employees income taxes, Social Security and Medicare contributions, and other amounts (such as employee contributions to a retirement fund, union dues, and health insurance premiums). The employer sends these amounts to the government, a union, an insurance company, or an investment fund on the employees' behalf.

A person's gross income is the total of all taxable income, while his net income is what he receives after deductions are taken out. Net income is sometimes called a worker's take-home pay. Income from a job is called earned income. Other income, such as that from an investment or from rental properties, is called—unfortunately—unearned income. It is unfortunate because the person has probably worked to put money into the investment and has worked to be able to buy and maintain the rental property, but tax jargon labels it as unearned.

Different Pay for Different Work

Just as jobs are different, different jobs receive different rates of pay. Here are just a few median rates that people in certain positions earned in 2015 (median means that half of the workers earned above this figure and half earned below it):

Floral Designer	$25,010
Emergency Medical Technician	$31,980
Sheet Metal Worker	$45,750
High School Teacher	$57,200
Computer Programmer	$79,530
Elevator Installer and Repairer	$80,870
Electrical Engineer	$95,230
College Administrator	$88,580
Attorney	$115,820
Dentist	$158,310

Pay scales for different jobs are the result of a number of factors. First, different levels of income reflect the principle of supply and demand: relatively fewer people are attorneys, so that work earns a relatively higher salary. What jobs earn is also an indication of how society values those jobs, the training that those jobs require, the effort required to do the work, or the difficulty or danger involved.

People choose to do jobs for a number of reasons. What people earn in a job is a reflection of choices people have made regarding education, training, and skill development. A major factor in what a person earns is productivity, the ability to produce goods or services in a specific period of time. More productive workers are more valuable to employers and tend to earn more income. People with fewer marketable skills—in other words, people who are less productive—are more likely to have lower income.

A change in demand for a product or service will affect the income for workers in that industry. A change in the price for a productive resource can also affect the pay that an employer offers for a job, since the employer might decide to use more machines and hire fewer people. If wages increase, workers will tend to increase the labor they supply; but at the same time firms may demand less total labor in order to limit costs. As we indicated in Lesson 46, the equilibrium is the pay that the employer offers for the labor that the employer requires.

Income Distribution

Economists study income in several different ways. One way is by functional distribution of income, which measures the distribution of income among different businesses and occupations in the economy. The median rates of pay shown at left are a measure of the functional distribution of income. When you determine how many people are sheet metal workers, high school teachers, attorneys, and so forth, you can see the total income that people in each category earn.

Lesson 49 - Income

Income Distribution by Household in the United States (as of 2014)

Quintile	Lower Limit	Average	Upper Limit
Lowest 20%	$0	$11,676	$21,432
Second 20%	$21,433	$31,087	$41,186
Third 20%	$41,187	$54,041	$68,212
Fourth 20%	$68,213	$87,834	$112,262
Highest 20%	$112,263	$194,053	(none)

Another way to study income is by household distribution of income. This is a measure of the distribution of income among groups of households according to income ranges, regardless of what jobs the people in those households do.

In 2014 (the last year for which information was available at the time of publication), the median household income in the United States was $53,657. This statistic is helpful in determining how family income rises or falls in a given year.

A common way that economists study household distribution of income is by quintiles, or groupings of one-fifth of the total. Consider the chart above that shows household income distribution in 2014. Each quintile contains about 65 million people.

The twenty percent of U.S. households (households of any size) that earned the least in 2014 earned between zero and $21,432. The next one-fifth of households earned from $21,433 to $41,186. So forty percent of American households earned $41,186 or less. Within the highest quintile, the top 5% of households earned an average of $332,347 (this data is not shown on the chart).

Another way to study the household distribution of income is to determine the share of national income that each quintile earns. The pie chart at right shows data from 2014.

As the chart shows, in 2014 the 20% of American households with the highest income earned just over half of all national income. But before you become incensed at the unfairness of this and think that the solution to all of our problems would be to tax the rich and give the money to the poor, we need to add a few more statistics.

First, poorer households tend to be smaller and have fewer people working while wealthier ones are larger and have more people working. The lowest quintile has one-fifth of the households but only about one-sixth of the population, while the top quintile had one-fourth of the population. Second, the highest quintile has the highest education level and contributes most of the investments that create jobs and grow the economy. Third, the idea of taxing the rich heavily is already happening.

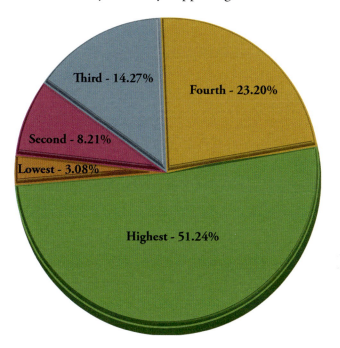

According to these figures, in 2014 the highest income quintile received 51.3% of the nation's income and paid 83.9% of all federal income taxes. The middle quintile received 14% of the national income and paid 9% of federal income taxes. The lowest quintile received 5% of the nation's income and paid 1% of federal income taxes.

Percentage of Federal Income Taxes Paid

Quintile	Percentage
Lowest 20%	-2.2%
Second 20%	-1.0%
Third 20%	5.9%
Fourth 20%	13.4%
Highest 20%	83.9%

The one-fifth of households with the highest income already pays almost 84% of all federal personal income taxes. The lowest forty percent on balance actually receive money from the federal government in the form of tax credits and transfers (assistance payments and other federal programs) that exceeds their income tax burden. Thus they receive more than they pay, hence the negative figures. We will talk more about tax policies and redistribution of income in the next unit.

Minimum Wage

A controversial issue in economic and political circles is the minimum wage, which is a legally mandated minimum hourly wage that all employers (with some exceptions) must pay workers. The first federal minimum wage, established in 1938, required a rate of 25 cents per hour. The chart below shows how the minimum wage has increased by act of Congress over time. The most recent increase in 2009 raised the minimum wage to $7.25 per hour. Some states and cities set a higher minimum wage than the federal rate.

Employees that have traditionally been exempt from the federal minimum wage include administrative, professional, executive, and outside sales employees; full-time college students; workers in some farming and fishing enterprises, and certain service workers who receive compensation plus tips that at least equals the minimum wage.

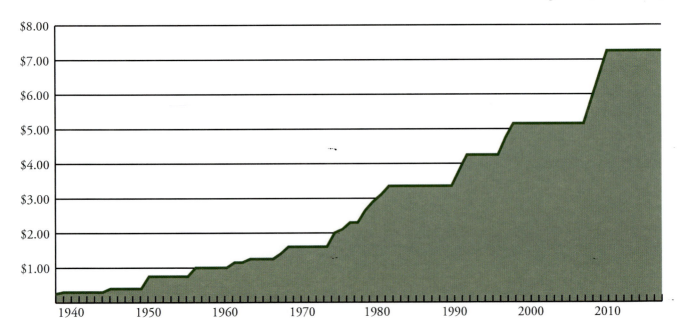

Federal minimum wage rate (1938-2016)

Many fast food restaurants are small businesses run by franchisees who pay a large corporation for the right to use the corporate name and system of operation. Many fast food workers start out at minimum wage, which allows young people and other inexperienced workers a chance to get started in the labor force.

Supporters of the minimum wage say that it ensures a decent income for working Americans; without it, supporters say, people would be at the mercy of business owners who might want to pay as little as possible. Advocates of a minimum wage argue that, since owners can always find someone who is willing to work for less, without a minimum wage the result would be people working in near-slavery conditions while business owners profit from the work of their underpaid employees.

A minimum wage helps the economy, advocates say, because it provides workers with more purchasing power, and greater consumer demand leads to more production. Proponents also claim that a minimum wage encourages low-wage workers by giving them a step up toward better-paying jobs. Higher wages can lead to a reduction in poverty, which means less of a need for income assistance (welfare) programs that the government provides. However, increases in the minimum wage have not generally kept pace with the cost of living.

Opponents of a minimum wage say that a mandated minimum wage is an artificial price floor for the cost of labor. Price floors tend to increase supply and decrease demand (see Lesson 28), so opponents say that firms will tend to hire fewer workers because of a mandated minimum wage. Requiring firms to pay their workers more will lead to higher prices to cover increased production costs, opponents argue, which lead to employers hiring fewer workers.

A required minimum wage, opponents charge, is a great challenge to small businesses. These companies hire most of the economy's entry-level workers, who are those in the labor market for the first time. If a business cannot afford to pay the minimum wage and cannot afford to increase prices, it will likely either hire fewer workers or have to close. Either eventuality leads to jobs lost. As these unemployed people look for other positions, the increased supply of potential workers tends to depress wages in job categories that the minimum wage law does not cover.

In an oversimplified example, imagine a small business with ten employees, each earning the minimum wage that we'll say is $4.00 per hour. Thus the hourly labor cost is $40.00. If the minimum wage increases to $5.00 per hour, it will mean a 25% increase in labor costs for the business owner. His choices would be to lay off two workers to keep his labor cost the same, decide to earn less profit, or increase prices. A marginal business with a low rate of profit would find either of the last two choices difficult.

The number of workers directly affected by the minimum wage is small. In 2013, 75.9 million workers age 16 or over were paid by the hour. Of that group, 1.5 million earned the minimum wage and 1.8 million earned less than the minimum because they worked in jobs not covered by the minimum wage law. In other words, only about 4.3% of the hourly-wage work force earned the minimum wage or less.

Currently, a full-time worker earning the minimum wage would have an annual income of $15,080 ($7.25 per hour x 40 hours per week x 52 weeks). The 2016 federal poverty level is $11,880 for a single person, $16,020 for a household of two, and $24,300 for a household of four. However, relatively few people are in the position of trying to support a family with the income from one minimum wage job. In addition, a family with income at this level generally has access to tax credits and other government programs that serve to boost their functional income level.

About one-third of those who earn the minimum wage are children from higher income families who are working at part-time jobs. Another one-sixth of minimum-wage workers come from poor families. Many minimum wage workers are in food preparation and service-related industries. Those who receive the minimum wage also tend to be under age 25.

Most economists agree that the most vulnerable category of workers as a result of the minimum wage are those age 16 to 19. These are people whom employers are least likely to hire at a required minimum wage rate because their productivity for the business will likely not justify the cost to the employers. The group most significantly affected appears to be black males, who as a result of the minimum wage law find it difficult to acquire the work skills and the experience they need to move up to higher paying jobs.

The minimum wage law is an attempt to ensure a decent income for workers. However, many economists believe that the minimum wage law does not accomplish its stated purpose. Rather than guaranteeing a living wage, it tends to cost people jobs and to depress wages for other low-paying positions by increasing the supply of workers for those jobs. The minimum wage law is an example of how actual government policy sometimes does not accomplish the good intentions of policy advocates and how unintended consequences occur instead. When we judge a government practice, we should not go by the desired results but by the actual results.

Labor unions tend to be big supporters of minimum wage increases in the name of "helping the working people of America earn a living wage." However, their support appears to have a hidden agenda. Only about 2% of union members earn the minimum wage, while most earn much more than that. The result of a minimum wage is that employers hire fewer low-skill workers, who tend to earn the minimum, and instead will hire higher-skill workers, who are more likely to be union members, to increase productivity. Thus despite the stated reason for supporting the minimum wage—to help

In 2015 the City of Los Angeles passed a law to raise the local minimum wage gradually to $15 by 2020. After ongoing demonstrations in support of the move, Los Angeles County passed a similar plan later that year.

---

all workers—the law actually helps unions and hurts non-union workers.

We cannot know what would have happened without a minimum wage law. The effect of the law has probably been to increase the wage level overall, even though the cost of the policy has been that some people have not had jobs. It seems reasonable to think that not having a minimum wage law would depress wage rates overall, perhaps closer to the equilibrium rate but certainly lower than what we have been used to.

Some economists, politicians, and commentators support a higher minimum wage. President Barack Obama signed an executive order raising the minimum wage to $10.10 an hour for employees of contractors doing work for the federal government effective January 1, 2015. In 2015 and 2016, many people urged raising the minimum wage significantly, to as much as $15.00 per hour. These ideas are politically popular, but advocates did not address the question of where the money for the higher wage would come from. Increasing prices for goods and services to pay for it will hurt the public. Lowering profits to pay for it will hurt marginal businesses and will likely hurt prospects for employing more workers.

Proposals for an alternative to a required minimum wage include a staggered minimum wage, one rate for teen workers and a higher rate for adults, and tax and regulatory breaks for small businesses to help them maintain profits while they pay the minimum wage. Another alternative is to increase the Earned Income Tax Credit, which decreases the amount of federal income tax low-income workers have to pay.

Those who believe in a free market say that supply and demand should be allowed to work in the labor market and take their course. They would say that if people want to work for ten cents per hour, they should be free to do so.

Those workers will be motivated to move on to higher paying jobs, and companies who cannot hire enough people at a lower rate will have to increase what they offer in order to attract better workers. Firms that do pay more would attract more workers, and others firms would have to follow. The result would be wage and employment equilibrium.

The Christian approach for an employer is to pay a worker what he is worth and to trust that the Lord will provide what the employer needs.

> The elders who rule well are to be considered worthy of double honor, especially those who work hard at preaching and teaching. For the Scripture says, "You shall not muzzle the ox while he is threshing," and "The laborer is worthy of his wages."
> 1 Timothy 5:17-18

Assignments for Lesson 49

Making Choices — Read the excerpt from *My Life and Work* (pages 116-119).

Literature — Continue reading *The Travels of a T-Shirt in the Global Economy*.

Project — Continue working on your project for this unit.

Student Review — Answer the questions for Lesson 49.

Texas tenant farmers displaced by tractors (1930s)

50 Out of Work

*Of all the aspects of social misery,
nothing is so heartbreaking as unemployment.*

— *Jane Addams*

The level of employment in an economy is an indicator of productivity, in other words, of how well producers are using the resources available. This is especially true for the most valuable factor of production, human labor. Humans use raw materials, machinery, and other factors of production to create goods and services.

In an economy where many people work for others, from time to time some of those people will find themselves without a job. Unemployment occurs when people who are willing and able to work do not have jobs. A high level of unemployment is an indication that the economy is not being as productive as it could be. Persons and machines are standing idle and are not producing goods and services that people could use.

Since employee earnings make up seventy percent of national income, and since so many people (workers and their families) depend on income from employment, unemployment is an important issue in economics and in life.

Economists have identified several different classes of unemployment. *Frictional unemployment* refers to those who simply have not had the time to find a job. They have the required skills and jobs exist for them, but the process of matching jobs to people takes time. The imperfect flow of information—people finding out about available jobs and applying for them, and employers finding the right people and hiring them—causes a delay. Someone might have been laid off from a previous job, and he or she has to go through the application and interview process to find other work. Recent graduates from school who have not yet found work are also in this category.

A second category is *structural unemployment*. This occurs because of a mismatch between the skills that people have and the needs that employers have. Technological change or jobs sent overseas might have caused some people to lose their jobs, and they have not had the opportunity to learn new skills to be able to perform a different kind of work. The level of structural unemployment, which is a result of the structure of the economy, indicates the dynamic or changing nature of the economy.

Third is *seasonal unemployment*. This happens after especially busy seasons pass, such as the Christmas shopping season or summer vacation

An unusual cold snap hit California in January of 2007. Freezing temperatures had a major effect on the agriculture industry, which forced many people out of work. The Federal Emergency Management Agency funded an unemployment assistance program.

season. Employers let go employees they hired temporarily, and those workers may need time to find other work.

Fourth is *cyclical unemployment*, which occurs as a result of downturns in the business cycle (see Lesson 45). Economists usually see this kind of unemployment as the result of a lack of aggregate demand.

The Austrian School of Economics cites another category that it calls *classical unemployment*. This is a result of wages being above the equilibrium rate, and as a result some people cannot find work. Minimum wage laws and the power of unions in raising wages above equilibrium are examples of why this happens. Some observers consider this an aspect of structural unemployment, since the structure of the economy causes this unemployment to occur.

How Full Is Full?

The rate of unemployment is a percentage determined by dividing the number of people who are without a job but wanting to work by the total work force.

Unemployment rate = number unemployed / total labor force

The goal for the business and political leaders of an economy is full employment, when everyone who wants to work is working and when the only people who are unemployed are those changing jobs. This is the description of an economy that is primarily dealing with frictional and seasonal unemployment and perhaps also structural unemployment to the degree that the economy is in transition.

Economists differ on what constitutes full employment, but they often say that an economy has achieved full employment when the unemployment rate is between 1% and 5%. This is also called the natural rate of unemployment. In a time of full employment, employers in expanding businesses sometimes have difficulty finding workers with the required skills since most of them are already working. Cyclical unemployment introduces a different dynamic, since it results from an economic recession. In that situation, people who want to work and have appropriate skills are not able to find work.

Two other factors that are not as obvious also affect the unemployment picture. One is called underemployment, which refers to people who are working at jobs that are beneath their skill level but are the only work they can find, as well as people who can only find part-time work when they want to work full-time. Another issue involves discouraged workers, who have not been able to find work and have stopped actively looking. These groups are not calculated in the usual rate of unemployment.

Who Is Looking for Work?

Unemployment does not cut across society evenly. It affects some groups more that others. On the whole, teens, blacks, and Hispanics have higher unemployment rates than the national average. Adult women and Asians, on the other hand, are two groups that often have a lower rate of unemployment. College graduates usually have a relatively lower rate of unemployment; high school dropouts have a higher rate.

In addition, different areas of the country can have more or less unemployment than the nation as a whole. This variation depends on the nature of the economy in individual states. A downturn in oil prices will lead to layoffs in Texas or North Dakota. Changes in the computer and technology industry hit California hard. Different regions within a state can also have different unemployment rates. A rural area with few industries will be hard hit if a factory or two closes. This can happen even while a more diversified urban area or a popular tourist location in the state is growing rapidly.

The length of time that people are out of work is important. In 2016 about 60% of those unemployed found work within fourteen weeks. The other 40% were without a job for fifteen weeks or longer, about one-fourth of the total longer than 27 weeks. In other words, over half of the unemployed find new work fairly rapidly, while another, smaller portion of those without work remain unemployed for a long period of time. Government and private programs to address unemployment differentiate between the short-term and the chronically unemployed.

Unemployment is not just a statistical and macroeconomic issue. It has a personal dynamic as well. Once again, the cold economic categories and statistics represent real human beings and their families. An individual can experience a deep personal loss by losing a job. Many people derive a great sense of self-worth from their work. When someone loses his or her job, the temptation is great to think that one must be a failure or less worthwhile as a person.

Sign at a construction site (2009)

Our society places great emphasis on being productive. When a person cannot be productive, through losing a job or becoming disabled, it can be a great blow. Our real worth is given to us by God, of course; but unemployment leads to genuine struggles for many people.

In the parable of workers in the vineyard, Jesus described men who went to the market place every day wanting someone to hire them. The owners of the vineyard hired men at different times during the day; in other words, the potential workers were unemployed for different lengths of time. Working or not working for a day would have a significant impact on these men and their families. They wanted to work; they just needed someone to hire them.

And he went out about the third hour and saw others standing idle in the market place; and to those he said, "You also go into the vineyard, and whatever is right I will give you." And so they went. Again he went out about the sixth and the ninth hour, and did the same thing. And about the eleventh hour he went out and found others standing around; and he said to them, "Why have you been standing here idle all day long?" They said to him, "Because no one hired us." He said to them, "You go into the vineyard too."
Matthew 20:3-7

Assignments for Lesson 50

Making Choices — Read the excerpt from *Random Reminiscences of Men and Events* (pages 120-122).

Literature — Continue reading *The Travels of a T-Shirt in the Global Economy*.

Project — Finish your project for this unit.

Student Review — Answer the questions for Lesson 50, take the quiz for Unit 10, and take the second exam.

Willis J. Ballinger, economic advisor to Federal Trade Commission (1939)

11 Government

The extent of government involvement in the economy and the form that involvement takes are significant factors in the American economy. In the United States, actions of Congress, the president, and many departments and agencies in the executive branch can protect or restrict economic freedom. Those people in government impact the economy by policies, regulations, and taxes. The majority of federal revenue comes from personal and corporate income taxes. Tax policies, government budgets, and budget deficits have a major effect on the economy.

Lesson 51 - Government Departments and Agencies
Lesson 52 - Government Policies
Lesson 53 - Regulations, Regulations
Lesson 54 - Taxes, Taxes
Lesson 55 - Making and Breaking the Budget

Books Used

The Bible
Making Choices
The Travels of a T-Shirt in the Global Economy

Project

1) Write 300 to 500 words on one of the following topics:

- How do you feel that the government should or should not be involved in providing public goods as described in Lesson 52: security, infrastructure, education, and health care?

- Suppose you are a member of your county's governing body. You've been asked to deliver a report and recommendation at the next meeting regarding the proposal of a large chemical company. The company wants to build a plant in your county which will bring hundreds of jobs to the area. They are asking that the county build a road from the proposed site to the nearest highway. They are asking for an exemption on property taxes for ten years. The local community is concerned about safety for the environment and potential employees. Write your report, responding to the proposal and all related issues.

2) What is a business, product, or service that you think needs to be less regulated or more regulated by the government? Design an attractive flier that succinctly explains your views.

3) Write and perform a skit that creatively explains taxes: who pays them, who gets the money, and what the money is used for. Recruit siblings or friends to perform with you.

Occupational Safety and Health Administration agreement to protect airline ground workers (2012)

51 Government Departments and Agencies

> *Government's view of the economy could be summed up in a few short phrases: If it moves, tax it. If it keeps moving, regulate it. And if it stops moving, subsidize it.*
>
> — Ronald Reagan

Those who advocate a completely free market believe that government should play no role in the economy other than making sure it is free (which is a policy decision in itself). Those who promote a command economy or socialism believe that the government should control everything related to the economy. Both sets of advocates have their reasons why they think their idea is best for the people who take part in that economy. History has shown that neither extreme position works without flaw, so the ideal goal is to find the proper balance—the best way for government to be involved in the economy.

As we have already learned, different people define that balance in different ways because they have different views on the goal of economic activity. One group says that the primary goal of economic activity is economic freedom, by which they mean that people should be free to work, buy, save, and engage in all other economic activity without any hindrance, regulation, or oversight by the government. They believe that this will bring about economic efficiency, which is the widest distribution of goods and services to those who can afford them at the lowest possible cost. They say that this is best for the people in that economy. Whatever limited government intervention in the economy takes place should be in pursuit of this goal.

The other group says that the primary goal of economic activity is economic security, by which they mean that the economic system should provide the essentials of life for every member of society whether or not they can afford to pay for those essentials themselves. The principle of economic security assumes and necessitates a redistribution of some wealth from those who have an abundance to those who have a need. The proposals to accomplish this usually take the form of taxation followed by dispersion of the money (or the goods and services that money can buy) to those in need through government programs. This group believes that this is the best policy for the people in the economy.

The track record of economic history shows that pursuing the principle of economic freedom accomplishes the most economic good for the most people. However, this pursuit does cause or allow

319

for economic difficulties for some people in the economy, so governments have instituted programs and policies to lessen that negative impact. The problem comes when a government enacts too many regulations or policies that are too restrictive. The result is economic inefficiency. In other words, we're still looking for just the right balance of government involvement in the economy.

Freedom . . . With Regulation

The basic principle that has guided the American economy has been economic freedom. On those occasions when economic freedom has led to or allowed a failure in the market in some way, the people in charge of government at the time have stepped in to create some degree of regulation. For instance, when the safety of food and drugs was a concern in the early 1900s, Congress created the Food and Drug Administration. After the stock market crashed in 1929, Congress created the Securities and Exchange Commission.

Mary Jo White became the 31st Chair of the Securities and Exchange Commission in 2013.

At times, those in government have initiated policies to bring about a desired end in economic activity that met a perceived need. Examples include founding Social Security to help the economic needs of seniors and creating the Occupational Safety and Health Administration to address safety in the workplace, even if improved safety regulations meant a greater cost to producers.

The generally-accepted principle in economics is that government intervention in the economy is justified when the benefit of intervention outweighs the cost. This involves conducting a cost-benefit analysis, but we have to expect some degree of subjectivity in that analysis. We cannot know for sure what initiating a policy will cost or what not taking action will mean. We can only go by what experience has taught us and what generally-accepted economic principles indicate will likely be the case.

In this unit, we will consider the role of government in the economy. We will discuss what the American government actually does, but we will also suggest some ideas about what government should or should not do. The overriding principles in this perspective include a belief in economic freedom but also a desire for government to engage in those policies that will further what is good, compassionate, and fair.

The economic policy of the federal government consists of two parts: monetary policy and fiscal policy. The Federal Reserve Board of Governors oversees monetary policy. We looked at monetary policy and the role of the Fed in Lesson 35. Congress participates in fiscal policy by enacting laws related to taxing, spending, and regulations. The executive branch participates in fiscal policy through the executing of laws, through regulatory activities, and through implementing policy goals. This lesson identifies the individuals and groups of people in the federal government who are involved in fiscal policy. Later lessons describe what these individuals and groups do.

The Congressional Budget Office (CBO) has an internship program for students pursuing graduate degrees in economics, public policy, health policy, finance, or a related field. This photo shows interns from 2008 with then CBO director Peter Orszag.

Congress

As the legislative branch of the federal government, Congress passes laws that set fiscal policy. The Senate and the House of Representatives use committees of their members as the first step in considering proposed legislation and as a way to gather information that might be relevant to congressional action.

Most of the committees in each house have some involvement in and interest in economic issues. The Senate committees that have the most direct relevance to economic policy are: Agriculture, Nutrition, and Forestry; Appropriations; Armed Services; Banking, Housing, and Urban Affairs; Budget; Commerce, Science, and Transportation; Energy and Natural Resources; Environment and Public Works; Finance; Health, Education, Labor, and Pensions; and Small Business and Entrepreneurship.

Committees in the House that deal most directly with matters pertaining to the economy are: Agriculture, Appropriations, Armed Services, Budget, Education and the Workforce, Energy and Commerce, Science, Small Business, Transportation and Infrastructure, and Ways and Means.

The Congressional Budget Office, according to its website (www.cbo.gov), has the responsibility of providing "independent analyses of budgetary and economic issues to support the Congressional budget process."

The President and the Executive Branch

The president, Cabinet departments and agencies within those departments, and independent federal agencies carry out the laws that Congress passes. Agencies in the executive branch often have considerable authority in formulating and enforcing specific regulations under the broad powers that Congress grants to them.

In addition to this formal authority, the president can use his position to promote economic policies to Congress and to the American people. The president has considerable power in appointing advisors and creating groups that help formulate economic policy. These advisors can speak for the president in various venues (giving speeches, granting interviews, and so forth).

The Executive Office of the President includes the Council of Economic Advisors, the National Economic Council, the Office of the United States Trade Representative (a Cabinet-level position), and the Office of Management and Budget. The Council of Economic Advisors is a three-member group of economists that advises the president on domestic and international economic policy. The National Economic Council has a more political function. It coordinates the president's economic agenda with the various departments that economic policy affects. The United States Trade Representative is responsible for developing trade and for conducting trade negotiations with other countries. The Office of Management and Budget heads the development of the federal budget and sees that the executive departments follow through on budget guidelines.

Treasury Department

The Department of the Treasury is the Cabinet department that is most involved with federal economic policy. The department manages the government's finances, insures the safety of the nation's financial system, and promotes economic growth and stability. One way it pursues the last goal is through the Community Development Financial Institution Fund, which expands credit and capital services in distressed rural and urban communities. The Internal Revenue Service enforces the tax code, and it has considerable authority to formulate specific tax regulations. The Alcohol and Tobacco Tax and Trade Bureau is also an agency in the Treasury Department.

One important function of the Treasury Department is the financing of the public debt. The Bureau of the Fiscal Service sells five kinds of marketable securities by which people loan money to the government, money that they expect to get back with interest. Treasury Bills (T-Bills) are short term obligations with maturity dates of up to one year. Treasury Notes (T-Notes) are intermediate term debt securities that mature in two to ten years. Treasury Bonds (T-Bonds) are long term obligations of thirty years that pay interest every six months. Treasury Inflation-Protected Securities (TIPS) have maturities of five, ten, and thirty years. The amount of principal invested in TIPS is adjusted upward with inflation but the value cannot go below the original investment. Floating Rate Notes (FRNs) pay varying rates of interest every quarter until they mature after two years. The Treasury Department also sells traditional savings bonds to individuals.

Other Departments and Agencies

Economic policy involves several of the Cabinet departments in the executive branch. Some agencies enforce policy while others carry out programs to enhance economic activity. Below are some Cabinet departments and agencies within them, as well as some independent agencies, that deal with economic issues.

Agriculture. Inspection services for animal and plant health, grain production, stockyards and meat packers, and food safety; payment of subsidies to farmers.

Commerce. Economic Development Administration; Minority Business Development Agency; and the Census Bureau and the Bureau of Economic Analysis, which collect and publish data related to the economy.

Health and Human Services. Food and Drug Administration, Low Income Home Energy Assistance Program.

In September 2016, the U.S. Department of Transportation issued new guidelines for the testing and deployment of automated vehicles. Secretary of Transportation Anthony Foxx spoke at a press conference about the policies.

Housing and Urban Development. Community Development Block Grants; agencies that are involved with home mortgages or with selling mortgage-backed securities, including the Government National Mortgage Association (Ginnie Mae), Federal Home Loan Mortgage Corporation (Freddie Mac), Federal National Mortgage Association (Fannie Mae).

Labor. Mine Safety and Health Administration, Occupational Safety and Health Administration.

State. Bureau of Economic and Business Affairs.

Transportation. National Highway Traffic Safety Administration (which enforces safety standards and vehicle fuel efficiency standards); agencies that enforce regulations related to air, railroad, highway, and maritime transportation.

Independent Agencies. Securities and Exchange Commission, Federal Trade Commission, Social Security Administration, Farm Credit Administration, Small Business Administration, Environmental Protection Agency, Equal Employment Opportunity Commission, National Labor Relations Board, Consumer Products Safety Commission, Amtrak, Tennessee Valley Authority, Export-Import Bank (which finances sales of exports to international buyers when potential problems might impede trade), United States Agency for International Development.

In addition to these federal agencies, state governments have departments of economic development that encourage the growth of state economies, regulatory agencies that supervise insurance and other specific industries, and other government bodies that oversee environmental and other issues related to the economy.

Free Market or Government-Controlled?

Does the United States have a free market economy or a government-controlled economy? Obviously, it has neither exclusively. People who participate in the American economy have many freedoms regarding what they produce, what they purchase, and how their businesses can operate. At the same time, the above list of government officials and agencies involved in the economy shows us that the federal government plays a significant role in our free market economy, from Congress to the president to numerous executive and independent agencies.

We usually say that the United States has a free market economy. However, the government is heavily involved in the economy through its taxing and spending policies, regulations it enforces, and encouragement of specific economic goals. The other lessons in this unit provide more detail on how the government carries out its fiscal policies.

The large number of government entities that are involved in the economy represent, serve, or regulate a wide array of particular groups, each of which has its own perspective on what the government should do with regard to the economy. In addition to what private groups want, some government employees can be more interested in exercising their own power in applying regulations than in what is best for the group they supposedly represent or serve.

Scripture teaches that Christians should help people in need of economic security. However, it also teaches that individuals have responsibility to provide for themselves.

For even when we were with you, we used to give you this order: if anyone is not willing to work, then he is not to eat, either.
2 Thessalonians 3:10

Assignments for Lesson 51

Literature — Continue reading *The Travels of a T-Shirt in the Global Economy*. Plan to finish it by the end of this unit.

Project — Choose your project for this unit and start working on it.

Student Review — Answer the questions for Lesson 51.

San Diego County Building Inspector (2007)

52 Government Policies

> *Nobody spends somebody else's money as carefully as he spends his own. Nobody uses somebody else's resources as carefully as he uses his own. So if you want efficiency and effectiveness, if you want knowledge to be properly utilized, you have to do it through the means of private property.*
>
> — Milton Friedman

In the previous lesson, we listed some of the economic policy makers and some of the departments, agencies, and programs that play a part in the federal government's role in the economy. Now we want to know what those officials, departments, agencies, and programs do. What are the overall policy goals of the federal government with regard to the economy?

The goals of the fiscal and monetary policies of the federal government are to promote economic growth while avoiding significant upswings and downturns, to reduce inflation and unemployment, to encourage international trade, and to provide equal access to a fair and free market.

As we consider government policies that pursue these goals, we need to keep some basic principles in mind. First, government policies are what we the people allow and what we forbid, what we encourage and what we make more difficult, through our elected representatives and through appointed personnel in the government. If citizens want government to pursue different policies, they can work to elect representatives who agree with them; and the representatives can then work to change laws. Changing long-standing laws and regulations is difficult, but it is possible.

Second, not all government policies are even-handed attempts to help all Americans to the same degree. Often a government action, whether a law that Congress enacts or a regulation that an executive agency formulates, is an attempt to benefit one particular group, such as business, labor, environmentalists, farmers, or the poor. In addition, some government policies can be contradictory. For instance, a policy against the drilling for oil in certain areas for environmental reasons conflicts with the goal of energy independence. Also, some government policies are counterproductive. For instance, heavy government borrowing to pay for deficit spending takes money from the money supply that the private sector could use to grow businesses.

Third, we need to remember that elected officials and government workers do not personally pay for the policies that they enforce. Policies are

325

not approaches that people in government decide to do with their own money. Instead, elected representatives and those who work in government decide what to do with other people's money, namely that which the government collects in taxes and fees.

Part of their consideration of policies is the political impact those policies might have. Because this is true, some policies have economic costs that outweigh economic benefits. However, since those policies have political benefits, they remain in place. Political leaders like policies that distribute costs widely and that benefit politically important groups directly. People who fund government policies don't always feel those costs directly, but people who benefit from government policies do feel the benefits. Therefore, political leaders tend to enact expensive policies that continue for a long time.

In the remainder of this lesson we will look at three general policies of government that seek to accomplish the overall fiscal and monetary policy goals listed above.

A Policy of Correcting for Market Failure

At times, the market does not accomplish economic equity, economic security, and economic stability. Recessions occur and millions of people lose their jobs, or inflation develops and prices go up. Sometimes industries struggle as a result of changes in the market or poor management, and thousands endure lower pay or lose their jobs. At other times, some people are not able to afford certain goods or services. An industry might cause pollution that harms people, but the polluter pays no cost.

People in government often respond to such situations by attempting to correct for these market failures. One rare response is to nationalize an industry, which means having bureaucrats run a business. The problem with this approach is that government ownership is not as efficient as private ownership. Bureaucrats do not have to be concerned about making a profit. So government's most frequent response to market failure has been to tinker rather than to take over. Government responds by enacting new regulations or by empowering a federal agency to formulate new rules.

Here are some examples of how government might respond to market failure or try to prevent market failure. An environmental policy might call for taxing or charging fines to polluters, or it might require companies to clean up toxic waste dumps and to pay the expenses for reducing their level of pollution. An energy policy might fund research into renewable sources of energy and at the same time forbid drilling for oil in the Arctic National Wildlife Refuge or forbid additional offshore oil production. When corn-based ethanol did not prove to be an economically feasible energy alternative to petroleum, the government began paying subsidies to farmers and producers for its production.

A Policy of Providing Public Goods

In Lesson 30, we explained that public goods are goods that government provides which more than one person can use at a time and whose use cannot be restricted to people who have paid for them. The government provides public goods when the social cost of not having them outweighs the fiscal cost of having them. People generally believe that government providing public goods creates a social benefit.

The free market does not provide some goods and services for two reasons: (1) because private companies cannot make a profit doing so or (2) because it would be inefficient or unreliable for a private company to do so. For example, private firms do not manage the armed forces. What might happen if another country made a higher bid than our government did for the private company that provided our military defense? That could be catastrophic.

Lesson 52 - Government Policies

The public perception of what public goods government should provide changes from time to time, as opinions about public versus private ownership change. Nevertheless, here are some general areas in which government provides public goods.

Security. National defense and local law enforcement have long been services that most people believe government should provide. We want these services for society as a whole and not just for those who can pay for them. The American people in general believe that having the government provide these is better than relying on private companies. However, the government contracts with private firms for certain jobs when those companies can provide those services at lower cost. For example, federal agencies hire private security services in certain situations and some states hire private companies to operate prisons.

Infrastructure. In the past, American businesses commonly built private roads and ferries, recouping their costs by charging people tolls to use them. However, this approach was inconsistent, unreliable, and inefficient. Besides, a competitor could hardly build a road next to an existing road. Now governments usually funds roads and bridges with tax revenue, although private contractors do the construction work. In some places the government still collects tolls to help pay for projects. Sometimes private companies operate tollbooth systems.

The Dulles Greenway is a 14-mile toll road that connects Leesburg, Virginia, with Washington Dulles International Airport. Opened in 1995, it is the first privately-owned toll road built in Virginia since 1816. As of 2016, the road is managed and partially-owned by Maquarie Atlas Roads, an Australian company which also operates private roads in France, Germany, and the UK. The owners pay property taxes and pay for Virginia State Police protection on the road. The state of Virginia is scheduled to assume ownership of and responsibility for the road in 2056.

In the early 1800s, government promoted public roads and canals as a way to encourage trade and to provide the intangible benefit of bringing our huge country closer together. Railroads developed using the same rationale. The Interstate system also helps to accomplish these purposes. Fuel taxes pay for much of the cost of highway construction and maintenance to provide this public good.

Education. For much of American history, parents directed the education of their children at home or funded schools in their communities. Local school boards built buildings, hired teachers, and oversaw instruction. Over the course of the nineteenth century and into the early twentieth century, many people came to see education as a worthwhile public good that state government should fund for the good of children and of society as a whole. State governments increasingly funded public education and state government employees oversaw the educational system.

Poster produced during World War II by the Office of War Information

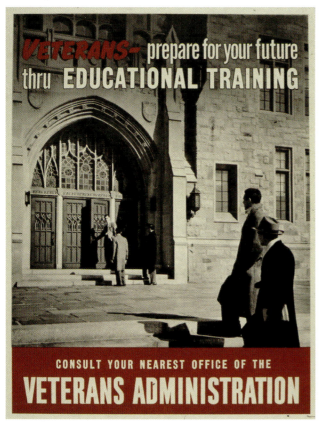

During the latter half of the 20th century the federal government began to fund education, enforce racial integration laws in schools, and create federal education standards. Near the end of World War II, the federal government passed the Servicemen's Readjustment Act (known as the G.I. Bill) which helped fund college education for veterans, created loans and grants for college students, and funded research grants for professors. Private schools and homeschooling are alternatives to public education. However, families who choose those options must pay taxes to support public schools in addition to paying for the education their children receive.

Health Care. Government has provided some level of health care for many years. Cities and counties once owned many hospitals, although more recently private corporations have come to own most hospitals. Public health clinics provide care for people based on their ability to pay. Medicare provides health care for seniors, and Medicaid provides health services for people who are unable to pay the full cost of coverage or care. State governments operate the Medicaid programs, but the federal government provides much of the funding. The Affordable Care Act of 2010 greatly increased the government's role in health care. The nature of the government's involvement in providing health care is a major issue that we will discuss later in the curriculum.

A Policy of Income Support and Redistribution

Wealth is not distributed evenly among the American people. This is the result of many factors, some of which we will discuss in a later lesson. In previous generations, families, religious groups, and other voluntary associations provided much of the care and assistance that the elderly, the poor, the disabled, and the unemployed received.

President Lyndon Johnson signed the Economic Opportunity Act in 1964 as part of his War on Poverty.

Today the government provides these goods and services in great measure. Income support programs that the government operates include unemployment benefits, government-funded job retraining, the health services mentioned above, as well as retirement and disability payments provided through Social Security. Tax revenues pay for these benefits, and government agencies distribute them to people who qualify for assistance.

Since the 1960s, the federal government has provided what has been broadly called welfare to low-income families and individuals. For many years, the federal government had no regulations that limited how long a person could receive welfare benefits. As a result, a culture of welfare dependency came to exist in a portion of the population. People in this culture came to depend on their welfare checks as their permanent source of income, and this dependency sometimes extended over more than one generation.

Reforms that Congress enacted in 1996 changed how the federal welfare assistance programs operate. The basic federal welfare program is called Temporary Assistance for Needy Families (TANF). States administer the program, which has a five-year limit on cash assistance. Participants who are actively searching for employment can receive a monthly payment.

The Supplemental Nutrition Assistance Program (SNAP) replaced the former food stamp program. SNAP uses Electronic Benefit Transfer (EBT) cards that people who receive them can use at participating grocery stores. As of 2015, about 45.8 million people received an average of $126.83 per month each in SNAP assistance. The total cost of the SNAP program that year was almost $74 billion.

The Women, Infants, and Children (WIC) program provides nutritional funding for low-income women who are expecting or who are new mothers, and also for low-income children.

These programs are a redistribution of wealth, from those who have more to those who have less. Economists call these government programs transfer payments. Politicians refer to them as entitlements because these programs offer assistance to recipients who are entitled to it, according to the criteria established by law. Some people believe the government should redistribute more income, while others believe that the government already transfers too much.

The question at the heart of the policy debate is whether government redistribution of income is really the best way for more people to be reasonably better off. Income support and redistribution does give more purchasing power to some people in the short run. However, many economists believe that government redistribution of the economic pie results in a smaller pie in the long run because it removes the incentive for economic success. In the long run, the economy is worse off because economic success produces investment, job creation, and other factors that help to grow the economy.

The question becomes whether a smaller pie that is more equally divided or a pie that has the freedom to grow larger by the free market, accompanied by private forms of assistance (namely voluntary redistribution of income, otherwise called charitable giving), is the better way to help the most people. However, the practice of income support and redistribution is well-entrenched. Congress might modify it in marginal ways, but it is not likely to end it altogether.

The voluntary sharing of assistance with those in need in the early church was an important part of the way that the spread of the gospel changed the world.

And in the proportion that any of the disciples had means, each of them determined to send a contribution for the relief of the brethren living in Judea.
Acts 11:29

Assignments for Lesson 52

Making Choices — Read the Program for Economic Recovery speech (pages 123-132).

Literature — Continue reading *The Travels of a T-Shirt in the Global Economy*.

Project — Continue working on your project for this unit.

Student Review — Answer the questions for Lesson 52.

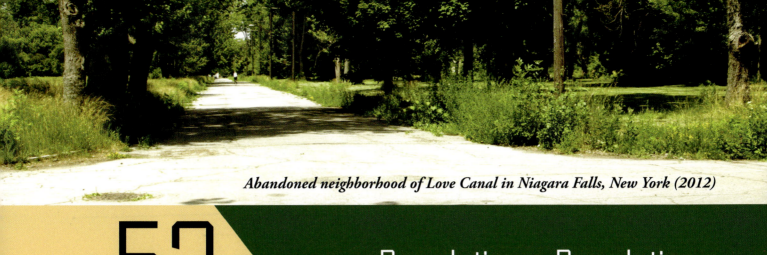

Abandoned neighborhood of Love Canal in Niagara Falls, New York (2012)

53 Regulations, Regulations

People who believe in evolution in biology often believe in creationism in government. In other words, they believe that the universe and all the creatures in it could have evolved spontaneously, but that the economy is too complicated to operate without being directed by politicians.
— *Thomas Sowell*

People have long been victims of fraud in the marketplace. The classic example is the snake oil salesman who comes to town selling a concoction that he claims will cure any ailment. People line up to buy it; but by the time the people learn that the snake oil is worthless, the salesman is long gone and the people have lost their money. Does the public need a government agency to regulate traveling salesmen, or should this be a matter of "Buyer, Beware"? People eventually discover the fraud and stop buying the snake oil, but what if someone in your family was a victim?

At times throughout the years, companies have made false or misleading claims in advertisements about their products. In the 1940s and 1950s, some cigarette companies placed ads in magazines that featured physicians who talked about how cigarette smoking was healthy and helped them feel great. Weight loss products have sometimes made exaggerated claims about what buyers can expect from using their products. Is there a need for truth-in-advertising laws?

After scientists discovered x-rays in the late 1800s, shoe stores commonly had x-ray machines that customers used to see how their foot fit inside a shoe. Not only was this level of direct exposure to x-rays harmful, but poorly-built machines often leaked radiation into the surrounding area. The government eventually banned this use of x-ray machines. Was government action appropriate?

From the 1930s to 1950s, in an area known as Love Canal in the city of Niagara Falls, New York, a chemical company buried about 21,000 tons of toxic waste in containers about twenty feet underground. The containers deteriorated and began to leak. Later, when the city was growing, developers built housing on the contaminated land and the city bought property there for a school. According to some reports, the city ignored warnings from the company about the waste.

In the late 1970s, people noticed a high incidence of birth defects and other health problems among people who lived in Love Canal. Both the city and the company denied responsibility.

The federal government undertook a major cleanup and relocated residents. Many costly lawsuits resulted from this public health disaster. Should the government have done anything at any point in the process, from prohibiting the dumping of the waste to requiring the company to pay for the cleanup?

Because of the risks that these and many other incidents have posed, government enacts and enforces regulations on the economy.

Regulating Economic Activity

The federal government regulates many areas of the economy in an effort to protect the American people. The Federal Register contains hundreds of thousands of pages of standards, guidelines, and rules that have the power of law in such areas as worker safety, product labeling, food handling, drug warnings, and advertising.

Regulations are a limitation on the free market, but the government puts them in place in the name of the public welfare. As we have already learned, complying with regulations puts an additional cost on producers, who pass the cost on to consumers in the form of higher prices. These costs push the market prices for goods and services above the equilibrium price. We all pay directly and indirectly for government regulation of the economy. The benefit is that we can live in a safer economy.

The Food and Drug Administration (FDA) sometimes takes years to approve a new pharmaceutical. At times other countries give their approval for the drug many years sooner. Less regulation would mean cheaper drugs more easily available, but the tradeoff would be the risk of taking a drug that turned out to be unsafe.

The Toy Review Committee in the FDA Bureau of Product Safety evaluated potentially dangerous toys in the 1960s. This committee included two engineers, a pediatrician, an injury data statistician, an injury guidance officer, and a compliance officer. The newly-created Consumer Product Safety Commission took over this responsibility in 1973.

Southwest Airlines took advantage of airline deregulation to expand its business outside of its home state of Texas. In 2015 it carried 145 million passengers to destinations from Seattle, Washington, to San Juan, Puerto Rico.

Federal law requires that automobiles sold in the United States have seat belts and air bags for passenger safety and catalytic converters as part of the emission control system. These requirements increase the cost of automobiles, but the tradeoff is safer travel and a cleaner environment.

The Occupational Safety and Health Administration (OSHA) regulates employee exposure to dangerous chemicals. The required protection suits and other safety materials cost companies money. The Environmental Protection Agency tells businesses that they cannot produce Product X without complying with Regulation Y. Complying with Regulation Y involves considerable expense, but the alternative is to allow companies to operate without full evaluation of potential impacts on their workers or the general public.

Sometimes regulations go too far. For instance, the federal government began regulating the trucking industry in 1935. Strict rules limited pricing, zones, routes, and competition. In some cases, regulations forbade a truck that carried goods from point A to point B to carry other goods back to point A, so it had to travel back empty, which meant increased cost to the trucking company. Sometimes a truck had to go hundreds of miles out of the way of a direct route because it had to follow a route that the company owned.

The federal government deregulated the trucking industry in 1980. Competition increased and transportation costs fell dramatically. A similar deregulation of the passenger airline industry in 1978 reduced or eliminated federal rules regarding ticket prices, routes, and the ability of new companies to begin offering service. The reforms led to lower fares by increasing the ability of airlines to compete in a freer market.

My father worked for a newspaper for many years. When Congress created OSHA and the agency began issuing safety regulations, one rule said that workers could not stand between the rolls of paper on a large press while the rolls were moving. However, workers had to stand between the rolls to adjust new rolls of newsprint, and the press had to be rolling slowly for them to do this. In other words, the regulation was impossible to follow given the needs of the industry. At an OSHA presentation explaining the regulations, newspaper representatives commented that, according to the regulation, the paper rolls on the presses were the last rolls that they would be able to use since putting new ones on would be impossible. OSHA later modified the regulation.

Sometimes the government establishes regulations to make life fairer for the disadvantaged, the "least of these" (Matthew 25:40). The Americans with Disabilities Act, for instance, requires businesses to provide accommodations for employees and customers with disabilities. The ramps and elevators that the law requires cost businesses thousands of dollars. The benefit is more equal physical access for all.

President George H. W. Bush (center) signed the Americans with Disabilities Act in 1990. From left to right are Evan Kemp, Chairman of the Equal Employment Opportunity Commission, who had suffered from spinal muscular atrophy since age 12; Harold Wilke, a minister who was born without arms; Swift Parrino, Chairman of the National Council on Disability and mother of two sons with disabilities; and Justin Dart, co-founder of the American Association of People with Disabilities, who had contracted polio as a teenager.

Issues Regarding Regulation

People engage in serious debate about the nature and extent of government regulations. Many businesspersons believe that too many and too restrictive regulations hamper their ability to run their businesses as they see fit, in a way that will allow them to earn a profit. Those who favor regulations believe that the public cannot always trust businesspersons to do the right thing. Sometimes businesses make mistakes; sometimes it takes years to know the full effect of using certain chemicals or taking some other action. Those who favor regulation say that the public needs protection from those who just want to make a profit whatever the cost. As with many issues, we must find a reasonable balance regarding regulations. Here are some specific questions about the topic.

Lesson 53 - Regulations, Regulations

Is government regulation more effective than self-regulation in a free market in which producers and consumers police themselves? In an unregulated market, if products do not do what firms claimed or if the products are actually harmful, people would find out and simply stop buying them. Producers would then have to change their products or go out of business. Victims could sue the companies for damages. On the other hand, such lawsuits are expensive and do not always serve justice. Even if companies and industries regulated themselves, there would always be someone who would try to skirt the rules in order to make a larger profit. The incidents of carmakers programming computers in their cars to falsify emissions test results are examples of this. And none of us would want to be the first user of a potentially faulty product and risk being its first victim.

Should the government seek to protect us from ourselves? Some claim that seat belt laws and motorcyclist helmet laws are an infringement on personal liberty. If someone wants to ride recklessly, they say, he should be free to exercise his choice. On the other hand, the preventable medical costs that occur as a result of unsafe travel add to the medical costs of everyone in the form of increased premiums and higher medical charges for the insured population to cover the costs that hospitals do not recover from uninsured accident victims. Some may even believe that if parents want to put their children at risk by not using a child restraint system, that is a choice that parents should be able to make without interference from the state. However, courts have held that the state has a compelling interest in protecting the health and lives of minor children and thus is justified in requiring automobile safety restraint systems for children under a certain age.

Do government regulations actually protect consumers? Government agencies do not always produce regulations in objective isolation. Producers sometimes pressure government agencies to write regulations that can be misleading. For instance, regulators have defined the term "natural flavors" so that it allows producers to use artificial ingredients in flavoring products. As a result, a company can label and advertise a product as having natural flavoring, which appeals to many consumers, even though it actually has artificial additives. In another example, the United States Department of Agriculture has standards that farmers must meet to be able to label a product as organic. However, standards for organic farming in other countries are not the same as those that American producers must follow. If a food product is grown in another country by its standards, should American stores sell the product as organic? Can the average consumer know what regulations actually protect him or her?

How can the cost of regulations be distributed fairly among producers of different size? For instance, if the government says that all companies that make Product X have to buy a $50,000 scanner to check for the presence of contaminants, larger companies can absorb the cost more easily than small companies can. A larger company can also usually more easily afford to pay an additional worker to complete paperwork requirements than a smaller company can. It would seem that this kind of regulation favors larger businesses, which often have more political influence with elected officials.

Regulations cost money and interfere with free trade. Historically, trade took place on the principle of *caveat emptor* (let the buyer beware). Even though many consumers do not have enough information or expertise to be able to determine for themselves whether, for instance, automobile tires, over-the-counter medications, or children's toys are safe before they purchase such items, private groups help promote safety in the market. For example, UL (formerly Underwriters Laboratories) has been testing products and giving its seal of approval since 1894. The Consumers Union, publisher of *Consumer Reports*, was founded in 1936 and gives consumers a source for impartial product reviews.

Some argue that the market will not regulate itself, so government must step in to regulate it. The continuing dilemma is trying to determine which regulations are necessary and which are burdensome. A key issue is determining the tradeoff involved with having a regulation and the tradeoff involved with not having a regulation. We want to know the cost of a particular regulation and the cost of not having a particular regulation. Regulations have a cost, but so does a lack of regulation.

The Lord put regulations regarding business practices in the Law of Moses for the protection of consumers. He wanted His people to do what was right from the heart, but He also knew the wrongs that people are capable of committing. Doing what is right, just, and fair in business honors the Lord.

You shall do no wrong in judgment, in measurement of weight, or capacity. You shall have just balances, just weights, a just ephah, and a just hin; I am the LORD your God, who brought you out from the land of Egypt.
Leviticus 19:35-36

Assignments for Lesson 53

Literature — Continue reading *The Travels of a T-Shirt in the Global Economy*.

Project — Continue working on your project for this unit.

Student Review — Answer the questions for Lesson 53.

Jefferson County Tax Collector, Monticello, Florida (2014)

54 Taxes, Taxes

Any tax is a discouragement, and therefore a regulation so far as it goes.
— *Oliver Wendell Holmes Jr.*

When a person or a firm wants to generate income, that person or firm engages in economic activity. The person or company produces goods and services and sells them to consumers. However, when a government wants to generate income, it usually does not engage directly in economic activity. Instead it taxes the economic activities of individuals and firms. Some agencies such as TVA and Amtrak that the government started actually engage in providing services; but these are rare. Amtrak actually operates at a loss and requires government subsidies.

Taxes are an additional cost on goods and services that is not related to the cost of production and distribution. As a result, taxes move prices away from equilibrium and thus have an impact on economic activity. Both buyers and sellers pay taxes. In a taxed exchange, buyers pay more and sellers get less than they otherwise would with the same money if no taxes were involved.

However, as Oliver Wendell Holmes Jr. said (elsewhere from the quotation above), "Taxes are the price we pay for civilization." Government cannot provide the services that people expect from it without incurring a cost, so taxes are the cost of having a government. This principle has historically meant that most people wanted a small government, providing only essential services, with as little taxation as possible. The definition of minimal services has expanded over the years, and as a result so has the level of taxation.

The primary purpose of taxes is to generate revenue for the government. This means that those who hold power in government turn to taxes to pay for programs that they want government to carry out. Sometimes governments use taxes to influence or regulate economic behavior. For instance, protective tariffs influence the behavior of exporters and importers. Taxes on particular items influence decisions by consumers on whether or not they want to buy those items. In addition, government uses taxes to redistribute wealth from people who have relatively more money to people who have relatively less money. This affects the economy by reducing the amount of money that wealthier people have to invest and by increasing participation in the economy by poorer people.

Sources of Federal Revenue

About 58% of federal revenue comes from personal and corporate income taxes. You might think that the federal income tax is simply a percentage of a person's income, but the law is more complicated than that.

A taxpayer or a tax-paying couple adds up all taxable income from wages, salaries, self-employment income, taxable investment income, and so forth to determine gross or overall income. Then taxpayers receive either a standard deduction from gross income or itemized deductions for charitable contributions, medical expenses that exceed a certain percentage of taxable income, property and sales taxes paid, interest paid on a home mortgage, and certain other expenses, if the total of itemized deductions is greater than the standard deduction. Taxpayers also have personal exemptions for themselves and their dependents. Each year taxpayers deduct from their gross income the amount the federal government allows for these personal exemptions.

When the taxpayer subtracts all exemptions and deductions from his or her gross income, the result is taxable income.

The federal government taxes income at different rates depending on the amount of income. Here are the marginal tax rates as of 2016 on the taxable income of a married couple filing jointly. Remember that taxable income is not the same as gross income. Marginal means that an additional dollar of taxable income puts the taxpayer into a higher tax bracket.

- 10% of the taxable income between $0 and $18,550.

- $1,855 (the tax on the income of the previous bracket) plus 15% on the taxable income between $18,551 and $75,300

- $10,367.50 (the total tax on the two previous brackets) plus 25% on the taxable income between $75,301 and $151,900

- $29,517.50 plus 28% of the taxable income between $151,901 and $231,450

- $51,791.50 plus 33% of the taxable income between $231,451 and $413,350

- $111,818.50 plus 35% of the taxable income between $413,351 and $466,950

- $130,578.50 plus 39.6% on the income over $466,950

The original Form 1040 tax return in 1913 had 31 lines on three pages with one page of instructions (see page 1 below). For the 2015 form, the IRS squeezed 79 lines onto two pages but provided 100 pages of instructions. An individual may have to file up to thirty extra forms and schedules to complete a return.

Government officials mailed 60,000,000 paper tax forms to U.S. citizens in 1939. The number of tax returns has more than doubled since then, but the IRS stopped mailing paper forms in 2010. Today about nine out of ten individual tax returns are filed electronically.

A taxpayer whose taxable income falls in the second bracket, for example, pays 10% on the first $18,550 of taxable income plus 15% of the additional taxable income he makes up to $75,300. Someone in the third bracket pays all of the taxes due on the amounts up to $75,300, plus 25% of his income above $75,300 but below $151,900.

This kind of increasing tax rate is called progressive, which means that the percentage of taxes to be paid increases as income rises. The opposite form of taxation is called regressive, which means that a higher percentage of income is paid in taxes at lower income levels. The justification behind progressive tax rates is that wealthier people are able to pay a greater percentage of their income in taxes without having to go without the essentials. Sales taxes are considered regressive since everyone has to pay the same tax rate for purchases; thus, sales taxes make up a greater percentage of a poor person's income than a rich person's income.

The second highest source of federal revenue, 33% of the total, is the payroll tax. Employers withhold part of these taxes from workers' wages, and employers pay another portion based on the employee's wages or salary. Employers withhold income taxes from an employee's check also, but payroll taxes are earmarked for Social Security and Medicare contributions.

In 2016, an employee had to pay 6.2% of his income up to $118,500 in Social Security taxes, while the employer contributed another 6.2%. The employee paid 1.45% of his wages in Medicare taxes with no maximum earning level, and the employer paid an additional 1.45%. So the typical employee had 15.3% of his income sent to the United States Treasury for Social Security and Medicare, half deducted from his earnings and half paid by his employer. A self-employed person was responsible for the entire 15.3%; but he paid it on only 92.35% of his earnings, and he could deduct half of this payment from gross income.

Some argue that payroll taxes are not actually taxes but are contributions to accounts from which people will draw funds later. However, payroll taxes do not go into separate funds earmarked for Social Security and Medicare. Instead, they go into the federal government's general revenue to pay for current expenses. In addition, all employees and self-employed persons must pay these taxes, even if they never receive the payments or services that these taxes supposedly fund.

The other 9% of federal revenue comes from excise taxes collected on the manufacture of specific goods such as cigarettes, alcohol, and gasoline (collected from the manufacturer but passed on to the consumer as higher prices); and fines, penalties, license fees, and other sources of revenue.

Economic Tax Policy Issues

Taxes are always a hot topic in politics and economics. Here are some important questions about the government's tax policies.

What is the balance between efficiency and equity? Taxes impose an efficiency cost on taxpayers. This cost consists of the taxes themselves, the administrative burden of record-keeping and filing tax returns, and the way that taxes influence the economic decisions of consumers. The counterweight to the efficiency issue is the question of equity or fairness. This involves determining the fairest way to share the cost of government among citizens who have different levels of income.

Is it best to tax income, savings, or consumption? Some argue that, since taxing income discourages earning and taxing interest on savings discourages saving, the better approach would be to drop the income tax in favor of a national sales tax that would tax consumption. Some have suggested a tax of as much as 23% of purchases. If you wanted to avoid paying as much in taxes, you could choose not to buy as much (low income Americans could receive a rebate of a certain amount that they paid in taxes). You could earn as much as you like without tax consequences, and your savings could be invested in economic growth. People would save a great deal of time and money in not having to file individual tax returns. A consumption tax could also reach the underground economy. People who earn income from dealing in drugs or other illegal activities will not report that income nor pay taxes on it; but they would pay taxes when they make purchases.

Those who oppose a national sales tax reply that some consumption is inelastic. Requiring a sales tax on necessities seems to violate the principle of equity. Trying to develop a national policy on what are necessities and what are luxuries could be a nightmare. In addition, a black market could develop that would be an attempt to bypass payment of the national sales tax.

Would a flat tax stimulate economic growth? Some have argued for a vastly simpler federal income tax code. This proposal calls for designating a certain level of income that would not be taxed, eliminating most or all of the complicated system of deductions and exemptions, and collecting a flat percentage of all income above the no-tax floor. Proponents say that the release from the oppressive burden of tax compliance would stimulate economic growth since compliance would be greatly simplified (although accountants and other tax professionals would likely suffer significantly).

Citizens demonstrate in support of different ideas about taxes and spending at the Minnesota State Capitol in April (left) and May (right) of 2011.

Opponents of the flat tax argue that, since the wealthy are able to build their wealth under our economic system, it is fair that they pay a greater share in income tax.

Are taxes a good way to regulate the economy? We have said that taxes affect decisions that consumers make. Some argue that taxes are preferable to regulations for influencing economic activity. Regulations necessitate paying for a huge bureaucracy; they engender lawsuits that attempt to define, apply, limit, or expand regulations; and they create an economic system that inefficiently distributes goods and services to those who can avoid or afford the fines that the regulations impose. Taxes, on the other hand, utilize the level of government we already have; they let people decide how they want to spend their money; and they allow the market to determine social priorities.

A Pigovian tax (named for economist Arthur Pigou) is a tax that attempts to correct for negative externalities in market activity. For instance, rather than impose and attempt to enforce pollution control regulations, the government could simply impose a tax on emissions that would increase the cost of production. Such a tax would cause less government expense than enforcing regulations, and it would give polluters an economic motivation to police themselves.

In 2009 Congress increased the excise tax on a pack of cigarettes from 39 cents to $1.01. Lawmakers intended for the additional revenue that the increase generated to help pay for an expanded health care program for children. The tax was an attempt to influence behavior without imposing additional government regulations on the purchase of cigarettes (other tobacco products also received large tax increases). A possible consequence was that, if people bought fewer cigarettes and other tobacco products, revenue for the health program would fall short of the goal. However, fewer people smoking would mean lower health costs, including health costs for children.

Do tax cuts stimulate economic growth? This is a matter of continuing debate among economists. Considerable evidence indicates that lowering taxes increases economic activity because taxes affect economic decisions. In general, people are more likely to work harder and to save and invest more if taxes are lower. Tax increases generally discourage economic growth. Over the long run, increased economic activity should lead to increased government revenue. Lowering taxes to increase revenue is something like a store having a sale to increase its sales total.

One related issue involves how large the tax cuts should be, since rates below a certain point could result in decreased revenue regardless of the increase in economic activity, just as sale prices at a store could result in less revenue than the store would otherwise collect. Another related issue is the need to keep government spending within government revenue, since deficit spending can have a negative effect on the economy.

Taxes were a hot topic of debate in first-century Israel. The Jews resented having to pay taxes to the pagan Roman Empire, especially since Rome used the money to finance the occupation forces it maintained in Israel. To support paying the taxes seemed to endorse Roman occupation, while refusing to pay the tax seemed to constitute rebellion against the government. In addition, Roman coins bore the image of Caesar; and many Jews believed that this violated the Second Commandment prohibiting graven images.

The National Chamber of Commerce was one business organization that opposed New Deal programs during the Great Depression. They put up this billboard in 1939 in the Washington, D.C., area.

Lesson 54 - Taxes, Taxes

When the Jewish leaders confronted Jesus over the question of whether it was in keeping with the Law to pay taxes to Caesar, they thought they had trapped Him by forcing Him to give an answer with which at least some people would disagree. Jesus noted that the Roman coins bore the image of Caesar and so belonged to him. The more central issue for Jesus was the fact that human beings are made in the image of God and thus ought to be given to Him.

"Is it lawful for us to pay taxes to Caesar, or not?"
But He detected their trickery and said to them, "Show Me a denarius.
Whose likeness and inscription does it have?"
They said, "Caesar's." And He said to them,
"Then render to Caesar the things that are Caesar's,
and to God the things that are God's."
Luke 20:22-25

Assignments for Lesson 54

Making Choices — Read "The Legitimate Role of Government in a Free Society" (pages 133-138).

Literature — Continue reading *The Travels of a T-Shirt in the Global Economy*.

Project — Continue working on your project for this unit.

Student Review — Answer the questions for Lesson 54.

Secretary of Defense Chuck Hagel meets with Representatives Chris Van Hollen and Paul Ryan of the House Budget Committee (2013)

55 Making and Breaking the Budget

Deficits mean future tax increases, pure and simple. Deficit spending should be viewed as a tax on future generations, and politicians who create deficits should be exposed as tax hikers.

— Former U.S. Congressman Ron Paul

Early in every calendar year, the president proposes a budget for federal spending to begin October 1, which marks the beginning of the federal government's fiscal year. Congress considers the proposal and generally approves it, although Congress often makes some changes in the final figures to reflect the interests of the majority party in Congress.

Budget Priorities

A budget reflects priorities—not just economic priorities, but issues that the budget maker believes are important and wants to see happen. A budget is a demonstration of an agenda, or, as in the case of a government budget, the collected agenda of many people over many years who have agreed to fund various programs.

The federal government spent $3.7 trillion in fiscal year 2015. The pie chart on this page shows a breakdown of the main spending areas.

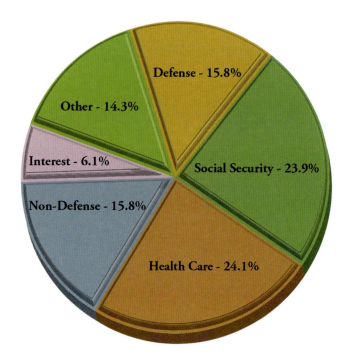

Spending for some federal programs, such as Social Security, Medicare, and the SNAP food assistance program, is called mandatory spending because the federal government has committed to funding those programs over time, and recipients depend on them. As mentioned before, these

344

programs are also sometimes called entitlements. Funding for non-entitlement programs is called discretionary spending.

Caring for older Americans is a key priority reflected in the federal budget, specifically through Medicare and Social Security outlays. These federal programs benefit specific groups, but the taxpayers at large bear the costs. Social Security, Medicare, and welfare payments are the principal means by which the federal government redistributes wealth from those with greater income to those with less income.

Government spending has a ripple effect throughout the economy. Increased spending by the government increases aggregate demand as those who receive federal dollars then use those dollars to buy goods and services. This is called the multiplier effect. Of course, spending by private consumers ripples through the economy also; but government spending is an important multiplier for two reasons. First, the spending by the government is so large and, second, the government can target its spending to achieve certain policy goals. When spending in the private sector takes place, the market determines where the ripples spread.

Deficits and Debt

A deficit is the amount that the government spends each year which exceeds revenue that it receives. In fiscal year 2015, the federal government collected $3.2 trillion and spent $3.7 trillion, which meant a budget deficit of about $500 billion. Whenever the government runs a deficit, it must borrow the difference and pay interest on what it owes. The federal government has had a deficit every year since 1970 with the exception of the years 1998-2001.

The accumulated annual deficits are called the national debt. The federal government went into debt soon after it was formed. The debt was reduced to zero in 1835, but in most years the government has run a budget deficit which increased the debt. The total federal debt as of 2016 was over $19 trillion.

Kathleen Sebelius, Secretary of Health and Human Services, meets with senior citizens at an apartment building in Washington, D.C., to discuss Medicare coverage (2010)

In political terms, most of the spending that the federal government does pleases people who receive immediate benefits from the government. Deficit spending defers full payment for the benefits until later, perhaps many years later.

In philosophical terms, deficits are the government's attempt to defy the principle of scarcity on which the study of economics is built. Who says we have to make choices about allocating scarce resources? Congress seems to be saying, "Let's just spend more! Let's give people more of what they want without having to make hard choices."

In economic terms, deficit spending takes loanable funds from the money supply that could be used by businesses and allocates them to government programs. This is called the crowding out effect. Potential private investment is crowded out by the borrowing that the federal government does. The crowding out effect neutralizes the multiplier effect to some degree. Deficit spending tends to drive up interest rates, as the demand for money increases and causes the price for money—interest—to increase also.

Deficit spending and the accumulation of debt cause concerns among potential investors who might want to buy public and private bonds, since the debt can have an adverse effect on the entire economy. Foreign investors can begin to worry about the strength of the dollar and become reluctant to invest in the United States. When the government finances the debt by borrowing from investors in other countries, the U.S. begins to face economic and national security concerns.

The government can simply print more money, but this brings on the possibility of inflation when more money chases goods and services that have not likewise increased in quantity. All else being equal, the increase in the money that is available will tend to result in higher prices as producers and providers seek to capture some of that increased supply of money.

Imagine a family that has for years spent more than its income and as a result is deeply in debt. A growing percentage of its income has to be devoted to paying the interest on the loans it has taken out. As its debt grows, the family finds that its options are increasingly limited. It cannot take on additional expenses because its income is already less than what it spends. If serious emergencies strike, such as health costs and repairs needed on the house, the family faces difficult choices. Economically healthy options, such as saving or paying cash for emergencies, are crowded out because of the deficit spending that the family is already doing. The same is true with government spending.

What Is the Answer for Deficits and Debt?

The federal government got to the position it is in by spending more than it took in. The remedy is to bring spending in line with revenue and to reduce the debt by means of spending cuts, tax increases, or some combination of both. But are politically unpopular solutions. It is much easier in the short run for Democrats to blame Republicans for not taxing the rich more, and for Republicans to blame the Democrats for wanting to spend more, and for Congress and the president to agree to spend more.

Some people believe that tax cuts can solve the problem by generating increased revenue from greater economic activity. For this to work, government has to control its spending. Congress enacted tax cuts during the administrations of Ronald Reagan and George W. Bush. Revenue increased, but spending increased more. Cutting taxes is the easier choice to make; but Congress has to reduce spending to maintain a balanced budget.

One major problem is how politicians and the general public have come to accept and excuse deficit spending. Most people used to see deficit spending in any amount as bad policy. More recently, politicians

Lesson 55 - Making and Breaking the Budget

have been willing to accept deficit spending as long as the overall debt is kept to a low percentage of the gross domestic product (GDP), the business activity that is the source for the government's tax revenue. In 1974, the total national debt amounted to about one-fourth of the GDP. By 2016 federal debt was about equal to the GDP. As long as elected officials accept deficit spending, and as long as voters keep sending those same elected officials back to office, the trend is likely to continue.

Nobel laureate economist James Buchanan has pointed out the moral issue that deficit spending raises. It is one thing, Buchanan said, to go into debt for something you can pay for yourself. Many people buy a house with a fifteen or thirty year mortgage and expect to pay it off themselves. It is also understandable for government to finance capital projects such as bridges and highways over a long period since the government expects those projects to serve the public for many years.

However, to finance current expenses by imposing a legacy of debt on future generations is morally irresponsible. Buchanan drew the parallel to environmental policy. If the current generation lived irresponsibly, polluted the environment significantly, and left it to later generations to clean up the mess, that would be a moral failure. How is it any less morally irresponsible for the current generation to spend and spend and leave it to future generations to deal with the resulting fiscal mess?

Federal Budget Deficits and Surpluses (1991-2015)

We must add, however, that the experience of the early twenty-first century has called into question classic theories about deficit spending and inflation. We said earlier that the government dealing with deficits by simply printing money can cause inflation, and we saw this in the late 1960s into the 1970s. However, since the major recession of 2007-2009, the federal government has run huge, unprecedented deficits while printing vast amounts of money, but inflation has remained low. If the politicians of the 1960s and 1970s had overseen rates of inflation that we have seen since 2009, they would have been wildly popular. Why are things different now?

Economist Gregory Mankiw has suggested two reasons. One, the Federal Reserve has not increased the money supply to finance federal debt. Instead, the increased money supply has helped support a weak economy and strengthen the financial system. Two, banks initially held on to much of the increased supply of money to strengthen their reserves instead of loaning it out. In addition, the Fed has additional tools to keep inflation in check: selling financial assets to drain money from the banking system, and paying interest on the reserves that banks hold to limit lending. This situation is a reminder that the economy is always changing and that economists are still learning the best way to manage an economy.

We have heard for years that the trend of federal deficit spending is unsustainable, but somehow we keep sustaining it. When will it actually become unsustainable? The answers that Congress and the president need to implement are already difficult for politicians and citizens to swallow; a worse situation might be even more difficult to correct. Sadly, we might have to endure a crisis before our leaders take meaningful action.

Many believe that the American economy is doing well despite the huge federal debt, but we can't know how much better things might be if we didn't have the debt looming over us. We do know that a family that does not saddle itself with debt will be in much better financial shape than one that does carry a burden of debt, even if the family with debt might appear to be doing fine. Despite the justifications regarding deficit spending, the warning of Proverbs still holds true.

The rich rules over the poor,
and the borrower becomes the lender's slave.
Proverbs 22:7

Assignments for Lesson 55

Literature — Finish reading *The Travels of a T-Shirt in the Global Economy*. Read the literary analysis of the book beginning on page 39 in the *Student Review* and answer the questions over the book.

Project — Finish your project for this unit.

Student Review — Answer the questions for Lesson 55 and take the quiz for Unit 11.

Union Pacific train in Corinth, Mississippi (2013)

12 Measuring the Economy

Economists have developed many ways to measure economic activity, growth, and decline. Some of the most widely used are gross domestic product (GDP), the rate of inflation, the rate of unemployment, the Index of Leading Economic Indicators, and increases or decreases of values on stock and commodity markets. The determination of recessions and depressions may be the most dramatic economic indicator. Wealth and poverty are the subjects of considerable discussion and debate.

Lesson 56 - What's Gross About the Domestic Product?
Lesson 57 - A Few Important Numbers
Lesson 58 - What Goes Up Must Come Down
Lesson 59 - What's a Recession?
Lesson 60 - Rich and Poor

Books Used

The Bible
Making Choices
Mover of Men and Mountains

Project (choose one)

1) Write 300 to 500 words on one of the following topics:

- Should a Christian pursue wealth? Do you think that a wealthy, luxurious lifestyle is acceptable for a Christian? What is the Biblical perspective on material goods?

- Why do you think people tend to look upon the wealthy with suspicion and distrust? What are ways that wealthy people in the history of our country have helped others increase wealth and quality of life?

2) Work with one of your parents to determine what your household spent during the last full month in the categories shown in the Consumer Price Index pie chart on page 357. With this information, create a pie chart that reflects your household's spending.

3) Research to find out the top three products produced by each of the top ten nations ranked by Gross Domestic Product as shown on pages 352-353. Make a photo essay creatively conveying this information.

Literature

R. G. LeTourneau was born in 1888 into a Christian family then living in Vermont. He moved around a great deal in his boyhood and adult life, spending significant time in California. Though strong-willed and rebellious in his youth, he came to Christ in his teens and spent his life serving Him.

Mover of Men and Mountains is LeTourneau's autobiography, published in 1959, and since translated into multiple languages. LeTourneau's purpose for the book is to glorify God through the testimony of His faithfulness.

LeTourneau was a businessman and inventor. His passion was large earth-moving and material-handling machines. He helped to transform the industry in his lifetime, and his impact continues to this day. He channeled his wealth into many causes for the Gospel, supporting mission work and many charities, distribution of a Christian newsletter, and the founding of LeTourneau Technical Institute, now LeTourneau University, still in operation in Longview, Texas.

R.G. LeTourneau died in 1969.

Ekonk Turkey Farm, Moosup, Connecticut (2014)

56 What's Gross About the Domestic Product?

> *Productivity is never an accident. It is always the result of a commitment to excellence, intelligent planning, and focused effort.*
>
> — Paul J. Meyer

The field of macroeconomics looks at the big picture of the overall economy: production, sales, employment, income, spending, investment—everything of an economic nature that individuals, households, businesses, and the government do. The single most important and most comprehensive measure of the overall economy is the gross domestic product (GDP), which is the market value of a nation's total domestic output of all final goods and services over a period of time. The GDP consists of these components: purchases by consumers, purchases of capital goods by businesses, purchases of goods and services by government, and net exports (total exports minus total imports).

The definition is fairly simple, but we need to emphasize several aspects of it:

- The GDP measures economic activity within a country. Even if someone from another country owns a business, its sales are included in the total.

- The GDP does not include purchases of production materials that are used to make other products. Those sales are assumed to be part of the purchase price of the final products. Items that businesses put into inventory to sell later are included in the total.

- The GDP does not include sales of used products. While the total of these sales is significant, such sales say nothing about the production of new goods in the economy.

- The GDP does not include Social Security payments. These payments do not reflect any kind of production, and it is assumed that this money will be counted in consumer purchases.

The GDP is different from the gross national product (GNP). The GNP is the production of a nation's permanent residents, whether that production occurs within the country or elsewhere.

Top Ten Nations by GDP (2015)

- [United States]
- [China]
- Japan (4.1)
- Germany (3.4)
- United Kingdom (2.8)
- France (2.4)
- India (2.1)
- Italy (1.8)
- Brazil (1.8)
- Canada (1.6)

Market in Goa, India (2014)

The sales of a company owned by an American but located in another country, or the services that an American citizen provides in another country, are included in the GNP but not in the GDP.

You can think of the difference between GDP and GNP in this way. The GNP measures production by the "*nationals*" or citizens of a country, wherever they might live; whereas the GDP measures production that occurs *domestically* or within a country, regardless of who owns the business. Usually the two figures are not significantly different; but the GDP more accurately reflects economic activity taking place within a country, and this information is of greater interest to economists and the government.

How the Government Measures GDP

In the United States, the Bureau of Economic Analysis (BEA) in the Department of Commerce measures the GDP. The bureau gathers information from businesses and from the government and gives an estimate of the production total for every three months of the year. As the BEA obtains more complete data, it issues a revised GDP estimate for a previous quarter.

We can determine the GDP either by totaling all expenditures or by totaling all income. This is true because one person's expenditure is another person's income. Any exchange has two parties, the seller and the buyer. If Doug makes an object and sells it to Olivia for $100, then Olivia's expenditure is $100 and Doug's income is $100. This exchange has increased the GDP by $100.

Most economists believe that a healthy average rate of growth for a nation's GDP is about 3% per year. This allows the economy to absorb and provide for population growth by new births and by immigration. Economies that are growing rapidly by an emphasis on modernization can grow as much as twice that fast. The U.S. GDP grew about 2.4% in 2015.

Lesson 56 - What's Gross About the Domestic Product?   353

United States (17.9 trillion US$)

China (10.9)

The Rule of 72 gives a rough estimate of the number of years it will take for a country to double its GDP at a given annual rate. The Rule of 72 is performed mathematically by using this formula: 72 divided by the percentage of growth in the GDP = number of years a country can expect to take to double its GDP. At a 3% average annual growth rate, a country can expect to double its GDP in about 24 years.

We can express the gross domestic product in nominal or real terms. The nominal GDP is the actual total figure of the value of the nation's output in terms of current prices. The real GDP expresses output in terms of a comparison with the prices of goods and services in the previous year. A comparison of nominal GDP to real GDP produces a statistic called the GDP deflator. The formula for the GDP deflator is: (nominal GDP/real GDP) x 100.

The Bureau of Economic Analysis calculates the GDP in this way because nominal GDP does not take inflation into account. A country might sell $100 worth of widgets in one year and $103 worth of widgets the next year. This might look like a 3% growth rate. However, if inflation was 6%, the value of widgets sold actually declined the second year if we use the previous year's value as the basis. Inflation might cause the second year's value to be higher even if the country sold fewer widgets. The deflator helps economists know whether the economy is truly growing or just inflating. Most economists and media talk about real GDP growth.

Another refinement of GDP measurement is called seasonal adjustment. This takes into account changes in economic activity that occur routinely throughout the year. For instance, retail sales totals are almost always lower in January than in December because people spend a great deal for Christmas and then do not spend as much in January. To say that the GDP for January fell from December would not be news. The question is whether sales fell more or less than they usually do for January. The BEA makes seasonal adjustments in its GDP estimates.

World Comparisons

The total world gross domestic product for 2015 was estimated to be just over $73.4 trillion, expressed in U.S. dollars. The estimated 2015 GDP for the United States, the largest national economy in the world, was $17.9 trillion, almost one-fourth of the world total. Government spending on all levels accounted for about one-third of U.S. GDP. The countries of the European Union had a combined GDP of $18.1 trillion.

The chart on this page shows the ten countries with the largest GDPs for 2015. The data used for this chart is provided by the World Bank with GDP values given in trillions of US dollars for comparison. GDP comparisons are at best a rough estimate because of data collection methods and currency exchange rate fluctuations. Other sources such as the International Monetary Fund and the United Nations give slightly different figures.

Another way to compare the economies of the world is with the per capita GDP, which is determined by dividing a country's GDP by its population. A corrective factor applied to GDP figures is called purchasing power parity (PPP).

The PPP takes into account the differences in the cost of living in various countries by using the long-term exchange rate between currencies to arrive at a common currency of expression.

Here are the 2015 world rankings of several countries based on national per capita GDP, PPP adjusted, in U.S. dollars. The World Bank estimated the world average per capita GDP in 2015 as $9,996.

National Per Capita GDP, PPP Adjusted (2014 estimates)		
Rank	Country	Per Capita GDP
1	Qatar	$132,100
2	Luxembourg	$99,000
6	Singapore	$85,300
19	United States	$55,800
28	Germany	$46,900
32	Canada	$45,600
39	United Kingdom	$41,200
55	Israel	$33,700
73	Russia	$25,400
94	Mexico	$17,500
103	Brazil	$15,600
113	China	$14,100
158	India	$6,200
206	Afghanistan	$1,900
229	Somalia	$400

What the GDP Shows and What It Doesn't Show

The gross domestic product is the broadest single measurement of a nation's economy. It indicates the overall health of an economy, including productivity. Yearly comparisons of a nation's GDP show whether an economy is experiencing growth or contraction and how large the changes are.

On the other hand, the GDP does not show everything of significance about a nation. It does not indicate the status of individual industries within an economy, nor does it show how wealth is distributed among the population. In addition, the GDP does not reflect the value of many things that are important to people, such as families where the wife and mother works at home, people caring for a sick or elderly relative, or citizens doing volunteer work. Nor does the GDP directly give us an indication of such quality of life factors as leisure time, environmental quality, literacy, or personal health.

However, the GDP does tell us something about such factors. The citizens of countries with a higher per capita GDP do tend on average to have better health and education, longer life expectancy, and other factors that contribute to a higher standard of living that cannot be measured in economic terms. A stronger economy makes more options available to more people, options which enable a better quality of life.

Modern skyline of Doha, Qatar, with traditional wooden boats in the foreground

Lesson 56 - What's Gross About the Domestic Product?

For a country to be truly prosperous, the people need more than money. The Old Testament book of 1 Kings described the economic well-being of Israel and Judah during the reign of Solomon.

Judah and Israel were as numerous
as the sand that is on the seashore in abundance;
they were eating and drinking and rejoicing.
1 Kings 4:20

Assignments for Lesson 56

Literature — Begin reading *Mover of Men and Mountains*. Plan to finish it by the end of Unit 15.

Project — Choose your project for this unit and start working on it.

Student Review — Answer the questions for Lesson 56.

57 A Few Important Numbers

Sunrise in Denver, Colorado (2013)

> *An "acceptable" level of unemployment means that the government economist to whom it is acceptable still has a job.*
>
> — Anonymous

The three most important macroeconomic variables are the gross domestic product, the rate of inflation, and the rate of unemployment. The GDP gives the best comprehensive picture of the overall economy. The rate of inflation affects the purchasing power of just about everyone. Unemployment puts the economy on a personal level. The strength of an economy rests in great measure on productivity, and people are not productive in a strict economic sense if they are not working. Unemployment affects both supply and demand. People have to be working to create goods and services for others to buy, and most people have to be working to be able to buy goods and services themselves.

These three variables are relatively easy to quantify and to understand. They are easy for the media to report. These are the economic statistics that the political party in power hopes will vindicate their policies or that the opposition party will use to condemn the economic policies of the administration in office at the time.

We considered the gross domestic product in the previous lesson. We have looked at inflation and unemployment in previous lessons, so here we will focus on how the government collects this information.

Inflation: The Consumer Price Index

The Consumer Price Index (CPI) is an estimate of what a typical urban consumer has to pay for a sampling of typical goods and services. The Bureau of Labor Statistics in the Department of Labor reports this estimate around the middle of each month for the preceding month. The BLS reports the CPI as a percent change from the previous month or from the same month of the previous year. When prices are said to have increased "at an annual rate of x%," that percentage figure is what most people consider to be the current rate of inflation. The focus is on urban consumers because they make up about 89% of the population. The CPI for urban consumers (CPI-U) is slightly different from the CPI for urban workers (CPI-W).

Lesson 57 - A Few Important Numbers

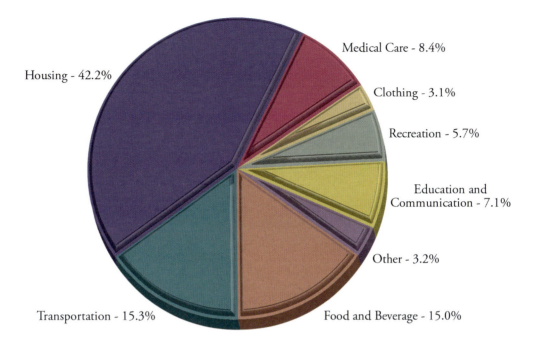

The basis for the CPI is what is called a market basket of goods and services. The items in the market basket are constant. (The BLS website has a five-page, single-spaced list of items included in the survey.) The BLS takes samplings of prices in several different cities, and they weight different categories to reflect their importance in a typical consumer's budget. The main categories and the percentage that each had in the market basket for December 2015 are shown in the chart above.

As comprehensive as the CPI is, it does have some limitations. The index does not include taxes. It does not reflect consumer prices in rural areas. Nor does it reflect changes in buying habits, such as when people decide to buy hamburger instead of steak when times are hard. The BLS constantly reviews the CPI to reflect consumer buying more accurately, but it does not immediately reflect new products that come onto the market or how consumers respond to changes in existing goods and services.

The CPI is a key indicator of changes in the cost of living as a result of inflation. Changes in the cost of living lead to cost of living adjustments (or COLA) in such things as the payments that Social Security recipients receive. Some labor contracts have annual COLA provisions.

How the Government Measures Unemployment

The rate of unemployment is another economic factor that the BLS measures. The basis for this figure is a monthly survey of 60,000 homes. Another BLS survey looks at the payrolls of about 146,000 businesses and government agencies. The Bureau of Labor Statistics reports its unemployment figure early in a month for the preceding month.

At best, the unemployment figure is an approximation of the percentage of the labor force that is out of work and looking for a job. As we indicated in Lesson 50, the survey does not reflect the percentage of discouraged persons who have given up looking for work or the percentage of persons who are underemployed and working less than they want. The payroll survey does not consider self-employed persons and does not reflect the number of people who have more than one job.

Economist Arthur Okun determined a direct correlation between changes in the real GDP and changes in the unemployment rate. Using the 3% annual rate of growth in the GDP as a benchmark, Okun found that for every two percentage point change in the real GDP above or below the benchmark figure, the unemployment rate will increase or decrease by about 1%. In other words, if the GDP grows by 6% (3% above the average), the unemployment rate will likely drop by about 1.5%. On the other hand, if the real GDP grows by only 1% (2% below the average), the unemployment rate will likely increase by about 1%.

Leading Economic Index

The Conference Board, founded in 1916, is "a global, independent business membership and research association working in the public interest . . . to provide the world's leading organizations with the practical knowledge they need to improve their performance and better serve society." The Board conducts research and holds conferences on business and economics.

For many years, the Conference Board has published the Leading Economic Index, also known as the Index of Leading Economic Indicators. The Index gathers information concerning ten areas of the economy and produces a single figure in an attempt to forecast future economic activity. The indicators are leading in the sense that movements in these areas can indicate the beginning of an overall economic trend. See the list below.

Lagging and Coincident Indicators

Some economic indicators are lagging in the sense that they change more slowly and as a result react to trends. Their value is not in predicting future economic activity but in providing information for assessing economic activity in the past. The Conference Board's seven lagging indicators are shown on the next page. Unemployment is a lagging indicator because layoffs generally occur after sales have started to decline, while hiring increases after the level of sales has begun to rise.

Still other economic indicators are called coincident because they occur about the same time as the economic trends they reveal. For instance, changes in personal income generally coincide with changes in the overall economy.

Leading Economic Indicators

1. Average length of work week for manufacturing workers
2. Number of first-time applications for unemployment benefits
3. New orders received by manufacturers for consumer goods and materials
4. New orders by manufacturers for capital goods (not related to defense contracts)
5. How quickly new merchandise is sent from suppliers to vendors
6. Number of new building permits for residential buildings
7. The Standard and Poor index of 500 stocks
8. The Leading Credit Index, which measures six financial and investment indicators
9. The difference between long-term and short-term interest rates (also called the yield curve)
10. Consumer expectations (or consumer confidence)

Lagging Economic Indicators
1. Average length of unemployment
2. Value of commercial and industrial loans that are outstanding
3. Change in the CPI for services
4. Change in labor cost per unit of output in manufacturing
5. Ratio of manufacturing and trade inventories compared to sales
6. Ratio of outstanding consumer credit compared to personal income
7. Average prime rate charged by banks

Other Economic Indicators

Since a nation's economy is complex, economists have devised many different ways of measuring economic activity in specific areas. Here are some other assessments and the sources for them.

Income. The Bureau of Economic Analysis in the Department of Commerce collects figures monthly on personal income, which is the gross income of households, and disposable personal income (DPI), which is the money that households have available for discretionary spending after taxes (because paying taxes is not a matter of choice).

Spending. The Census Bureau conducts surveys throughout the year and the Bureau of Labor Statistics (BLS) in the Labor Department reports the data from the surveys on consumer spending, focusing on retail sales. As we have indicated, retail consumer spending makes up about 70% of economic activity.

Producer Prices. The BLS gathers information to publish the monthly Producer Price Index (PPI), which reflects wholesale prices that producers charge to retail establishments. Changes in producer prices usually indicate that a change in retail prices will occur soon.

Durable Goods. The Census Bureau reports monthly on orders for durable goods. Durable goods are not consumable and typically remain in service for longer than one year. These are usually more expensive than goods that people consume quickly. An increase in orders for durable goods generally indicates that manufacturing activity is growing and that consumers have more disposable income and are more confident about their economic prospects.

Home Sales. The National Association of Realtors reports each month on the sale of new and existing homes and how the rate of sales compares with one year earlier. The Census Bureau and the Department of Housing and Urban Development announce each month the rate at which construction of new homes is beginning. We will see in a later lesson why home construction and home sales are an important indicator of economic activity.

Productivity. The Bureau of Labor Statistics provides a quarterly reading of worker productivity, which is a statistic that reveals average output per labor-hour. Productivity reflects how well producers are using raw materials, technology, and improvements in machinery and how well workers are trained to do the work they are performing. We will discuss the importance of productivity in economic activity and growth in a later lesson.

People want to know what is going to happen in the future. Economists study surveys and reports to try to identify trends that indicate what is likely to happen in the economy. The Pharisees and Sadducees wanted to see indicators from Jesus that would reveal His identity to them. Jesus gave plenty of signs showing who He was, but the Jewish leaders were unwilling to accept what those signs revealed.

The Pharisees and Sadducees came up, and testing Jesus, they asked Him to show them a sign from heaven. But He replied to them, "When it is evening, you say, 'It will be fair weather, for the sky is red.' And in the morning, 'There will be a storm today, for the sky is red and threatening.' Do you know how to discern the appearance of the sky, but cannot discern the signs of the times?"
Matthew 16:1-3

Assignments for Lesson 57

Literature Continue reading *Mover of Men and Mountains*.

Project Continue working on your project for this unit.

Student Review Answer the questions for Lesson 57.

BM&F Bovespa Stock Exchange, São Paulo, Brazil (2016)

58 What Goes Up Must Come Down

I never attempt to make money on the stock market. I buy on the assumption that they could close the market the next day and not reopen it for five years.
— *Warren Buffett, billionaire investor*

When you want to buy or sell vegetables, you go to a vegetable market. The supply and demand of vegetables in the market determine the prices for the vegetables.

When you want to buy or sell shares of stock (that is, shares of ownership) in publicly traded corporations, you go to a stock market. The supply and demand of those stocks in the market determine the prices for the shares of stock.

New York Stock Exchange

The New York Stock Exchange (NYSE) is the largest actual stock market in the world. It traces its roots to business dealings on Wall Street in 1792, and the NYSE headquarters is still located on Wall Street. The nature of its operations has changed significantly over the years, but traders still buy and sell shares of stock on the exchange. The classic image of the exchange involves hundreds of stock brokers shouting buy and sell orders, with piles of paper mounting on the floor, and stock ticker tapes spitting out changes in stock prices. Today's trading floor is not as frenzied, since computerized electronic trading has become the order of the day. The NYSE itself is owned by Intercontinental Exchange, a publicly traded, for-profit company based in Atlanta that also owns exchanges in Canada, Europe, and Singapore.

The prices for shares on the stock market rise and fall. These changes occur not only as a result of economic developments but also because of world political events. An old Wall Street saying holds that greed and fear are the two main emotions driving the buying and selling of stocks.

The two most famous declines in U.S. stock values occurred October 28-29, 1929, when the market lost 23.6% of its value, and October 19, 1987, when the market lost 22.6% of its value, the largest single-day loss in its history. One reason the losses were so great on that day in 1987 was program trading, which involved automatic sell orders by many brokers that took effect when the market declined by a certain amount. The exchange halted trading early that day to avoid further losses.

Trading floor of the New York Stock Exchange in 1936 and in 2014

The New York Stock Exchange did not open on September 11, 2001, after terrorists flew planes into the World Trade Center in New York. The stock market remained closed until the next week. The first week it was open, the market lost about 14% of its value, or about $1.4 trillion dollars in stock value.

On the other hand, the long term trend of the market has been one of growth. Historically, the combined value of stocks has increased by an average of about 10% annually. Most non-experts who "play the stock market" by constantly buying and selling the stocks of individual companies are hoping—some would say gambling—to catch favorable trends. The more reliable way for average Americans to invest in the stock market is through a mutual fund that professional investors manage. Wise investors plan to keep their investments in the fund for several years.

The Dow Jones Averages and the S&P 500

In 1896, Charles Dow, editor of the *Wall Street Journal*, and Edward D. Jones created the Dow Jones Industrial Average (DJIA). The DJIA takes the stock values of thirty key companies out of the thousands that are traded and uses a formula to determine a cumulative value for those stocks. This value of the Dow, as it is sometimes called, is a composite index which gauges how well these businesses are doing.

The New York Stock Exchange publishes its own composite index of all the stocks listed on the exchange, but the Dow is probably the best known index of the value and performance of the New York Stock Market.

The Dow began in 1896 with a value of 40.94. Its value is updated continuously, and during the day it can rise or fall dramatically before settling on its closing value at the end of the trading day. Here are some landmark high closings:

Date	Closing Value
January 12, 1906	100.25
March 12, 1956	500.24
November 14, 1972	1003.16
November 21, 1995	5023.55
March 29, 1999	10,006.78

The all-time high close as of the publication of this book was on July 12, 2016, when the Dow closed at 18,347.67.

Lesson 58 - What Goes Up Must Come Down

Dow Jones Industrial Average Companies and Stock Ticker Symbols (September 2016)

AAPL	Apple	KO	Coca-Cola
AXP	American Express	MCD	McDonald's
BA	Boeing	MMM	3M
CAT	Caterpillar	MRK	Merck
CSCO	Cisco	MSFT	Microsoft
CVX	Chevron	NKE	Nike
DD	E I du Pont de Nemours and Co	PFE	Pfizer
DIS	Disney	PG	Procter & Gamble
GE	General Electric	TRV	Travelers Companies Inc
GS	Goldman Sachs	UNH	UnitedHealth
HD	Home Depot	UTX	United Technologies
IBM	IBM	V	Visa
INTC	Intel	VZ	Verizon
JNJ	Johnson & Johnson	WMT	Wal-Mart
JPM	JPMorgan Chase	XOM	Exxon Mobil

The company that owns the Dow changes the businesses listed in the DJIA periodically to reflect the changing economy and changing demand for specific stocks. The thirty companies that made up the Dow Jones Industrial Average at the time of writing are shown in the table above.

The Dow Jones Company publishes other stock averages in addition to the industrial average. The Dow Jones Transportation Average, begun in 1884, predates the DJIA. It measures the stock values of twenty companies involved in transportation, such as railroads, trucking companies, airlines, United Parcel Service, and Federal Express. The Dow Jones Utilities Average began in 1929 when the Dow Jones Company private utility companies were separated from the DJIA. The Utilities Average considers the share values of fifteen utility companies, mostly providers of electricity, such as Consolidated Edison, Pacific Gas and Electric, and American Electric Power Company.

The Standard and Poor 500 (S&P 500) is the second most widely followed stock index after the Dow. In 1860, H. V. Poor published his first reference book with information on railroad companies. In 1906, the Standard Statistics Bureau company was organized to publish information about businesses other than railroads. Standard and Poor, now a part of McGraw Hill publishing company, produces materials that provide financial research and analysis. The S&P (Standard and Poor) 500 tracks the value of the stocks of 500 large companies that are listed either on the New York Stock Exchange or on NASDAQ.

NASDAQ and NYSE MKT LLC

Other stock exchanges trade the stocks of other companies. NASDAQ (National Association of Securities Dealers Automated Quotations), founded in 1971, is headquartered in New York City. It is an electronic stock market and is the second largest stock exchange in the United States. The NASDAQ maintains its own index of the stock prices of companies traded on it.

The NYSE MKT LLC, formerly known as the American Stock Exchange, is also based in New York. It began in 1842 with brokers gathering on the sidewalk to shout buy and sell bids. The noise was so loud that brokers developed hand signals to indicate their wishes. As a result of its outdoor origin, it was sometimes called the Curb Exchange. Trading did not move indoors until 1921. The NYSE MKT LLC maintains an index of the stocks traded through it.

Other countries have stock markets and related indices. For instance, the best-known index for the London Stock Exchange is the FTSE (pronounced footsie) 100. The Nikkei 225 is an index for the Tokyo Stock Exchange.

Commodity Exchanges

Another specialized market is that for commodities. Several commodity markets exist, including ones for agricultural products, such as grains, hogs, and cattle; oil and natural gas; precious metals; and metals industries use, such as zinc and copper.

Probably the most famous commodity market is the Chicago Mercantile Exchange. The Chicago Board of Trade (CBOT) was founded in 1848. The Chicago Butter and Egg Board began as a spin-off of the CBOT in 1898 and was eventually renamed the Chicago Mercantile Exchange (CME or the Merc). The CBOT and the CME merged in 2007 to become the CME Group.

Trade on the commodity exchanges once involved traders standing in pits and shouting their bids or using hand signals. Now nearly all trading is done electronically. Traders call electronic trading "on screen" trading.

Futures

The buying and selling of commodities takes place by means of futures contracts. In a futures contract, a speculator agrees to buy a commodity from a producer at a specified time in the future for a price agreed upon today. Such an agreement protects the producer against a price decline in the market for that commodity between now and the time the commodity sells, and it protects the buyer against a price increase over the same period. If the price in the market does go up by the sell date, the speculator will make a profit when he sells the commodity to a third party. The risk with a futures contract is that the buyer of the contract could lose money if the market price of the commodity falls below what he has agreed to pay the producer and then tries to sell the commodity to a third party.

Here is a simple example. A corn farmer plants his crop not knowing what the price for corn might be at harvest time. The market might experience a shortage and the price could be high, or there might be a bumper crop and the price could be low. A speculator who studies the overall corn market offers the farmer a contract to buy his crop at a certain price at a specified future date. It will be something less than what the speculator hopes to sell it for at harvest time, but at least the farmer knows for sure what he will make from the crop. The difference between the buying price and the selling price might only be a few cents per bushel; but if the speculator can buy a large amount of corn, he stands to make a great deal of money. Speculators do lose money sometimes, so it is to their benefit to know the market well and to bid accurately.

Chicago Mercantile Exchange

The actual buying and selling of commodity futures and stock futures is more complicated than this simple example. Futures are usually bought on margin, which means that the buyer only pays a fraction of the purchase price up front. Traders can buy and sell stock futures also. Stock futures can involve agreements to buy stock or agreements to sell stock, depending on what the speculator thinks the market will do. Futures investors try to make money by taking risks on what stock and commodity prices will be in the future.

How the Stock Market Is the Economy—And How It Isn't

Each business day brings a report on how the Dow Jones Industrial Average has changed in that day's trading. Usually the report also includes the NASDAQ index and perhaps the S&P 500. These numbers are fairly good indicators of the perceived success of large companies that employ millions of people and that have a major impact on the economy.

On the other hand, the stock markets are not the whole story of the economy. The closing numbers from Wall Street are easy to report; but the longer term trends that we described in the previous lesson that the government and other agencies report monthly, quarterly, or yearly provide a broader and more accurate reading of the overall economy. The Wall Street numbers are especially important to investors, and many average Americans who participate in mutual fund accounts are small investors.

But the NYSE and NASDAQ do not directly reflect what is happening with small businesses and with the self-employed. A large disconnect can exist between big businesses and people who invest in them on the one hand and the lives of middle income and poor Americans on the other. The economic situation of the latter groups, less wealthy but more numerous, is important also.

The Lord taught this lesson about what is of far greater importance than economics.

Sell your possessions and give to charity; make yourselves money belts which do not wear out, an unfailing treasure in heaven, where no thief comes near nor moth destroys.
Luke 12:33

Assignments for Lesson 58

Making Choices — Read about the US Foods IPO (pages 139-140).

Literature — Continue reading *Mover of Men and Mountains*.

Project — Continue working on your project for this unit.

Student Review — Answer the questions for Lesson 58.

Abandoned hotel sign, Las Vegas, Nevada

59 What's a Recession?

> *The media has correctly predicted 36 of the last 2 recessions.*
> — *Zig Ziglar*

Of all the measurements of economic activity, the one that economists, politicians, and journalists watch and discuss with the most interest is the determination of a recession.

One reason for the discussion is that economists differ over the precise definition of a recession, including when it starts and when it is over. What the various definitions have in common is that they use some combination of the measurements we have discussed in this unit. Adding to the interest is the often-hyped media coverage of economic activity.

News outlets have a hard time coming up with an exciting news story when the economy is growing at a decent pace and no calamities are taking place. As a result, the media sometimes seize upon one indicator or one economist's dire predictions to make things appear to be bleak throughout the economy. This creates a story that the media can use to attract viewers, readers, and listeners, regardless of what is actually happening in the economy. Hence the quotation by Zig Ziglar above.

Defining a Recession

A business cycle consists of a period of expansion, a peak of activity, a period of significant decline that most economists consider to be a recession, and a trough or turning point when expansion begins again.

The traditional definition of a recession is when the gross domestic product has declined for at least two consecutive quarters or six months. However, many economists do not like this definition because it does not consider any other variables such as unemployment or consumer confidence and because they prefer to identify a more precise starting point for a recession.

During a period of economic downturn, most or all of the major measures of economic activity—stock prices, employment, personal income, business profits, and so forth—decline or show only small growth. Most business and economic experts can tell when a general decline is taking place. However, the closest thing to an official definition of a recession comes after the fact by the National Bureau of Economic Research.

The National Bureau of Economic Research (NBER) is a private, non-partisan, and non-profit organization founded in 1920 that conducts research on the economy. It published its first business cycle dates in 1929. The official definition of a recession by the NBER is "a significant decline in economic activity spread across the economy, lasting more than a few months, normally visible in real GDP, real income, employment, industrial production, and wholesale-retail sales." The NBER Business Cycle Dating Committee, formed in 1978, considers what it believes to be the relevant economic data and determines when a recession began. Most economists accept the committee's determination of the beginning and ending points of a business cycle.

Since World War II, recessions have lasted an average of just over eleven months from peak to trough. The periods between low points have generally gotten longer. The recession that lasted from December 2007 until June of 2009 was the deepest and longest-lasting slowdown of economic activity in the U.S. since the year that World War II ended.

In the latest recession, the Business Cycle Dating Committee of the NBER determined that domestic production and employment were the main factors; but they also considered personal income, manufacturing output, and wholesale and retail sales. The peaks for all of these factors did not converge in December of 2007, but that is when the committee felt that the overall decline in the economy began. We will discuss this recession more in Lesson 70.

U.S. Business Cycles (1945-2009)				
Peak (when decline started)	Trough (low point before recovery began)	Number of months of contraction or recession (from peak to trough)	Number of months from previous trough to this trough	Decline in GDP during contraction
February 1945	October 1945	8	88	12.7%
November 1948	October 1949	11	48	1.7%
July 1953	May 1954	10	55	2.6%
August 1957	April 1958	8	47	3.1%
April 1960	February 1961	10	34	1.6%
December 1969	November 1970	11	117	0.6%
November 1973	March 1975	16	52	3.2%
January 1980	July 1980	6	64	1.1%
July 1981	November 1982	16	28	3.6%
July 1990	March 1991	8	100	1.4%
March 2001	November 2001	8	128	0.3%
December 2007	June 2009	18	91	5.1%

Unemployed workers in a "Hooverville" in New York City, January 1938

Defining a Depression

A joke, sometimes attributed to Harry Truman, says that a recession is when your neighbor loses his job and a depression is when you lose your job.

Before the 1930s, people referred to every economic downturn as a depression (a common term in the 1800s was panic). The United States had experienced many downturns earlier in its history, so what happened in the 1930s was called the Great Depression. The term recession came to be used after the Great Depression to describe less severe downturns.

The NBER does not have a set definition for an economic depression. A depression is generally understood to be a period of economic downturn that is more severe than a recession. One common rule of thumb is that a depression involves a decline in the GDP of more than 10%.

The NBER has determined that two periods of significant decline occurred during the 1930s. The first extended from the peak in August of 1929 until the trough of March of 1933. During that time, real GDP declined 27% and was the worst downturn in American history. After a time of relative (though by no means complete) recovery, the second decline of the decade occurred from the peak in May of 1937 until the trough in June of 1938. As the chart at left indicates, the recessions that have occurred since then do not come close to the severity of the downturns during the 1930s.

The impact of economic downturns spreads throughout the country, although not all parts of the country feel the effects to the same degree or in the same way. While it is true that the large majority of people do not lose their jobs, almost everyone knows of a family that endures significant hardship because of a recession or depression. This is yet another reminder that the study of economics is not about impersonal numbers but about real people enjoying success and enduring setbacks.

The opening verse of the Old Testament book of Lamentations expresses Jeremiah's sad appraisal of what had happened in Jerusalem, a city that once bustled with economic activity.

How lonely sits the city that was full of people!
She has become like a widow who was once great among the nations!
She who was a princess among the provinces has become a forced laborer!
Lamentations 1:1

Assignments for Lesson 59

Literature — Continue reading *Mover of Men and Mountains*.

Project — Continue working on your project for this unit.

Student Review — Answer the questions for Lesson 59.

Ten members of the De Marco family lived in this shack near Pemberton, New Jersey (1910)

60   Rich and Poor

*The fellow that has no money is poor.
The fellow that has nothing but money is poorer still.
— Billy Sunday, American evangelist (1862-1935)*

The United States is a wealthy nation. As of the end of 2015, total net household worth was about $86.8 trillion (most of the figures in this lesson come from the U.S. Census Bureau). Total annual household income as of mid-2016 was just over $16 trillion. As of 2014 (the last year for which data was available at the time of publication), the median household income was $53,657.

However, income in America is not equally distributed. About 20% of American households have an income of $100,000 or more, while another 20% have household income under $20,000. Transfer payments from government programs add to that latter figure in practical terms.

In this lesson, we examine the reality of income inequality. We will consider what has brought about this situation, what is the nature of poverty in America, and what can and should be done about income inequality.

In 1963 Mollie Orshansky, the daughter of immigrants, was an economist and statistician working in the Social Security Administration. She developed the first official guidelines for defining poverty in the United States. Her basic standard was three times the amount of income needed for an economical food budget, adjusted for the number of persons in a household.

Over the years, the basis for the calculation has changed in some ways; but the basic approach is the same. Each year, the U.S. Department of Health and Human Services issues poverty guidelines, which the government uses to determine whether citizens are eligible for certain federal programs designed to help the poor.

Mollie Orshansky (1915-2006)

2016 Poverty Guidelines Based on Number of Persons in Household

1	$11,880	5	$28,440
2	$16,020	6	$32,580
3	$20,160	7	$36,730
4	$24,300	8	$40,890

For families with more than 8 persons, add $4,160 for each additional person.

The table above shows the 2016 income guidelines for the 48 contiguous states and the District of Columbia. The economies of Alaska and Hawaii are different enough to justify separate guidelines. The meaning of the chart is that a family with this many members with income at that level or below is considered to be in poverty.

In 1964, 19% of the U.S. population lived in poverty. Fifty years later, after $22 trillion spent in the War on Poverty, the poverty rate was still 15%. Social welfare programs have provided real benefits for real people in need. Poverty rates for African Americans and for seniors have dropped more sharply than for the population as a whole. However, while these programs have alleviated some of the symptoms of poverty, they have not been able to eliminate the root causes.

Identifying the wealthy is more difficult. The federal government has not established official guidelines to determine who is wealthy. Different people have different ideas about how much annual income makes a person wealthy: $100,000, $250,000, one million dollars, or some other amount. The typical person would probably define a wealthy person as being someone who makes or who has more than he or she does.

The trend of the first decade and a half of the twenty-first century was that the percentage of total income earned by the wealthiest 1% of Americans increased, while the percentage of total income earned by the rest of Americans declined.

The Lorenz Curve

The Lorenz curve, developed by Max Lorenz in 1905, is a graph showing actual income distribution compared to perfect distribution. The diagonal line A from (0,0) to (100,100) illustrates perfect distribution: twenty percent of the population has twenty percent of income, sixty percent has sixty percent of income, and so forth. Any point along the line shows the percentage of income which that percentage of the population receives. The curved line B below the diagonal line shows the actual distribution of income by households in a certain population.

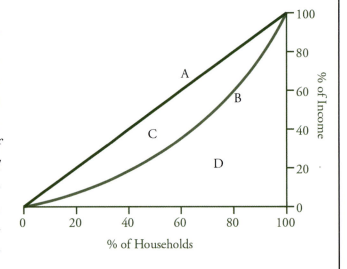

For instance, the lowest 20% of households might have 10% of income, the highest 20% might have 40% of income, and so forth. The Gini coefficient, developed by Corrado Gini in 1912, is the ratio of the area (C) between the line of perfect distribution and the Lorenz curve compared to the total area below the line of perfect distribution (C+D). The smaller the ratio, the closer actual distribution is to perfect distribution. Recent calculations of the Gini coefficient for countries of the world show that the United States has the highest ratio, which means that we have a greater degree of income inequality than any other country.

Lesson 60 - Rich and Poor

Important Factors in Defining Rich and Poor

As we consider wealth and poverty, we need to keep certain facts in mind. First, we must recognize the difference between wealth and income. Income is what a person earns during a certain period, say one year. Wealth, on the other hand, is the total value of a person's assets, which often includes a house and property, investments, bank accounts, and other useful goods, acquired over several years. A person might have little or no income in a year but still be wealthy because of what he owns. A person just starting a career might have a good income but little wealth because he has not had time to save or acquire much. Income can lead to wealth, but the two are not the same in economic terms. In calculating wealth and poverty, we usually measure income, since accurate information about a person's wealth beyond an estimate is usually not available until someone dies and his estate is settled.

Second, terms such as "the rich" or "the poor" do not always communicate the real situation. The same people are not always rich or always poor. A large number of people have good years with high income but also lean years with much less income. Thomas Sowell has said that 54% of Americans will be in the top 10% in income at some point in their lives; many of them just don't stay there. In the same way, most people qualify as poor at some point. Someone who is just starting out, or who is without a job for a year or more, would qualify as poor; but they probably won't stay in that category. A small percentage of Americans are chronically poor.

Third, to a degree poverty is a relative measurement. Most people classified as poor today have it much better than people whose income classified them as poor in previous decades. A 2005 survey revealed that 46% of families in poverty owned their own home. The typical home of a family in poverty had three bedrooms, one and a half bathrooms, a garage, a porch or patio, and was in good repair. Seventy-six percent had air conditioning, three-fourths owned cars, 97% owned at least one television set (over half had two or more), and 73% owned a microwave oven. Only 2% said they often did not have enough to eat. The image of a family with gaunt children living in a shack and wearing ragged clothes does not apply to the vast majority of cases. The face of poverty in the United States has changed.

Most of those who live in the lowest income quintile in the U.S. live in conditions that are vastly superior to the conditions in which most impoverished people in the world live. Still, it does not change the fact that people living in poverty in the United States today do not have as much income or wealth as many other people in America today.

Fourth, it is important to note that in world history, poverty is the norm and wealth is the exception. Most people worked hard to live very simply, while the very few had abundant income and wealth. We will note later in this lesson what has created the different situation in our world today.

Why Are Some Poor and Some Rich?

Some say the poor are just lazy, while others say they are victims of an unjust system. The reason that this debate continues is that both sides have valid claims and can point to examples that support their arguments.

Many factors can influence a person's earning power. Where a person grows up can make a difference. A child who grows up in a remote Appalachian town has more obstacles to wealth than a child who grows up in a wealthy suburb on Long Island. The Appalachian child can overcome the obstacles and the Long Island child can throw his opportunity away; but the likelihood is strong that their backgrounds will play a part in their lifetime income. Education can make a difference, especially one that prepares a child for a productive adult life. Family culture can make a difference: a child who grows up with his or her mom and dad and who has books in the home and abundant cultural opportunities has a better chance of a good income than a child who lives with one parent, watches lots of television from a young age, and has little verbal interaction with adults.

The key issue for determining wealth and poverty is productivity. Some people are more productive than others. Income is a by-product of productivity; more productive people have higher incomes. Sometimes people have low productivity because of their own choices: they choose to leave school, they choose not to work, or they make other choices that limit their productivity. In some cases, a person might want to be more productive but cannot. For instance, if someone cannot get a job because of discrimination, he or she cannot be productive. If a husband leaves his wife and children, the mom will find it hard to be economically productive while caring for her children. Some disabled persons find work difficult or impossible.

We will look at productivity in more detail in a later lesson.

The question of why some are poor does not have one simple answer for every situation. However, two factors are clear. In many poor households, people in the household do not work many hours and the father is absent. The members of an average poor family only work about 16 hours per week. The reasons for this can vary; but if the poor who could work did work, their situation would be greatly improved. Two-thirds of children in poor families live in one-parent homes. If their fathers would take the responsibility to provide for their children, this would greatly reduce poverty. Some are poor because of systemic injustice. Some are poor because they live in a culture of poverty that makes it hard for them to see another way of life. Personal attitudes also play a major role.

Volunteers at the Food Bank of Central and Northeast Missouri, Columbia, Missouri (2013)

Lesson 60 - Rich and Poor

The reasons why some are rich are to a great degree the mirror images of the reasons why some are poor. Most of those who are wealthy have sought out educational opportunities, have decided that they are not going to be victims, have worked hard, and have kept their families intact. Many do what many poor do not do, and as a result they achieve different outcomes. According to economist Thomas Sowell, 80% of millionaires earned their money during their lifetime. Only 20% of millionaires, which is a tiny percentage of the total U.S. population, inherited their wealth. Even this does not make them the "idle rich" as others sometimes call them. A large number of those with inherited wealth work hard and are active in philanthropic causes.

Many factors lead to income inequality, but most poor Americans are not poor because other people prevent them from earning much money. By and large, the poor do not have much money because of their own decisions. They need something besides money to help them alleviate their poverty.

Are the Poor Poor Because the Rich Are Rich?

When I toured the Biltmore Mansion in Asheville, North Carolina some years ago, I was impressed with its beauty and immensity; but I had a nagging thought. It seemed to me that the Vanderbilts could have paid their workers more and made do with fewer rooms. The idea of one family living in such luxury while their employees had to get by with a relatively low hourly wage haunted me.

Today we hear reports of corporate CEOs getting huge bonuses and retirement packages, sometimes after their companies have lost money and after people who trusted them with their life savings have been badly hurt financially. As justifiably valuable as the executives might be to their companies, it does seem as though the table is tilted in favor of the few who become wealthy and away from the millions who struggle to get by.

The facts, however, say otherwise. Those who take the risk of building companies provide jobs for many others. The Vanderbilt wealth did not make others poor; instead, the Vanderbilt wealth enabled many others to have more by providing jobs for them. The same is true about Henry Ford, Bill Gates, and other entrepreneurs. Yes, the wealthy could pay their employees more and keep less wealth for themselves; but who is to say how much wealth that should be? What if someone in government decided how much wealth you should have?

In addition, the wealthy pay a huge portion of the personal income taxes that the federal government collects every year; and much of that revenue goes to fund government income redistribution programs. In addition to starting and growing companies, the wealthy make donations to fund hospitals, museums, and other charitable and cultural organizations.

The argument that the poor are poor because the rich are rich assumes a stagnant, limited economic pie and that the wealthy find it to their benefit to starve the poor. Wealth, however, grows a bigger pie that helps more people. Even the so-called "idle rich" spend and invest, both of which give economic opportunity to others.

Why must the wealthy be the villains? Why is the answer that many propose to tax more heavily people who have worked the hardest, sacrificed and risked the most, and been willing to do what they needed to do to be successful economically? Why not see them as heroes who help instead of selfish people who abuse others? We can find examples of the wealthy who do take advantage of others, but these are the exception and not the rule.

Can We Eliminate Poverty?

We live at a remarkable time in world history. Fewer than ten percent of the world population live in extreme poverty, defined as living on the equivalent of $1.90 per day or less. In 1990, that figure was about 37%.

May 1 is International Workers Day, and on May 1, 2012, protestors in cities around the world demonstrated in favor of workers' rights. People at a rally in San Francisco criticized the wealthiest 1% of Americans for having what they consider excessive wealth and disproportionate influence. A few people used the protest as a cover for violence, causing property damage to cars and small businesses in the area.

As noted earlier, the poor in America today live much better than the poor in America a generation or two ago. In real terms, we have taken huge strides toward eliminating poverty in the United States. The poor in America live better, have better health care, and have better nutrition than the poor anywhere else in the world. The poor in America today also have a better life in material terms than the vast majority of people who have ever lived.

Immigrants have come to America with nothing and by their hard work have been able to enjoy economic success. In the twentieth century, many people left the poverty of Appalachia, found work in the industrial cities of the North, and achieved economic success. Immigrants (legal and illegal) still come to the United States because they see here their best hope for a better future for themselves and their children.

Why has this happened? Because people had ideas about doing things better, the freedom to do something with those ideas, and the belief that every individual deserved to have access to those ideas. It has been because places such as China and India discovered the power of markets and because governments have gotten out of the way of people using their talents to help others and by doing so helping themselves. The U.S. did not become the richest country in the world by government handouts. Some industries have managed to get preferential subsidies and tax breaks, and the government has done some things right to correct injustices; but government programs did not cause the rising tide that has lifted all boats the way it has.

Nevertheless, we can probably never completely eliminate poverty. I have been in many cities, and there never fails to be a poor section of town, with run-down housing, idle people, and a generally depressed atmosphere. Try as we might, with government transfer programs, work training programs, and encouragement for businesses to hire people, Jesus' observation that we will always have the poor with us is evident. The best that the United States can do is offer equality of opportunity, and this is more true today than it has ever been. No one, however, can promise equality of results. As Friedrich Hayek said in *The Road to Serfdom*, to guarantee equality of outcome, we would have to treat people unequally because they do not start out in the same place.

Can the richest country in the world keep everyone from living in poverty? Probably not, as long as people are free to choose how they live. If the government gave every poor person $50,000, some would invest that in building a strong financial foundation, while others would squander it. If the government protects freedom and encourages businesses to give people a chance, that will give more people a chance to succeed economically.

Some people choose to become entrepreneurs, while others choose to work as a laborer. One choice is not better than the other. There will always be inequality of results. No system of forced equality will bring true equality because even in such a system some will use the system to their own benefit. And as we said above, forced equality limits the pie instead of helping the pie to grow larger.

Many believe that the government needs to "do something" to make income more equal, specifically tax the rich and redistribute it to the poor. But we cannot trust the government to carry out such a program perfectly. There will still be inequities. It won't work, but the idea wins votes from the poor and from those who want to feel good for thinking this way.

Those who believe the government should redistribute wealth could just do it themselves. They could give 50%, 60%, or 90% of their income (or wealth) to others. They could do it for a small community if necessary and see how it works.

What Spiritual Obligations Do Christians Have to the Poor?

Some are poor because of systemic injustice in our society. Some are poor because they grew up in a culture of poverty and haven't left. Some are poor because of their own bad decisions. Some are poor who are unable to work because of physical limitations or mental health challenges.

So what do we do? Can we who follow the One who came to redeem us simply shake our heads, turn away, and ignore the problem? Can the children of poverty look for any help from people who worship the God of compassion, the God who gave them another chance when they did not deserve it? Can Christians build ever larger buildings in which to assemble while many of their fellow citizens see few opportunities to lead productive lives? Should Christians assume that the government will take care of the poor, while those same Christians lament boondoggle government programs and handouts?

Christians can work to promote justice and equal opportunity, and they can offer practical assistance to the poor to help them address the real reasons for poverty in their lives. Christians can support educational opportunities that can help the next generation break the cycle of poverty.

Believers can also work through their churches to provide benevolent help, to offer training in productive skills, and to provide a new vision for what is possible in people's lives. Poverty is not just a financial issue. People living in poverty frequently face other problems such as a broken family, drug dependency, illiteracy, and crime. Christians can offer the possibility of a different way of life, but they have to be in touch with the people who need a different way of life to be able to offer it.

Christians can also look carefully and honestly at their own rising expectations of material well-being and decide how much is really enough. The poor aren't poor because some Christians are better off, but Christians who are better off can commit themselves to helping others in the name of Jesus (Acts 4:34-35). The Bible does not condemn wealth as such. For example, Abraham was wealthy, Job was wealthy, and some believers that Timothy knew were wealthy (1 Timothy 6:17-19). The Bible does teach the importance of righteousness in obtaining wealth and in using it, and the Word also warns against the dangers of greed for wealth and against the dangers of depending on wealth. Generous and compassionate Christians will not eliminate poverty, but they can make a difference in the lives of the people God places in their path.

The wealthy can be humbled, the poor can be encouraged, and they both can be brought closer together by this truth:

The rich and the poor have a common bond,
The Lord is the maker of them all.
Proverbs 22:2

Assignments for Lesson 60

Making Choices — Read "Poverty and Wealth" (page 141).

Literature — Continue reading *Mover of Men and Mountains*.

Project — Finish your project for this unit.

Student Review — Answer the questions for Lesson 60 and take the quiz for Unit 12.

Geothermal power plant in Northern California (2011)

13 - Economic Issues, Part 1

Health care makes up about one-sixth of the American economy. The Social Security and Medicare programs make up a major portion of the federal budget. Energy costs, federal energy policy, and determining sources for future energy needs are all important economic issues. The automotive and housing industries make up sizable portions of the American economy.

Lesson 61 - The Business of Health Care
Lesson 62 - Social Security and Medicare
Lesson 63 - Energy
Lesson 64 - On the Road Again
Lesson 65 - O Give Me a Home

Books Used

The Bible
Making Choices
Mover of Men and Mountains

Project (choose one)

1) Write 300 to 500 words on one of the following topics:

- What do you think America's top five energy priorities should be? What are the economic implications of these priorities? What can be accomplished by the government and what by the private sector? (see Lesson 63)

- With your parents' permission, survey at least five adults, preferably of different ages, about their experiences and thoughts on the health care system in the United States. Ask: 1. How well do you feel that the health care system in the United States has served you? 2. Do you feel that health care comes at a reasonable price? 3. How would you change our health care system? Write an article about your findings.

2) Create a large painting (at least 11"x14") that reflects the many different types of energy in use in the United States (see Lesson 63).

3) Working with your parents to arrange details, make a mini-documentary (three to five minutes) about the work of someone who serves the housing industry, such as a real estate agent, mortgage broker, contractor, or government employee.

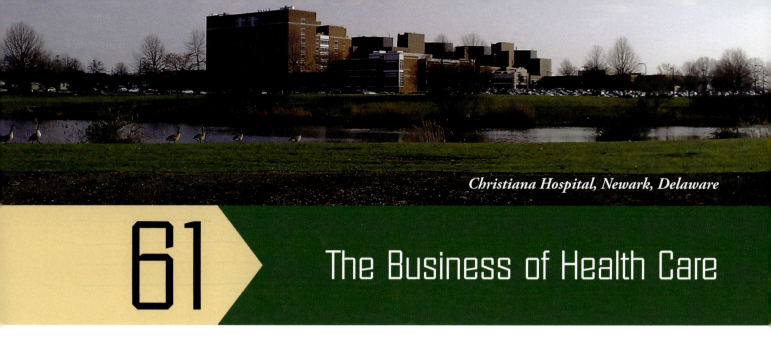

Christiana Hospital, Newark, Delaware

61 The Business of Health Care

The greatest wealth is health.

— *Virgil*

The economic impact of health care in the United States is enormous, besides the physical and emotional impact:

Health care in the United States accounts for about one-sixth of the gross domestic product.

The average cost of health care for a family of four with employer-provided health insurance, counting the costs that the employer, the insurance company, and the family pay, is over $25,000 per year. The cost has more than tripled since 2001. Of that total, the family pays over $9,000 in premiums and out-of-pocket expenses.

About one-fourth of the federal budget goes to pay for health care, mostly through Medicare (care for the elderly) and Medicaid (care for the poor).

Federal, state, and local governments pay about half of all medical costs.

The annual rate of increase in health care costs is consistently greater than the overall rate of increase in the consumer price index.

The passage of the Affordable Care Act in 2010 did not end discussion of and debate over health care in the U.S. Health care costs will continue to be a major economic issue, and the changes that Congress enacted will almost certainly not be the last ones that Congress and the public will consider.

The issues involved with health care are numerous and interrelated. Part of the confusion and frustration that come with dealing with the subject is that different people emphasize different issues. In this lesson we will emphasize the economic aspects of health care, but separating economics from politics and personal impact is difficult.

Paying for Health Care

Before the days of widespread health insurance and government involvement in paying health care costs, medical care was simply a service that physicians provided and that patients paid for.

If someone could not afford to pay for medical care, either he did without, or the doctor reduced or eliminated his fee. Often the patient paid what he could, or the patient received help from a charitable hospital or a church, or some combination of these alternatives. Medical insurance was not common before World War II.

As we learned in Lesson 49, during World War II, government wage and price controls meant that companies could not increase wages to keep or attract workers when unemployment was low. They began to offer benefits that the government did not tax as income. One of these benefits was employer-provided health insurance.

Typically the company paid the insurance premium or a portion of it, and the insurance companies began paying the major part of health care costs on behalf of employees and their families. Individuals who had health care expenses usually had to pay a small portion of the charges, called a co-payment or out-of-pocket expense. This amount may have been 20% of the charges up to a total out-of-pocket amount for the year, after which the insurance company paid all of the expenses.

The purpose of insurance is to share the risk of expense. Rather than every family paying its own medical expenses, with some paying nothing and others having to pay large amounts, insured families (or the company for whom a family member worked) would pay monthly premiums to an insurance company. The insurance company assumed the majority of the risk and paid most of the expenses for individuals and families. Insurance companies set their premium rates high enough to pay the medical expenses of those who paid premiums, to cover the expenses of operating the insurance company, and to make a profit.

The growth of health insurance had two economic effects. First, since insured individuals did not have to pay all of their medical expenses, the demand for medical treatment increased. The employer paid all or part of the premiums. The employers who did not pay the entire premium deducted the employee's part of the premium from his or her paycheck. Thus the employee never felt the financial impact of the premiums.

If an insured family had to pay a $10.00 co-payment for a doctor visit instead of the entire actual cost of $50.00, the family was more likely to go to the doctor for less urgent medical needs. Insurance companies paid providers on the basis of what insurers called "usual and customary charges," or

---

The Taos County Cooperative Health Association started in New Mexico in 1942, supported by payments from participants and funding from the Farm Security Administration. The association provided routine and emergency medical care to local residents, most of whom were Hispanic. A clinic waiting room is shown at left below. At right a seventy-seven-year old doctor puts chains on his tires to drive on snowy roads.

Lesson 61 - The Business of Health Care

the amounts that insurers believed were reasonable for specific medical procedures, such as an office visit, a tonsillectomy, or setting a broken arm. Over time a little over half of all Americans came to have employer-provided medical insurance coverage. The percentage is slightly lower today, but employer-provided medical insurance still covers almost half of all Americans. Employees who change employers can keep their insurance coverage.

Employer-provided health insurance brought about what economists call a *moral hazard*, which is the tendency of people to engage in riskier behavior if other people bear or share the cost of that behavior. For instance, if someone's parents pay his utility bill or his car insurance, that person might be less responsible about using electricity or less careful about his driving. In the same way, if someone has health insurance coverage provided for him or her, he or she might be less conscientious about pursuing a healthy lifestyle since someone else will be paying most or all of his medical expenses.

The second impact of employer-sponsored health insurance was that the increased demand drove up prices for medical care. This in turn increased the demand for insurance coverage by people who did not have employer-provided insurance. Insurance companies began providing more individual policies. These individuals had to carry more of the risk than someone who had employer-provided coverage because they were not part of a large pool of people at a business who paid premiums, but they still carried less risk since the insurance company could lump them together with other individuals who were of the same age or who lived in the same part of the country. Having health insurance coverage became the norm, and a smaller percentage of Americans did not have coverage.

As private, profit-making businesses, insurance companies could decide who they would be willing to provide insurance for. An insurance company could handle the medical costs for a few people who worked at a large company and who had chronic illnesses because the majority of employees would be generally healthy. However, the insurance company could reject or charge higher premiums for individuals who had expensive, pre-existing medical conditions or who developed chronic illnesses that required considerable medical treatment. Sometimes companies canceled coverage for people who had expensive surgeries or who needed continuing care.

In the 1960s, the federal government began providing Medicare insurance coverage for the elderly and Medicaid coverage for the poor. Health care costs skyrocketed as the government for the most part began simply paying the bills that providers submitted. Excessive charges were common and some providers committed fraud by charging for services never provided. Attempts to rein in the payments that the federal government made began not long after Medicare and Medicaid went into effect.

Medical costs have continued to rise faster than the overall rate of inflation ever since, as the amounts for usual and customary charges have changed. Since the federal government now pays such a large portion of medical expenses, the government for the most part determines what are acceptable medical charges and how providers itemize and bill medical procedures.

Why Is Health Care So Expensive?

Health care is more expensive per capita in the United States than in any other country of the world. In addition, our health costs have been rising rapidly. In 1950, five percent of all household income was spent on health care; now it takes 16% of all income. Health care expenses have caused many people to file for bankruptcy. Bankruptcy hurts the patient and it hurts the providers who do not get paid. Many factors contribute to our expensive health care system.

So much is possible. Health care providers can use hi-tech scanners, complex lab tests, robotic surgery, and many more products of medical technology. You would expect such care to cost more than it would if the tools available to a health care professional consisted of a stethoscope and a tongue depressor. We have come a long way in health care, but the progress has not been free. We have better health care, but someone has to pay for it. This a major reason for rising health care costs.

Someone besides the patient pays most costs. The doctor and the patient are the two main parties in a medical situation. A third party, either the insurance company or the government or both, actually pays most of the bill. If you spend your own money for something, you are likely to shop for the best price. If someone else is paying for it, you will likely not be as concerned about the price.

Our system of developing prescription drugs is costly. A drug company must spend millions of dollars to develop a new drug. Then to be able to sell the drug, the company must receive approval from the Food and Drug Administration in the U.S. Department of Health and Human Services, which can take more years of testing and more millions of dollars. Once a drug receives approval, the patent for it is good for only a limited time, so the company must recover its costs during that period. The company may spend more millions in advertising and in making free samples available to doctors in order to let people know about the drug's availability and effectiveness. After the patent expires, companies that paid nothing for research and development can produce generic equivalents that cost much less.

Doctors practice defensive medicine. When a patient has a problem, doctors sometimes order many tests. Some of those tests are probably not necessary, but the doctor wants to use all tools available to help the patient, and the doctor wants to avoid the possibility of a malpractice lawsuit. Medical malpractice insurance is a major expense for physicians.

Medical care is not free. Some experts estimate that the administrative costs of health care in America comprise as much as one-fourth of health care expense. Another estimate says that care provided to patients without charge adds up to $1,000 per year to the cost of premiums for a typical health insurance policy. We must expect doctors and other health professionals, hospitals, drug companies, and insurance companies to make a profit on their work; otherwise, they would not be available to provide health care or to improve their products and services. Many in the health care industry do earn high incomes, but putting limits on how much they make means further government involvement.

The Affordable Care Act

The 2010 Affordable Care Act (ACA, often called Obamacare) brought a huge change in how the health care system operates and it has brought about some unintended consequences.

The Affordable Care Act requires every American (with a few exceptions) to have health insurance coverage or face the disincentive of having to pay a penalty. This is called the health insurance mandate. The federal government set up health insurance exchanges in which health insurance companies compete for customers, and the federal government offers subsidies for people with low income to help them pay for the insurance. Employers who have more

Lesson 61 - The Business of Health Care

than a certain number of full-time employees must offer health insurance coverage or pay a penalty.

Insurance companies may not refuse coverage to people with pre-existing conditions, and they may not cancel coverage because of an illness. To pay for this coverage, insurance companies have raised premiums.

The Affordable Care Act expanded the number of people who qualify to take part in Medicaid, which the federal government pays for but the states administer. Several states have exercised the option extended to them of not increasing their Medicaid programs.

The government allowed the creation of insurance co-ops, which are non-profit consumer-operated health insurance companies that compete with for-profit companies. Twenty-three co-ops entered the market, assisted by $2.4 billion in federal loans to get started. As of mid-2016, all but seven co-ops have folded because they were not able to meet expenses. Thus a considerable amount of the federal loans will not be repaid.

The largest health insurance companies pulled out of the exchanges because they were losing money. Many of the new health insurance customers are high-risk, which means that they have high medical costs.

Some businesses are moving toward hiring part-time employees so that the companies will not have to provide health insurance for those employees.

The federal government contracted with multiple technology providers to create the HealthCare.gov website to let Americans compare and choose options for health care coverage under the Affordable Care Act. Despite costing some $1.7 billion, the site has suffered from serious technical problems since its launch in 2013.

Economic Issues Regarding Health Care

In a free market, sellers offer goods and services and buyers pay for them at the prices the sellers set. The forces of supply and demand push the prices toward equilibrium. However, the field of health care has so many other factors at work, such as government regulation and third-party payers, that health care is what economists call a *distorted market*. Typical free market principles do not work the same way in a distorted market. A true health care market seems to be a better way to provide goods and services than government involvement and oversight, but this is not the direction American healthcare is going. Unless major reforms take place, we will have to deal with this distorted market.

Government regulation tends to put ceilings on prices that health care providers charge. These ceilings may mean that health care recipients do not pay the full true cost of health care. Price ceilings tend to increase demand—since people pay less than market value for a service—but they also tend to decrease supply, since providers cannot provide services at a loss. One short-term solution is for the government to make up the difference, but this means rising government expenses. The longer-term result will likely be a shortage of medical care and perhaps rationing of care in an attempt to limit costs. Rationing means that someone will have to decide who receives care, which can lead to a change in how our society values life. It can also lead to corruption as people utilize a black market in health care or make secret deals to obtain care.

The ACA purports to make health care "affordable," which is usually presented as offering lower costs to consumers. A consumer might pay less than he did before, but if government and insurance payments make up the difference, the cost is simply spread among other people. If an office visit costs $100 and a consumer used to pay $100, but now his cost is lowered to $20 while government pays $40 and the insurance company pays $40, the cost is the same but taxpayers (and creditors holding federal debt) and those who pay premiums to the insurance company share the cost. The office visit might be more affordable for the consumer, but whether the office visit is affordable for the society at large is another question. Savings on health care costs are possible, but achieving those savings would require major changes in approach.

An increased demand for health care is taking place as the result of three factors. (1) Most medical expenses occur in the last years of a person's life. (2) Life expectancy is increasing. (3) The baby boomer generation is reaching retirement age, meaning a large increase in the number of people needing and using medical care. Thus more people will need more care for more years. This will place increased demand on health care providers, addressing needs for people in a time of life when the government is already the major payer of health expenses.

One option available for Americans who do not want to purchase health insurance under the ACA are health care sharing ministries. These organizations bring together people who share common beliefs and commit to certain practices that promote good health. Members then share medical expenses among themselves. Health care sharing ministries help members reduce medical costs by working directly with providers instead of going through a third-party insurance system.

Unless our country makes a dramatic shift to a viable free-market system, we are likely moving toward a single-payer system, in which the government provides or pays for nearly all health care. This will not solve all of the issues, but it will be the alternative of last resort. Some single-payer systems in other countries use private companies, while others are completely government-run.

Lesson 61 - The Business of Health Care

Is health care a public good that government should provides? Enough people believe it should be to have moved the health care industry in that direction. However, many people still believe that a free market approach is a better answer.

Greater competition and less direct government involvement could help to bring down costs while also providing better care. The free market has made a higher standard of living available to an increasing number of people, and it could contribute to a higher standard of health care as well.

Often lost in the shuffle of issues and payments are the hurting people who need care. The Lord has a heart of compassion for those with physical needs as well as spiritual needs. He applied this passage from Isaiah to His ministry.

The Spirit of the Lord God is upon me,
Because the Lord has anointed me
To bring good news to the afflicted;
He has sent me to bind up the brokenhearted,
To proclaim liberty to captives
And freedom to prisoners.
Isaiah 61:1

Assignments for Lesson 61

Making Choices — Read "Will We Heal with Living Water or Snake Oil?" (pages 142-145).

Literature — Continue reading *Mover of Men and Mountains*. Plan to finish it by the end of Unit 15.

Project — Choose your project for this unit and start working on it.

Student Review — Answer the questions for Lesson 61.

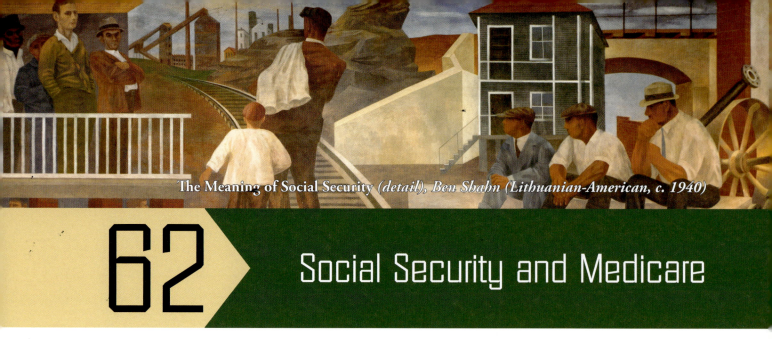

The Meaning of Social Security (detail), Ben Shahn (Lithuanian-American, c. 1940)

62 — Social Security and Medicare

> *The greatness of America is in how it treats its weakest members: the elderly, the infirm, the handicapped, the underprivileged, the unborn.*
> — William Federer

Social Security and Medicare are programs of the federal government. They primarily provide transfer payments (redistribution of wealth as money, goods, or services) to older Americans. Both programs are accepted parts of American life, and both need significant reform if they are to continue in anything like the form we have known them.

Social Security

Social Security began in 1935 to provide retirement benefits for workers and survivor benefits to families of deceased workers. The plan called for a small amount in taxes to be taken out of payroll checks to provide a fund from which eligible recipients would receive monthly payments. Payroll deductions began in 1937, and monthly payments to the first recipients began in 1940. At the time, the United States had over forty workers for every one retiree. Life expectancy for those born in 1935 was sixty-one years.

The Social Security Administration calculates retirement benefits on the basis of a worker's income during his years of work. The benefits formula tends to favor lower-income workers, since Social Security payments replace a greater percentage of income for those whose income is relatively less. Recipients can begin receiving reduced benefits at age 62, full benefits at age 66 (the full retirement age is slowly increasing from its original 65 to age 67 in 2022), and even more benefits if the recipient waits until 70 to start drawing payments. A spouse and children of a deceased worker receive full survivor benefits if a worker paid Social Security taxes for at least ten years.

Social Security disability payments began in 1957. In 2016 some 43.8 million retirees and dependents received benefits, about six million received survivor benefits, and about 10.6 million others received disability benefits. Social Security paid out about $75 billion every month in benefits, and the average monthly benefit was about $1,237 per person.

Politicians have suggested that Social Security taxes (which are also called FICA, Federal Insurance Contributions Act taxes or payroll taxes) are placed in a lock box for beneficiaries. There is no lock

Lesson 62 - Social Security and Medicare

box. The government collects FICA taxes as part of general federal revenues, and Social Security payments are part of general federal expenditures. If FICA taxes collected one year exceed Social Security benefits paid out that year, the Treasury Department issues bonds in that amount to the Social Security Administration. These bond holdings are called the Social Security Trust Fund.

This is not money. The money has been spent. These are debts that the government owes itself. If and when FICA revenues one year fall below the benefits that Social Security pays out that year, the Social Security Administration will go to the Treasury Department to redeem the bonds to obtain additional funds. At that point the Treasury Department will (or should) pay the bonds off with money from general federal revenues. As of the end of 2015, the Trust Fund held about $2.8 trillion worth of Treasury bonds.

Potential Problems for Social Security

The Social Security system faces a looming financial disaster for several reasons. First, more retirees are now living longer, so Social Security needs more money to be able to pay benefits. The life expectancy for children born in 2015 was 78.8 years of age. Second, the pool of workers paying into Social Security is shrinking since birth rates declined after the Baby Boomer generation. The amount of money workers pay into the system each year is declining. Third, the first members of the Baby Boomer generation (the generation born between 1946 and 1964) have become eligible for retirement. The oldest Boomers turned 62 in 2008. The retirement of the Baby Boomer generation will further increase the number of people wanting to receive Social Security benefits.

This Social Security exhibit at the FDR Presidential Library and Museum opened in 2010, the 75th anniversary of the program.

As of 2016, instead of forty workers for each retiree, there were fewer than three. By 2030 the ratio is expected to be a little more than two workers for each retiree. In 2010 Social Security paid out more in benefits than it took in with payroll taxes. Social Security expects this to continue for a few years, although interest income for the Trust Fund continues to provide a positive annual balance. However, benefit payments are expected eventually to exceed Trust Fund income. Unless something changes, the Trust Fund is expected to run out of money sometime in the 2030s.

One problem with estimates of future revenues and payments is that reality gets in the way. For instance, the 2007-2009 recession added to the problems facing Social Security in two ways. First, the millions of jobs lost meant that even less FICA revenue was paid into the system than had been predicted. Second, the recession caused many more people to apply to begin receiving benefits than had been anticipated. These two problems led to the shortfall in 2010. We cannot know what events will affect the already foreboding future estimates we now have.

Potential Solutions for Social Security

Social Security has long been considered an untouchable federal program. Politicians call it the "third rail" of American politics. The term comes from the third or middle rail of an electric train system, which provides the electricity for the train and thus cannot be touched safely. Workers look forward to receiving benefits after paying into the system for decades, retirees depend on the payments, and both workers and retirees vote.

Everyone knows that Social Security cannot continue indefinitely the way it currently does. The people who can do something about it are Congress and the president. They need to make the courageous political decisions that a continuation of Social Security requires. These are possible changes that might keep the program functioning.

Full retirement age could be raised beyond the current target of 67 in 2022. The standard of 65 was reasonable in 1935, but now many people can continue to work effectively well beyond that age.

Social Security could use a means test to determine what level of benefits a person actually needs.

Social Security could lower the amount it pays in benefits to individuals. Such a decrease would likely disappoint workers who had been counting on more, but a slight decrease is better than receiving nothing.

The government could increase the payroll tax rate, but current workers would likely see such an increase as merely a tax and not a contribution toward their own future benefits.

Currently the government collects payroll tax only on the first $118,500 of a person's annual income. Congress could raise or eliminate that ceiling.

Instead of current workers just paying for the benefits of current retirees, Social Security could adjust benefits so that each generation could realistically understand that it is providing for its own retirement. This change would mean saving Social Security surpluses as investments and not spending them as general tax revenue.

Medicare

Medicare began in 1965 to cover physician visits and hospitalization for Americans age 65 and older. In 2003 Congress added a prescription drug benefit to the Medicare program.

As of 2014 it covered about 44.9 million seniors in addition to about 8.9 million persons younger than 65 who are permanently disabled. The total cost for Medicare in 2015 was about $632 billion, or about one-fifth of the total national health care expense. Medicare comprised about 15% of the federal budget.

These costs were paid for through payroll taxes that working Americans pay (37%), premiums that participants pay (13%), general federal tax revenues (42%) and a few other sources, including payments from states and interest earned by a trust fund devoted to the program. Some Medicare charges require a small co-payment from patients. Medicare spends on average between $10,000 and $11,000 per recipient each year.

Medicare is a fee-for-service program. In other words, the more medical services a doctor orders, the more the doctor gets paid. Medicare guidelines have a large influence on how the rest of the health care system operates.

Medicare faces many of the same problems that Social Security does: increasing demands, decreasing sources of revenue, and future commitments that the program cannot pay for under current practices. The key issue for Medicare is how it can provide quality medical care while keeping costs from overwhelming the federal budget. Raising the Medicare payroll tax, premiums, or co-payments are possibilities; but those ideas face the same political risks that ideas for reforming Social Security face.

One suggested reform is giving participants at least some of the money Medicare now spends on them, so that they can make more cost-effective decisions in the medical marketplace. Care networks similar to health maintenance organizations that recipients could join could pool funds and provide more economical (and perhaps more effective) treatment.

Artists John Ahearn and Rigoberto Torres created a series of life-size busts in 1997 called "Homage to Medicare and Medicaid." The pieces are located at the Centers for Medicare & Medicaid Services Building in Maryland.

Medicare has no viable competition. A small number of Americans over 65 pay for their own health care. If a person does not sign up for all parts of Medicare when he or she turns 65 and then chooses to enroll later, he or she must pay a penalty every month thereafter. This is an incentive for a person to enroll in Medicare as soon as possible. As a result of this lack of competition, Medicare suffers from its insulation from market forces. Like Social Security, Medicare is a significant part of the economy and of our society. For it to continue, it must be reformed.

The Bible teaches the importance of showing respect for the elderly, and our society needs to figure out how to coordinate private and public efforts to do that.

> *A gray head is a crown of glory;*
> *It is found in the way of righteousness.*
> Proverbs 16:31

Assignments for Lesson 62

Making Choices — Read the "Security in Your Old Age" pamphlet (pages 146-148).

Literature — Continue reading *Mover of Men and Mountains*.

Project — Continue working on your project for this unit.

Student Review — Answer the questions for Lesson 62.

Wind turbines in Power County, Idaho (2012)

63 Energy

We've embarked on the beginning of the last days of the age of oil. Embrace the future and recognize the growing demand for a wide range of fuels or ignore reality and slowly—but surely—be left behind.
— *Mike Bowlin, oil company executive, 1999*

Modern economies need abundant sources of energy. In former times, people could operate an abacus or make horseshoes by sunlight; but today, industries, office buildings, agricultural production, homes, and means of transportation require energy from oil, coal, nuclear facilities, and other types of energy.

The economics of energy involves many concepts we have discussed earlier: choices people make about sources of energy and how they use energy, the impact of supply and demand, the impact of supply and demand shocks (such as the Arab oil embargo of the 1970s), the influence of prices, energy as a cost of production, international trade, government regulations and taxes, and more.

One of the most important realities to remember regarding energy is the fact that, whatever source of energy individuals, companies, or nations use, they will have to face tradeoffs and make decisions about what they gain and what they give up.

Renewables: Earliest Energy Sources

For most of world history, mankind depended on renewable sources of energy to accomplish work. These included humans and animals that did work after gaining energy by eating plants and meat, wind that moved ships and operated windmills, water that powered mills, the sun that dried clothes and food, and wood that fueled fires to cook food and (as when made into charcoal) provided more intense heat when needed.

Mankind accomplished a great deal using these renewable sources. However, they face tradeoffs. The speed at which humans co depended for centuries on how fast the w and how fast horses could pull. Technolog enable large production facilities. And, o of human energy was the terrible practice o not only in the United States but in many countries around the world. Change was slow.

Coal

Coal fueled the Industrial Revolution of the 1700s and 1800s. The steam engine, powered by burning coal, transformed manufacturing and transportation. Large industrial facilities allowed more people to accomplish more work more efficiently. Railroads and steamships brought the world closer together through travel and trade.

Today coal is the most abundant known fossil fuel resource in the world. The United States has about 26% of the world's known coal reserves, the most of any nation. In the U.S., almost all the coal that is mined is used to produce electricity.

Coal provided about 21% of America's total energy needs in 2016. At current consumption rates, and without any major changes in mining technology, America's known recoverable reserves of coal are expected to last for 250 years.

The tradeoffs with using coal include the harm caused to the health of miners, the devastation of the land caused by strip-mining, and the air and water pollution that has resulted from burning it.

Natural Gas

Natural gases found underground that have high levels of hydrocarbons are also used to generate electricity. Preparing the natural gas used at electric generation plants releases quantities of other gases such as propane, butane, and nitrogen. As extraction methods improved in the 2000s and prices dropped, natural gas became a major component of U.S. energy usage.

Electricity is a secondary source of energy. This means that we must use primary sources of energy to produce it. In 2016 natural gas surpassed coal as the largest fuel source for electricity production in the United States. The chart at right shows the major methods of U.S. electricity production for the twelve months ending in July 2016.

Sources of U.S. Electrical Generation

- Natural Gas - 34.4%
- Coal - 30.0%
- Nuclear - 19.8%
- Hydropower - 6.5%
- Wind - 4.7%
- Biomass / Solar / Geothermal / Other - 4.6%

Lesson 63 - Energy

Oil

Production. Economies change. For many years, the most common fuel oil used in the United States was whale oil, and most of that fueled lamps. As the country and the economy grew, whale oil became insufficient. People knew about petroleum because it seeped from underground in some places, but its main uses were for medicines and kerosene. In 1859, workers drilled the first petroleum well in the United States in Titusville, Pennsylvania (and thus we have oil companies named Pennzoil and Quaker State). People in other parts of the world were already extracting oil, and, of course, explorers have since discovered additional sources of oil in many places around the globe.

A barrel of crude (unrefined) oil contains 42 gallons. From each barrel, refiners produce about 19 or 20 gallons of gasoline; industries use the rest for many other petroleum-based products. Fuel derived from petroleum (gasoline and diesel) enabled the automotive revolution because it provides the energy for the internal combustion engine.

Today, the top five oil producing countries are Saudi Arabia, Russia, the United States, China, and Canada. As mentioned in Lesson 26, the Organization of Petroleum Exporting Countries (OPEC) is a cartel. The cartel includes twelve oil-producing countries: Algeria, Angola, Ecuador, Iran, Iraq, Kuwait, Libya, Nigeria, Qatar, Saudi Arabia, United Arab Emirates, and Venezuela. OPEC produces about 40% of the world's oil and controls about 80% of the world's known oil reserves.

U.S. oil production peaked at ten million barrels per day in 1970. After dropping to five million barrels per day in the early 2000s, production is back up to almost nine million barrels per day in 2016. This is a little less than half of total U.S. petroleum consumption per day (almost twenty million barrels). Most of the oil that we import comes from Canada, Saudi Arabia, Mexico, Venezuela, and Nigeria.

Price. Though many factors affect the prices for oil and oil products, supply and demand is the key factor. Oil producing nations must make millions of barrels of oil available every day to fuel the world economy. An increase in demand causes prices to rise. As the world population grows and developing nations increase their use of oil, demand is growing rapidly. Any disruption in drilling or refining, such as war, political turmoil, or weather, can cause prices to increase quickly.

Seasonal demand affects oil prices also. Demand in the United States, for instance, is highest during the summer travel season and lowest in winter. Any decline in the value of the dollar in world currency exchange markets affects oil prices in the U.S. If the dollar declines in value, Americans need more dollars to buy oil on the world market. This increases the price of oil products in the U.S.

Oil pipeline pumping station in Saline County, Nebraska (2013)

Average Gasoline Prices Per Gallon in Select Countries (September 2016)

In 2015 the four main factors that influenced the average price for a gallon of gasoline in the United States were the cost of crude oil (48%); refining (19%); federal and state taxes (19%); and distribution, marketing, and dealer costs and profits (14%). Included in these factors are the cost of environmental regulations, additives that refiners put into gasoline, competition among gas stations, and the distance that a distributor has to transport gasoline to each station.

The United States is a relatively inexpensive place to buy gasoline, when compared with the prices citizens of other countries must pay. Fuel taxes that governments impose are a major factor in the prices that retailers charge in other countries. The chart above shows average gasoline prices in September 2016 in selected countries. Prices are expressed in U.S. dollars per gallon of 95-octane gasoline.

Use. The United States is the world's leading consumer of petroleum products. In 2015 the U.S. used about 385 million gallons of gasoline per day, about 70% of it for powering automobiles, trucks,

Filling station in Venezuela (2013)

farm equipment, airplanes, and so forth. Energy produced from oil is about 36% of total U.S. energy consumption.

The Strategic Petroleum Reserve is an emergency supply of oil that the United States government has maintained in underground storage facilities along the Gulf of Mexico since 1975 to cushion the effect of a supply shock when normal sources are unavailable. It is the largest emergency supply of petroleum in the world. With a capacity of some 700 million barrels, it could supply oil to the country for about a month based on current usage levels. The president decides when to release oil from the reserve. Releases have taken place to help bring down oil prices during crises in the Middle East and after hurricanes shut down production in the Gulf of Mexico.

Lesson 63 - Energy

Economic Issues of Energy

Continued dependence on fossil fuels. The United States will probably continue to depend on coal, natural gas, and oil for much of its energy needs for many years. Since this is the case, domestic production of these fuels is important. The potential tradeoff to domestic production is possible harm to the environment, which is what some people fear might happen in the Arctic National Wildlife Refuge in Alaska or as a result of drilling in waters off American shores. Technology and careful oversight can limit environmental concern, although we cannot completely eliminate the possibility of accidents.

If we restrict oil production within the United States but continue to import oil that other countries produce, we simply shift the location of the potential environmental impact. The United States can develop other energy sources, but while we do that it seems in our strategic best interest as a country to lessen our dependence on foreign oil. Increased domestic production would also be a way to provide more jobs for American workers.

Another lingering question regarding fossil fuels involves how much is left. In the 1970s, many people believed that the world was running out of petroleum and had enough for only a relatively few more years. Though this was a common perception, it turns out to have been wrong.

Despite increasing population and increasing use of petroleum, the world still has an abundant supply and prices have fallen significantly. Technology has enabled better discovery and recovery of oil (although the fracking process for recovering oil does have negative environmental tradeoffs). People have also developed more fuel-efficient vehicles. Though we may eventually run out of fossil fuels, no one knows the actual available supply.

Nuclear energy. As of 2016, nuclear power generated about 20% of our electricity. In France, that number was 77%. We make this comparison merely to show what is possible. The two main tradeoffs with nuclear power are (1) the possibility of an accident that could release harmful radiation and (2) the problem of what to do with radioactive waste that nuclear plants generate. Another tradeoff is that, because of regulations, nuclear facilities are very expensive to build and maintain.

Vermont Yankee Nuclear Power Station in Vernon, Vermont, opened in 1972 and eventually provided about one-third of electricity for the state. Because of economic dynamics in the energy market, the plant closed in 2014.

Energy companies have to conduct a careful cost-benefit analysis before building a nuclear power plant. The Watts Bar nuclear plant in Tennessee began producing electricity in 1996 after 23 years of construction. No new construction of a nuclear plant took place in the U.S. until 2013.

The specters of past accidents understandably haunt discussion of expanded use of nuclear energy. Three major nuclear incidents have occurred: in 1979 at Three Mile Island in Pennsylvania, in 1986 at Chernobyl in the Ukraine (then part of the Soviet Union), and in 2011 at the Fukushima power plant in Japan following an earthquake and tsunami.

The small amount of radiation released at Three Mile Island had no detectable health effects. The United States actually received more radiation from Chernobyl than from Three Mile Island. Chernobyl was a terrible accident, but the conditions under which it occurred no longer exist. The Fukushima disaster was the result of human error in failing to meet safety standards.

Experts can reprocess nuclear waste and bury it safely in sparsely populated areas, if the people and politicians in those areas agree to it.

Alternative sources of energy. We can cheer the cleanliness of renewable sources of energy, such as solar and wind. Besides enabling less dependence on fossil fuels and causing less pollution, the development of renewable sources of energy has the possibility of creating new jobs.

Creative humans will continue to explore and innovate with various methods of energy production. Improved battery technology that can store energy produced from renewable sources is one important area of research. The introduction of driverless cars may also radically transform American dependence on automobiles.

However, at this point the extensive use of alternative sources has significant tradeoffs. The cost of building the required facilities is still a major issue, especially when oil prices are relatively low. Developers of alternative energy sources have depended on large government subsidies, which change the market dynamics. Wind and solar energy development also requires large areas of land to have a significant number of wind turbines and solar panels.

Because of relatively high energy costs and abundant sunshine, Hawaii produces more solar electricity per capita than any other state. In addition to large arrays like this, more than ten percent of homes have solar panels installed.

Lesson 63 - Energy

The economics of energy involves many other issues. Conservation efforts and updating the power grid are important and could provide additional new jobs. Developing reliable energy sources to support the U.S. economy is a long term goal that will require patience and perseverance. We also need to be aware of what is happening in the rest of the world and encourage wise use of energy resources in every country.

In the future, as the Lord wills, we will not just need different energy. We will need more energy. We expect world population and the world economy to grow; and both of these trends will require additional sources of energy. Whatever happens, private enterprise and entrepreneurship will fuel the changes that we will need and want.

The Bible speaks of a different kind of power, spiritual power, that is available in Christ.

Now to Him who is able to do far more abundantly beyond all that we ask or think, according to the power that works within us, to Him be the glory in the church and in Christ Jesus to all generations forever and ever. Amen.
Ephesians 3:20-21

Assignments for Lesson 63

Literature — Continue reading *Mover of Men and Mountains*.

Project — Continue working on your project for this unit.

Student Review — Answer the questions for Lesson 63.

New Chrysler cars in Detroit (1973)

64 On the Road Again

Our national flower is the concrete cloverleaf.
— *Lewis Mumford*

The American auto industry is the single largest manufacturing industry in the United States. It generates the most retail business and employment of any industry. It alone makes up about 3-4% of the gross domestic product, and at its height it employed over two million people in some capacity. It has been a mainstay of the American economy for over one hundred years.

Putting It in Reverse: A Brief Automotive History

Inventors and entrepreneurs dabbled with engine-powered carriages or cars in the late 1800s. When Henry Ford's company introduced the Model T in 1908, the modern automobile industry was born. Cars became a major part of American life, and Henry Ford was America's industrial genius. The key to his success was making the car available to the mass market at a price that many people could afford.

A group of small car companies began coming together in 1908 to form what became General Motors. GM surpassed Ford as the nation's (and thus the world's) largest car manufacturer in 1931. By the 1950s, over half of the new cars sold in America were General Motors products. GM became the largest business in the country. Automobile manufacturing was centered in the area of Detroit, Michigan, where Ford and other entrepreneurs lived and worked. The Chrysler Motor Company began in 1925. Other car makers came onto the scene at various times and either merged with one of the larger companies or went out of business.

Through the 1950s and 1960s, gasoline was cheap, Americans loved their cars, and automakers built the cars big. The United Automobile Workers union became a powerful entity as it negotiated contracts with automakers that gave its members high wages and attractive benefits. A few imported models, such as the Volkswagen from Germany, were a minor part of the American auto business.

A major change took place in 1973, when oil-producing countries in the Middle East stopped selling oil to the United States because of U.S. support for Israel. Gasoline prices quadrupled, and long lines formed at gas pumps as drivers tried to get whatever gasoline they could. Suddenly gas-guzzling American cars were a liability; and small, fuel-efficient, foreign-made cars started to make sense.

The percentage of foreign cars sold in America increased, and the domination of the U.S. car market by domestic manufacturers began to weaken. By 1979 Chrysler was in financial trouble. The company asked the federal government to guarantee $1.5 billion in loans so the company could turn itself around. Congress agreed, Chrysler turned around, and the company paid off the loans several years ahead of schedule. In 1983, Chrysler introduced the minivan, the model that revolutionized American car buying. Meanwhile, in 1982 in Ohio the Japanese automaker Honda opened the first foreign-owned car manufacturing plant in the United States.

During the 1970s and 1980s, Americans came to appreciate the quality and efficiency of Japanese autos. At the same time, many models that American companies built were of poor or mediocre quality. More Japanese companies built assembly plants in the U.S. during the 1980s and 1990s. Many of them were in the southern part of the United States and employed non-union workers. The workers earned about the same wages as union employees of domestic car companies, but the retirement and health insurance benefits were not as lavish as those that UAW members received from American companies. Meanwhile, American producers continued to lose market share.

The Big Three (General Motors, Ford, and Chrysler) eventually improved the quality of their vehicles; and more people began buying domestically-made trucks and sport utility vehicles (SUVs), which were highly profitable for the companies. But foreign makers introduced their own trucks and SUVs. American companies carried heavy obligations from union contracts, not only for current wages but also for future pension payments and for health insurance for retirees. During the 2007-2009 recession, auto sales declined significantly, and the price of gasoline reached $4.00 per gallon. GM and Chrysler declared bankruptcy, and Ford barely hung on. Many autoworkers lost their jobs. In 2008 Toyota surpassed GM as the world's best-selling automaker.

For a short time the federal government became majority stockholder in General Motors. The government bought 500 million shares of GM stock in 2010 as the company reorganized and became more efficient. GM discontinued the Saturn, Pontiac, and Oldsmobile brands. The government sold the last of its shares in GM in 2013. The federal government injected almost $12 billion in Chrysler and helped other related companies as well. The automobile industry bailout program resulted in a loss of $9.3 billion for U.S. taxpayers.

Auto workers founded the UAW in 1935. The full name of the organization is The International Union, United Automobile, Aerospace and Agricultural Implement Workers of America

Getting the Feel of the Interior: The Auto Industry and the Economy

The automotive industry plays a large and multifaceted role in the American economy, not to mention its role in the world economy. In 2015, Americans purchased or leased about 17.5 million new cars and light trucks, which amounted to $570 billion in sales. But that is literally not the half of it. Americans also bought 38.3 million used cars and trucks that year. In 2015 cars and light trucks registered to owners totaled about 253 million. The average age of a registered car or truck was 11.5 years. A little over half were cars; the rest were light trucks (the light trucks classification includes pickups, vans, and SUVs). Over 90% of American households owned at least one vehicle.

Whereas GM used to have over half of the American market itself, in 2014 the Big Three domestic makers together accounted for only 45% of domestic sales. GM's share was about 18%. This means that foreign-owned companies assembled over half of the new vehicles sold in the United States in 2014, even though many of the vehicles were built in the U.S. Japanese-owned auto companies accounted for about 40% of new sales. About 70-75% of cars made by Japanese-owned companies and sold in the U.S. were built in factories in the U.S. American car companies also own assembly plants in other countries.

The auto industry employs a large labor force. In 2016 about 925,000 Americans had jobs involved in some way in making vehicles or vehicle parts. About half worked for parts manufacturers. Carmakers do not make all the parts for their vehicles. Other companies make parts (lights, transmissions, airbags, seats, and so forth) through contracts with the large automakers.

The impact of the automotive industry extends beyond the assembly of new vehicles. Automobiles provide work for manufacturers, parts makers that are located in many places around the country and in other countries, distribution companies that deliver vehicles and parts to retail locations, and advertising companies. Vehicles are the reason for new car dealers, used car dealers, repair shops, auto insurance companies, parts stores, gas stations, car washes, and drive-in restaurants. The United States spends billions on building and repairing roads and parking lots. One estimate says that the auto industry accounts for one in every 22 jobs in the American economy.

German automaker BMW opened a plant in Greer, South Carolina, in 1994. Eight thousand workers produce about 1,400 vehicles per day, most of which are exported outside the United States. The facility also includes a BMW museum.

Lesson 64 - On the Road Again

Are We There Yet? Economic Issues

Many of the economic issues we discuss in this curriculum are at work in the automotive industry. As with other industries, a major issue is supply and demand. For many years, American carmakers did not supply what a large number of Americans demanded while foreign carmakers did. The auto industry is another example of how economies change; in this case, not only have the relative positions of manufacturers changed in terms of their sales, but also the energy needs for vehicles are changing. Autos that use some or all electric power have come onto the market, which means a possible decline in the demand for oil and gasoline. Employment needs in the industry are also changing as manufacturers need more highly trained workers.

Decisions about transportation can show the importance of substitute goods. Consumers can find incentives to buy other goods instead of the ones they have been purchasing. They can buy cars that are less expensive to operate, repair a car instead of buying a new one, ride public transportation, or use ride-sharing services such as Uber or Lyft. We also see the importance of complementary goods. If you buy a vehicle, you will also buy fuel and car insurance. An increase or decrease in auto sales will mean an increase or decrease in the sale of complementary goods as well.

Government regulations influence the automotive industry. The government sets exhaust emission standards for cars and trucks. The federal government also sets fuel efficiency regulations that are called Corporate Average Fuel Economy (CAFE) standards. The government sets a minimum miles per gallon standard and an average miles per gallon rate for a company's entire production. The average fuel efficiency of vehicles that a company produces must meet that standard. California has generally set even stricter standards than the federal government does. These environmental and fuel efficiency regulations have an impact on how companies build vehicles and on the cost of new vehicles.

GM launched the Chevrolet Volt, an electric hybrid vehicle, in 2010. The Volt can only drive about 35 miles on a full charge, but it has a gasoline engine for additional range. The all-electric Chevrolet Bolt EV, released in 2016, has a range of over 200 miles.

Foreign trade is a major issue in the automotive industry. In addition to the growing segment of the American vehicle market that foreign-owned companies control, GM, Ford, and Chrysler have production and marketing agreements with companies based in other countries. GM has begun importing cars made in China to the U.S. During the 2007-2009 recession, while sales in the United States fell, sales of General Motors products increased in other parts of the world. On this issue we again face the economic reality that if it is good for American companies to export goods to other countries, the United States has to be willing to import goods from other countries.

While the auto industry continues to play a major role in the American economy, it faces many changes and uncertainties. The state with the most auto-related jobs is no longer Michigan, but Tennessee. New kinds of cars meet consumer demands and lessen American dependence on oil. With help from the federal government (meaning the American taxpayers), the industry has for the most part rebounded from the 2007-2009 recession; but as has been the case in other industries, the firms and the workers in the automotive business must be willing to adapt, or they risk being left in the rearview mirror.

Don't you think the description of an urban battle by the prophet Nahum sounds like traffic in an American city?

The chariots race madly in the streets,
They rush wildly in the squares,
Their appearance is like torches,
They dash to and fro like lightning flashes.
Nahum 2:4

Assignments for Lesson 64

Making Choices — Read "How Detroit's Automakers Went from Kings of the Road to Roadkill" (pages 149-157).

Literature — Continue reading *Mover of Men and Mountains*.

Project — Continue working on your project for this unit.

Student Review — Answer the questions for Lesson 64.

Construction of The Moderne luxury apartments in Milwaukee, Wisconsin (2011)

65 O Give Me a Home

You know, George, I feel that in a small way we are doing something important: satisfying a fundamental urge. It's deep in the race for a man to want his own roof and walls and fireplace, and we're helping him get those things in our shabby little office.

— Character of Peter Bailey,
executive officer of Bailey Brothers Building and Loan,
in the movie It's a Wonderful Life *(1946)*

Housing plays a major role in the economy for a number of reasons. Just about everybody wants and needs a place to live, so housing is in great demand. This demand stimulates many suppliers to build and offer single-family residences, condominiums, and apartments. The home construction industry has a major impact on the demand for lumber, home appliances, furniture, roofing materials, and other goods in related industries. More homes and larger homes also increase the demand for energy.

Most families want to own their own home. About two-thirds of all American households and about 80% of married couple households own a home outright or are making payments on a mortgage. Buying a home is usually the single largest purchase that a family will make. It is also usually the largest investment—that is, purchasing something in the hope that it will increase in value—that a family will make. This investment affects many areas of their lives, such as how much they can save or spend on other things and how well a couple is prepared for retirement. The ability to buy a home has traditionally been an indication that a family is doing well financially, specifically that one or both of the parents have steady income. Because of the importance of housing in the economy, the number of home sales and the number of new home construction starts in a given month are key statistics in determining the strength of the economy.

In more intangible terms, homeownership best exemplifies the institution of private property. Owning a home is an essential part of what has been called the American Dream, the goal of a materially secure life that many Americans have pursued. More people owning homes instead of renting homes tends to bring stability to a neighborhood, since owners are less likely to move than renters. Owning a home encourages people to take care of their property, since people generally take better care of housing that belongs to them than housing they rent. This better care in turn increases property values, which helps to make a family's investment in a home worth even more.

Many factors contribute to the value of a home, such as the cost of construction materials, the cost of labor, and the value of the land on which a house sits. A common saying about house prices is that the three most important factors are location, location, and location. In other words, where a house is located has a major impact on its value. Location includes the part of the country in which a house is located, the popularity of the neighborhood in which a house is located, whether the community is growing or declining, and many other factors. The very same houses, made of exactly the same building materials and with the same floor plan, can have widely varying values as a result of these factors.

Two statistics clearly indicate the importance of home ownership to the economy. In 2015 the total value of all American housing was approximately $27.5 trillion dollars, and housing constituted about one-third of all American wealth.

How a Home Mortgage Works

Most people—and especially most first-time home buyers—do not have the cash on hand to pay the full purchase price for a home, so they borrow the money from a bank to buy a house from a builder, a developer, or the current owner. A loan to purchase a home is called a mortgage.

The home buyer pays off the mortgage with monthly payments over a period of years. These monthly payments include the principal (the amount borrowed) and the interest that the lending institution charges for the loan. The monthly payment on a fixed-rate mortgage remains the same throughout the life of the mortgage, but the amount of the payment applied to the principal gradually increases over time while the amount applied to the interest gradually decreases over time because the buyer owes less and less on the mortgage.

Historically, the most common kind of mortgage has been a loan for thirty years at a fixed rate of interest. If a couple buys a house for $100,000 and pays 20% as a down payment, they must take out a mortgage for $80,000 to pay the person (or institution) from whom they are buying the house.

If the bank charges five percent interest, the monthly total payment for principal and interest will be $429.46. In the first month's payment, only $96.13 is applied to the principal while $333.33 goes to pay interest on the amount owed. The payment at the end of ten years will apply $157.66 to the principal and $271.80 to interest. Payment number 360 at the end of thirty years pays off the last $427.69 of principal and only needs $1.77 for interest. An amortization table shows the relative amounts of principal and interest in each payment over the life of the loan.

Taking out a mortgage means that, to borrow $80,000 at 5% interest, the couple will actually have paid $174,000, including $74,000 in interest and the $20,000 down payment. In other words, the home costs them almost 75% more than the actual purchase price. If on the other hand a couple borrows $80,000 for only fifteen years, their monthly payment will be $632.64; but they will only pay about $34,000 in interest because they are paying off the loan much more quickly. Even though the interest cost is significant, most people believe that purchasing a home with a mortgage is a better financial decision than renting, since no part of rent payments goes toward buying the property and making it one's own.

Banks and other lenders have traditionally followed certain guidelines regarding how they approve loans for home buyers. A common rule of thumb is that a family should only buy a home if its price is less than three times the family's annual income. In addition, lenders have usually

Lesson 65 - O Give Me a Home

wanted the total paid out for principal, interest, property taxes, and home insurance to be no more than 28% of a family's gross income. Banks have also wanted a buyer's total debt payments (for the mortgage, car loans, student loans, and other debt) to be no more than 36% of gross income. Home ownership involves other costs, such as utilities and maintenance expense; and a family has to be able to meet these costs within its budget.

Few home buyers stay in the same house for the life of a thirty-year mortgage. Young home buyers generally want more room as they have children; so most homeowners sell their homes after a few years to buy a larger home. At that point, they use the equity they have in the home (equity is the value that the home has above what they owe on it) as down payment on another house, take out another mortgage for the remainder of the purchase price, and the process begins again.

We could discuss many more details regarding mortgages. For instance, if the mortgage amount is 80% or less of the home's appraised value, the borrower usually will not have to pay private mortgage insurance (PMI). The monthly PMI premium buys insurance that will pay off the loan if the borrower defaults on the mortgage. Lenders who want to be protected against loss require PMI. The premium is usually about one-half of one percent of the loan, or about $40.00 per month on a mortgage of $80,000. A relatively smaller loan that is made to someone who can make a relatively larger down payment means less risk for the lender, so PMI is not normally required on loans that are for less than 80% of appraised value. This is why a down payment of 20% or more saves the borrower money.

Another issue related to a mortgage is the question of borrowing money at all. In general, although it is usually not wise to borrow money, borrowing to buy a house does not involve as great a risk because you are borrowing for something that is expected to increase in value. Borrowing to buy a car, on the other hand, is unwise because the car will almost certainly decrease in value over time; and you might face a situation in which the car is worth less than what you owe on it.

During the 1930s, the Economics and Statistics Division of the Department of Commerce collected data about population growth, rates of residential construction, and funds available for home mortgages.

Residential neighborhood in Mesa, Arizona

Home Mortgages and the Macroeconomy

As we mentioned above, Americans place great importance on owning a home. A combination of factors, including a rising standard of living, a greater willingness by banks to make mortgage loans, and federal policy that encourages homeownership, has led over time to more people taking out mortgages to buy homes. In 1900, about one-third of owner-occupied homes had a mortgage. Most people either owned their homes outright or lived in rented property. A century later, about two-thirds of owner-occupied homes had mortgages. Going into debt to purchase a home has become much more possible and acceptable in American society. In 2015 lenders held mortgages that were worth a total of about $13.8 trillion. Obviously, homeownership and the issuing of home mortgages play a significant role in the economy.

The federal government has created several entities that encourage and assist homeownership. The Federal Housing Authority (FHA) insures some mortgages that private banks make to homeowners. The Department of Veterans Affairs (VA) insures a portion of home loans that veterans obtain at private banks to help veterans get better terms.

Government-sponsored investment corporations such as the Federal National Mortgage Association (FNMA, nicknamed Fannie Mae) and the Federal Home Loan Mortgage Corporation (FHLMC, nicknamed Freddie Mac) help make money available for home mortgages by buying mortgages that lending institutions issue. This allows lenders to make other loans to additional homebuyers.

Lesson 65 - O Give Me a Home

The Government National Mortgage Association (Ginnie Mae) is a govenment-owned corporation that guarantees bonds that are backed by home mortgages that are insured by a government agency, usually the FHA or the VA.

The federal tax code encourages homeownership in several ways. When the modern personal income tax began in 1913, almost all interest payments for any debts could be deducted from taxable income. In 1986 the government removed most interest payment deductions except for home mortgage interest. Economists generally believe that the ability to deduct home mortgage interest from taxable income encourages people to buy homes instead of renting. Some experts question this, since homeownership rates in Canada are about the same as in the United States and Canada does not have a mortgage interest deduction. Also, most people do not itemize their deductions, so they cannot take the mortgage interest deduction. However, most people perceive the deduction as a benefit to homeowners. A taxpayer can also deduct property taxes from taxable income when he or she itemizes deductions.

In addition, when a homeowner sells his house, he does not have to pay capital gains tax on the first $250,000 in value that his house has gained since he bought it ($500,000 for a married couple filing jointly). Most people do not see that much gain, so they do not have to pay federal tax on this profit that comes from an increase in their home's worth. These provisions in the tax code help make the buying and selling of homes a major part of economic activity in the United States.

As we mentioned earlier, mortgages are an asset that lenders use as the basis for making loans to businesses and others. But the story does not end there. Some banks sell the mortgages they hold to larger investment companies for immediate profit. For instance, a bank that makes an $80,000 mortgage loan might sell that loan to an investment company a year later for $90,000. We have seen how that mortgage has a potential value of over $150,000 to a lender when interest payments are added in.

When a bank sells a mortgage, it makes an immediate (although lesser) profit and hands over the risk for the loan to a larger company. The larger company then has the mortgage on its books as an asset, and that company uses the asset to make other loans. Sometimes an investment company bundles many mortgages into large financial packages that investors purchase in the hope of making a profit. Fannie Mae and Freddie Mac purchase large numbers of mortgages that they then sell to investors. As of 2015 these two corporations owned or guaranteed about $4.6 trillion dollars worth of mortgages, or a little less than half of the nation's total mortgage debt. Private banks carry about 39% of mortgage loans, and Ginnie Mae backs about 15% of U.S. mortgages.

However, home mortgages can also have a negative impact on the economy. If a family pays too much for a home relative to their income, they wind up using a large part of their income paying the mortgage and have to cut back on other purchases. This can lower the demand for other goods and services in the economy. In addition, the encouragement of home ownership can go too far and can lead to too much risk on the part of home buyers. Some lenders have lowered their requirements for down payments to 5% or 3% of the loan value, or even to requiring zero down. Some lending companies have offered mortgages in which the borrower only pays interest for as much as ten years. The assumption behind such a mortgage is that the house will increase in value, so the borrower will still be better off when he wants to sell the house. However, such loans saddle borrowers with huge payments that do not build equity in the home.

Another approach by lenders has been to offer adjustable rate mortgages. These mortgages offer an enticingly low teaser interest rate for the first year or first few years, then the interest rate is adjusted (usually upward) in later years. The result is often that borrowers find their house payments increase more than they can comfortably afford.

When a homeowner cannot afford to make mortgage payments, the loan is said to be in default. When this happens, the owner loses the house and it becomes the property of the lending agency. This process is called foreclosure. The lending agency will usually have to sell the home for less than it is worth in order to get something out of it since lenders do not want to be homeowners. When this happens frequently over a short period of time, it has a serious negative impact on the economy. We will see in Lesson 70 how these factors contributed to the recession of 2007-2009.

Where a person builds a house is an important factor in its worth and stability. Jesus encouraged His followers to build their houses (that is, their lives) on the solid rock of His teaching.

> *Therefore everyone who hears these words of Mine and acts on them, may be compared to a wise man who built his house on the rock.*
> Matthew 7:24

Assignments for Lesson 65

Literature — Continue reading *Mover of Men and Mountains*.

Project — Finish your project for this unit.

Student Review — Answer the questions for Lesson 65 and take the quiz for Unit 13.

Harvest time in Laramie County, Wyoming (2015)

14 Economic Issues, Part 2

The way that farmers practice agriculture has changed drastically over time, but farming remains a key part of the American economy. A delicate balance exists between economic activity and protecting the environment. Productivity is a key factor in economic growth. Two of the most significant economic events of the past one hundred years are the Great Depression and the Great Recession.

Lesson 66 - Old MacDonald Had a Farm
Lesson 67 - The Environment
Lesson 68 - Productivity and Growth
Lesson 69 - What Happened in the Great Depression?
Lesson 70 - What Happened in the Great Recession?

Books Used

The Bible
Making Choices
Mover of Men and Mountains

Project (choose one)

1) Write 300 to 500 words on one of the following topics:

- How could America do a better job of providing a quality food supply for its people? How could the negative environmental and health impacts of modern agriculture be reduced? How should government, large business, small business, and consumers be involved in the process?

- Write a short story set in the Great Depression or the Great Recession (see Lessons 69 and 70).

2) Plan a meal that celebrates U.S. agricultural productivity. Use recipes that reflect specific parts of the country. Find out where the main foods used in the meal were grown. Create a menu for the meal that gives this information. Prepare this meal for your family.

3) What is one concern you have about a negative environmental impact? Create a full-page magazine advertisement that encourages personal responsibility in this area. You can design it on a computer or by hand using the medium of your choice (paint, pastels, pencil, colored pencil, marker, ink, chalk, etc.).

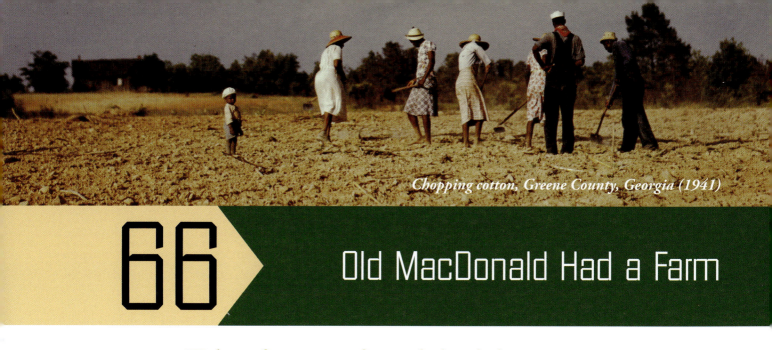

Chopping cotton, Greene County, Georgia (1941)

66 Old MacDonald Had a Farm

We learn from our gardens to deal with the most urgent question of the time: How much is enough?

— Wendell Berry

Before the computer industry, before the automotive industry, before the petroleum industry, there was agriculture. We could not produce the other things we do without farming because farming gives people the energy we need to live. Farm products are important to the domestic economy and are a major U.S. export to other countries.

The United States is blessed with an abundance of productive land, a long growing season, and adequate rainfall. Farmers have also had the support of the people as a whole and, since the 1930s, the support of government policies. Even so, the success of agriculture also depends on variables such as the weather and the possibility of infestations of insects and disease.

Even though agriculture has existed since Adam and Eve tended the Garden of Eden, the nature of the farming industry has changed significantly since the mid-1800s. In agriculture, many of the same issues are at work that we have seen in other areas of the economy: supply and demand, prices, trade, and government policies and regulations. We have also seen the impact of technological changes on farm productivity as well as the conflict between what is best in economic terms and what is best for human beings.

Historical Perspective

By far the majority of settlers in the American colonies were farmers. Even most of those who operated shops in town still worked the land to feed their families. Before the Civil War, family farms were the norm in the North. The majority of farms in the South were also sustenance family farms, but owners of large plantations who relied on slave labor dominated the economy and the political life of the South. In 1860, the nation had about two million farms (remember that number). Agricultural products made up 82% of American exports, and much of that was cotton grown in the South.

Following the Civil War, northern farms prospered, especially in the Midwest. Southern agriculture took several years to recover from the devastation of the war. Tenant farmers and sharecroppers, most of whom were poor, provided much of the post-war farm labor force in the South.

Unit 14: Economic Issues, Part 2

Farm in Kansas covered by blowing dust (1936)

Congress established land grant universities after the Civil War, which states financed by the sale of public lands. These universities taught college courses in improved farming methods and conducted scientific research to aid farming.

During the last third of the 1800s, American farmers frequently struggled. Prices for farm goods rose and fell, many farmers were in debt, and the nation's economic interest was drawn to the rapidly developing industrial sector and away from agriculture. Farmers organized groups such as the Grange and political movements such as the Populist Party to exert greater influence on government policies. The U.S. Department of Agriculture received Cabinet status in 1889.

The first two decades of the twentieth century were prosperous times for American farmers as the demand for food grew with the rapidly increasing population. However, farmers faced more difficult times in the 1920s as prices declined. Farming as a whole entered an economic depression well before 1929.

In the New Deal, the federal government became involved in agricultural policies and production in an unprecedented way. Congress created the Rural Electrification Administration in 1935 to encourage extending electricity to farming areas. The primary means of federal involvement were price supports, which guaranteed minimum prices for farm products, and crop restrictions, which limited the number of acres in production so that decreased supply would increase demand and raise prices.

Because of New Deal programs, farmers plowed under thousands of acres of crops and killed thousands of head of livestock in order to raise prices, even as millions of Americans were going hungry. Government involvement in agricultural prices and production continues today. In fact, almost all countries with a sizable farm economy have a high level of government assistance.

Today the United States government makes agricultural payments amounting to billions of dollars each year. It also funds food assistance programs such as school lunches and the Supplemental Nutrition Assistance Program for low-income families. The ironic result is that the farmer, who has long been the symbol of independence and self-support, is highly regulated and depends heavily on government money.

The Numbers

Trends in the farm economy are clear: fewer farms, larger and more productive farms, and fewer workers. In 1940 the United States had some six million farms that averaged about 166 acres each. In 2014 the U.S. had just over two million farms (remember that number from 1860?), and the average size was 438 acres. In 1930 farms employed about 12.5 million workers. In 2012 the farm workforce was just over one million, even though the national population doubled over the same period. In 1900 half of the American labor force was in agriculture. In 2012 hired farm workers constituted about 1% of the wage and salary workforce.

The reason for these dramatic changes is a significant increase in farm worker productivity brought about by developments in technology. The steel-tipped plow, the reaper, and the combine became available in the nineteenth century.

Lesson 66 - Old MacDonald Had a Farm

Railroads, especially refrigerated rail cars, created national markets for farm goods. Motorized farm equipment in the twentieth century brought even more growth to farm output.

Agricultural science developed seeds, fertilizer, and pesticides that increased yield. Today farmers regularly use computers and even satellite technology. Changes in how companies processed, packaged, and distributed food encouraged more agricultural production.

Family farms still exist, but American agriculture today takes place mostly on large, efficient, agribusiness operations. Whereas many children of farmers once continued the family farm, today those children might work for a farm equipment manufacturer, an implement dealer, or a food processing company.

Here are some recent U.S. agricultural production figures:

- 2015 value of farm products (crops and livestock): $375 billion

- 2014 corn production: 14.2 billion bushels (most in the world)

- 2014 soybean production: 4 billion bushels (most in the world)

- 2014 wheat production: 2 billion bushels (third behind China and India)

- 2015 meat production: 23.8 billion pounds of beef, 46.5 billion pounds of poultry, 24.6 billion pounds of pork

- 2014 total farm exports: $152.5 billion (11% of all U.S. exports)

- Total imports of agricultural goods: $109.2 billion (5% of U.S. imports)

As of 2016, farmers in Iowa raise about one-third of the nation's pigs. Dean Folkmann, pictured below, feeds his pigs a homemade blend of food. The farm has been in his family since 1854.

USDA researchers explore ways to reduce the cost of ethanol production (2013)

Two Farm Issues: Ethanol and Organics

Ethanol. Corn is America's largest crop. It is an ingredient in many food products, a feed for livestock, and a source of ethanol. Ethanol is grain alcohol, produced in the United States mostly from corn. About 97% of gasoline sold in the United States is blended with ethanol, most of it with a 10% mix of ethanol. E85 fuel is 85% ethanol and 15% unleaded gasoline and is designed especially for newer flex fuel vehicles. In 2005 Congress established the Renewable Fuel Mandate that requires oil refiners to include ethanol in an increasing percentage of the gasoline they produce.

Advantages of using ethanol include enabling the U.S. to be less dependent on foreign oil and reducing some harmful emissions. On the other hand, ethanol is relatively expensive to make and producing it requires considerable energy, it tends to make motor fuel more expensive, many people believe it hurts the performance of automobile engines and does not help the environment, and it drives grain prices up as a greater percentage of corn is used for ethanol instead of for food. Farmers have decided to plant corn on thousands of acres that had been set aside for conservation.

The federal government paid out billions of dollars in subsidies to the ethanol industry before those direct payments ended with the 2014 Farm Bill. However, the government continues to use other ways to encourage ethanol production, such as the Renewable Fuel Mandate. The ethanol issue includes questions about the economics of corn production and use, energy policy, and government involvement in economic and farm policies.

Organic farming. Many people fear that scientific advances in farming such as pesticides, chemical fertilizers, and artificial livestock growth hormones have come with tradeoffs. These tradeoffs include unintended health consequences caused by eating foods grown with such chemicals and environmental externalities caused by water runoff from fields treated with these chemicals.

One response to these concerns has been the growth of organic farming, which uses non-chemical means to produce foods. Organic foods are available in specialty food stores, some conventional grocery stores, and at many of the over 4,000 farmers' markets in the country. Organically-grown products are a rapidly growing part of the United States food market, although they are still a small part of total farm production.

Produce from Meadow's Mirth Farm in Stratham, New Hampshire

In 2015 organic retail sales totaled $43.3 billion, which was about 3.3% of U.S. food sales. Most organic farm operations are relatively small. Many organic farmers have banded together in cooperatives to enable more effective marketing to consumers. Locally-grown food is becoming a more important part of local economies. The larger issue is how and to what extent organic products can successfully compete with the huge agribusiness firms that dominate the American food industry.

The American farm is part of our national ethos. It symbolizes hard work, initiative, dependence on God, and the balance between independence and interdependence as a people. Farmers have to maintain a delicate balance between using such advances as chemicals and genetically modified seeds to increase production while at the same time protecting human and animal health.

We can trace the importance of agricultural production back to the earliest people.

---

*And Abel was a keeper of flocks,
but Cain was a tiller of the ground.
Genesis 4:2*

Assignments for Lesson 66

Literature — Continue reading *Mover of Men and Mountains*. Plan to finish it by the end of Unit 15.

Project — Choose your project for this unit and start working on it.

Student Review — Answer the questions for Lesson 66.

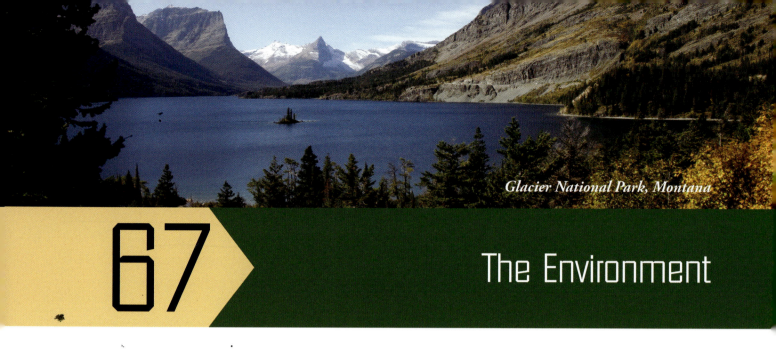

Glacier National Park, Montana

67 The Environment

Man cannot create a species, but he can destroy one.
— *James Buckley*

Charles Dickens' description of nineteenth-century Birmingham, England, in his 1841 novel *The Old Curiosity Shop* is a vivid picture of what can happen, what has happened, and what is happening today in some parts of the world:

A long suburb of red brick houses—some with patches of garden-ground, where coal-dust and factory smoke darkened the shrinking leaves and coarse rank flowers, and where the struggling vegetation sickened and sank under the hot breath of kiln and furnace, making them by its presence seem yet more blighting and unwholesome than in the town itself—a long, flat, straggling suburb passed, they came, by slow degrees, upon a cheerless region, where not a blade of grass was seen to grow, where not a bud put forth its promise in the spring, where nothing green could live but on the surface of the stagnant pools, which here and there lay idly sweltering by the black road-side.

Advancing more and more into the shadow of this mournful place, its dark depressing influence stole upon their spirits, and filled them with a dismal gloom. On every side, and far as the eye could see into the heavy distance, tall chimneys, crowding on each other, and presenting that endless repetition of the same dull, ugly form, which is the horror of oppressive dreams, poured out their plague of smoke, obscured the light, and made foul the melancholy air. On mounds of ashes by the wayside, sheltered only by a few rough boards, or rotten pent-house roofs, strange engines spun and writhed like tortured creatures; clanking their iron chains, shrieking in their rapid whirl from time to time as though in torment unendurable, and making the ground tremble with their agonies. Dismantled houses here and there appeared, tottering to the earth, propped up by fragments of others that had fallen down, unroofed, windowless, blackened, desolate, but yet inhabited.

Lesson 67 - The Environment

Men, women, children, wan in their looks and ragged in attire, tended the engines, fed their tributary fire, begged upon the road, or scowled half-naked from the doorless houses. Then came more of the wrathful monsters, whose like they almost seemed to be in their wildness and their untamed air, screeching and turning round and round again; and still, before, behind, and to the right and left, was the same interminable perspective of brick towers, never ceasing in their black vomit, blasting all things living or inanimate, shutting out the face of day, and closing in on all these horrors with a dense dark cloud.

Americans who remember smog-covered days in Los Angeles and New York, and those who have experienced industrial air pollution in major cities today, know that environmental damage is a real issue with real human consequences.

Environmental problems still happen. In 2014 the city of Flint, Michigan, was in transition to a different water source as a cost-cutting measure. The city began utilizing the Flint River, which officials had not properly treated for contaminants, including lead. Many residents began experiencing health problems. Several officials were indicted for their failure to fulfill their duties, which put the health of thousands of people at risk.

The United States has some of the most stringent environmental regulations in the world; but these have come with a fight, primarily between environmentalists and conservationists on one side and business interests on the other. In the years leading up to the founding of the Environmental Protection Agency in 1970, voices of concern over damage to the environment competed with howls of protest from business groups who said that they could not survive if they had to meet pollution control standards.

The threat of damage to the environment because of economic activity is real. Strip mining, sometimes accompanied by the use of processing chemicals, did serious damage to the land in many parts of the U.S. and made later economic activity (not to mention healthy living) in those areas difficult or impossible. Many cities have dealt with industries dumping waste into streams as a routine practice.

After its introduction during World War II, farmers in the United States made extensive use of the pesticide DDT. In her 1962 book *Silent Spring*, Rachel Carson pointed to serious negative environmental consequences of widespread use of the pesticide. The U.S. banned the use of DDT for most applications in 1972, and most other countries followed suit over the next decades.

Poster made during World War II encouraging the use of DDT in home gardens

The issue comes down to this: can the United States and the world have a healthy economy and a healthy environment? The following situation illustrates the tradeoffs about which people must decide. Southwest Alaska has a large deposit of gold and copper. The proposed open-pit Pebble Mine to retrieve the precious metals would be the largest in North America but operating the mine using current technology would ruin a salmon habitat and release toxic mine waste into the environment. Do we turn away from developing the mine, or do we cause permanent damage to a beautiful location and cause the loss of thousands of jobs in the salmon fishing industry? Is there a way we can save the environment and operate a mine?

A healthy economy and a healthy environment are attainable at the same time. The alternative of settling for one or the other (or neither) does not do justice either to the natural resources God has given us or to the economic needs and realities of our world.

Reviewing Some Economic Principles

To get a handle on the relationship between the environment and the economy, we must review some basic economic principles we have discussed earlier.

Most choices involve marginal decisions, not all-or-nothing decisions. Few people seriously propose that we return to a non-industrialized economy, and few people seriously propose the elimination of all environmental regulations on industry. The issue is one of margins: how can we improve environmental protection without hurting the economy, and how can we increase economic output without hurting the environment?

Unfortunately, advocates on the two sides in the environmental debate sometimes caricature those on the other side as tree-huggers who value animals over humans or as greedy industrialists who do not care how much they pollute. This kind of public posturing and attacking does not get us closer to the goal of a meaningful and workable policy.

People make choices, and no choice is without cost. Even though we try to minimize the opportunity cost of an economic decision, there is still a cost. We have to decide if the cost of doing something is worth making the choice to do it, which is what cost-benefit analysis is about. We cannot do just one thing. Choosing to do something means we are choosing not to take action on something else. Everything we do affects someone or something else in some way. In any given situation, the decision to make the environment the top priority or the decision to make economic output the top priority has a price.

Environmental protection is a kind of public good. In Lesson 30, we described a public good as something that many people can use at one time, including those who do not pay for its use. However, each user of a public good enjoys the benefits directly but others share in the costs indirectly.

For example, an industry can pollute the environment without paying the cost of that pollution. The public at large pays the cost in having to pay for cleaning up the environment with taxpayer funds, in having to deal with health problems that occur as a result of the pollution, in lower property values, and in other ways. A greater accountability for misuse can help protect the environment for all.

Another principle that we have not directly stated previously is that economic activity and growth require energy and result in waste. This is true for all human activity. The people who lived in non-industrialized cities in the Middle Ages required energy (horses, wood fires, and so forth) and produced animal and human waste that was a health concern that affected the environment. People have to find ways to provide energy and to handle waste in ways that help the economy without hurting people and the environment.

Lesson 67 - The Environment

Cap and Trade: An Economic and Environmental Issue

Of the many issues we could discuss, we will consider one that relates to energy, the environment, and the economy, namely the desire to control carbon emissions and the proposal to do so with a policy called cap and trade.

The ideal way to control pollution is for industries to regulate themselves. Unfortunately, this does not always happen. One way to control harmful emissions is by the government formulating regulations, but this generally has negative consequences. Regulations require a bureaucracy to enforce them, they result in endless legal battles, and they usually wind up costing everybody money that could be put to better use.

Sometimes regulations are the best option; but in the case of cutting carbon emissions, as with many environmental issues, another option is to use a market-based solution. One market solution for carbon emissions would be for the government to enact a tax on those emissions that producers of the emissions would pay. Producers could cut their carbon emissions and thus lower their taxes by cleaning up their wastes or by changing to a non-carbon-producing energy source.

Paying the tax, lowering emissions, or changing to another energy source would increase the cost of production, which would increase the price of the product to the consumer. The market forces of price, profit, and competition would encourage producers to cut emissions as economically as possible. Consumers could also choose to buy less carbon-intensive products. Government could use the revenue that the tax generated to lower other taxes, pay down the debt, or provide needed services.

Gathering in Washington, D.C., in 2013 to protest the Keystone XL pipeline and to call for cleaner energy

Air pollution in Beijing, China (2015)

However, politicians do not usually come out in favor of increasing taxes, so one step away from imposing a tax is the cap and trade idea. In this policy, government grants allotments to industries of how much carbon emissions the industries can produce (the cap), and then issues permits that companies buy at auction which allow the companies to produce carbon emissions above their initial allotments.

When a company reduces its carbon emissions, it can sell or trade its permits to other companies (the trade). As government lowers the overall cap over time, the permits become less numerous and thus more valuable and should increase in price. Companies have a market-based incentive to lower their carbon emissions. Again, revenue that the government receives from the policy can be put to any number of uses.

This is how a cap and trade system could work in theory. However, to the extent that the government gives those permits away instead of auctioning them, they can be political favors to certain industries. Companies that receive free permits do not have the incentive of reducing costs; thus prices will not rise and consumption will not decline, but emissions will continue to be a problem.

Giving away permits decreases potential government revenue that can meet other priorities. Most economists assume carbon producing industries (often electricity-producing companies) will eventually pass on the cost of carbon reduction to consumers in the form of higher prices. Congress can offset the burden of these higher prices if it uses the auction revenue of permits to reduce taxes, but a lack of auction revenue eliminates the possibility of lowering taxes in response.

If the United States implements a cap and trade policy that results in higher production costs, the U.S. would put itself at an economic disadvantage compared to countries such as China and India that do not have such a cap and that could produce goods more cheaply with fewer environmental regulations. The result could be a loss of manufacturing jobs by the U.S. to other countries, and the increased production in less-regulated countries could actually increase the amount of carbon emissions into the world's atmosphere. The decrease in U.S. carbon emissions would be a tiny percentage of the world level of carbon emissions.

Lesson 67 - The Environment

Broad Issues about the Environment

Climate change. We have not addressed the issue of climate change (once called global warming) in this discussion of environmental issues. The climate is changing, as it has done many times over many centuries. The evidence available to us does not lead to a clear verdict about the exact causes or the best solutions. The need to limit pollution and to protect the environment is a worthwhile issue in itself, whether or not human activity is contributing to climate change. We have seen too much environmental damage to think that concern about the environment is misplaced.

The U.S. does not act alone, but the U.S. should lead. As with other aspects of economic activity, the United States does not act in a vacuum on environmental issues. China's growing economy, for instance, produces significant pollution. China's argument in reply is that it should have the opportunity to develop its economy with fewer regulations, as was the case in the United States and other developed countries in years past. However, all countries have more advanced technology available now, so China's desire to play by rules 50-75 years old is self-serving.

The United States can be a leader in dealing with environmental issues. In setting a positive example, the U.S. can help move the nations of the world toward a level playing field where all national economies have to work toward (and pay for) better environmental protection. The world needs substantive change, not posturing.

East Africa faced a severe drought in 2011 and 2012. International relief organizations attempted to assist those affected, such as Oxfam's work in Ethiopia pictured below. Despite these efforts, perhaps a quarter of a million people died, half of them young children.

Christians should care for the earth. Christians should be leaders in protecting the environment. We cannot focus exclusively on what happens in our own country and ignore what is happening in other parts of the world. Environmental issues related to food production and access to clean water have more dramatic impacts on people in countries with less economic development. More people in those countries depend on agriculture for their daily livelihood. Dealing with crises is more difficult when combined with limited infrastructure, limited surpluses, and limited mobility.

We cannot let the cries of business deafen us to the danger of environmental damage, nor should we turn away from the issue because of the presence among environmentalists of secularists and those who exalt so-called "Mother Earth" as a goddess. The earth is not a god, but caring for it is a stewardship that God has given to people. Our world is God's handiwork, and respecting it as such gives glory to Him.

The Scriptures express profound joy over the Lord's creation.

For every beast of the forest is Mine,
The cattle on a thousand hills.
I know every bird of the mountains,
And everything that moves in the field is Mine.
Psalm 50:10-11

Assignments for Lesson 67

Making Choices — Read "Ecology and the Economy: The Problems of Coexistence" (pages 158-169).

Literature — Continue reading *Mover of Men and Mountains*.

Project — Continue working on your project for this unit.

Student Review — Answer the questions for Lesson 67.

Orange juice bottling factory

68 Productivity and Growth

The way to get started is to quit talking and begin doing.
— Walt Disney

Some countries are wealthy, as measured by per capita income and per capita GDP, while other countries are poor by the same standards. Some individuals are wealthy and others are poor. The United States, which once sustained three million people, now sustains over three hundred million people. Why are these things true?

We usually measure economic growth by the increase in a nation's gross domestic product, its output of goods and services. The single most important factor influencing personal wealth, personal and national standard of living, the strength of the American economy, and economic growth is productivity. Companies can pay workers more when their productivity increases because the companies have more goods and services to sell as a result of the increased productivity.

Defining Productivity

We can express productivity in several ways. It is a measure of output per unit of input, or the ratio of output to inputs:

$$\frac{\text{output}}{\text{inputs}}$$

Inputs involve such factors as time, the number of people employed, and resources used. What an employee produces in an hour of labor is another common measure of productivity. This is sometimes expressed as *output divided by hours worked*, or:

$$\frac{\text{output}}{\text{hours worked}}$$

We express productivity for an economy as a whole with the following ratio:

$$\frac{\text{GDP}}{\text{aggregate hours worked}}$$

425

Factors in Productivity

Technology. Let's go to Ann's Apron Shop, which specializes in attractive kitchen aprons. Ann buys some fabric and thread and advertises for seamstresses to make aprons for her. Betty and Carol show up. Ann gives each of them the same amount of fabric and thread and tells them to come back in a week with their work.

A week later, Betty bounces in with twenty aprons that look sharp and crisp. Carol comes in at the end of the same day, flexing her tired fingers and carrying three aprons that look a little ragged in places. Upon investigation, Ann discovers that Betty has been using a sewing machine while Carol has been using her hands and a needle.

The two seamstresses had the same materials and the same amount of time, but the technology used in production made the inputs more productive for one of the workers. Apply this illustration to a factory or to an industry, and you can see why improvements in technology will result in greater productivity.

Education, training, and skill. Ann's heart goes out to Carol, so Ann buys her the same sewing machine that Betty has been using. A week later, Betty comes in with twenty more aprons while Carol comes in with five aprons, clipping loose threads on them as she enters. Upon investigation, Ann learns that Betty has taken sewing lessons and has been sewing for twenty years while this was the first time that Carol had been in front of a sewing machine. Carol had to start and stop, use trial and error, and undo most of what she did because she did not know how to operate a sewing machine.

A higher level of training and skill led to greater productivity. Multiply this illustration throughout a workforce, and you can see why education, training, and skills improve productivity. These factors help workers to gain from improved technology and to adapt to new work situations.

Lesson 68 - Productivity and Growth

Size of the work force. Carol finally catches on to using a sewing machine, and the next week proudly brings in her twenty aprons. When Betty arrives, however, she has fifty aprons to give to Ann. Upon investigation, Ann finds out that Betty has asked a friend to help her with the work, and the two women working together were able to more than double Betty's previous output. All else being equal, the larger the workforce—the more people working in an industry—the greater will be the productivity.

The growth of the American population has provided the increasing workforce that has helped the United States to grow in its productivity. Americans have usually enjoyed peace. They have not constantly had to go off to war because of an aggressive, militaristic leadership as citizens of many nations have, nor have they disappeared in the night because of a paranoid and ruthless leader. Instead, with a few notable interruptions, Americans have been able to go to work day by day and produce goods and services.

One major factor in the growth of the workforce has been immigration. The millions of people who came to this land, especially in the late 1800s and early 1900s, helped to staff the growing number of factories. This helped production to grow and provided a larger market for what those factories produced.

Hours worked. Tom and Hank are both landscapers. They meet for lunch once a month at their favorite restaurant. Tom usually comes in with a new shirt, a new cell phone, or a story about some new piece of equipment or a new customer he has lined up. Meanwhile, Hank usually scans the menu carefully for the cheapest items because he never seems to have much extra money. It turns out that Tom usually puts in about fifty hours per week while Hank gets rolling about nine most mornings and knocks off about three. It doesn't take an economics genius to realize that Tom is more productive than Hank because he works more hours.

This factor is most obvious when comparing national economies. When factories in a country have insufficient materials or unreliable electrical service or poorly-maintained machines (all of which are the result of other factors of productivity), the workers are not able to produce as much; so the per capita productivity will be low. The measure of hours worked does have a marginal limit, when a person becomes too tired to be productive; but within reason the more hours worked means more productivity.

Investment. Bill and Bob run competing widget factories. They both have about the same amount of profit. Bill uses his profits to buy a new home theater system, a new car, and a new boat. Bob makes do with his current toys, saves his profit, and after a couple of years invests in a new widget machine. Two years after that, Bill is making payments on his toys while Bob has almost doubled his profit as a result of his investment in his business; and now Bob can buy a few new toys of his own. Investment in training, new equipment, and new technology enables a business to be more productive. It requires the discipline of accepting deferred gratification or the ability to attract outside investors, but the long-term gain more than makes up for the wait.

The role of management. The factors that increase productivity do not just involve laborers. Management is also a key to increasing productivity. Business owners have to invest in new technology and capital goods in order for their workers to be more productive. Owners have to make sure that their workers receive good training. Managers have to use good people skills to motivate workers. Owners have to provide or to seek out investment so that their companies can grow.

A great deal of productivity involves personal choices and decisions that people make, and owners and workers both have to make good decisions and work together to improve their productivity. The bottom line is that when people are not productive, they do not earn much.

How Government Can Encourage Economic Growth

Government policies can encourage economic growth and greater productivity. A national government can encourage investment by keeping tax, debt, and inflation rates low and by maintaining stable financial markets. Government can provide economic and political stability and eliminate corruption that discourages hard work and entrepreneurship. The government can encourage education and job training programs as well as research and development. A nation's leaders can seek to expand international trade so that the goods and services that a nation produces will have growing markets.

One important way that the government can encourage economic growth is by staying out of the way as much as possible. Economic growth is the best way to lessen poverty because it creates new opportunities for employment and for entrepreneurs to make profits. A government policy that emphasizes redistributing wealth serves to limit and discourage growth and hampers advancement in the standard of living.

On the Other Hand . . .

We need to remember some other important truths to keep a clear and accurate perspective on productivity. A person needs to maintain balance with regard to his work and other aspects of his life, such as devotional and fellowship time, time with family, and time given to serving others and pursuing hobbies. A person needs to be productive but not to the point of becoming a workaholic.

UrbanPromise is a faith-based non-profit organization in Camden, New Jersey. Through educational programs, service projects, and mentorship, it seeks to "equip children and young adults with the skills necessary for academic achievement, life management, spiritual growth, and Christian leadership." The volunteers pictured below donated their time to save money on a rehabilitation project in 2012. UrbanPromise programs have spread to other U.S. cities and to Canada, Honduras, and Malawi.

Lesson 68 - Productivity and Growth

Someone who gives himself to excessive work activity can actually be less productive. Being busy does not necessarily mean being productive. Someone who "goes in all directions" might be accomplishing little of real value. Failing to take care of your health can decrease your productivity in the long run.

In addition, productivity does not measure the worth of persons. Some people's lives do not fit easily into a discussion of productivity. Those with different physical or mental abilities and the elderly may not be productive in the sense we have been discussing, but those people still have value. A minister or a stay-at-home mom might not be able to determine economic productivity by dividing their output by their inputs; but they have important roles to play in society and, as a result, in the economy. A minister can help others be productive by teaching them about their worth in God's eyes or by encouraging them to overcome habits that keep them from being productive, although again a person's worth is not determined by their economic productivity. A working dad enables a stay-at-home mom to do what she does, but in a very real and important sense the mom enables the dad to do what he does as well. A married couple should agree on how they want to use their lives together to accomplish what they believe God wants them to do in their family.

A growing economy challenges one of the fundamental principles in economics, namely the principle of scarcity. Increasing productivity pushes back the boundaries of scarcity and provides the necessities and more for a growing population. No matter how much an economy grows, its people will not be able to have everything and will have to make choices; but the ability to grow in productivity to provide more and more people with an ever higher standard of living tells us that even scarcity has its limits.

The writer of Proverbs expressed the idea of productivity.

Poor is he who works with a negligent hand,
But the hand of the diligent makes rich.
Proverbs 10:4

Assignments for Lesson 68

Literature — Continue reading *Mover of Men and Mountains*.

Project — Continue working on your project for this unit.

Student Review — Answer the questions for Lesson 68.

A hobo accepts a sandwich (1935)

69 > What Happened in the Great Depression?

I lived there [Texas] during the Great Depression. That's what they call it. I didn't see anything great about it.
— Addie Mae Farmer, my wife's great-aunt

The Great Depression began in 1929 and continued through the 1930s. Its causes and effects were widespread and complex. Because of its major impact on American attitudes and experiences, it has been a subject of debate among economists and politicians ever since. In our analysis of the Depression, we will refer to many economic principles that we discussed earlier in this curriculum.

Background of the 1920s

The economic recovery in the United States and the world during the early 1920s that followed the Great War (World War I) was not smooth. Many countries had gone off the gold standard to print more money during the war, and many people in other countries who owned gold sent it to the United States for safekeeping. At one point, the U.S. held about 40% of the world's gold reserves. As countries returned to the gold standard, gold began leaving the United States.

Economic activity in the United States was strong overall during the 1920s, but there were some bumps. The U.S. economy went into recession three times (1920-21, 1923-24, and 1926-27), although the last two were relatively mild. During the decade, wages and stock prices rose, businesses grew, and consumer buying increased. Many people invested in the stock market because of rising stock values.

Some people invested on margin. This meant that they only put down 10-25 percent of the stock values, borrowed the rest from the broker, and both investor and broker expected to make a profit as stock prices rose further. The increased demand for stocks drove their prices up, beyond their actual value relative to the worth of companies.

The Federal Reserve Board kept the money supply consistent with the output of goods and services in the economy, and inflation was not a serious problem during much of the decade. Many people believed that the historical business cycle was a thing of the past. President Herbert Hoover spoke of being nearer than ever to the complete elimination of poverty throughout the country.

Lesson 69 - What Happened in the Great Depression?

The Crash and the Aftermath

In 1928, the Fed raised interest rates to stem the flow of gold out of the country. This restricted economic activity, lessened the demand for capital goods, and lowered prices, although production did not decline. Business activity peaked in August of 1929 and then production began to decline. Agriculture, especially in the South, had already been suffering from low prices during the 1920s; and the overall drop in business activity made conditions worse for farmers.

The stock market suffered some declines in the early autumn. Investors began to have concerns about maintaining company values and stock prices, and so they began selling. The speculative bubble burst; and on October 29, 1929, the stock market lost 13% of its value (see photo on page 84). By the end of November, the market had lost 40% of its value.

The impact throughout the economy was not immediate, but by 1930 things were looking bleak. People began withdrawing money from banks, which decreased the supply of loanable funds. The response of the government was almost a textbook case of what not to do in an economic downturn. The Fed did not maintain an adequate money supply; and as a result, businesses could not borrow money to invest in their operations. Because banks operated on a fractional reserve basis (see Lesson 32), they began to fail because they did not have enough cash to meet depositor's demands.

President Hoover proposed an increase in tariffs to protect American industries. The Smoot-Hawley Tariff that passed Congress in 1930 went further than Hoover had requested, and the president signed it only reluctantly. The result was a sharp drop in trade with other countries, many of which were having economic difficulties of their own. This led to a further decline in U.S. business activity.

Protesters in New York City hold signs in the rain hoping to get their money back after a 1931 bank failure.

Congress lowered income tax rates during the 1920s because the federal government had begun running a surplus. With the economic downturn, the surplus vanished and the government began running a deficit. Congress raised income tax rates in 1931 to try to cut the deficit. Higher taxes do not promote recovery; instead, they do the opposite. Higher taxes leave people with less income, so consumers have less to spend. Also in 1931, the Fed again raised interest rates to try to halt the flow of gold out of the country; and this too hurt chances for recovery.

Between 1929 and 1933, unemployment rose from less that 5% to about 25% of the labor force. Real GDP fell 30.5%, and retail prices fell 24.4%. The stock market fell to about one-sixth of what its value had been in 1929. Of the almost 25,000 commercial banks in the country, 10,763 failed. This was before FDIC insurance, and many people simply lost their money. The money supply continued to be inadequate and actually fell by one-third.

The Response of the New Deal

During the 1932 presidential campaign, Franklin Roosevelt criticized Herbert Hoover's administration for too much taxing and spending and for trying to control the country from Washington, D.C. After Roosevelt became president, his administration ended up implementing policies similar to Hoover's that went even farther.

Thirteen-year-old sharecropper at work (1937)

Lesson 69 - What Happened in the Great Depression?

Many Americans had come to believe that active government intervention in the economy by increasing government spending was the way out of the Depression. This was the rationale for the numerous New Deal programs such as the Works Progress Administration and the Civilian Conservation Corps.

Regarding economic activity, the Roosevelt Administration believed that too much competition had led to overproduction, so a major goal was to decrease production in order to raise prices. But production had declined anyway, so this further reduction only made the situation worse. Farm production was limited and, as we mentioned in Lesson 66, some crops and livestock were destroyed even as many people were going hungry. Government policies encouraged industries to set production limits. Still, the money supply was inadequate for business activity to expand very much.

The economy experienced a minor recovery in 1933, but the pace of recovery slowed over the next two years. In 1935 and 1936, the Supreme Court struck down the government's farm and industry regulations; and recovery was stronger from 1935 to 1937. Then another serious recession hit in 1937 and lasted into 1938. The annual unemployment rate was 14.3% for 1937 and 19.1% in 1938. In 1940, unemployment still stood at 14.6%.

The Depression lasted several years longer in the United States than it did in many other countries. Production and employment did not significantly increase until military production increased dramatically during World War II. However, domestic price controls and rationing kept a full recovery from occurring until after the war.

Did the New Deal Help or Hurt?

Debates about the Great Depression and the New Deal center on the causes of the downturn, the reasons for the slow recovery, and the real reason

An elderly woman sells pencils on the street (1938)

why the Depression ended. The economy in 1940 was certainly in better shape than it was in 1933, although opinions differ on whether that was because of or in spite of New Deal programs.

The New Deal is political and economic anathema to conservatives, who believe that it prolonged the Depression. We cannot say for sure, since we cannot know what would have happened if the federal government had not implemented the New Deal as it did. The United States had always recovered from panics and recessions with much less government intervention, although the Depression that began in 1929 was the worst that the nation had experienced.

Certainly the New Deal was not an unqualified success. Some decisions went against accepted economic theory. For instance, Congress increased the top marginal income tax rate (the rate paid by people with the highest incomes) from 25% to 63% in 1932 under the Hoover Administration, then to 79% in 1936 and to 90% in 1944 under Roosevelt.

Unit 14: Economic Issues, Part 2

Unemployed men in Scott's Run, West Virginia, attend a Workers Alliance Council meeting (1937)

This hurt the possibility of investment (those with the highest incomes had much less to invest), which would have helped to bring about growth. Also, the tendency of the Roosevelt Administration to experiment with programs resulted in uncertainty among the population as a whole and among business leaders in particular.

Republicans, Democrats, and the Federal Reserve must share blame for bringing the Depression about and for prolonging its effects. Actions in the free market and actions by the government probably helped to some degree and probably hindered to some degree. Many Americans came to believe that government intervention is the only way out of economic difficulty. A large percentage of the American population now depends on the federal government to provide an economic safety net that includes welfare, food assistance, health care, unemployment benefits, and other programs. The federal government's expanded role in the economy continued to grow long after the Depression ended.

A common tendency among people is to look to others for assistance during hard times. We should help each other in times of difficulty, but not even the rich and powerful can help us in the ways we need most.

*Do not trust in princes,
In mortal man, in whom there is no salvation.
Psalm 146:3*

Assignments for Lesson 69

Making Choices Read "The Rules of the Game and Economic Recovery" (pages 170-176).

Literature Continue reading *Mover of Men and Mountains*.

Project Continue working on your project for this unit.

Student Review Answer the questions for Lesson 69.

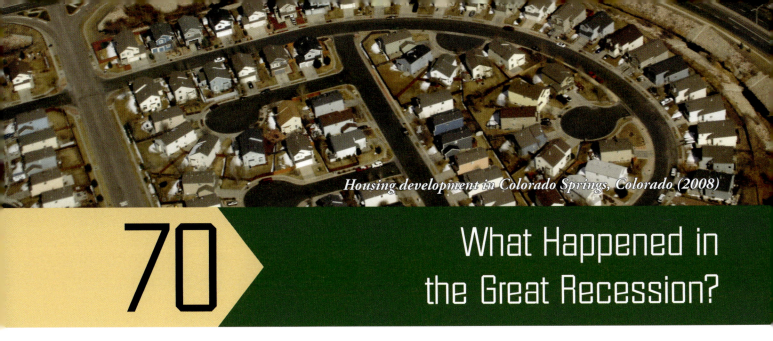
Housing development in Colorado Springs, Colorado (2008)

70 | What Happened in the Great Recession?

Governments never learn. Only people learn.
— Milton Friedman

The Great Depression did not end the pattern of business cycles. The United States experienced several recessions after the Depression. The recession that occurred in the early 1980s was described at the time as the worst downturn since the Great Depression. Because of debt and greed, the recession that officially began in December 2007 now holds that unwanted title.

Underlying Causes

Debt. Imagine that you spend your life up to your chin in water. It is how you live. You become used to it, and you forget that the situation is dangerous. However, a small rise in the water level can be fatal. For a man who is six feet tall and is up to his chin in water, the water level would only have to rise ten inches, or 16%, for him to be completely submerged. If he were standing on dry ground, a rise of ten inches in the water level would not even come to his knees. With water already up to his neck, a rise of a few inches puts him in trouble; ten inches will do him in.

This is an illustration of the extent to which the American economy is dependent on debt. Large, successful businesses carry billions of dollars in debt. Families have tens of thousands of dollars in mortgage debt, credit card debt, and school loan debt. The federal government sets the example for this way of life with deficit spending every year and a rapidly growing national debt. We have become used to it, but even a small increase in debt can cause big problems.

Greed. People like to make money. People like to make more money. People like to find new ways to make more money. The stock market crash of 1929 followed a period of speculation fueled by greed. The Savings and Loan crisis of the late twentieth century (see Lesson 20) was the result of greed. Do you see a pattern here?

Many people want to buy a house. Many people want to buy a bigger house. Many people are tempted to buy a house that is bigger than what they can afford.

Many people are willing to go into debt so that they can have more. Many people are willing to be in debt up to their necks . . . and that takes us back to the first point in this section.

Government promotion of homeownership. As we pointed out in Lesson 65, owning a home has long been part of the American Dream. It does have several economic advantages. Leaders in government like to make it possible for a greater percentage of Americans to own a home. But when too much debt mixes with unchecked greed, the results can be disastrous.

Occasionally Congress passes new laws that make it easier for people to qualify for a mortgage. Department of Veterans Affairs (VA) and Federal Housing Authority (FHA) loans are two examples. The purpose of the national mortgage companies Fannie Mae and Freddie Mac was to help more people own homes. Homeownership is an economic goal that many individuals desire, and leaders in the federal government want to encourage it.

The problem comes when political leaders encourage lenders to relax their rules to make mortgages available to people who are not good risks. In addition, the way that investors sell and resell mortgages throughout the investment world creates a situation in which many people depend on unreliable debt.

First Steps

In the late 1990s, the economic boom known as the high-tech bubble was beginning to burst. The stock market began to fall in 2000, and a recession began the next year. The Fed cut interest rates to encourage an economic recovery. Political leaders pressured Freddie Mac and Fannie Mae to loosen credit restrictions so that more people could become homeowners.

In the early years of the twenty-first century, many people who bought homes were not prime candidates for mortgages, so the loans they received were called subprime mortgages. Some of these mortgages carried variable interest rates that rose after the first year or two, which meant that the monthly payment increased also.

After the 2001 recession, the next several years were generally a prosperous time. House values increased, so many people bought larger homes than they could really afford with loans that carried more risk than the people could bear. Realtors and banks encouraged buyers by telling them that, if they had to, the buyers could always sell their houses and still make money.

Many mortgage loans were bundled into investment instruments called mortgage-backed securities. The value of these securities depended on house prices continuing to rise and on people being able to continue making their mortgage payments. Mortgage-backed securities are also called derivatives, which are financial instruments whose value is determined by or derived from an underlying asset.

Encouraged by what appeared to be healthy business activity, the stock market rose for several years and reached its all-time high to that point in October of 2007.

The Unraveling

Then reality began to set in. Many houses did not increase in value as much as lenders and borrowers had anticipated. In fact, many were worth less than the mortgages people had taken out on them. Many owners found themselves unable to make their mortgage payments, so they defaulted on their loans. Banks took over the homes through the foreclosure process. These mortgages came to be called toxic assets.

The presence of cheaper foreclosure homes on the market brought down house values in general. This hurt responsible homeowners whose homes also declined in value. Mortgage-backed securities based on toxic mortgages lost value, so investors and investment companies began to lose money. Two investment funds owned by the company Bear Stearns collapsed in June of 2007.

As investments began to lose value, banks were not able to loan as much money, so economic

Tamarack Village Plaza was planned to be part of a ski resort in Idaho. The developer ran into financial trouble and construction stopped in 2008, when this photo was taken. Appraisers valued the resort at over $200 million in 2008 during foreclosure proceedings. The unfinished buildings were sold at auction for $13 million in 2013.

activity began to slow down. Many companies routinely obtain short term loans (sometimes called commercial paper) to make their payroll and then pay the loans back when they have sold some of their inventory of goods. With the economy slowing down, however, sales were not good so companies could not repay the loans. This credit crunch, the restriction in lending activity, was a major factor in the financial downturn.

In early 2008, the federal government began to consider ways to stimulate the economy. In February Congress passed the Economic Stimulus Act. The government borrowed money and sent checks totaling about $152 billion to taxpayers. Other provisions in the law were intended to encourage economic growth as well, but the decline continued. In March the government assumed $30 billion in liabilities from Bear Stearns, and the company was sold to the financial company JPMorgan Chase.

By August of 2008, stock prices for Fannie Mae and Freddie Mac had declined sharply. The Treasury Department took over their operation on September 7. Less than a week later, the investment company Lehman Brothers neared bankruptcy. Federal officials decided against rescuing the company as they had Bear Stearns, so Lehman Brothers went bankrupt. Officials arranged for Bank of America to purchase another investment company, Merrill Lynch.

A few days later, the government rescued the giant insurance company American International Group (AIG) with $85 billion from the federal government. AIG was brought low by a financial instrument called a credit default swap (CDS).

This is a kind of insurance arrangement in which a bank or investment company that holds a debt makes a payment like a premium to an insurance company, for which the insurance company assumes the risk if the debt goes bad. AIG carried billions of dollars in CDS obligations; and when so many loans went into default, AIG did not have the assets to pay its obligations.

Meanwhile, stock prices were falling dramatically. Treasury Secretary Henry Paulson announced a $700 billion proposal for the federal government to buy so-called toxic assets from banks. This would remove the bad loans from the books of the banks and allow them to resume making loans. The House of Representatives defeated the proposal on September 29, but an amended version passed Congress in early October. Meanwhile, national economies elsewhere in the world were declining also.

While all of this was happening, gasoline prices hit record highs, reaching over $4.00 per gallon in June of 2008. This sharp increase in fuel costs hurt economic activity even more. Gas prices declined in the fall and fell below $2.00 per gallon by December. The economic decline served as a dramatic backdrop to the 2008 presidential election. Democrat Barack Obama defeated Republican John McCain, at least partly because many people blamed the Republicans for the nation's economic woes.

Problems continued into December 2008 and then into 2009. The Fed lowered its federal funds target rate to between zero and .25% to encourage borrowing in the still tight credit market. The Christmas shopping season was the worst for retailers in thirty years. Homeowners experienced over three million home foreclosures in 2008, up 81% over the previous year. The federal government extended aid to banks, and it appeared that the government might take over the banking industry.

Because of declining sales, General Motors and Chrysler slid into bankruptcy in 2009. Remember the illustration of living in debt up to your neck? Both companies had carried significant debt for years. General Motors, for instance, had operated its Saturn division for almost twenty years even though Saturn had never made an annual profit. The federal government took over controlling interest in GM and ordered a major reorganization. The Italian carmaker Fiat bought Chrysler.

In 2009 the home of Tecora Parks in Minneapolis went into foreclosure. The case drew attention from people who thought that if anyone was going to be bailed out, it should be average Americans instead of big banks and insurance companies. Leslie Parks, Tecora's daughter, was able to arrange for her mother to stay in the home and purchased the house with a new mortgage in 2011.

Lower tax revenues and another $787 billion bailout package pushed the fiscal year 2009 federal budget deficit to $1.42 trillion, the largest ever. Unemployment reached 10.2% in October 2009, the highest level in 26 years. The news that top executives in some failed companies received large bonuses angered many Americans.

The year 2008 saw 25 bank failures, including Washington Mutual, the largest single bank failure in U.S. history. One hundred forty banks failed in 2009 and 157 in 2010. The rate started to decline in 2011 with 92 failures and then 51 in 2012. However, the presence of FDIC insurance helped to prevent bank runs like those that took place during the worst years of the Great Depression.

The Dow Jones average hit bottom in March of 2009 but by October had regained considerable ground. The housing market began to show signs of recovery at times during the year. The Federal Reserve pursued a policy it called quantitative easing, which was the introduction of new money into the money supply. This helped the country avoid the problems that had occurred with the restricted monetary supply during the Great Depression.

The National Bureau of Economic Research determined that the recession began in December 2007 and hit the trough or lowpoint of economic activity in June of 2009. Then an expansion began. The eighteen months duration made the recession the worst that has occurred since World War II.

Recovery from the recession was painfully slow, but by mid-2016 the stock market had recovered almost all of its value, Americans' total household worth had surpassed its pre-recession peak, and unemployment was back down below 5%. The Fed kept interest rates low, which was a boon to borrowers but an irritation to investors, who usually wanted a higher rate of interest on their investments.

The Aftermath

Why didn't more people see the recession coming? Some did, and some economists voiced warnings about the dangers of subprime mortgages. As a rule, however, economists, like everyone else, are better at analyzing the past than predicting the future. Economist John Kenneth Galbraith once joked, "The only function of economic forecasting is to make astrology look respectable." Too many people are wishful thinkers, seeing only what they want to see and hoping that they can avoid the law of reaping what they sow.

Was a lack of regulation the problem? Probably not. A bigger problem was the encouragement by members of both political parties for lenders to bend the rules and approve subprime mortgages. Risk means that failure is possible. Lenders and borrowers assumed too much risk, and failure occurred.

Washington Mutual branch in Brooklyn, New York (2007)

Did the stimulus programs help? As with the New Deal, this will be hard to prove because we cannot know what would have happened if the stimulus spending did not take place. The Obama Administration said that their goal was that through their programs three million jobs would be created or saved. This was a nebulous goal because it is difficult to prove that jobs that were not lost would have been lost. The stimulus spending probably helped in some ways, but what we do know for sure is that the federal government has become involved in the economy in unprecedented ways and that the national debt has increased enormously.

In some ways responses to the recession were good. In 2010 Congress passed the Dodd-Frank Act that increased regulations on the financial industry. However, a lack of regulation was not the cause of the recession. A failure to maintain regulations and guidelines already in place, especially regarding who should obtain a mortgage, was more to blame.

In 2014 Fannie Mae announced its willingness to back loans with as little a down payment as 3% of a home's value, provided that the borrower had private mortgage insurance on the loan. This ignored the experience of a few years earlier and the clear evidence that borrowers who make down payments of 20% or more have a much smaller default rate than those whose down payments are less.

What can we learn? Risk is dangerous, greed is damaging, and the rules are in place for a reason. We should also learn that, unless this was truly a unique situation, the economy will recover from the downturn and then somewhere down the road people will push the limits and another downturn will occur.

Jesus' words to a man who was concerned about an inheritance address anyone who allows greed to dominate him.

> *Then He said to them, "Beware, and be on your guard against every form of greed; for not even when one has an abundance does his life consist of his possessions."*
> *Luke 12:15*

Assignments for Lesson 70

Making Choices — Read the speech on the Economic Bailout Proposal (pages 177-181).

Literature — Continue reading *Mover of Men and Mountains*.

Project — Finish your project for this unit.

Student Review — Answer the questions for Lesson 70 and take the quiz for Unit 14.

15 ME-conomics: The Ultimate Microeconomy

An economy is made up of individuals who live in the material world with the eternal world before them. Every individual has a responsibility to live by spiritual priorities and moral obligations. People have many decisions to make regarding personal finances, including the choice of one's life's work. In the Sermon on the Mount, Jesus taught his disciples about money, possessions, and the priority of seeking the kingdom of God and His righteousness.

Lesson 71 - What Difference Can One Person Make?
Lesson 72 - What Should I Do?
Lesson 73 - Me and My Money
Lesson 74 - When I Grow Up
Lesson 75 - "Seek Ye First . . ."

Books Used

The Bible
Making Choices
Mover of Men and Mountains

Project (choose one)

1) Write 300 to 500 words on one of the following topics:

   - What does it mean to seek first the kingdom of God?

   - Write an article directed at teenage Christians about our moral responsibilities regarding money.

2) If you were choosing right now, what would you choose as your career? Make a commercial about one minute long recruiting for that career. Include ways that particular career benefits society and individuals.

3) Make a poster with the title, "One Person Can Make a Difference." Include at least ten pictures or photos of individuals you know and/or from history. Represent in words and/or pictures the way or ways each person has made a difference. Use the medium of your choice (paint, pastels, pencil, colored pencil, marker, ink, chalk, collage, etc.).

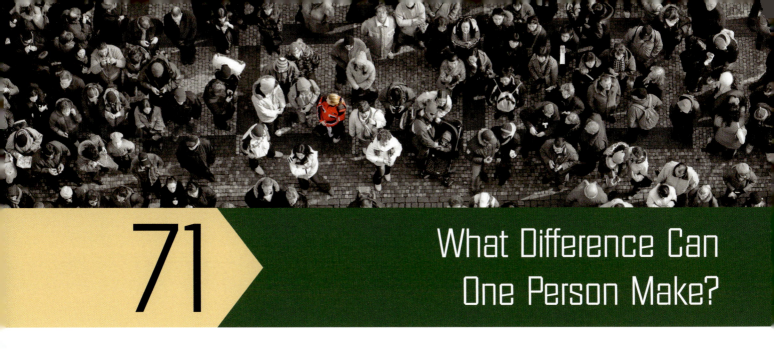

71 What Difference Can One Person Make?

I came to realize that my money problems, worries, and shortages largely began and ended with the person in my mirror. I realized also that if I could learn to manage the character I shaved with every morning, I would win with money.

— *Dave Ramsey*

Economics studies national and worldwide activity. It talks about billions and trillions of dollars and uses terms like aggregate and macro. What difference can one person make?

The individual makes all of the difference. "The market" doesn't make decisions; individuals do. "The government" doesn't determine a policy; the president, or a leader in Congress, or someone in an executive department does. Individuals, either singly or as part of a group, make all economic decisions. If something happens in the United States economy, it happens because of individuals.

If an economic activity is large enough for many people to notice it, many people are likely engaged in it—and that is the point. Individuals—not groups, not social classes, not governments, not societies, but individuals—make decisions, develop products and services, consider opportunity costs, face tradeoffs, and deal with unintended consequences. Sometimes an individual makes a decision that affects millions of people, but it is still an individual decision. The largest companies, the most powerful labor unions, and the actions of government all involve individuals.

So you as an individual make a difference in economics. The economy is made up of millions of individuals like you, none of whom has any greater or lesser worth before God than you do. In this last unit, we will consider decisions that you as an individual will have to make regarding economic issues. Some of the topics we discuss in this unit slip over from being strictly economics into the area of personal finance, but those topics have a place in economics nonetheless.

This World and the Other World

Christians live in a constant tension between two realities. On one hand, we believe that the eternal is what ultimately matters. Paul considered all of the worldly accomplishments he had achieved as rubbish compared to knowing Christ (Philippians 3:8). Jesus warned against gaining the world and losing one's soul (Matthew 16:26). John reminded us that the world is passing away, but the one who does the will of God lives forever (1 John 2:17).

On the other hand, we live in the physical world. We live in a world of buildings, markets, commodities, automobiles—trillions and trillions of dollars worth of stuff all around us, and some of it in our own homes. The Bible says that God will judge people's lives in terms of how they live in this world, "according to their deeds" (Revelation 20:12). How we treat other people, whether we work productively and resist the temptation to steal (Ephesians 4:25-28), and how we handle the abilities and opportunities given to us regarding the things of this world (Matthew 25:14-30)—all are important to God.

Economics has everything to do with our lives before God. In His wisdom, God places us spiritual beings in this physical world and tells us to live well—to live exceptionally—in it. Jesus told His followers to be "shrewd as serpents and innocent as doves" (Matthew 10:16). We are to have hearts of compassion for the poor and for victims of injustice (1 John 3:17, James 5:4). We are to work to provide for ourselves and to teach others to do the same (2 Thessalonians 3:6-13). We follow a Lord who condemned those who made a business out of the worship of His Father (Mark 11:15-17).

Our calling is to figure out what this tension between two worlds means for us in terms of eternity and in terms of our lives in this world, and to live responsibly before the Judge of the universe. This calling, to live a Spirit-based life in a material-based world, gives us a lifelong challenge. Perhaps the following ideas will help you on this journey.

The Responsibilities You Have

Depend on God and on your efforts. This sounds like a contradiction, but it is not. You are dependent on God for your life and everything you have, whether you admit it or not. Admitting it, however, gives God the glory and allows you to work with Him instead of against Him. As you depend on God, you live as a steward to use well the life He gives you.

God did not make a world in which no one needs to do anything while He provides housing, clothes, and food for everyone regardless. We live in a world that requires people to work. Since God gave you abilities, you have a responsibility to use them to support yourself and to bless others. You can decide that you are not going to be dependent on others, including the government. Instead, you can decide to be a contributor to making your world better and your economy healthier.

Live by the priorities you say you believe. You might say that you believe in various principles and that certain activities are important to you, but you demonstrate what you really believe by what you do. How you spend your time and how you spend your money are two of the most reliable demonstrations of what you really believe, regardless of what you say. Make sure that how you spend your time and money matches what you say you believe. Otherwise, people will have little faith in what you say.

Do the right thing regardless of what others do. Christians are committed to doing what is right whether other people do right or not. People sometimes make excuses for cutting corners and fudging on the truth as the way to get ahead. They may say that that is just how business is done. Swimming against the stream is difficult, but you don't have to follow those lower standards. You can trust that God's way, the way of integrity, will serve you well, even in an economic world that follows a worldly standard.

Christians in the first century, as they lived in a pagan world, faced the same challenge. You can't let the decisions that others make turn you aside from the decisions you know you need to make. Don't blame others for a lack of integrity in yourself; instead, seek to be a light to others as you pursue God's will.

Decide on your level of involvement in the world. You might decide that the course of events in the world is in God's hands and that you can live with whatever happens without voting in elections or trying to influence economic policies. On the other hand, you might decide that God has given you political and economic freedom and that you have a responsibility to use your freedom to further the cause of justice, equality, and freedom by taking part in political campaigns, voting in elections, and working to influence elected officials.

You will have to make decisions about the work you do and about how you spend the money that God grants you. You don't have a choice about living in the world, but you must make a choice about how you are going to live before God in this world. Be able to be at peace with your decision.

We might like an easier ride through life, but that is not why we are here and that is not how we grow. Life is sometimes daunting, but it is also a thrilling challenge to realize that God gave us life for a purpose. He does not expect anything of us that is impossible; and yet He calls us to live up to our potential, with no excuses.

In handling your relationships, in dealing with your dollars and cents, and in relating to the world in which you live, you have a responsibility before God. Decide to fulfill that responsibility to honor Him, and in that way enjoy the fullest life He can give you.

News Release Basketball is a ministry run by Christians that sends teams of college basketball players to interact with young people in other countries by conducting training clinics.

*Therefore I urge you, brethren, by the mercies of God,
to present your bodies a living and holy sacrifice, acceptable to God,
which is your spiritual service of worship.
And do not be conformed to this world,
but be transformed by the renewing of your mind,
so that you may prove what the will of God is,
that which is good and acceptable and perfect.
Romans 12:1-2*

Assignments for Lesson 71

Making Choices — Read "What Makes for Success?" (pages 182-195).

Literature — Continue reading *Mover of Men and Mountains*. Plan to finish it by the end of this unit.

Project — Choose your project for this unit and start working on it.

Student Review — Answer the questions for Lesson 71.

72

What Should I Do?

To see what is right and not to do it is want of courage.
— *Confucius*

The moral economy is a term that describes economic activity based on moral principles such as goodness, fairness, honesty, and justice. Moral economics holds, for instance, that it is better to do what is right than to achieve the most profit a person could potentially make. In moral economics, selling defective goods at full price or selling goods produced by slave labor are morally wrong actions.

The free market works best when people in the market follow moral principles, although the study of economics does not always explicitly express these principles as the best basis for market activity. The principles are implicit, however, in the understanding that markets have to be based on trust if market activity is to bring about mutually satisfying exchanges.

Moral economic standards were easier to maintain when market activity was concentrated in local communities. Before global communication and a global economy became the way that goods and services are distributed, local communities and local economies served people in a small area. The people in those communities generally shared common beliefs and values. If a merchant became known as someone who cheated customers, buyers would likely avoid doing business with him. This helps us understand the practical implications of provisions in the Law of Moses requiring true weights and measures and forbidding usury. A society in which people routinely take advantage of each other and which operates in an atmosphere of distrust will not foster economic, personal, or spiritual growth.

As economic activity expanded and as producers and consumers became connected over long distances and with different moral standards, people could not know as easily if buyers and sellers followed moral principles in their economic activity. Consumers increasingly did not know the suppliers with whom they engaged in transactions. Addressing issues of product quality and honesty became more difficult; a frustrated consumer could no longer just go to the next booth at the market to make a satisfying purchase.

Today we often do business with people we never meet, people who might or might not share the same values we do. Many people do not seem to have as many close personal friendships as their ancestors did; instead, they have virtual social networks. This challenges our ability to engage in morally-based economics, but it does not remove our responsibility to do what is right regardless of what others do. If anything, the need is even greater to engage in personal and business practices that follow God's teachings.

Moral Obligations

Here are some economic practices that reflect choices based on God's principles. The overriding principle is the Golden Rule, to treat others the way you want to be treated (Matthew 7:12).

Keep the long term in mind. Patience and sacrifice have practical benefits. If you save part of your income instead of spending everything you have, you will be better off in the long run. You will be able to afford things that you want and need instead of having to go into debt for them. If you pay the opportunity cost now to pursue training and preparation, you will reap the benefits of those efforts later. It's never too early to start saving for retirement. You might not want to retire the way many people do (leave your job, draw a pension, and engage mostly in recreational activities). You and others will be better off if you stay productive for as long as you can. However, you might think differently if you have grandchildren come along or if you become physically unable to work as you would like. Saving now will give you more options later in life.

Respect others. Be honest in business and in everything you do. Do not pressure people to try to get them to respond the way you want them to. Have enough respect for others, enough faith in your product, and enough faith in God to give people the information they need and let them decide. Respect the needs of others by always paying your bills on time.

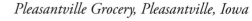

Pleasantville Grocery, Pleasantville, Iowa

Lesson 72 - What Should I Do?

Use your position to bless others. Whether you are self-employed, work in a local store, work in government, work for a major corporation, hire other people, or run a large business, you have the opportunity to do good. Treat well those who work with you or for you and do not take advantage of them for your benefit. Be aware of your impact on the environment, from how you dispose of trash to how you participate in recycling programs to how you handle pollution emissions from your factory. Look for ways that you can give to other people or to good causes out of the income that God gives you through your work.

Respect your conscience. The conscience is the capacity a person has to determine right and wrong. Everybody has a conscience; but a conscience must be trained, and people's consciences are trained differently. As a result, people will have different scruples on some issues. These issues are different from the matters that the Lord has specifically addressed in Scripture, which everyone is responsible to follow. Paul discussed some matters of conscience in Romans 14 and said that, bottom line, we each answer to the Lord.

One example of respecting your conscience is in the matter of investments. The Bible does not say "Thou shalt (or thou shalt not) invest in mutual funds," so whether and how you invest in a mutual fund is your decision. Most mutual funds include the stock of companies that you would probably not support. If you invest in a typical mutual fund and the fund increases in value, you will be profiting from the economic activity of companies you would probably not buy from directly. You need to decide whether your conscience will allow you to invest in that mutual fund.

In the parable of the talents, the master told the fearful slave that he should have put the money in the bank so that it could have gained interest (Matthew 25:27). The master did not deal with the question of whether the bank might have invested the money in improper activities. On the other hand, Christians are admonished to avoid any association with evil (for instance, Ephesians 5:3).

So, the Bible has no law against investing in mutual funds. However, if you want to invest money but have a conscientious objection to typical mutual funds, you will have to choose something else. People have created socially responsible mutual funds, sometimes called conscience funds, that only invest in businesses that meet certain moral standards. Or, you might invest in the business of someone you know and trust. Whatever you do, stay true to what you know to be right and what you believe is your obligation before God. Stay close to God, and keep learning and seeking His will.

Buy Responsibly

Your purchases do not just benefit you. They also benefit the supplier from whom you buy them. You can often choose to make purchases that will bless people close to you instead of following the easy default setting of buying everything from big retailers. You can make at least some of your purchases at a local hardware store or a local grocery store. You can buy organic fruits and vegetables at a local farmers market or from people you know. I prefer to do business with a local banker and a local insurance agent. These are people I can sit down with and look in the eye.

Christians have an obligation to be good stewards of the resources God gives us, but this does not necessarily mean that we must only buy at the lowest possible price. We are more than consumers, and we should be concerned with more than just maintaining or increasing our standard of living. For instance, spending another dollar or two locally can help keep a small-town grocery store open. One reason to do so might be that elderly people depend on that store. Buying responsibly maintains the diversity and accountability that have helped to make our economy great.

One way to sum up the principles and practices we have discussed in this lesson is the way Paul said we are to live: following the example of our wonderful, exalted, self-sacrificing, loving Savior.

Therefore I, the prisoner of the Lord, implore you to walk in a manner worthy of the calling with which you have been called.
Ephesians 4:1

Assignments for Lesson 72

Literature — Continue reading *Mover of Men and Mountains*.

Project — Continue working on your project for this unit.

Student Review — Answer the questions for Lesson 72.

"Mr. Micawber delivers some valedictory remarks," Hablot Knight Browne (English, 1850)

73 — Me and My Money

> *"My other piece of advice, Copperfield," said Mr. Micawber, "you know. Annual income twenty pounds, annual expenditure nineteen nineteen six, result happiness. Annual income twenty pounds, annual expenditure twenty pounds ought and six, result misery."*
> — *Charles Dickens,* David Copperfield *(1850)*

The financial decisions we make cause us to be part of the economy. This lesson discusses some of the typical decisions that Americans have to make with regard to their money. Being aware of these decisions will help you to be a wiser participant in the economy.

You will bless yourself, your family, and others if you develop a good grasp of godly financial wisdom. Many Christian writers and speakers provide valuable and reliable guidance. The important thing, however, is not just to read books or listen to podcasts but to put what you learn into practice. You have to be absolutely determined that you and the Lord are going to be victorious in the Battle of the Budget.

A married couple needs to be together in their thinking. Disagreements over money are one of the leading causes of marital conflict. A husband and wife will likely have different experiences and different expectations regarding money. They have to come together to develop a plan that is better than either one of them could have devised individually. Addressing this issue honestly and openly before and throughout marriage will help a couple avoid many conflicts.

One key principle is to keep it simple. Christian writer Charlie Shedd said that his plan was to give ten percent, save ten percent, and live on the rest with thanksgiving and praise. You can find more detailed financial advice, but you will be hard pressed to find wiser advice.

The Basics

Set financial goals. You have to know where you want to go; otherwise, how will you know if you get there? Satisfying financial outcomes do not just happen; they take planning, prayer, and action. A husband and wife have to be clear with each other on what their goals are. The goal of "a nice home" might mean a condominium to one and a ranch-style house with a large yard to the other. You will probably have to revisit your goals from time to time because your thinking will change and reality never fails to happen, but you have to start where you are.

Make and keep a budget. You have to plan realistically how to meet your expenses and how to pay for the things you desire. A budget is essential for financial responsibility. It sets out what you want and need to accomplish with your income, and it lets you know how you are doing on achieving your goals. As with your financial goals, you will need to revise your budget from time to time in view of new realities that come into your life.

The two most important elements of a budget are making it and keeping it. A budget is not a guess or a flexible guideline. You do not achieve a worthy goal by sort of aiming in that direction; instead, you accomplish your purpose by conscientious, diligent work toward the specific goal you set.

Books and online resources give typical budget categories and the percentage that each category should have in your budget. Common categories for spending include: giving, saving, housing (which includes rent or mortgage payment, utilities, insurance, maintenance, furnishings, and improvements), food, transportation (car, fuel, insurance, maintenance, and repairs, or mass transit passes or other options), medical expenses, clothing, life and health insurance, and personal activities (recreation, vacations, and so forth). Families also have to budget for the educational expenses of their children. Another major category is taxes. While employers deduct taxes from employee paychecks, self-employed persons have to save up so they can send to the United States Treasury quarterly estimated payments of income tax and Social Security and Medicare contributions.

Live within your means. Mr. Micawber's advice, quoted at the beginning of this lesson, is sound (even though Mr. Micawber did not follow it). Avoid debt. Proverbs 22:7 says that the borrower becomes slave to the lender, and slavery is not pretty or fun. If it is wrong for the government to spend beyond its means, the same is true for families.

If you can't afford a purchase within your budget, save up for it or generate more income. Buying more house than you can afford is easy to do. However, over time the payments and the inevitable associated expenses can begin to put a strain on your budget. You will also find more financial peace if you pay cash for a car and budget for the inevitable expenses associated with it. Wise saving will help you be ready for the rainy days that will come and will enable you to help others when they have needs.

Keep your eyes on the Lord and off of other people. Comparison is a deadly game. You will always be able to find someone who has more than you do, and you will always be able to find someone who has less than you do. Do not be envious of someone's bigger house or newer car. You do not know what else might be going on in that person's life. That other person might be envious of your peaceful, godly life. Trust the Lord to provide, and trust His timing to provide what you need when you need it. If you are tempted to compare your lot to someone else, think about Jesus, who during His time on earth, had nowhere to lay His head.

Some Difficult Specifics

Insurance is a way to manage risk. Cost-benefit analysis will help you see whether the benefit of insurance outweighs the cost. You face many risks in life: getting sick, having an auto accident, becoming disabled, and having a business loss or liability. Because you face the certainty of dying, you risk leaving dependents who have counted on you to provide income for them and who will face the certainty of funeral expenses. Because these risks and certainties are real, you need to provide for their occurrence responsibly.

Many people purchase insurance to manage these risks. They purchase health insurance, disability insurance, business insurance, and/or life insurance. Many states require car owners to purchase auto insurance. Of course, just as it is possible to be house-poor (feeling poor because you are paying for too much house), it is also possible to be insurance-poor (feeling poor because you have too much insurance); so you need to plan carefully to know how much insurance you need.

Insurance does not have to take the traditional form. It is possible to be self-insured, which means having enough money on hand to cover the expenses of illness, disability, a business loss, or your death. Christians have started health expense sharing plans and other different organizations that provide alternative options to standard forms of insurance.

Debt involves owing money to someone. Debt occurs when you borrow money or when you have expenses that are more than what you can pay. People in our society are eager to lend you money: banks, check cashing companies, auto dealers, appliance stores, and credit card companies. They offer you the opportunity to have something while you are paying for it. This creates an obligation for your money tomorrow (usually for many tomorrows) when you do not know what tomorrow might bring. Debt also costs you more money than you would spend by just paying the purchase price for things because those friendly people who are waiting to loan you money charge you interest for using it. Those interest charges are the price you pay for not saying no or for not waiting until you can pay cash. Going into debt to start a business can be unwise because you put yourself under great financial obligation from the very beginning.

Bankruptcy is the inability to pay one's debts. It is the worst financial situation a person can be in. United States law recognizes different kinds of bankruptcy. In some forms, creditors take what they can get from your property, while in other kinds the bankrupt person develops a plan to pay off his debts over time. Bankruptcy is a seriously negative mark on a person's credit history, something that you should work hard to avoid.

A person can recover from bankruptcy, but it is a terribly painful experience for the people who go through it. Christians should feel a moral obligation to pay all of their debts however long it takes. Other people are counting on receiving what you have said you will pay them. The sure way to avoid bankruptcy is to avoid going into debt.

The Real Standard of Living

In this curriculum, we have talked a great deal about people being consumers and about the rising standard of living that is possible in a free market society. We have done so because these concepts are important in economics, not because they are the most important matters in a person's life. The Bible mentions many economic concepts—such as making choices, counting the cost, making investments, making trades, suffering loss, engaging in labor, being rich and being poor, and experiencing growth and change—to describe matters that are far more important than money and economics.

This should remind us that the standard of living that Jesus offers is eternal life. This eternal life is life on a higher plane; it is something we can enjoy now, not just in heaven. It is not dependent on budgets, bank accounts, or the gross domestic product. His offer is not one that the media and advertisers shout at us, but the choice He puts before us is the most important decision we will ever make. It should be the decision that guides every other decision we will ever face, financial or otherwise.

Christ experienced what He did so that we might experience it also.

---

*Therefore we have been buried with Him through baptism into death,
so that as Christ was raised from the dead through the glory of the Father,
so we too might walk in newness of life.*
Romans 6:4

Assignments for Lesson 73

Making Choices — Read the excerpts from "The Art of Money Getting" (pages 196-203).

Literature — Continue reading *Mover of Men and Mountains*.

Project — Continue working on your project for this unit.

Student Review — Answer the questions for Lesson 73.

74 When I Grow Up

*The place God calls you to is the place where
your deep gladness and the world's deep hunger meet.*
— Frederick Buechner

You will do something with your life.

You might be the person who discovers a medical breakthrough, casts a crucial deciding vote on the U.S. Supreme Court, or creates the next big product in technology. Somebody will, and it might be you.

You might run a major corporation, teach at a large university, or represent your state in Congress. Somebody will, and it might be you.

You might be a well-respected local business leader, a beloved minister in a church, or the organizer of an effective homeschool cooperative. Somebody will, and it might be you.

You might be a wonderful mother, a reliable worker in a factory, or a trusted website builder. Somebody will, and it might be you.

You might flounder your way through life, wind up deep in debt, and leave people wondering what happened to someone with so much potential. Somebody will, and it might be you.

At this point in your life, you cannot know where the Lord will lead you. You can know, however, that you have opportunities and decisions ahead of you in which you will be called upon to honor God and to make the best use of your life. In this lesson we will consider some questions that you will face as you determine your life's work.

What Do You Really Want to Do?

Taking off from the quotation by Frederick Buechner (pronounced BEEK-ner), what is your deep gladness? What great need in the world do you believe you can fill? You could work at a job you hate that pays you well, but that is no way to live. On the other hand, you could give yourself to a work that you love but that does not provide what your family needs. If you decide to honor God with your life, He will provide what you need; you will need to decide how you want to spend your days.

You might feel pressures from some people to do what they think you ought to do, but trying to fulfill other people's dreams can be frustrating and disappointing. You should listen to your parents and to wise counsel from respected friends because they might be giving voice to God's will for you.

Nic Vujicic (pronounced Vooycheech) was born in 1982 without arms or legs. His parents were Serbian immigrants to Australia. Vujicic is a Christian who learned how to accomplish his goals in spite of his disability. He is now a husband and father who travels around the world inspiring others to overcome obstacles in their lives. Vujicic spoke at the World Economic Forum in Davos, Switzerland, in 2011.

Wise parents will consider how God has molded and equipped you. They will encourage you, and they will open doors for you; but they will not push you through a door.

How might you start? How might you receive training? What life experiences will help to make you what you can become? What price are you willing to pay now to have a more fulfilling life later? To whom should you be listening? In an earlier lesson we discussed some of the essential questions involved in starting a business. Perhaps you will spend some time working for others and then at some point launch out on your own; or perhaps you will start out on your own and then work for someone else.

You can change your mind later about what you want to do. Many people do. Some people know exactly what they want to do at the point you are in your life, but many do not. Some people think they know, but they later see God opening a different door. All of your experiences count in the process of helping you reach the goal God has for you. You can probably count on the fact that your life will not look exactly like the way you now think that it will, but that is good. God is in the business of making things better than we can ask or imagine.

You Are a Leader

Whatever you do, you will be a leader. Some people have this as a goal. They want to be a mover and shaker, they want to have an impact, they want to make a difference. Others might read this and think, "Me? No way! I just want to . . ." and then they complete the statement with their personal goal.

It doesn't matter. Whatever you do, you will be a leader. A leader is someone who influences others, and you will do that. For instance, if God gives you children, you will be a major influence in their lives. Never look past this primary opportunity and responsibility. Some people are so focused on what they want to accomplish in the business world, or the political world, or the virtual world, that they fail to see the huge impact that they will have on the world under their own roof. The world around you will have thousands of doctors and millions of computer programmers, but your children will only have you for a mommy or a daddy. Be their leader.

You might not own the company you work for, but you can be a leader in the factory or the office. You can be one of the few people who show up whenever your community needs volunteers. You can be someone who humbly shows others what it looks like to live for God. You can be an example of the best that homeschooling has to offer and thus influence the thinking of those who have questions about that educational choice.

Rest assured that others will be watching you. It might be your younger brother or sister—and it might be your younger brother or sister who sits on the Supreme Court, runs the successful local business, or builds great websites. You can be one of the influences who help to make that happen.

Impacting the Economy from Home

The decisions you make at home—whether you decide to rent or buy a home, where you decide to shop, whether you decide to save or borrow—will have an impact on the economy. Take some time to consider a home-based business. You might offer a service or perhaps raise organic produce and poultry. The Internet has opened up new possibilities for home-based businesses. A home-based business can be a great opportunity to mentor your children in the ways of the business world and to teach them responsibility and the heart of a servant.

Never doubt that the life and work of a wife and mother at home is tremendously important. Remember that the Greek word from which we get economy described someone who was the manager of a household. The English word economics used to mean the management of a home. In this sense, to impact the economy from home is to return economics to its roots.

You can make a difference. You have responsibilities and obligations. You have financial decisions to make. You have work to do, a life to live. You are an *oikonomos*, a steward of what God has given you.

In the final lesson, we will look at your first priority.

*Now as to the love of the brethren, you have no need for anyone
to write to you, for you yourselves are taught by God to love one another;
for indeed you do practice it toward all the brethren
who are in all Macedonia. But we urge you, brethren,
to excel still more, and to make it your ambition
to lead a quiet life and attend to your own business
and work with your hands, just as we commanded you,
so that you will behave properly toward outsiders
and not be in any need.
1 Thessalonians 4:9-12*

Assignments for Lesson 74

Making Choices   Read "The Wanamaker Name" (pages 204-207).

Literature   Continue reading *Mover of Men and Mountains*.

Project   Continue working on your project for this unit.

Student Review   Answer the questions for Lesson 74.

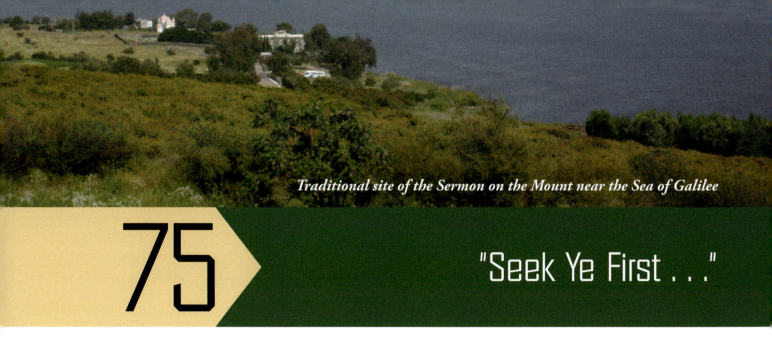

Traditional site of the Sermon on the Mount near the Sea of Galilee

75

"Seek Ye First..."

Katrin: But Mama, wouldn't you like to be rich?
Mama: I would like to be rich the way I would like to be ten feet high.
Is good for some things, bad for others.
— Dialog from the movie *I Remember Mama* (1948)

For this last lesson in economics, we are going on a field trip. It is a scene described in Matthew chapters 5, 6, and 7. We are going to a mountain in Israel in the first century. Large crowds are here. The people are mostly poor. Some are diseased and disabled. For the most part, these are not the financially successful nor the economically powerful. We passed by those types on the road as we were coming. They seem to be standing apart from the thousands of everyday people who are streaming into the area around the mountain.

In the distance, we see Jesus climbing up the mountain, followed by twelve other men. Jesus sits down, and we see that He is going to have a teaching session. We move closer because we want to hear what Jesus has to say.

He begins by telling us that some surprising people are blessed: the poor in spirit, the humble, those who hunger and thirst for righteousness, the persecuted—these are the ones whom Jesus says are blessed. He goes on to talk about a greater righteousness, one that surpasses the righteousness of the religious leaders. What He describes is a righteousness of the heart and not just outward actions, but also being right in one's thoughts, motivation, and intent. Not only is murder wrong, Jesus says; so is hatred. It's not enough to bring your sacrifice to the altar to be right with God; you need to be right with your brother before you approach the altar. Sure, adultery is wrong, He tells the crowd; but so are lustful thoughts. Don't pile up vows to try to make your words impressive; just say yes or no and mean it. It's not enough to love the people you like and the people who are similar to you; you need to love your enemies, the social outcasts, even the Gentiles. This will make you like God, since He sends rain on all people, the evil and the good. In other words, be complete: do what is right in thought as well as in action, just as God is complete and is good in His thoughts and His actions.

Having set this high standard, Jesus goes on to tell us and the rest of the crowd not to make a show of our religion. Don't give to the poor to create a media event, He says; give secretly—so secretly that your left hand doesn't even know what your right hand is doing. God will notice. Don't pray to be seen by others so that they will admire your piety; instead, pray secretly, and talk to God as your Father. He will hear you. Don't make a show of fasting so that others will be impressed by your devotion. Instead, when you fast, just go about your day as usual. God will see what you are doing.

Then Jesus talks to us about money, and stuff, and the ways that our desires for money and stuff show a lack of faith in God. So, having come all this way to hear Jesus teach, we now hear Jesus talk to us about economics. We need to listen (Matthew 6:19-34).

What Do You Want?

We've said that economics is the study of production, distribution, and consumption of goods and services. Jesus wants you to think about why you are acquiring and consuming stuff. We've talked a great deal about the value of saving. Jesus wants to know what you are saving for, and what you are storing up. Saving up and acquiring stuff just to have more stuff is futile. Stuff rusts out; it gets stolen; it becomes obsolete; it declines in value through recessions.

Jesus has a better deal. He says to store up heavenly riches. Thieves can't break into heaven. Heavenly things are never obsolete; instead, they are eternal. And there is no business cycle in heaven. The reason this talk about heaven is important is the same reason Jesus talked about hatred and lust and love. Where your treasures are shows where your heart is, and getting your heart right is the most important thing you can do.

Having the right perspective on money and stuff involves your judgment, your discernment, how you look at things. If your judgment is wrong, you won't know what is of real value and what is just temporary. What a shame to put your most valuable investment—your life—in a bank that is definitely going to fail. If you can tell the difference between light and darkness, you will know what is most important and where you should put your investments.

A worker cannot have ultimate loyalty to two bosses. You will not be able to have a part-time job with Jesus. He's very demanding; He wants an exclusive contract. But He wants this because it is best for you. He is the best person you could ever work for, and you would be miserable if you constantly tried to choose between which boss you wanted to work for on a given day, and in a given situation.

Besides, wealth makes a lousy god. It doesn't give you what it claims it can; it won't be there when you need it; and somebody else's god will always seem to be more powerful than yours. Wealth wasn't intended to be a god, so it fills the position poorly.

The first question Jesus wants you to think about is: What is your motivation for your labor? What are you trying to achieve? One way of living—putting money first—can lead to material wealth; but that is the way of spiritual poverty. The other way, putting God first, leads to spiritual wealth; and you can have that wealth regardless of how much you have in material terms.

What Are You Worrying About?

Since getting your heart right is so important, Jesus tells us not to be preoccupied with goods and services, acquisition and consumption. Life is more than acquiring and consuming. As an illustration, Jesus points to the bird economy. In the bird economy, God takes care of the production and distribution phases; and as a result the birds have all they need to consume.

Birds are terribly busy, but they do not fret. God provides everything they need. People get fretful and concerned about the markets, but all of that fretting does not do any good. Markets rise and markets fall. Most of us are price takers, but God is the ultimate price maker; and we can trust Him over the long term.

Lesson 75 - "Seek Ye First . . ."

Jesus then points out the flowers in the field. They are glorious, but their beauty is from no effort on their own part. If God takes care of the birds, and if God arrays the flowers in such splendor, can't we count on Him to provide for us? We're His children; we're made in His image. Of course He is going to take care of us. Where is your faith?

So what are you worried about? Worrying about how you are going to have the goods and services that you need is the worldly—frankly, the pagan—way of thinking. God knows what you need. He has no scarcity, He has no production costs, and He is reliable.

What Is Your First Priority?

Your first priority should be to make sure that God is your king and that His way of righteousness is your way of living. You take care of these, and God will take care of you. Be a good steward of the talents and opportunities that God gives you, and trust that God will take care of your needs in just the right way.

Many people seem to be preoccupied with what they have, what they want, what they might lose, and what others have. Caught up with those preoccupations, they seem to think that their walk with God and their spiritual growth will somehow take care of themselves. Jesus says that we need to reverse those priorities. Be preoccupied with the durable goods of God's kingdom, and trust that He will take care of all those mere consumer goods that you need day by day.

That sounds good, you might think; but there is always tomorrow. Tomorrow might bring another recession, another business cycle, other shocks, other unintended consequences. Jesus says that is no problem. God is God of tomorrow also. The same rules apply.

White-throated kingfishers in Israel

He Intends for Us to Listen and Obey

Throughout His sermon, Jesus expresses high expectations for people: "Be perfect, love your enemy, do not judge." He gives the crowd high goals: "Rejoice when you are persecuted, forgive others, and do not worry." Then Jesus ends with a challenge. He says that if we hear His words and act on them, we will be like a wise man who built his house on a firm rock; but if after listening to Him we do not act upon His words, we will be like a foolish man who built his house on uncertain sand.

Jesus does not want us just to think about His words, to be inspired by them, or to discuss how the world might be different if people actually lived this way. He expects us to act upon His words, to put them into practice, to do them. As we head home from our field trip, we discuss what an economy based on all the teachings of Jesus would look like.

Such an economy would have suppliers and consumers, markets and prices. People would make choices. Some would have absolute advantages and comparative advantages, but everyone would acknowledge God as the real supplier of every worthwhile good and service. Each person would be productive, using the talents God had given him or her to bless others. Those who oversaw others in their work would be fair, kind, understanding, and encouraging.

Those who could not work would be provided for generously and cheerfully. Some people would probably have more than others because some are more productive than others, but being rich and acquiring stuff for the sake of having stuff would not be matters of concern. People would take part in the material economy without being materialistic, learning to be happy with less.

Economic exchanges would be based on trust, truthfulness, justice, and doing what is best for the other person. People would pay taxes, but they would be more concerned about giving to God what rightfully belongs to Him. Humans would respect each other as beings created in God's image and would respect the environment as His handiwork.

People would see themselves as *oikonomoi*, stewards of the resources God places in their care, working together in an abundant economy.

But seek first His kingdom and His righteousness, and all these things will be added to you.
Matthew 6:33

Assignments for Lesson 75

Literature Finish reading *Mover of Men and Mountains*. Read the literary analysis of the book beginning on page 49 in the *Student Review* and answer the questions over the book.

Project Finish your project for this unit.

Student Review Answer the questions for Lesson 75, take the quiz for Unit 15, and take the third exam.

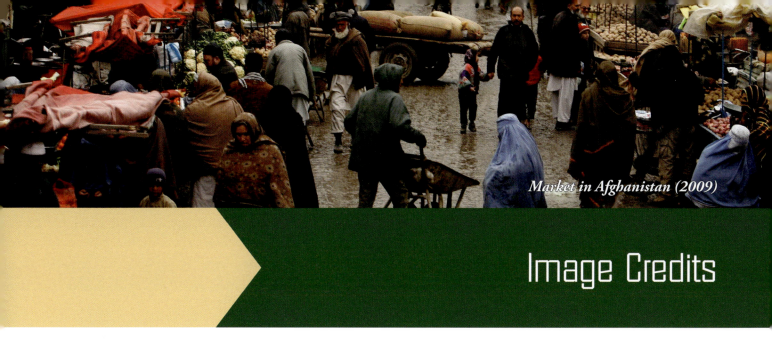

Market in Afghanistan (2009)

Image Credits

Images marked with one of these codes are used with the permission of a Creative Commons Attribution or Attribution-Share Alike License. See the websites listed for details.

CC-BY-2.0	creativecommons.org/licenses/by/2.0/
CC-BY-3.0	creativecommons.org/licenses/by/3.0/
CC-BY-4.0	creativecommons.org/licenses/by/4.0/
CC-BY-SA-2.0	creativecommons.org/licenses/by-sa/2.0/
CC-BY-SA-2.5	creativecommons.org/licenses/by-sa/2.5/
CC-BY-SA-3.0	creativecommons.org/licenses/by-sa/3.0/
CC-BY-SA-4.0	creativecommons.org/licenses/by-sa/4.0/

Charts and graphs by Nate McCurdy and John Notgrass.

i	Number1411 / Shutterstock.com
iii	Everett Historical / Shutterstock.com
v	Tricia Simpson / Wikimedia Commons / CC-BY-SA-3.0
vi	Swampyank at English Wikipedia / CC-BY-SA-3.0
ix	Fahad Faisal / Wikimedia Commons / CC-BY-SA-3.0
1	Everett Historical / Shutterstock.com
2	Wikimedia Commons
3	NorGal / Shutterstock.com
4	The Lyda Hill Texas Collection of Photographs in Carol M. Highsmith's America Project, Library of Congress, Prints and Photographs Division
6	Giovanni Vale / Shutterstock.com
9	RIA Novosti archive, image #878967 / Yuryi Abramochkin / CC-BY-SA 3.0
10	Richard Thornton / Shutterstock.com
12	Pixabay images arranged in diagram by Nate McCurdy
13	Pixabay images arranged in diagram by Nate McCurdy
14	Supertrooper / Shutterstock.com
15	revers / Shutterstock.com
17	Prasit Rodphan / Shutterstock.com
19	Pixeljoy / Shutterstock.com
20	Vacclav / Shutterstock.com
21	Charlene Notgrass
23	Gimas / Shutterstock.com
24	Library of Congress
25	Metropolitan Museum of Art (www.metmuseum.org)
26	Nikita Maykov / Shutterstock.com
28	rmnoa357 / Shutterstock.com
31	Kiev.Victor / Shutterstock.com
32	Ludwig von Mises Institute / CC-BY-SA-3.0
33	International Monetary Fund
34t	The Friedman Foundation for Educational Choice
34b	Mr. Granger / Wikimedia Commons
35	Holger Motzkau / Wikimedia Commons
37	Wikimedia Commons
39	3523studio / Shutterstock.com
41	Wikimedia Commons
42	Vadim Petrakov / Shutterstock.com
45	Protasov AN / Shutterstock.com
46	Everett - Art / Shutterstock.com
47	Andreas Praefcke / Wikimedia Commons / CC-BY-3.0
49	Wikimedia Commons
50	Wikimedia Commons
53	Oren Rozen / Wikimedia Commons / CC-BY-SA-4.0 (cropped)
54	Wikimedia Commons
55	Wikimedia Commons
57	Renata Sedmakova / Shutterstock.com
58	Chavdar / Shutterstock.com
59	Wikimedia Commons
60	Wikimedia Commons
61	Mefusbren69 / Wikimedia Commons
63	Chief Mass Communication Specialist Steve Carlson / U.S. Navy
65	Wikimedia Commons

Image Credits

66	Wikimedia Commons
67	cpaulfell / Shutterstock.com
69	jorisvo / Shutterstock.com
70	Wikimedia Commons
71	Wikimedia Commons
73	Library of Congress
75	Matyas Rehak / Shutterstock.com
77	Cylonphoto / Shutterstock.com
78	James R. Martin / Shutterstock.com
79	Elena Mirage / Shutterstock.com
81	Ken Wolter / Shutterstock.com
82	Wikimedia Commons
83	Library of Congress
84	Library of Congress
85	Carol M. Highsmith Archive, Library of Congress, Prints and Photographs Division
87	Everett Historical / Shutterstock.com
88	NYPL Digital Gallery
89	BeeRu / Shutterstock.com
90	Wikimedia Commons
91	Library of Congress
92	Daniel M. Silva / Shutterstock.com
93	National Numismatic Collection at the Smithsonian Institution
95	Rfj0906 / Wikimedia Commons
96l	Library of Congress
97	National Numismatic Collection at the Smithsonian Institution
98	new york public library
99	Dan Logan / Shutterstock.com
101	Architect of the Capitol
102	Library of Congress
103	Everett Historical / Shutterstock.com
104	Everett Historical / Shutterstock.com
106	Library of Congress
107	Library of Congress
108	Library of Congress
109	Library of Congress
110	Carol M. Highsmith Archive, Library of Congress, Prints and Photographs Division
110	Library of Congress
112	NARA
113	Library of Congress
114	Evan-Amos / Wikimedia Commons
115	bfishadow / Flickr / CC-BY-2.0
117	Rawpixel.com / Shutterstock.com
119	Pixfiction / Shutterstock.com
121	Settawat Udom / Shutterstock.com
123	GoodMood Photo / Shutterstock.com
124	Steven Vaughn, Agricultural Research Service / USDA
125	morisius cosmonaut / Flickr / CC-BY-2.0
126	StockStudio / Shutterstock.com
127	John Wollwerth / Shutterstock.com
129	Marc Bruxelle / Shutterstock.com
131	asharkyu / Shutterstock.com
132	Library of Congress
133	Amazon.com
135	Denis Linine / Shutterstock.com
136	seyephoto / Shutterstock.com
137	Cyiomarsina / Wikimedia Commons / CC-BY-SA-3.0
138	Library of Congress
139	Library of Congress
141	Scott Catron / Wikimedia Commons / CC-BY-SA-2.0
142	Attila JANDI / Shutterstock.com
144	LBJ Library
145	Marco Verch / Flickr / CC-BY-2.0
147	Matej Kastelic / Shutterstock.com
149	nborun / Flickr / CC-BY-2.0
150	DJ Mattaar / Shutterstock.com
151	Barry Blackburn / Shutterstock.com
152	Visitor7 / Wikimedia Commons / CC-BY-SA-3.0
154	Library of Congress
156	ValeStock / Shutterstock.com
158	OnlyZoia / Shutterstock.com
161l	US Army
161r	knyazevfoto / Shutterstock.com
162	Matyas Rehak / Shutterstock.com
164	Mark Turnauckas / Flickr / CC-BY-2.0
165	Teddy Leung / Shutterstock.com
166	User Bobak on en.wikipedia / CC-BY-SA-2.5
167	Patryk Kosmider / Shutterstock.com
169	Dragan Jovanovic / Shutterstock.com
171	Library of Congress
172	Htm / Wikimedia Commons / CC-BY-SA-3.0
175	iggy7117 / Pixabay
176	Karl Baron / Flickr / CC-BY-2.0
177	Florida Keys--Public Libraries / Flickr / CC-BY-2.0
179	OlegDoroshin / Shutterstock.com
180	Radu Bercan / Shutterstock.com
183	Frank J. Aleksandrowicz / EPA
184	Scott Edelman / US State Department
185	Mon Œil / Flickr / CC-BY-2.0
187	Library of Congress
189	Mikhail (Vokabre) Shcherbakov / Flickr / CC-BY-SA-2.0
190	User World Imaging / Wikimedia Commons
191	Popolon / Wikimedia Commons / CC-BY-SA-40
192	U.S. Government Printing Office
193	Boston Public Library
194	Targaryen / Wikimedia Commons / CC-BY-SA-3.0
196	Everett Historical / Shutterstock.com
197	Andrew Filer / Flickr / CC-BY-SA-2.0

Image Credits

198	Matthew G. Bisanz / Wikimedia Commons / CC-BY-SA-3.0
199	official-ly cool / Wikimedia Commons / CC-BY-SA-3.0
200	British Library
201	U.S. Department of the Treasury
203	larry1235 / Shutterstock.com
205	Downingsf / Wikimedia Commons / CC-BY-SA-3.0
206	OkFoto / Shutterstock.com
210	Everett Historical / Shutterstock.com
212	Library of Congress
214	James R. Martin / Shutterstock.com
216	Library of Congress
217	Nate McCurdy
218	Xnatedawgx / Wikimedia Commons / CC-BY-SA-4.0 (cropped)
219	Farragutful / Wikimedia Commons / CC-BY-SA-3.0
220	Federalreserve / Flickr / CC-BY-2.0
221	Justin Ruckman / Flickr / CC-BY-2.0
223	leungchopan / Shutterstock.com
225	Sheila Fitzgerald / Shutterstock.com
226	Port of San Diego / Flickr / CC-BY-2.0
228	AHMAD FAIZAL YAHYA / Shutterstock.com
231	Library of Congress
232	Library of Congress
233	Siyuwj / Wikimedia Commons / CC-BY-SA-3.0
234	rijans / Flickr / CC-BY-SA-2.0
235	Sesamehoneytart / Wikimedia Commons / CC-BY-SA-40 (rotated, cropped)
237	oksana.perkins / Shutterstock.com
238	Neil Ballantyne / Flickr / CC-BY-2.0
241	User Saforrest / Wikimedia Commons / CC-BY-SA-3.0
243	James R. Martin / Shutterstock.com
244	Sean Pavone / Shutterstock.com
245	Kelvinsong / Wikimedia Commons / CC-BY-3.0
247	Mike Gonzalez (TheCoffee) / Wikimedia Commons / CC-BY-SA-3.0
248	Cory Doctorow / Flickr / CC-BY-SA-2.0
249	Library of Congress
251	Pavel Bobrovskiy / Shutterstock.com
252	Alastair Wallace / Shutterstock.com
254	Hans Dinkelberg / Flickr / CC-BY-2.0
255	testing / Shutterstock.com
257	Jeffrey Beall / Wikimedia Commons / CC-BY-3.0
259	Walmart / Flickr / CC-BY-2.0
261	Jared / Flickr / CC-BY-2.0
263	Pete Souza / White House Photo
265	Donna Beeler / Shutterstock.com
266	Roman Boed / Flickr / CC-BY-2.0
267	Ruth Peterkin / Shutterstock.com
269	disq / Shutterstock.com
270	Erlo Brown / Shutterstock.com
271	Marcel Mooij / Shutterstock.com
272	Africa Studio / Shutterstock.com
273	Syda Productions / Shutterstock.com
274	Alliance / Shutterstock.com
275	kanchana_koyjai / Shutterstock.com
275	FLariviere / Shutterstock.com
277	antoniodiaz / Shutterstock.com
282	zhangyang13576997233 / Shutterstock.com
283	Patrickklida / Wikimedia Commons / CC-BY-3.0
284	EPA
285	Edwin Verin / Shutterstock.com
287	Joe Mabel / Wikimedia Commons / CC-BY-SA-3.0
289	Everett Historical / Shutterstock.com
291	USDA / Flickr / CC-BY-2.0
293	David Litman / Shutterstock.com
294	Arina P Habich / Shutterstock.com
295	Krista Kennell / Shutterstock.com
297	Library of Congress
299	Library of Congress
300	Everett Historical / Shutterstock.com
301	Atomazul / Shutterstock.com
302	EPA
303	Library of Congress
305	Library of Congress
309	Sorbis / Shutterstock.com
311	Dan Holm / Shutterstock.com
313	Everett Historical / Shutterstock.com
314	Michael Raphael / FEMA
315	Bart Everson / Flickr / CC-BY-2.0
317	Library of Congress
319	US Department of Labor
320	U. S. Securities and Exchange Commission
321	Congressional Budget Office
323	National Highway Traffic Safety Administration
325	Amanda Bicknell / FEMA
327	DrTorstenHenning / Wikimedia Commons
328	NARA
329	LBJ Library
331	Buffalutheran / Wikimedia Commons
332	U.S. Food and Drug Administration
333	Classic Colors / Flickr / CC-BY-SA-2.0
334	Executive Office of the President of the United States
337	Michael Rivera / Wikimedia Commons / CC-BY-SA-3.0
338	Everett Historical / Shutterstock.com
339	Library of Congress
341	Fibonacci Blue / Flickr / CC-BY-2.0
342	Everett Historical / Shutterstock.com
344	Erin A. Kirk-Cuomo / Department of Defense

345	Chris Smith / U.S. Department of Health & Human Services	413	Library of Congress
349	Ron Cogswell / Flickr / CC-BY-2.0	414	Library of Congress
351	Analia Bertucci (USDA NRCS) / Flickr / CC-BY-2.0	415	Carol M. Highsmith Archive, Library of Congress, Prints and Photographs Division
352	saiko3p / Shutterstock.com	416	USDA / Flickr / CC-BY-2.0
354	Fitria Ramli / Shutterstock.com	416	ilovebutter / Flickr / CC-BY-2.0
356	Robert Kash / Flickr / CC-BY-2.0	418	Carol M. Highsmith's America, Library of Congress, Prints and Photographs Division
361	Alf Ribeiro / Shutterstock.com	419	NARA
362l	Everett Historical / Shutterstock.com	421	Jmcdaid / Wikimedia Commons / CC-BY-SA-3.0
362r	lev radin / Shutterstock.com	422	testing / Shutterstock.com
365	Joseph Sohm / Shutterstock.com	423	Oxfam East Africa / Flickr / CC-BY-2.0
367	Dave Newman / Shutterstock.com	425	bikeriderlondon / Shutterstock.com
369	Everett Historical / Shutterstock.com	426	Agnes Kantaruk / Shutterstock.com
371t	Library of Congress	428	UrbanPromise / Flickr / CC-BY-2.0
371b	Social Security Administration	430	Everett Historical / Shutterstock.com
374	KOMUnews / Flickr / CC-BY-2.0	431	Everett Historical / Shutterstock.com
376	davitydave / Flickr / CC-BY-2.0	432	Everett Historical / Shutterstock.com
379	David Berry / Flickr / CC-BY-2.0	433	Everett Historical / Shutterstock.com
381	diaper / Flickr / CC-BY-2.0	434	NARA
382	Library of Congress	435	David Shankbone / Wikimedia Commons / CC-BY-SA-3.0
385	txking / Shutterstock.com	437	A.Davey / Flickr / CC-BY-2.0
388	Carol M. Highsmith Archive, Library of Congress, Prints and Photographs Division	438	Fibonacci Blue / Flickr / CC-BY-2.0
389	FDR Presidential Library and Museum	439	Jim.henderson / Wikimedia Commons
390	Carol M. Highsmith Archive, Library of Congress, Prints and Photographs Division	441	Rawpixel.com / Shutterstock.com
391	Photographs in the Carol M. Highsmith Archive, Library of Congress, Prints and Photographs Division	443	Henrik Winther Andersen / Shutterstock.com (modified by Nate McCurdy)
393	U.S. Department of Energy	445	Bob McElroy (USAG Brussels) / U.S. Army / Flickr / CC-BY-2.0
395	shannonpatrick17 / Flickr / CC-BY-2.0	447	vetre / Shutterstock.com
396	The Photographer / Wikimedia Commons	448	Ashton B Crew Photo taken for www.randomiowa.com
397	Entergy Nuclear - Nuclear Regulatory Commission	451	Wikimedia Commons
398	Xklaim / Wikimedia Commons / CC-BY-SA-3.0	452	Daxiao Productions / Shutterstock.com
400	EPA / NARA	455	Rawpixel.com / Shutterstock.com
401	John Lloyd / Flickr / CC-BY-2.0	456	Photo by Sebastian Derungs Copyright World Economic Forum / Flickr / CC-BY-SA-2.0
402	Ken Lund / Flickr / CC-BY-SA-2.0	457	Uber Images / Shutterstock.com
403	TheDigitel / Flickr / CC-BY-2.0	459	gugganij / Wikimedia Commons / CC-BY-SA-3.0
405	Jeramey Jannene / Flickr / CC-BY-2.0	461	Vladimir Kogan Michael / Shutterstock.com
407	Library of Congress	463	Staff Sgt. Russell Lee Klika / US Army National Guard
408	Tim Roberts Photography / Shutterstock.com	467	Dracaena / Wikimedia Commons / CC-BY-SA-3.0
411	Gates Frontiers Fund Colorado Collection within the Carol M. Highsmith Archive, Library of Congress, Prints and Photographs Division	471	Lane V. Erickson / Shutterstock.com

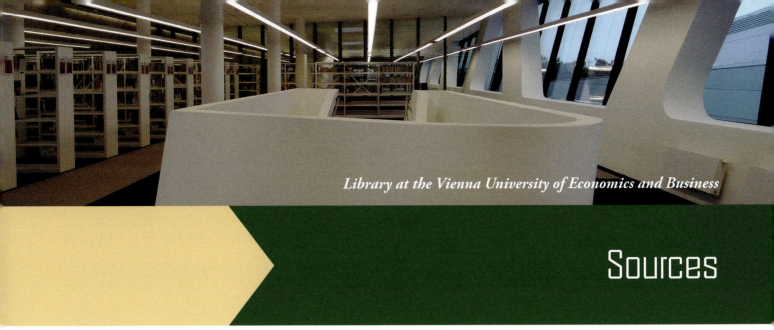
Library at the Vienna University of Economics and Business

Sources

The following sources provided general information. The lesson notes indicate when a lesson cites a specific quotation, fact, or perspective from a source.

Bookbinder, Steve and Lynne Einleger. *The Dictionary of the Global Economy.* New York: Franklin Watts (Scholastic, 2001).

Church History magazine, Vol. 6 No. 2 and Vol. 7 No. 3 (two issues devoted to the topic of Money in Christian History).

Friedman, Milton and Rose Friedman. *Free to Choose: A Personal Statement.* (New York: Harcourt, Brace, Jovanovich, 1980).

Hailstones, Thomas J. *Basic Economics.* Third edition. (Cincinnati: South-Western Publishing Company, 1968).

High School Economics Web-Based Curriculum. Center for Economics and Personal Finance Education, College of Business, New Mexico State University. http://cepfe.nmsu.edu.

Mankiw, N. Gregory. *Principles of Economics.* (Fort Worth: The Dryden Press, 1998. Seventh edition, 2014).

Rima, Ingrid. "Economics." *Academic American Encyclopedia.* (Danbury: Grolier, 1989. Volume 7), pages 47-51.

Sowell, Thomas. *Basic Economics: A Citizen's Guide to the Economy.* (New York: Basic Books, 2000. Fifth edition, 2015).

Other books that are worth reading include:

Clark, Anthony. *Economics Through Everyday Life.* Berkeley, CA: Zephyros Press, 2016.

Hazlitt, Henry. *Economics in One Lesson.* New York: Harper and Brothers, 1946, 1962, and 1979.

Sowell, Thomas. *Applied Economics: Thinking Beyond Stage One*, revised and enlarged edition. New York: Basic Books, 2009.

---. *Economic Facts and Fallacies.* New York: Basic Books, second edition, 2011.

---. *The Housing Boom and Bust.* New York: Basic Books, revised edition, 2010.

---. *Wealth, Poverty and Politics: An International Perspective.* New York: Basic Books, 2015.

Two Internet sources that provide excellent information are the Library of Economics and Liberty (econlib.org) and the Foundation for Economic Education (fee.org). Other Internet sites, especially websites of government agencies, can be good sources of information; but you should consult them carefully. We make no guarantees about the reliability or propriety of everything on all the websites cited in this work or of the links posted on those websites to other sites. Visit our website for updated links and information: notgrass.com/ee

Lesson 4

Reports on polls about capitalism and socialism:

http://www.gallup.com/poll/191354/americans-views-socialism-capitalism-little-changed.aspx

http://iop.harvard.edu/youth-poll/harvard-iop-spring-2016-poll

Lesson 22

The idea of the limited versus the unlimited pie is taken from Stephen Covey, *The Seven Habits of Highly Effective People* (New York: Simon and Schuster, 1990), pages 219-220

Lesson 24
Christopher Leonard, "College Grads Avoiding Brunt of Layoffs," Cookeville (TN) *Herald-Citizen*, January 12, 2009, page A-5

Lesson 26
Sowell, *Basic Economics: A Citizen's Guide to the Economy*, p. 308

Lesson 28
Mankiw, *Principles of Economics*, pp. 323-330
Sowell, pp. 33-38

Lesson 29
Sowell, pp. 59-60

Lesson 30
Mankiw, p. 10

Lesson 34
Friedman, *Free to Choose: A Personal Statement*, p. 254

Lesson 38
Mankiw, p. 191

Lesson 39
Department of the Treasury and Federal Reserve Board, "Major Foreign Holders of Treasury Securities," http://www.treas.gov/tic/mfh.txt

Lesson 42
"Small Business in the United States," http://economics.about.com
Small Business Administration, "Frequently Asked Questions," http://web.sba.gov/faqs

Lesson 42
This lesson includes statistics from the Small Business Administration.

Lesson 44
Illustration adapted from one used in the online curriculum provided by New Mexico State University (NMSU) College of Business, http://cepfe.nmsu.edu
Mankiw, pp. 272-274

Lesson 48
Morgan O. Reynolds, "Labor Unions," The Concise Encyclopedia of Economics, http://www.econlib.org/library/Enc/LaborUnions.html
Sowell, pp. 162-165

Lesson 49
Scott A. Hodge, "Tax Burden of Top 1% Now Exceeds That of Bottom 95%," http://www.taxfoundation.org/blog/show/24944.html, July 29, 2009, retrieved July 30, 2009
Sowell, p. 168
NMSU Curriculum, Chapter 15, Lesson 4
David Neumark, "Delay the Minimum-Wage Hike", *The Wall Street Journal Online*, http://online.wsj.com/article/SB124476823767508619.html, retrieved June 12, 2009
Median pay rates are from the Occupational Outlook Handbook, Bureau of Labor Statistics, U.S. Department of Labor, www.bls.gov
Information on Household Income Quintiles is from the Tax Policy Center, taxpolicycenter.org, January 28, 2016; accessed September 1, 2016
"Top 20% of Earners Pay 84% of Income Tax," Laura Saunders, *Wall Street Journal*, www.wsj.com, April 10, 2015, accessed September 4, 2016.
Drew Desilver, "Who Makes Minimum Wage?", Pew Research Center, www.pewresearch.org, September 8, 2014; accessed September 4, 2016

Lesson 50
U.S. Bureau of Labor Statistics, "Unemployed persons by duration of unemployment," http://www.bls.gov/news.release/empsit.t12.htm, September 2, 2016, accessed September 5, 2016

Lesson 52
Food and Nutrition Service, U.S. Department of Agriculture, http://www.fns.usda.gov/pd/supplemental-nutrition-assistance-program-snap, July 8, 2016, retrieved September 7, 2016.

Lesson 54
Roberton Williams, "The Numbers: What are the federal government's sources of revenue?", http://www.taxpolicycenter.org/briefing-book/background/numbers/revenue.cfm, retrieved September 22, 2009
"State and Local General Revenue by Source, Percentage Distribution," Tax Policy Center, www.taxpolicycenter.org, June 20, 2016, retrieved September 8, 2016

Sources

Lesson 55

Center on Budget and Policy Priorities, "Policy Basics: Where Do Our Federal Tax Dollars Go?", http://www.cbpp.org/cms/index.cfm?fa=view&id=1258

Economic Report of the President 2009, http://www.gpoaccess.gov/eop/tables09.html

U.S. Treasury, http://www.treasurydirect.gov/NP/BPDLogin?application=np

James Buchanan, "The Deficit and Our Obligation to Future Generations," *Imprimis*, January 1987, www.hillsdale.edu

Gregory Mankiw, "Bernanke and the Beast," *New York Times*, January 17, 2010

Lesson 56

CIA World Factbook, https://www.cia.gov/library/publications/the-world-factbook/

Lesson 57

"Relative Importance of Components in the Consumer Price Indexes," U.S. City Average, December 2015," Bureau of Labor Statistics, http://www.bls.gov/cpi/usri_2015.txt, retrieved September 9, 2016.

Zachary Karabell, "How Bad Is It, Really?", *Newsweek*, February 16, 2009, p. 30

Conference Board, www.conferenceboard.org/about/index.cfm?id=1980, retrieved September 9, 2016)

Lesson 58

Sowell, pp. 178-182

Ezra Klein, "Wall Street Isn't the Economy," *Los Angeles Times*, September 9, 2007, http://www.latimes.com/news/opinion/la-op-klein9sep09,0,1250969.story, retrieved September 29, 2009

Lesson 59

National Bureau of Economic Research, "Business Cycle Expansions and Contractions," http://www.nber.org/cycles.html, retrieved September 9, 2009

National Bureau of Economic Research, "Determination of the December 2007 Peak in Economic Activity," http://www.nber.org/cycles/dec2008.html, December 1, 2008; retrieved September 30, 2009

Lesson 60

Thomas Sowell, "Random Thoughts," syndicated column, May 27, 2014, https://www.creators.com/read/thomas-sowell/05/14/random-thoughts-d667c

Robert Rector, "How Poor Are America's Poor? Examining the 'Plague' of Poverty in America," http://www.heritage.org/Research/Welfare/bg2064.cfm, August 27, 2007, retrieved September 30, 2009

Kerby Anderson, "Wealth and Poverty," http://www.leaderu.com/orgs/probe/docs/poverty.html, August 5, 2003, retrieved September 30, 2009

Sowell, p. 168

"The Week," *National Review*, November 2, 2015

Deirdre N. McCloskey, "How the West (and the Rest) Got Rich," http://www.wsj.com/articles/why-the-west-and-the-rest-got-rich-1463754427, *Wall Street Journal*, May 20, 2016, retrieved May 22, 2016

Thomas Sowell, *Wealth, Poverty and Politics: An International Perspective.*

Lesson 61

"2016 Milliman Medical Index," www.milliman.com/mmi/, May 24, 2016, retrieved September 19, 2016.

David Goldhill, "How American Health Care Killed My Father," http://www.theatlantic.com/doc/200909/health-care, September 2009

Jim Kuhnhenn, "Health Care Issues: Preventive Measures," http://news.yahoo.com/s/ap/20091203/ap_on_go_co/us_health_care_briefing_3, September 28, 2009

N. Gregory Mankiw, "Beyond Those Health Care Numbers," http://www.nytimes.com/2007/11/04/business/04view.html, November 4, 2007

Robert J. Samuelson, "Getting Real about Health Care," *Newsweek*, September 15, 2008, p. 73

Lesson 62

Jeffrey S. Flier, "Health care reform: without a correct diagnosis, there is no cure," http://www.jci.org/articles/view/41033, September 10, 2009

Alan Greenspan, "Future of the Social Security program and economics of retirement," Testimony before the U.S. Senate Special Committee on Aging, March 15, 2005, http://www.federalreserve.gov/boarddocs/testimony/2005/20050315/

"Medicare," *New York Times*, http://topics.nytimes.com/top/news/healthdiseasesconditionsandhealthtopics/medicare/index.html, September 25, 2009

Robert Samuelson, "Obama's Health Care Will Make It Worse," http://www.realclearpolitics.com/articles/2009/08/10/obamas_health_care_will_make_it_worse.html, August 10, 2009

Thomas R. Saving, "Social Security," The Concise Encyclopedia of Economics, Library of Economics and Liberty, http://www.econlib.org/library/Enc/SocialSecurity.html

Meena Thiruvengada, "Medicare, Social Security Trusts Dwindling Faster Than Expected," Dow Jones Newswires, www.dowjones.com, May 12, 2009

Lesson 63

U.S. Energy Information Administration. "What is U.S. electricity generation by energy source?" www.eia.gov, April 1, 2016; retrieved September 21, 2016)

Prices for the week of September 26, 2016, retrieved October 3, 2016. http://www.globalpetrolprices.com/gasoline_prices/

Kevin Bonsor and Ed Grabianowski, "How Gas Prices Work," http://auto.howstuffworks.com/fuel-efficiency/fuel-consumption/gas-price.htm

Daren Briscoe, "Obama's Nuclear Reservations," *Newsweek*, December 1, 2008, p. 48

Robert J. Samuelson, "Let's Shoot the Speculators!" *Newsweek*, July 7-14, 2008, p. 18, and

"The Bias Against Oil and Gas," *Newsweek*, May 18, 2009, p. 46

William Tucker, "The Case for Terrestrial (a.k.a. Nuclear) Energy," *Imprimis*, February 2008, https://imprimis.hillsdale.edu/the-case-for-terrestrial-aka-nuclear-energy/

Lesson 64

"Automotive Industry: Employment, Earnings, and Hours," http://www.bls.gov/iag/tgs/iagauto.htm, retrieved October 10, 2009

Kendra Marr, "Toyota Passes General Motors as World's Largest Carmaker," *The Washington Post*, January 22, 2009, http://www.washingtonpost.com/wp-dyn/content/article/2009/01/21/AR2009012101216.html, retrieved October 4, 2009

U.S. Census Bureau, "Facts for Features: Model T Centennial," August 7, 2008, http://www.census.gov/Press-Release/www/releases/archives/facts_for_features_special_editions/012439.html, retrieved October 10, 2009

Bureau of Transportation Statistics, "New and Used Passenger Car Sales and Leases," http://www.bts.gov/publications/national_transportation_statistics/html/table_01_17.html, Retrieved October 5, 2009

U.S. Department of Commerce International Trade Administration, "The Road Ahead: An Assessment of the U.S. Motor Vehicle Industry," April 2009, http://trade.gov/wcm/groups/public/@trade/@mas/@man/@aai/documents/web_content/auto_report_roadahead09.pdf, retrieved October 10, 2009

Lesson 66

2016 World Almanac. (New York: Infobase Learning, 2016)

Steven Rattner, "The Great Corn Con," *The New York Times*, June 24, 2011, http://www.nytimes.com/2011/06/25/opinion/25Rattner.html, retrieved June 27, 2011

Dina Cappiello and Matt Apuzzo, "The secret, dirty cost of Obama's green power push," NBC News, November 12, 2013, http://www.nbcnews.com/business/secret-dirty-cost-obamas-green-power-push-2d11577495, retrieved November 12, 2013.

"American Agriculture: Its Changing Significance," http://economics.about.com/od/americanagriculture/, retrieved October 11, 2009

Lesson 67

"Environment and the Economy: A Curriculum from the Foundation for Teaching Economics," http://www.fte.org/teachers/programs/environment/curriculum/, Copyright 2005; retrieved October 12, 2009

Martin Feldstein, "Cap-and-Trade: All Cost, No Benefit," *The Washington Post*, June 1, 2009, http://www.washingtonpost.com/wp-dyn/content/article/2009/05/31/AR2009053102077.html, retrieved October 13, 2009

N. Gregory Mankiw, "A Missed Opportunity on Climate Change," *New York Times*, http://www.nytimes.com/2009/08/09/business/economy/09view.html, August 8, 2009; retrieved October 13, 2009

Lesson 69

Burton W. Folsom Jr., "Do We Need a New New Deal?" *Imprimis*, January 2009, https://imprimis.hillsdale.edu/do-we-need-a-new-new-deal/

Gene Smiley, "Great Depression," The Concise Encyclopedia of Economics, Library of Economics and Liberty, http://www.econlib.org/library/Enc/GreatDepression.html, retrieved October 14, 2009

Lesson 70

"Credit Crisis—The Essentials," New York Times, http://topics.nytimes.com/top/reference/timestopics/subjects/c/credit_crisis/index.html, September 22, 2009

Matthew Philips, "The Monster That Ate Wall Street," *Newsweek*, October 6, 2008, p. 46

Index

A
- Absolute advantage, 229-230
- Accounting profit, 276
- Afghanistan, 354, 463
- Aggregate demand, 32, 163, 212, 214, 284, 290, 314, 345
- Aggregate supply, 163, 173, 212, 284
- Agriculture, 90, 97, 314, 321-322, 335, 411, 413-417, 431
- Alabama, 154
- Alaska, 267, 372, 397, 420
- American International Group (AIG), 219, 437-438
- Americans with Disabilities Act, 333-334
- Amtrak, 10, 323, 337
- Arbitrage, 254
- Arizona, 248, 408
- Arkansas, 166, 259, 262
- Articles of Confederation, 92-94
- Austrian School of Economics, 31-32, 284, 314
- Automotive industry, 107, 166, 300, 333, 400-404
- Average marginal cost, 279

B
- Bangladesh, ix, 234
- Bank of the United States, 95, 97, 102-103
- Banking industry, 97-98, 102-105, 107, 109-110, 196-208, 210, 348, 406-409, 431-432, 437-438, see also Federal Reserve
- Bankruptcy, 95, 109-110, 219, 383, 401, 437, 453-454
- Barter, 15-16, 190
- Belgium, 27, 239, 244
- Belize, 21
- Blue collar, 293-295, 300
- Bonds, 93, 96-97, 106, 109, 203-208, 221, 244
- Boycott, 78, 153, 154

- Brazil, 233, 244, 352, 354, 361
- Budget (personal), 137, 357, 452-453
- Budget, Federal, 115 143-144, 321-322, 344-348
- Bush, George H. W., 32, 114-115, 334
- Bush, George W., 35, 115, 346
- Business cycle, 102, 143, 282-286, 367-368, 430

C
- California, 10, 105, 225-226, 245, 262, 291, 293, 311, 314, 325, 403
- Canada, 92, 115, 129, 156, 230, 239-241, 352, 354, 361, 395-396, 409, 428
- Cap-and-trade policy, 421-422
- Capital account (trade), 245
- Capital gains, 207-208, 409
- Capital goods, 7, 150, 270, 358, 427, 431
- Capitalist/capitalism, 9-10, 23-30, 73-75, 154, 179, see also Free market
- Cartel, 153, 302, 395
- Central bank, 19, 110, 216-222, 255
- Chicago School of Economics, 34-35
- Child labor, 83, 297, 305
- China, 10, 17, 172, 191, 223, 225, 229, 233, 239, 244-246, 248, 255-256, 353-354, 395-396, 403, 415, 422-423
- Chrysler, 400-403, 438
- Circular-flow diagram, 12-13
- Civil War, United States, 73, 106-109, 413
- Coal, 83, 107, 232, 302-303, 393-394, 418
- Coincident economic indicators, 358
- Collusion, 153
- Colorado, 247, 294, 356, 435
- Columbus, Christopher, 89
- Command economy, 9-11, 141-143, 153, 155, 184-185

471

Commodity exchanges, 364-365
Commodity money, 191
Communism, 27-30, 65, 184-185, 225, 254
Communist Manifesto, 27
Comparative advantage, 12, 229-230, 246
Competition, 24-25, 141, 152-155, 165, 179-184, 231-232, 270-271, 333, 392
Complementary goods, 158, 403
Connecticut, 262, 351
Constitution of the United States, 95-96, 146
Consumer choice theory, 137
Consumer goods, 150-151, 229, 358
Consumer Price Index, 209, 356-357, 359
Consumer spending, 283, 359
Consumption, 7, 129, 135-136, 161, 340
Corporation (business structure), 172, 204, 262-263
Cost-benefit analysis, 125-127, 139, 246, 398, 453
Council of Economic Advisors, 35, 322
Credit, 54, 95, 97, 102-103, 196, 199, 207, 284, 358-359, 436-438, 453
Credit cards, 112, 125, 195, 199, 252
Credit default swap, 437
Credit rating, 201
Credit union, 199, 218
Croatia, 6
Cross-price elasticity of demand, 176
Current account (trade), 245

D *Das Kapital*, 27
Deadweight loss, 280
Debt financing, 205
Debt, 43, 53-54, 93, 95, 102-104, 109, 125, 199-201, 203-205, 207, 260, 273, 407-409, 435-438, 452-454
Debt, Federal (national), *see* National debt
Deficit, Federal, 32-33, 110, 113, 115, 211, 325, 342, 344-348, 432, 435, 438
Deflation, 174, 211-212, 220
Delaware, 381
Demand curve (graph), 159-160, 174, 177, 290
Demand, law of, 7, 14-15, 41, 47, 150, 156-170, 173-185, 200, 204, 212-215, 251-254, 290-291, 306, 386, 395, 403
Depression, *see* Great Depression and Recession
Deregulation, 199, 333
Determinants of demand, 158
Determinants of supply, 156
Diamond-water paradox, 168-170
Diminishing marginal utility, 137-138
Discount rate, Federal, 220-221

Discrimination in work force, 80, 297-298, 374
Discrimination, price, *see* Price discrimination
Disincentive, 136, 156, 384
Disposable income, 156, 163, 359
Distribution of goods and services, 7, 123, 129, 133, 149-151
Distribution of income, 306-308, 328-330, 372
Dow Jones Industrial Average (DJIA), 362-363, 438
Durable goods, 150-151, 359

E Economic goals of government, 141-146
Economic profit, 276
Economy of scale, 132-133
Economy of scope, 133
Elasticity, 175-177
Energy, 107, 326, 393-399, 403, 416, 420-421
Entrepreneur, 98, 155, 171, 180, 227, 265-274, 375, 400, 428
Environment, 19, 80, 132, 144, 325-326, 333, 347, 396-397, 416, 418-424, 449
Equilibrium interest rate, 203
Equilibrium labor wage, 290, 302, 311-312, 314
Equilibrium price, 160, 164, 168, 174, 182, 235-236, 240-241, 280, 332, 337, 386
Equity financing, 205
Ethanol, 123-124, 150, 326, 416
Ethiopia, 127, 423
Exchange rate, currency, 192, 251-256, 353-354
Externalities, 19, 183-184, 341, 416

F Factors of production, 129-130, 173, 276
Fair trade, 240-241
Fannie Mae, 262, 323, 408-409, 436-437, 440
Federal Deposit Insurance Corporation (FDIC), 198, 432, 438
Federal funds rate, 202, 220-221
Federal Open Market Committee, 217, 220-221, 253
Federal Reserve System (Fed), 35, 105, 110, 211, 215-222, 253, 320, 348, 430-432, 436-439
Fiat currency, 191-194
Finland, 172
Fiscal policy, 320-321
Florida, 177, 337
Ford Motor Company, 262, 400-403
Ford, Gerald, 113, 192
Ford, Henry, 107, 166, 259, 275
Fracking, 397
Fractional reserve banking, 198, 200, 431
France/French, 24-25, 50, 89, 91, 101, 161, 192, 239, 267, 296, 327, 352, 397

Index

Freddie Mac, 323, 408-409, 436-437
Free market, 9-10, 24, 29, 31, 35, 84, 116, 149-151, 159, 180, 237, 259, 275, 311, 319, 324, 326, 332, 335, 386-387, 447, *see also* Capitalist/capitalism
Friedman, Milton, 34-35, 211, 237, 284, 325, 435
Full employment, 314-315
Futures, 206, 364-365

G Galbraith, John Kenneth, 439
General Agreement on Tariffs and Trade (GATT), 33, 238
General Motors (GM), 262, 283, 400-403, 438
Georgia, 33, 99, 261, 413
Germany, 19, 32, 47 110, 210, 221, 239, 244, 252, 254, 261, 327, 352, 354, 400
Gibbons v. Ogden, 103
Gini coefficient, 372
Gold standard, 191-193, 430
Government regulation, 18-19, 25, 31, 35, 108, 183-184, 240, 260, 290, 319-324, 331-336, 341, 386, 396-397, 403, 419-422, 439-440
Great Depression, 35, 84, 110-111, 197, 212, 219, 238, 342, 369, 430-434
Great Recession (2007-2009), 8, 29, 85, 139, 348, 390, 401, 403-404, 435-440
Greed, 43, 69-71, 82-86, 116, 281, 361, 378, 435-436, 440
Gross domestic product (GDP), 21, 112, 266, 282-283, 347, 351-358, 367-369, 381, 400, 425, 432

H Hamilton, Alexander, 95-98, 238
Hawaii, 20, 372, 398
Hayek, Friedrich, 33, 377
Health care, 144, 149, 328, 341, 381-387, 391-392
Hedge fund, 207
Hegel, George F. W., 26
Home mortgage, *see* Mortgage
Home sales, 21, 359, 405
Homeownership, 107, 122, 405-410, 436-438
Human resources, 130
Honduras, 226, 230, 254, 428
Hong Kong, 137, 165, 223, 239, 244, 396

I Idaho, 393, 437
Illinois, 34, 262, 301, 364-365
Immigration, 290, 296-297, 352, 427
Imperfect competition, 152, 179-185
Incentive, 18, 114, 135-136, 139, 144, 156, 167-168, 200, 207, 285, 290-291, 330, 392, 403, 422

Income distribution by quintiles, *see* Distribution of income
Income elasticity of demand, 176-177
Income redistribution, 145, 319, 328-330, 375, 388
India, 149, 161, 190, 239, 241, 244, 246, 352, 354, 415, 422
Indiana, 164, 305
Inflation, 113, 209-215, 356-357
Insurance, 198-199, 323, 381-388, 402-403, 407, 437-438, 452-453
Interest, 43, 51, 56, 69, 93, 114, 165, 196-205, 208, 210-215, 218-221, 253, 322, 345-346, 406-409, 431-432, 436, 453
International trade, 17, 223-256
Investment banks, 199, 205
Invisible hand, 25-26
Iowa, 124, 415, 448
Ireland/Irish, 167, 244, 296
Israel (modern), 42, 45, 53, 113, 211, 354, 461
Israelites (ancient), 41-56
Italy/Italian, 41, 57, 65, 200, 239, 352, 438

J Jackson, Andrew, 103-104
Japan, 126, 137, 221, 229, 233, 239, 244, 251, 352, 396, 398, 401-402

K Kansas, 265, 414
Kentucky, 191, 193
Keynes, John Maynard, 32-33, 162

L Labor unions, *see* Unions
Labor, 13, 17-18, 24, 27-28, 49-52, 83-84, 99, 130-132, 165, 169, 190, 277-278, 287-316, 357-359, 413-414, 425
Lagging economic indicators,
Laissez faire, 25
Law of Moses, 41-44, 336, 447
Leading Economic Index, 358
Leverage, 207
Liberation Theology, 74-75
Liquidity, 189, 201
Loans, 43, 54, 93, 97, 102-104, 109-110, 114-115, 125, 196-205, 220-221, 322, 328, 346, 385, 401, 406-410, 435-440, 453
Lorenz curve, 372
Louisiana, iii, 235
Luther, Martin, 71
Luxembourg, 244, 354

M Macroeconomics, 21, 32, 282, 351
Maine, 266
Margin, buying on, 207, 365, 430
Marginal analysis, 277-279, 291
Marginal decisions, 127, 137, 420
Marginal income tax rates, 4, 338, 433
Marginal propensity to consume,
Marginal rate of substitution, 137
Marginal utility, 169
Margins (profit), 28, 310-311
Market (definition), 14-15
Market economy, *see* Free market
Market failure, 179-185, 326
Marx, Karl, 26-30, 289
Marxism, 33, 74-75
Maryland, 94, 249, 302, 390-391
Massachusetts, 71, 90-91, 93, 123
Material resources, 40, 129
Medicaid, 328, 381-385, 391
Medicare, 144-145, 306, 328, 339-340, 344-345, 381-383, 391-392
Menger, Carl, 31
Mercantilism, 24-26, 89
Mexico, 115, 172, 239, 354, 395
Michigan, 262, 283, 300, 400-404, 419
Microeconomics, 21, 275
Minimum wage, 18, 290, 308-311
Minnesota, 205, 262, 341, 438
Mises, Ludwig von, 31-32
Mississippi, 349
Missouri, 374
Mixed economy, 10
Monastic movement, 70-71
Monetary policy, U.S., 108-110, 214, 217-222, 320
Money market funds, 198, 201, 207
Money multiplier, 197
Money supply, 191-192, 201, 211-212, 218-220, 348, 430-433, 439
Money, 5, 15-16, 40, 57-62, 85-86, 92-93, 95-97, 102-104, 108-109, 113, 130, 187-222, 251-256, 346-348, 371, 443
Monopoly, 25, 103, 179-182, 227, 280, 303
Monopsony, 182
Montana, 110, 418
Morocco, 147
Mortgage-backed securities, 323, 436
Mortgage, 198-199, 213, 221, 323, 405-410, 436, 438-440, 452
Multiple-deposit expansion, 197
Mutual funds, 205-207, 362, 365, 449

N NASDAQ, 115, 363-366
National Bureau of Economic Research (NBER), 367-369, 439
National debt, 33, 96, 102, 107, 114-115, 145, 211, 244-245, 255, 322, 345-348, 440
Natural gas, 364, 394
Natural monopoly, 181
Nebraska, 262, 395
Nepal, 228
Netherlands, The, 69, 74, 176, 194, 239
Nevada, 367
New Deal, 33, 110, 342, 414, 432-434
New Hampshire, 33, 416
New Jersey, 92, 103, 108-109, 371, 428
New Mexico, 382
New York Stock Exchange, 84, 96, 109, 361-366
New York Stock Exchange, 96, 109, 361-363
New York, 1, 82, 84, 87, 96-97, 99, 103-105, 109-110, 196, 199, 262, 331, 361-366, 369, 431, 439
New Zealand, 238
Nominal exchange rate (currency), 252
Non-durable goods (soft goods), 151
Non-profit corporation, 263, 281, 303
North American Free Trade Agreement (NAFTA), 115, 238
North Carolina, 221, 375
North Dakota, 197, 315
North Korea, 142, 234
Nuclear energy, 394, 397-398

O Obama, Barack, 263, 311, 438, 440
Offshore, moving production, 246-247
Ohio, 183, 262, 401
oikonomia/oikonomos, 5-6, 56, 62, 457
Oil (petroleum), 107-108, 113, 132, 150, 153, 211, 229, 239, 246, 280, 302, 326, 393-398, 400, 403-404, 416
Oklahoma, 257
Oligopoly, 181
Oligopsony, 182
Opportunity cost, 7, 11-12, 131-132, 139, 229-230, 247, 276, 420, 448
Oregon, 152, 237
Organic farming, 335, 416-417
Organization of Oil-Exporting Countries (OPEC), 113, 153, 395

P Parks, Rosa, 154
Partnership, 260-261

Index

Paul the Apostle, 5-6, 40, 61, 66-68, 83, 86, 121, 195, 242, 268, 281, 298, 443, 449-450
Paul, Ron, 31, 344
Payment of taxes by income quintiles, 308
Peer-to-peer lending, 202
Pennsylvania, 95, 98, 107, 241, 262, 284-285, 395, 398
Per capita GDP, 353-354
Perfect competition, 152
Philippines, 137, 246-247
Phillips curve, 213
Portugal/Portuguese, 89, 225, 229, 232, 297
Poland, 167, 184-185, 254-255
Poverty guidelines, Federal, 310, 371-372
Poverty, 43, 49-50, 55, 61, 69-72, 74-75, 80, 155, 309-310, 329, 371-378, 428, 430
Price ceiling, 168
Price controls, 112-113, 162, 168
Price discrimination, 166-167
Price elasticity of demand, 175-177
Price elasticity of supply, 176
Price floor, 168, 241, 309
Price maker, 165, 276
Price stability, 174
Price supports, 168, 414
Price taker, 165
Price, 7, 14-15, 110, 135-137, 141, 149-152, 156-170, 173-183, 209-213, 225, 231-232, 240-241, 246, 254, 276-277, 356-359, 364-365, 395-396
Producer goods, 150
Producer Price Index, 359
Production possibilities frontier or curve, 130-132
Production resources, 129-130, 306
Production, 7, 18-19, 27, 98-99, 123-124, 129-138. 150-163, 171-185, 225-230, 243-250, 275-281, 351-355
Productivity, 49-50, 228-230, 277-279, 292, 351, 359, 373-374, 425-429
Profit, 3-4, 13, 17-18, 24, 27-28, 74, 89-90, 164-168, 178, 203-208, 259-263, 275-281, 291, 309-311, 326, 334-335, 427-428
Property rights, 47, 80, 183-184
Protectionism, 231, 238, 249
Protestant Ethic and the Spirit of Capitalism, The, 73-74
Proverbs, 36, 49-51, 53-55, 72, 80, 86, 202, 264, 348, 378, 392, 429, 452
Public choice theory, 145
Public goods, 182-184, 326-327
Purchasing power parity (PPP), 353-354
Purchasing power, 5, 210, 213, 266, 309, 330
Puritans, 71-72

Q Qatar, 354, 395
Quintile, 307-308, 373
Quota (trade), 233

R Railroads, 83, 105-109, 302, 363
Reagan, Ronald, 32-33, 114, 149, 211, 233, 319, 346
Real exchange rate (currency), 254
Recession, 32, 114-115, 211, 215, 282-285, 367-370, 430, 435-440
Reconstructionism, 76
Relative price, 166
Renewable sources of energy, 294, 326, 393-399, 416
Rent control, 168
Revelation, Book of, 68, 444
Rhode Island, vi, 93, 98-99, 262, 297
Rich Young Ruler, 60-61, 134
Romania, 180, 184
Rule of 72, 201, 353
Russia, 9, 70, 77, 179, 189, 354, 395, *see also* Soviet Union

S Salary, 213, 290, 305-306
Sanction (trade), 233-234
Savings and loan (thrift), 115, 199
Savings bonds, 203, 207, 322
Say, Jean-Baptiste, 161, 267
Scarcity, 7, 39-41, 123-124, 153, 164-169
Securities, 205-207, 220-221, 244, *see also* Mortgage-backed securities
Sermon on the Mount, 57-58, 459-462
Shays' Rebellion, 93-94
Shocks, supply and demand, 178, 192, 211, 284, 393
Shortage, 159-162, 168, 182, 185, 364, 386
Singapore, 17, 244, 354, 361
Slavery, 66, 73, 91, 96, 393
Small business, 90, 265-274, 309-310
Smith, Adam, 23-30, 89, 168-169, 208, 225
Social gospel, 73
Social Security, 145, 210, 306, 320, 340, 344-345, 351, 357, 371, 388-391
Socialism, 9, 27-30, 154, 179, 299, *see also* Command economy
Sole proprietorship, 260-261
Solomon, 46-47, 50
Somalia, 354
South Carolina, 402
South Dakota, 291
South Korea, 225, 239
Soviet Union, 32-33, 112, 184-185, 234, 240, *see also* Russia

Spain, 89, 94, 137, 229
Specialization, 11, 227-228
Sri Lanka, 169
Stagflation, 211
Standard and Poor (S&P) 500, 358, 363
Sticky prices and wages (menu costs), 177-178
Stock/Stock Market, 96, 110, 115, 204-207, 263, 361-366, 430
Student loans, 125, 139, 407, 435
Subsidies, 10, 135, 156, 235-237, 326, 384, 398
Substitute goods, 136-137, 156, 158, 180
Supply and demand, 14-15, 150, 156-163, 168-170, 173-174, 177-178, 182-183, 290-292, 403
Supply curve (graph), 157, 159-160, 174, 182, 290
Supply schedule, 157
Supply-side economics, 114
Surplus (economic), 159-161, 168, 241
Surplus (government budget), 104, 115, 347, 432
Surplus (trade), 245-246
Switzerland, 19, 31, 135, 229, 244, 456

T T-account, 197
Tariffs, 18, 96-97, 104, 106, 231-233, 237-238, 431
Taxes, 4, 57-58, 73, 91-92, 95-96, 98, 106, 110, 112-115, 136, 144-145, 156, 182-184, 204-208, 260, 263, 265-266, 305-311, 319-322, 326-328, 337-348, 388-391, 396, 409, 421-422, 432-433
Tennessee, 214, 243, 398, 404
Tennessee Valley Authority (TVA), 10, 337
Texas, 4, 27, 63, 262, 299, 313, 333
Thailand, 121, 137
Theonomy, 76
Trade balance, 245
Tradeoff, 132, 137, 140, 247, 304, 332-333, 336, 393-394, 397-398, 416, 420
Transaction costs, 240
Transition economy, 10-11
Treasury (U.S.), 33, 96, 105, 109, 187, 201, 219-220, 244, 253, 282, 322, 388, 437-438
Treasury bonds, 230, 244, 322, 389

U Unearned income, 306
Unemployment, 32, 109, 113-115, 139, 192, 210-211, 213-214, 249, 282-283, 313-316, 329, 356-359, 432-433, 438-439
Unintended consequences, 121, 132, 136, 139, 249, 310, 384, 416
Unions (and labor organizations), 18, 27-28, 108, 153, 213, 290, 299-304, 306, 310-311, 400-401
United Kingdom, 137, 239, 244, 352, 354, 396
Utah, v, 141
Utility-maximizing conditions, 138
Utility, economic, 137-138, 168-169

V Velocity of money, 201
Venezuela, 162, 395-396
Vermont, 397
Virginia, 89-90, 106, 151, 327
Virtual monopoly, 180-181

W Wage-price spiral, 213
Wages, 5, 9, 13, 18, 27-28, 82-83, 112-113, 154-155, 177, 210, 212-214, 243, 247, 259-260, 275-278, 290-312, 314, 338-340, 400-401, 430
War of 1812, 101-102
Washington Mutual (bank), 438-439
Washington, D.C., 85, 217, 219, 262, 303, 342, 345, 421
Washington, George, 98
Washington, 237, 262, 287
Wealth of Nations, The, 23-24, 89, 168-169
Weber, Max, 73-74
Welfare (social programs), 144, 211, 309, 329-330, 372, 434
West Virginia, 83, 110, 138, 434
Whiskey Rebellion, 98
White collar, 293-295, 300
Whitney, Eli, 99
Wisconsin, 405
Women in the work force, 161, 294-296, 315
World Bank, 33, 353-354
World War I, 32, 110, 120, 192, 210, 430
World War II, 33, 112, 120, 161, 194, 305, 328, 382, 419, 433
Wyoming, 411

Also Available from Notgrass History

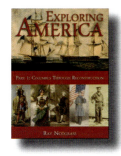

Exploring America by Ray Notgrass

Your child can earn one year of credit in American history, English (literature and composition), and Bible. Engaging history lessons, combined with primary sources, provide a rich understanding of our nation's past. High school.

Exploring World History by Ray Notgrass

Engaging lessons, combined with primary sources, survey history from Creation to the present. Your child can earn one year of credit in world history, English (literature and composition), and Bible. High school.

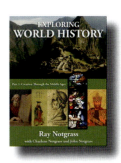

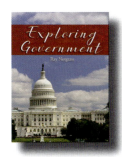

Exploring Government by Ray Notgrass

This one-semester course provides a half-year credit in government and English (literature and composition). Learn about the operations of government and about issues facing our nation today. High school.

America the Beautiful by Charlene Notgrass

This one-year American history, geography, and literature course combines the flexibility and richness of a unit study with the simplicity of a textbook-based approach to history. Engaging, fascinating, and fun. Ages 10-14.

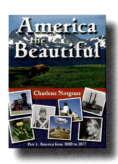

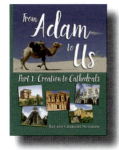

From Adam to Us by Ray and Charlene Notgrass

This one-year world history and literature course combines narrative lessons, full-color photographs, primary sources, literature, and hands-on activities to help the student connect with world history in a personal way. Ages 10-14.

Uncle Sam and You by Ray and Charlene Notgrass

This one-year civics and government course has daily lessons that teach your child about the foundations of American government, the elections process, and how Federal, state, and local governments work. Ages 10-14.

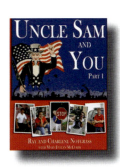

For more information about our resources, call 1-800-211-8793 or visit notgrass.com.